# Mark Twain & Company

LELAND KRAUTH

# Mark Twain & Company

## SIX LITERARY RELATIONS

The University of Georgia Press
Athens and London

© 2003 by the University of Georgia Press

Athens, Georgia 30602

All rights reserved

Designed by Mindy Basinger Hill

Set in Bauer Bodoni by Bookcomp, Inc.

Printed and bound by Maple-Vail

The paper in this book meets the guidelines for
permanence and durability of the Committee on
Production Guidelines for Book Longevity of the
Council on Library Resources.

Printed in the United States of America

07   06   05   04   03   c   5   4   3   2   1

Library of Congress Cataloging-in-Publication Data

Krauth, Leland.
Mark Twain & company : six literary relations / Leland
Krauth.
p. cm.
Includes bibliographical references (p. ) and index.
ISBN 0-8203-2540-6 (alk. paper)
1. Twain, Mark, 1835–1910—Friends and associates.
2. American literature—19th century—History and criticism.
3. English literature—19th century—History and criticism.
4. Twain, Mark, 1835–1910—Contemporaries.   5. American
fiction—English influences.   6. Influence (Literary, artistic,
etc.)   I. Title: Mark Twain and company.   II. Title.
PS1333 .K73 2003
818'.4'09—dc21                                    2003004608

British Library Cataloging-in-Publication Data available

FOR BARBARA, *the best of company*

# Contents

# Acknowledgments

*Mark Twain & Company* is a study of Twain in relationship to several other creative writers and thinkers of his time. It seems apt to acknowledge those scholars and critics, colleagues, friends, and family members who have in one way or another kept me company. The number is in fact large, and any attempt to single out the most important would be doomed, for they have all mattered. The bibliography here—almost larger than I would wish but no larger than necessary—is the fullest recognition of my scholarly debts. Those whose work is most seminal to my study appear in the introduction. More generally, I want to say that one of the pleasures of working on Twain is reading those who have already written on him and his marvelously varied and engaging work.

It is a pleasure to acknowledge a very few specific obligations. Alan Gribben's *Mark Twain's Library: A Reconstruction* established many new vantage points from which to view Twain, including the one assumed here. While my attention to Twain's culture has a genre emphasis remote from his own work, Louis J. Budd's *Mark Twain: Social Philosopher* and *Our Mark Twain* continue to provide the indispensable context for Twain in his time. Robert Weisbuch's *Atlantic Double-Cross: American Literature and British Influence in the Age of Emerson* is a groundbreaking study from which I have profited greatly.

As always, Michael B. Frank at the Mark Twain Project has provided useful advice and information. I continue to admire—and benefit from—the work the project is doing. The Elmira College Center for Mark Twain Studies, especially under its former director, Gretchen Sharlow, involved me in Twain events and gave me a forum for airing some of the notions finally embedded in this study. As long ago as 1987, I presented at the center's Summer Lecture Series some ideas about Twain's humor that eventually worked their way into various parts of this study. My paper on Twain and Kipling, given at the center's Conference on the State of Mark Twain Studies in 1993, was the start of "Wandering Devious." I had the pleasure of serving on the planning committee for the center's 2001 conference and listening to the stimulating ideas of the other committee members: Louis J. Budd, Alan Gribben, Susan K. Harris, Michael J. Kiskis, Lynne Rusinko, Gretchen Sharlow, Nina Skinner, and Mark Woodhouse.

A paper on Twain and Howells given at the American Humor Association's conference in 1988 formed the basis for a part of "Creating Humor," and one on Twain and the Gothic given in 1999 at the International Gothic Studies Association conference shaped some of "Exposing the Body in Protest." A version of the final section of "Creating Humor" appeared in *Ball State University Forum* 24 (winter 1983): 368–84; and a small part of "Wringing the Human Heart" and "Assaying Manliness" appeared in *American Literature* 54 (1982): 368–84.

Several of my colleagues here at the University of Colorado at Boulder have been especially helpful. The chair of the English department throughout the making of this book, John Stevenson, has been unfailingly accommodating and gracious. Two Victorian specialists, Kelly Hurley and Sue Zemka, offered useful observations about Matthew Arnold. Mary Klages, an Americanist, had insightful things to say about Harriet Beecher Stowe, and Nan Goodman, another specialist in American literature, was more helpful than she realizes. She not only endorsed the design of the study when I had doubts about it, but also provided the metaphor for its conclusion. Much of the final chapter was written when I was a visiting professor at the University of Hawaii at Manoa. I want to thank the chair, Cristina Bacchilega, and the associate chair, Judith Kellogg, both for their cordial hospitality and for giving me the opportunity to talk about my project at a department colloquium

Over the long haul, my closest and most important company has been my family. I really owe them all more than I can acknowledge here. No matter what I attempt, my daughter Heidi insists that I can do it, and no matter what the topic, she is always a surprising and engaging conversationalist. My other daughter, Karin, and her husband, Paul, have been endlessly supportive, providing cheer and enthusiasm and dogs to care for. Their company keeps one's moral compass pointed in the right direction. Karin undertook to help with the checking of documentation (and learned in the process how much I needed the help). My son, Gregory, and his wife, Kathleen, have kept me aware of global issues as I worked on my American Mark Twain, and they, too, always believe in my work. Their two children, Sam and Sophie, are wonderful company, whether in the backyard or on board ship in Alaska. Sam has, to use a phrase of Kipling's from one of his Just-So stories, a "satiable curiosity" and a quiet fondness for humor that makes him a delight. Sophie has enough energy to light a small city and an unpredictable zaniness that makes her a joy.

Finally, I owe most to my wife, Barbara, the companion of my life for over forty years, whose humor, intelligence, and sprightliness constantly turn the ordinary into the magical. A superb editor and critic, she has improved everything in this book. Most of all, she has opened to me the joy of life in its smallest as well as its largest moments.

# Abbreviations

AMT        *The Autobiography of Mark Twain.* Ed. Charles Neider. New York: Harper and Row, 1959.

CH         *Mark Twain: The Critical Heritage.* Ed. Frederick Anderson. London: Routledge & Kegan Paul, 1971.

CY         *A Connecticut Yankee in King Arthur's Court.* Ed. Bernard L. Stein. Berkeley: U of California P, 1979.

ET&S1      *Early Tales and Sketches, Volume 1 (1851–1864).* Ed. Edgar Marquess Branch and Robert H. Hirst. Berkeley: U of California P, 1979.

ET&S2      *Early Tales and Sketches, Volume 2 (1864–1865).* Ed. Frederick Anderson, Lin Salamo, and Bernard L. Stein. Berkeley: U of California P, 1975.

FE         *Following the Equator: A Journey Around the World.* 1897. Rpt., New York: Dover, 1989.

HF         *Adventures of Huckleberry Finn.* Ed. Walter Blair and Victor Fischer. Berkeley: U of California P, 1988.

IA         *The Innocents Abroad, Roughing It.* Ed. Guy Cardwell. New York: Library of America, 1984.

L1         *Mark Twain's Letters, Volume 1 (1853–1866).* Ed. Edgar Marquess Branch, Michael B. Frank, and Kenneth M. Sanderson. Berkeley: U of California P, 1988.

L2      *Mark Twain's Letters, Volume 2 (1867–1868)*. Ed. Harriet Elinor Smith and Richard Bucci. Berkeley: U of California P, 1990.

L3      *Mark Twain's Letters, Volume 3 (1869)*. Ed. Victor Fischer and Michael B. Frank. Berkeley: U of California P, 1992.

L4      *Mark Twain's Letters, Volume 4 (1870–1871)*. Ed. Victor Fischer and Michael B. Frank. Berkeley: U of California P, 1995.

MTA      *Mark Twain's Autobiography*. 2 vols. Ed. Albert Bigelow Paine. New York: Harper & Brothers, 1924.

MTB      Albert Bigelow Paine. *Mark Twain: A Biography*. 3 vols. New York: Harper & Brothers, 1912.

MTBE      *Mark Twain at the "Buffalo Express": Articles and Sketches by America's Favorite Humorist*. Ed. Joseph B. McCullough and Janice McIntire-Strasburg. Dekalb: Northern Illinois UP, 1999.

MTC1      *Mark Twain: Collected Tales, Sketches, Speeches, & Essays, 1852–1890*. Ed. Louis J. Budd. New York: Library of America, 1992.

MTC2      *Mark Twain: Collected Tales, Sketches, Speeches, & Essays, 1891–1910*. Ed. Louis J. Budd. New York: Library of America, 1992.

MTE      *Mark Twain in Eruption*. Ed. Bernard DeVoto. New York: Harper & Brothers, 1940.

MTHL      *Mark Twain–Howells Letters*. 2 vols. Ed. Henry Nash Smith and William M. Gibson. Cambridge: Harvard UP, 1960.

MTL      *Mark Twain's Letters*. 2 vols. Ed. Albert Bigelow Paine. New York: Harper & Brothers, 1917.

MTLP      *Mark Twain's Letters to His Publishers*. Ed. Hamlin Hill. Berkeley: U of California P, 1967.

MTMS    *Mark Twain's Mysterious Stranger Manuscripts.* Ed. William
        M. Gibson. Berkeley: U of California P, 1969.

MTOA    *Mark Twain's Own Autobiography: The Chapters from the
        "North American Review."* Ed. Michael J. Kiskis. Madison:
        U of Wisconsin P, 1990.

MTSpk   *Mark Twain Speaking.* Ed. Paul Fatout. Iowa City: U of Iowa
        P, 1976.

MyMT    William Dean Howells. *My Mark Twain: Reminiscences and
        Criticism.* 1910. Rpt., Baton Rouge: Louisiana State UP, 1967.

N&J1    *Mark Twain's Notebooks & Journals, Volume 1 (1855–1873).*
        Ed. Frederick Anderson, Michael B. Frank, and Kenneth M.
        Sanderson. Berkeley: U of California P, 1975.

N&J2    *Mark Twain's Notebooks & Journals, Volume 2 (1877–1883).*
        Ed. Frederick Anderson, Lin Salamo, and Bernard L. Stein.
        Berkeley: U of California P, 1975.

N&J3    *Mark Twain's Notebooks & Journals, Volume 3 (1883– 1891).*
        Ed. Robert Pack Browning, Michael B. Frank, and Lin
        Salamo. Berkeley: U of California P, 1979.

RI      *Roughing It.* Ed. Harriet Elinor Smith and Edgar Marquess
        Branch. Berkeley: U of California P, 1993.

TS      *The Adventures of Tom Sawyer; Tom Sawyer Abroad; Tom
        Sawyer, Detective.* Ed. John C. Gerber, Paul Baender, and
        Terry Firkins. Berkeley: U of California P, 1980.

# Mark Twain & Company

# Introduction

In the last year of his life Mark Twain published in *Harper's Bazaar* a playful and provocative essay, "The Turning Point of My Life." Harper's had asked a number of distinguished people to write on the topic posed by the title. With typical comic perversity, Twain denied the very idea of a single turning point in anyone's life, arguing instead for a deterministic chain of events that leads inevitably to the life one has lived. Playfully, Twain stretches his chain back first to Caesar's crossing of the Rubicon and finally to what he calls the origin of all human chains: the Garden of Eden. At the same time as he elongates the sequence of causality he also fancifully enlarges the notion of significant event to include such ordinary occurrences as getting the measles. While Twain thus comically subverts the controlling concept of the magazine's series, he does in all seriousness define his life's centering. "To me," he writes, "the most important feature of my life is its literary feature." The events he invokes, large and small, plausible and improbable, are all aimed, as he puts it, at "launching" him "into the literary guild." There is nothing unexpected about Twain's assertion that the most important aspect of his life is its literary dimension (though in giving priority to his creative life, he sets aside such possible competitors as being married, being a father, or even becoming rich and famous), but Twain's description of his life's core is surprisingly phrased as becoming a member of a "guild." (He repeats the term three times.) In calling his creative life a matter of joining a guild, Twain underscores its communal nature: he is a part of a confederacy of artisans united by their craft (*MTC2* 931, 938).

In one sense Twain's insistence on his membership in a guild of literary workers is in keeping with his lifelong tendency to describe his creative processes in terms of laboring trades. From the first, his humor itself was conceived of as a workman's machine—"the talent is a mighty engine" (*L1* 323)—and achieving imaginative resurgence was always for Twain simply a matter of waiting for the "tank" to "fill up again" ("My Literary Shipyard" 407–8). Just as these metaphors de-romanticize creative endeavor, returning it to the world of ordinary work, so Twain's customary accounts of the sources for his writing habitually point to lived, nonliterary experience. In *Life on the Mississippi*, for instance, he insists that he knew on the river all the types of humanity with which he would later people his fiction. And in his famous contretemps with Paul Bourget he seems to set aside literary inventiveness, imagination itself, in favor of "*absorption;* years and years of unconscious absorption; years and years of intercourse with the life concerned; of living it" (*MTC2* 166). Twain did have, as Bernard DeVoto once observed, "a magnificent gusto for experience of all kinds" (107). But critics' attention to Twain's nonliterary experience—to boyhood joys and terrors, to vagabondizing, to riverboat piloting, to western prospecting, to literary traveling—sometimes obscures what Twain himself acknowledges so clearly and emphatically at the end of his career: he was for most of his life a man who worked alongside others at the craft—the trade—of literature.

Twain's literary relations, his interactions with his fellow guild members, quite naturally assumed two forms: friendship and reading. As his fame grew both at home and abroad, Twain met most of the major writers of his age. Although he formed few close relations with his fellow writers, he maintained a cordial acquaintance with many. And in a few cases he sustained a long-term animosity. Either way, through friendship or dislike, he remained literally and imaginatively—creatively—in touch with other writers throughout his career.

He not only knew them but also read their works. Beginning most significantly with Minnie M. Brashear's 1934 study, *Mark Twain: Son of Missouri*, which argued convincingly that Sam Clemens grew up in a highly literary culture and that he was an assiduous reader (see her chapter 6), Twain scholarship has gradually but steadily documented his wide reading. It has begun to establish the truth of William Dean Howells's observation that Twain "was always reading some vital book" (*MyMT* 15). Attested to in passing by various scholars, Twain's reading was finally brought into full view in Alan Gribben's monumental study (published in 1980 and now being revised and expanded), *Mark Twain's Library: A*

*Reconstruction.* Since then critical condescension to Twain as "unlettered" has been silenced, and Twain's own stance as a backwoods amateur has been exposed for what it was: a calculated pose, a part of the carefully created persona Mark Twain. No one now contests the fact that Twain was conversant with the literary culture of his time or that he knew—and made use of—the Anglo-American tradition in literature from the medieval period to his own unfolding moment. Though pretending not to be, he was a man steeped in letters.

Twain's own ideas about writing further underscore his absorption in the works of others. Although he was almost always ready with opinions about writers and individual works, he generally avoided formulating theories about literature. He preferred in fact to strike the pose of the novice who knew little and was just finding his way. Even in 1894, after over three decades of writing, he described himself as a "jackleg" novelist (author's note to "Those Extraordinary Twins," *Pudd'nhead Wilson* 119). However, beginning casually (and somewhat accidentally) in the 1870s, Twain struck an idea that he repeated and enlarged upon for the rest of his career. It became perhaps as close as he would come to a theory of creativity, and it too linked him to his fellow guild members.

In 1871, when a weak imitation of Bret Harte's poem "The Heathen Chinee" (a national sensation at the time) appeared in the *Buffalo Express* and was subsequently attributed to Mark Twain by Thomas Bailey Aldrich, Twain wrote Aldrich in hot denial of authorship.[1] He first demanded a retraction, noting that he was "not in the imitation business," and then retracted his demand, insisting that the issue was "not important." But as he tried to extricate himself from what must have seemed unnecessary and embarrassing complications, he insisted: "It *is* hard to be accused of plagiarism—a crime I never have committed in my life" (*L4* 304–5).

Eight years later, however, in a gracious speech delivered at the breakfast hosted by the *Atlantic Monthly* in honor of Oliver Wendell Holmes's seventieth birthday, Twain sang a different tune. He confessed to having "stolen" the dedication he used for *The Innocents Abroad* "almost word for word" from Holmes's own dedication to *Songs in Many Keys.* Noting that "pride protects a man from deliberately stealing other people's ideas," he explained away his own theft as the result of reading and rereading Holmes's poems so often that his "mental reservoir was filled up with them to the brim," so full that when he came to write a dedication he "unconsciously stole it." Twain thus turns his minor transgression into a graceful compliment, and he further mitigates it by reporting that Holmes himself, when told of the borrowing, said he believed all writers "unconsciously worked over ideas gathered in reading and hearing, imagining they were original" (*MTSpk* 135).

The idea that writers inevitably poach on each other's work (a notion perhaps poached from Holmes) became the keystone in the arch of Twain's thinking about literary activity. When pressed to contribute to a volume entitled *The Art of Authorship*, a collection of essays edited by George Bainton in 1890, Twain first humorously claimed not to have any methods of composition, then said that if he did, they were only a "jumble" that could not be described, and finally offered this "guess" about literary art: "Whenever we read a sentence and like it, we unconsciously store it away in our model-chamber; and it goes with the myriad of its fellows to the building, brick by brick, of the eventual edifice which we call our style." He suggested that the "training" most writers have is "of this unconscious sort" (*MTC1* 945). In a speech to the London Authors Club a few years later he acknowledged having read—and "absorbed," again "unconsciously"—the *Walpole Letters* and so used them in his own writing without quite realizing it (*MTSpk* 323). With the kind of playful candor that their intimacy invited, Twain once explained to William Dean Howells that he had rejoiced in discovering "a bran [*sic*] new & ingenious way of beginning a novel," only to realize that the idea was really Charles Dudley Warner's. He then added that he might be "the worst literary thief in the world, without knowing it" (*MTHL* 112). Writing to Helen Keller in March 1903 in response to her having sent him an inscribed copy of *The Story of My Life*, Twain brought up her trial for plagiarism to defend her by attacking her accusers. He vented his anger at the "solemn donkeys" full of "ignorant rubbish about plagiarism" and formulated in the midst of his tirade his most sweeping and dogmatic assertion of the unavoidable nature of literary—and even nonliterary—borrowing:

Oh, dear me, how unspeakably funny and owlishly idiotic and grotesque was that "plagiarism" farce! As if there was much of anything in human utterance, oral or written, *except* plagiarism! The kernal, the soul—let us go further and say the substance, the bulk, the actual and valuable material of *all* human utterances—is plagiarism. For substantially all ideas are second-hand, consciously and unconsciously drawn from a million outside sources, and daily used by the garnerer with a pride and satisfaction born of superstition that he originated them; whereas there is not a rag of originality about them anywhere except the little discoloration they get from his mental and moral calibre and his temperament, and which is revealed in characteristics of phrasing. (*MTL* 731–32)

In the book he liked to call his "bible," *What Is Man?*, he would, with equal dogmatism, declare: "A man's brain is so constructed that it *can originate nothing whatever.*" Ideas themselves, as well as literature and inventions, come, he said, from "a thousand unknown sources"—"mainly *unconsciously* gathered" (*WIM* 130, 164, Twain's emphasis).

What Twain thus variously insisted upon is more or less what today's theoretical discourse calls intertextuality. Prescient or just quirky, he was aware of the fact that texts of all kinds (but especially literary ones) are constructed out of other texts. If one work does not become directly involved with another through allusion, imitation, or parody, it inevitably does so by participating in a common culture: by sharing the same linguistic universe. As Kristeva puts it, with a certainty Twain would have admired, "in the space of a given text, several utterances taken from other texts, intersect"; "any text is constructed as a mosaic of quotations; any text is the absorption and transformation of another" (*Desire in Language* 36, 66). Barthes makes the same point even more comprehensively, and with more precision:

Every Text is an intertext; other texts are present in it, at variable levels, in more or less recognizable forms: the text of the previous culture and those of the surrounding culture; every text is a new fabric woven out of bygone quotations. Scraps of code, formulas, rhythmic patterns, fragments of social idioms, etc. are absorbed into the text and redistributed in it, for there is always language prior to the text and language around it. A prerequisite for any text, intertextuality cannot be reduced to a problem of sources and influences; it is a general field of anonymous formulas whose origin is seldom identifiable, of unconscious or automatic quotations given without quotation marks. ("Texte [Théorie du]," in *Encyclopedia Universalis*, vol. 15)

Mark Twain would surely have endorsed this formulation, especially its attention to the "unconscious or automatic," for he had, in his own vocabulary, said much the same thing throughout his career. Indeed, for him, such assimilation and reconstruction were at the core of creativity itself.

Given his friendships, his reading habits, and his notion of creativity, it is natural that Twain would think of himself as a member of the literary guild, his works as crafted products of a common trade, sometimes made with borrowed materials. Oddly, however, there have been few extended, critical studies of Twain in relation to his fellow guild members.[2] Some of his ties to broader literary movements have been examined. Perhaps the most familiar, though somewhat out of fashion at the moment, is the analysis of his participation in realism, a connection (and disconnection) examined in terms of cultural history by Michael Davitt Bell in *The Problem of American Realism*; in terms of contract law by Brook Thomas in *American Literary Realism and the Failed Promise of Contract*; and in terms of the aesthetics of race, class, and gender by Joe B. Fulton in *Mark Twain's Ethical Realism*. Twain's relationship to southwestern humor was established long ago by Kenneth S. Lynn in *Mark Twain and Southwestern Humor*, and more recently David E. E. Sloane has explored Twain's work in terms of the literary comedians in *Mark Twain as a Literary Comedian*. Kenneth R. Andrews places Twain among the literary luminaries of Hartford living adjacent to him in *Nook Farm: Mark Twain's Hartford Circle*; still within the confines of the New England region Albert E. Stone has considered Twain's boy-books in the context of mid-nineteenth-century writers of fiction centered on children in *The Innocent Eye*. On the purely personal level, two studies have illuminated Twain in relation to George Washington Cable, Guy A. Cardwell's *Twins of Genius* and Arlin Turner's *Mark Twain and George W. Cable*. Howard G. Baetzhold's *Mark Twain and John Bull* details Twain's mercurial feelings about England in part by tracking his acquaintances with contemporaneous British writers, including three taken up here. Finally, in *Mark Twain in the Company of Women* Laura E. Skandera Trombley has recently broken new ground by exploring the influence of women on Twain's creative process. These are all compelling and revealing studies. In their introduction to a recent collection of essays that maps new directions in Twain scholarship, Trombley and Michael J. Kiskis call attention to the still largely unexplored "generative power of Clemens's literary and personal associations" (7). *Mark Twain & Company* looks into six such associations.

My study investigates Twain's writings in terms of his literary relations. It examines Twain and his works, not in the broad field of some particular literary fashion or movement, but in the narrower corridor of his personal acquaintanceship. It pairs Twain with one writer at a time. Part of the rationale for examining pairs of writers is Twain himself. His mind was always stimulated by seeing one thing next to another. In his incisive study of Mark Twain as a literary critic, Sydney Krause captures half of Twain (which is all that concerns him in this instance) when he locates in Twain's "critical analysis" the "dynamics of contrast as a way of knowing" (248). This formulation takes us directly to the heart of Twain's epistemology, especially when we add that Twain knew not just by perceiving contrast but also by discovering similitude. But what is true of his critical thought is also true of his creative imagining. From *The Innocents Abroad* with its contrast between the old world and the new, through *Huckleberry Finn* with its opposition of slave and free (as well as Tom and Huck), to the final *Mysterious Stranger* with its clash between the angelic and the human, Twain's texts are structured by paired opposites. Even in his formless autobiography—the "law" of which, Twain says, is "that I shall talk about the matter which for the moment interests me" (*MTOA* 4)—he is inclined to write through contrast and similarity. He hoped to create a text in which "the past and the present are constantly brought face to face, resulting in contrasts which newly fire up the interest all along like contact of flint with steel" (*MTA* 2:245).

Examined here are the sparks and smolderings ignited by Twain's contacts with six writers, three American, three British, all prominent in their time: Bret Harte, William Dean Howells, and Harriet Beecher Stowe, on the American side; Matthew Arnold, Robert Louis Stevenson, and Rudyard Kipling, on the British. To be sure, other pairings—Twain and Shillaber, Twain and Holmes, Twain and Warner, Twain and Aldrich, Twain and Dickens, Twain and Browning, to mention only a few—are also worthy of study. But the writers selected here are especially important, for each writer was someone whose work in the guild of literary creators was compelling for Twain; it had the power to stimulate or provoke or reassure or annoy or confirm.

Some of the personal connections between Twain and these other guild members are slight. The tie in such cases is something less than a full-blown literary relationship. Examining it, however, provides an occasion for probing an important aspect of Twain's writing. The relation between Twain and Matthew Arnold is an obvious example. While Twain and Arnold met only once, and while Arnold commented briefly—and critically—on Twain, and Twain wrote sharply on him, further literary connection is scant. But there may be no better way to explore some of Twain's notions about literature, criticism, and culture than by approaching these through Arnold, perhaps the single most influential nineteenth-century critic of Anglo-American letters, not to mention civilization itself, after Carlyle and Emerson. At the other extreme, some relations—Twain and Howells is the case in point—are so extensive and fertile that only a few strands in a complex web of mutuality can be touched.

The writers paired here are chosen to reflect Twain's position in trans-Atlantic, Anglo-American culture. Happily, the once determinant national boundaries of literary study have collapsed (along with the belletristic definition of literature itself). We are in the process, as William Spengemann has put it, of "expanding our literary geography" (*A Mirror for Americanists* 22). The approach taken in this study is predicated on the necessity of such expansion, on the need to see writers—indeed, "American literature"—in a broader context.[3] Recent studies have begun to understand the Victorian ethos, the culture of Mark Twain, as an Anglo-American phenomenon. Daniel Walker Howe has argued, with convincing multiple examples, that "Victorianism was a transatlantic culture" (3–28); D. H. Meyer has explored the "crisis of faith" common on both sides of the Atlantic (59–77); and David D. Hall has illuminated what he calls "the Victorian connection" by seeing the American mugwumps as a version of English "liberalism" and the Genteel Tradition in America as an expression of "the idea of culture" promulgated by "Arnold, Mill, and other mid-century English Victorians" (82, 81–94). There were, to be sure, subcultures within the prevailing Victorian one. To cite the most obvious examples, America felt the shaping force of African Americans, first slave, then free; of immigrant (largely proletarian) peoples; of indigenous Native Americans; and of Spanish speakers in the Southwest and Far West. What in large measure created the hegemony of Victorian culture, however, was the control of the "printed word" (Howe 6). In the burgeoning age of print, control of newspapers, journals, and books fostered a Victorian ideology, familiar traits of which include the emphasis on hard work; the insistence on the postponement of gratification; the injunction to improve oneself;

the celebration of competition in business, politics, and even religion, as well as sports; the quest to create—and maintain—order, both social and, if possible, metaphysical; the drive to use time itself; the demand for seriousness; and the ever-present need to inform, instruct, and guide.

Despite the prevalence of such ideas and attitudes in England and America, there were rifts in Anglo-American culture, and there were also those who promoted fissures.[4] Stephen Spender has characterized Anglo-American literary exchanges, in the summarizing title of his book, as *Love-Hate Relations*. *Mark Twain & Company* does not attempt to gauge the broad sweep of cross-national response, but certainly Twain's relation to Arnold approaches hate, while his ties to Stevenson and Kipling are marked by a deep and abiding affection. In his compelling study, *Atlantic Double-Cross*, Robert Weisbuch, who finds more "enmity" than love (xviii), nevertheless makes an essential point about trans-Atlantic literature: "There is a huge, rough agreement between American and British writers in the nineteenth century. Each nation . . . produces a literature that is intolerant of the habitual understandings of its culture's daily social life" (xvii). An ocean apart, American and English writers still shared not just a language, determinant as that is, and a literary tradition, seductive as that is, but also a common probing of social values.

*Mark Twain & Company* takes up Twain in relation to six of his fellow guild members, and it proceeds by pairing Twain with each of the six. The subtitle, *Six Literary Relations*, is meant to suggest that something more than biography is being examined. The pairs were, to be sure, friends or at least acquaintances, so they related to one another on a personal level. But they also connected in literary ways, for each pair employed a common "relation"—that is, as the Latin root *relatio* reminds us, a mode of narration, a means of storytelling. It is this narrating or recounting or telling that is explored most fully. The attempt is not to discover influence or intertextuality but to see correspondences. The study whose methodology is closest to mine is James L. Johnson's *Mark Twain and the Limits of Power*, a compelling examination of Twain in relation to Emerson (its subtitle is *Emerson's God in Ruins*) that does not argue "any influence of Emerson on Twain" but looks instead at the "correspondences" between their works which arise from their common culture (8–9).

Unmistakably—with individual differences and with varying degrees of engagement—all six writers examined here in relation to Twain experienced a common culture. But their response to that culture was complex, for if on the one hand, as Weisbuch suggests, they undertook to challenge their society's ways of being and its norms, they tried, on the other, to satisfy its taste by writing books that would appeal to the general public. They exploited popular forms. All six were published, read, and criticized on both sides of the Atlantic. All six writers—and certainly Twain himself—courted the public; all of them were inspired or constrained by what was likely to sell in the marketplace. The forms they chose inevitably implicated them in cultural challenge or confirmation, for of course a form or genre is not an ahistorical category but a temporally specific expression of a particular cultural circumstance. The forms—the modes or genres—they use are themselves embodiments of the social system in which they have currency, reflecting, as Raymond Williams has argued, relative stability or instability, fixity or change (*Marxism and Literature* 189–90). In the very act of selecting a form, each writer embroiled himself or herself in a cultural tug-of-war between preserving the status quo and altering it. The forms taken up by Mark Twain & Company all reflect notable tremors, indeed deep shiftings, in the very ground of their culture. For as that sensitive seismograph, Henry Adams, avowed, the world changed profoundly in the second half of the nineteenth century: "My country in 1900 is something totally different from my own country in 1860. I am wholly a stranger in it. Neither I, nor anyone else, understands it. The turning of a nebula into a star may somewhat resemble the change" (qtd. in Jacobson 5).

Within their common and conflicted culture, then, each pair of writers examined here shared a friendship, a mode of literary relation, and an engagement with current ideas. The strategy pursued here is first to consider, usually quite briefly, the biographical relationship of each pair, then their common mode of relation as it functioned within the culture, and finally the larger issue of outlook or vision as registered in significant parallel texts.

The title, *Mark Twain & Company*, faintly echoes Kipling's 1899 account of boys' high jinks in a boarding school, *Stalky & Co.*, which was itself probably indebted to Twain's *Tom Sawyer* (Stewart 154). Of course, the six writers examined along with Twain formed nothing like the clique of unruly boys whose doings Kipling chronicles. Indeed, these writers constituted no school of common literary endeavor at all—far from it. Yet like Kipling's young men, they all rebelled against aspects of their society and all brought to bear upon the issues of their time the kind of moral seriousness finally embraced by Stalky and his comrades. The title is also intended to evoke the purely social dimension of their acquaintance with Twain. All but Stevenson were literally company in Twain's house (and Stevenson was invited there)—or, as in the case of Kipling, the house of his in-laws. They were—however briefly, as with Arnold and Stevenson, or frequently, as with Howells—Twain's companions. That Twain valued such association is made clear by the inscription from Emerson he had engraved in brass over the fireplace in his library: "The chief ornament of a house is the friends who frequent it." That Twain parted company with some of the six does not diminish his general delight in such acquaintance. Henry James, whose life and writings crystallize the trans-Atlantic Victorian culture, observed early in his career: "The best things come, as a general thing, from the talents that are members of a group; every man works better when he has companions working in the same line, and yielding the stimulus of suggestion, comparison, emulation" (*Hawthorne* 25). Although he once quipped that he would "rather be damned to John Bunyan's heaven" than have to read *The Bostonians* (*MTHL* 534), Twain would no doubt have agreed with James's suggestion that "companions working in the same line" were invaluable for a writer—likely to provoke "the best things."

In the final, eulogistic conclusion to *My Mark Twain*, William Dean Howells compares Twain to the other literary figures he knew (and he knew virtually every major writer of his time) and concludes: "They were like one another and like other literary men; but Clemens was sole, incomparable, the Lincoln of our literature" (*MyMT* 84). The idea that Twain was, to borrow a botanical term, a sport, a rare variation in the literary field, is a beguiling one. And it is one Twain himself cultivated. As Louis J. Budd has pointed out, he managed, paradoxically, to promote himself simultaneously as a representative American and a singular, indeed unique, personality (*Our MT* 12). Sustained first by the Romantic notion of creative genius and then by the modernist idea of the artist as alienated, the view of Twain as "sole," though arguable in terms of his achievement, nonetheless disguises the extent to which Twain was both stirred by other writers and interested in cooperative literary ventures. After all, he coauthored *The Gilded Age* with Charles Dudley Warner, wrote a play with

Bret Harte, planned several with Howells, co-edited with him a library of humor, toured the lecture circuit with George Washington Cable, and promoted a composite novel to be written in separate chapters, as he put it, by various "big literary fish" (*MTHL* 160). (Interestingly, Twain included Henry James in the "big fish" category.) Although one pictures Twain alone in his Hartford billiards room turned work-space or even more solitary in his octagonal study high up on Elmira's East Hill at Quarry Farm, the truth is that Twain enjoyed imagining—and sometimes even doing—his work with others. This is perhaps only natural for someone whose early years were spent in two highly communal workplaces: the print shop and the newspaper office.

Looking at Twain in terms of other writers is in keeping with who he was, and it may provide, if not new insights, at least new ways of entering into his works. As the ampersand in the title indicates, the focus of this study is Mark Twain. Some new, or at least interesting, notions about the other writers may also emerge, but this study is predominantly an examination of Twain: of how he related to some of his fellow guild members, of how his attitudes toward them—and their work—disclose important dimensions of his own writing, of how his writing corresponds with their works having similar forms and congruent subjects. The interest is finally in Mark Twain, defined by some of the literary company he kept.

The sequence of chapters is loosely chronological, following Twain's encounters with his six other companions in the craft of writing, from his early association with Harte to his late friendship with Kipling. The first chapter examines Twain and Harte in terms of their sentimentality and considers how that mode affects their protest fiction. The second chapter defines the humor of Twain and Howells in their early travel narratives and explores how that humor informs their private correspondence as well as their late social critique. The third chapter examines the Gothicism of Twain and Stowe and investigates how they present racial issues through the Gothic. The fourth chapter looks at Twain and Arnold in terms of the role of the Victorian Sage and compares the conceptions of civilization they propound as sages. The fifth chapter describes the mode of sensational adventure in Twain and Stevenson and considers how it constructs masculinity. The sixth chapter explores the picaresque in Twain and Kipling and discloses how it supports or subverts imperialism.

William Dean Howells, who knew Twain about as well as anyone, once described him this way: "He saunters out into the trim world of letters, and lounges across its neatly kept paths, and walks about on the grass at will, in spite of all the signs that have been put up from the beginning of literature, warning people of the dangers and penalties for the slightest trespass" ("Mark Twain: An Inquiry" 146). This is an intriguing depiction of Mark Twain. Howells evokes the sense of Twain as a trespasser: a violator of conventions, literary ones, and a willful defier of traditional order, implicitly the social, moral, and political order. But Howells's image has a reverse side. For he depicts Twain in his leisure and sauntering as a gentleman, suggesting that instead of trespassing, aesthetically and normatively, he wanders—freely, to be sure, the way privileged gentlemen do—within traditional boundaries, the park itself. Implicitly, Howells's description raises the dual question: did Twain violate or honor traditional literary modes and conventional values? Howells's lovely metaphor also locates Twain firmly within the "world of letters," which is precisely where Twain placed himself when he described the centering of his life in "The Turning Point of My Life" and defined his work as that of a craftsman within the "literary guild." *Mark Twain & Company* traces some of Twain's saunterings in the "trim world of letters," notes several of the people he met along the way, and tracks a few of the paths they walked together.

WRINGING THE HUMAN HEART

# Mark Twain
# & Bret Harte

*I know it is a pity to wring the poor human*

*heart, and it grieves me to do it;*

*but it is the only way to move some people to reflect.*

MARK TWAIN, 1906

"Bret Harte was one of the pleasantest men I have ever known. He was also one of the unpleasantest men I have ever known" (*MTE* 264). Thus with a faint echo of Dickens's *A Tale of Two Cities*, Mark Twain began what has become one of the most famous tirades in the history of American letters. Dwelling mostly on the unpleasant, Twain goes on to recall incidents in his thirteen-year relationship with Harte that began convivially in San Francisco in 1865, grew into a mutually beneficial friendship, resulted in a collaboratively written play, *Ah Sin*, and ended with acrimony and recrimination on each side.

Twain's tale of two writers has sparked a number of biographical brush-fires. While most Twain commentators have accepted—or passed over—his remarks about Harte, some Harte critics have challenged Twain's account and undertaken to rectify it, occasionally by attacking Twain's character.[1] Yet there is by now something close to a critical consensus on the nature of the Twain-Harte relationship. They are viewed as writers from the same territory who exploited similar materials and became rivals,

14

competitors who vied with each other for national acclaim. It is clear that the two writers acted and reacted to each other, that they were stirred, sometimes positively, sometimes negatively, by each other. Beyond that, however, there is little sense of the exact nature of their ties as writers. The literary implications of their personal relationship have not been fully explored. What, one still wonders, did Twain hate so much about Harte's work? Or, if the answer to that is clear enough (and it probably is), why? What does Twain's response to Harte reveal about his own writing?

Although Harte (1836–1902) was a year younger than Clemens, he was as quick to dedicate himself to literature as Clemens was slow. Both men tried various nonliterary careers. Harte dabbled in western mining, taught school, clerked in a pharmacy, and worked as a Wells Fargo courier, a printer's devil, and an assistant newspaper editor, all before fully settling into the profession of writing. Clemens started somewhat closer to the world of letters, serving at the age of thirteen, after the death of his father, as an apprentice on a Hannibal newspaper, then as a printer's devil and occasional assistant editor on his brother Orion's newspaper, but he veered away from the print shop and editorial office to become a successful riverboat pilot, and then, after the Civil War closed down the river trade, a bureaucratic assistant in the Nevada Territory, a frenzied prospector, and finally a newspaper correspondent. With a striking mixture of ruefulness, pride, melodrama, and self-deprecation, Harte recorded, at age twenty-one, his commitment to literature:

In these 365 days [he is writing on New Year's eve] I have again put forth a feeble essay toward fame and perhaps fortune—I have tried literature albeit in a humble way—successfully—I have written some poetry: passable and some prose (good) which have been published. The conclusion forced upon me by observation and not by vain enthusiasm that I am fit for nothing else—must impel me to seek distinction and fortune in literature. (Harte's diary; qtd. in Stewart 68)

Clemens announced his own literary vocation with equal pride, melodrama, and self-deprecation, but he was twenty-nine when he did so:

I *have* had a "call" to literature, of a low order—*i.e.* humorous. It is nothing to be proud of, but it is my strongest suit, & if I were to listen to that maxim of stern *duty* which says that to do right you **must** multiply the one or the two or the three talents which the Almighty entrusts to your keeping, I would long ago have ceased to meddle with things for which I was by nature unfitted & turned my attention to seriously scribbling to excite the **laughter** of God's creatures. Poor, pitiful business! Though the Almighty did His part by me—for the talent is a mighty engine when supplied with the steam of **education**—which I have not got . . . (*L1* 322–23)

Just as his determination (or resignation) to become a writer preceded Clemens's, Harte's establishment as a literary figure came before his. Well before Clemens had arrived in the West and discovered his mother lode as Mark Twain, Harte was publishing poems and sketches in the optimistically named *Golden Era*. Before Mark Twain reached San Francisco as a harum-scarum writer of humorous sketches, on the run from Nevada, Harte had become not only a regular contributor to but also the occasional editor of the *Californian*, a weekly journal in which Twain would sometimes appear and which he touted to his family as "the best weekly literary paper in the United States" (*L1* 312). Harte had even published a story, "The Legend of Monte del Diablo," in the august *Atlantic Monthly*. Twain did fire off something of a skyrocket in 1865 with the publication of "Jim Smiley and His Jumping Frog," but he did not publish a book until an ill-fated collection of his sketches, *The Celebrated Jumping Frog of Calaveras County and Other Sketches*, appeared in May of 1867. He did not secure a true national audience until *The Innocents Abroad* began to sweep the homefront late in 1869. Harte, on the other hand, edited a controversial, widely discussed volume, *Outcroppings, Being Selections of California Verse*, in 1866; published his own popular *Condensed Novels and Other Papers* as well as *The Last Galleon and Other Tales* in 1867; became the founding editor of the *Overland Monthly* in 1868 (a journal designed to rival the *Atlantic Monthly*); published a national sensation, "Plain Language from Truthful James," in 1870; and brought out in the same year his most widely read work, *The Luck of Roaring Camp and Other Stories*. He was ahead of Twain in almost all ways: in finding his career, in creative output, in versatility, in recognition, and in the perfection of his artistry. (Only in genius—genius not yet realized—did Twain outstrip Harte.) Twain himself (never one to shower praise on others) acknowledged as much. "Though I am generally placed at the head of my breed of scribblers in this part of the country," he told his mother and sister in 1865, "the place properly belongs to Bret Harte" (*L1* 328).

Having the jump on Twain in accomplishment and recognition, Harte would speak from the Olympian heights of his early fame to rank Mark Twain graciously as "the most original humorist that America has yet produced" ("American Humor," *Writings of BH* 20:230). And Twain, having struck what he took to be the gold mine of subscription publishing, would urge the American Publishing Company to sign on Harte (*MTLP* 74, n. 1). Yet Twain was divided over Harte's sudden rise in the literary world. In one mood he insisted "indeed Harte *does* soar, & I am glad of it" (*L4* 248); in another, however, he proclaimed, "I will 'top' Bret Harte again or bust" (*MTLP* 58). Only after their fatal collaboration—one that has been called "the most ill-fated collaboration in the history of American letters" (Scharnhorst 60)—did Harte settle into indifference about Twain and Twain become entrenched in unmitigated scorn for Harte.

The collapse of their relationship was not a sudden plummet but a slow, accelerating downward spiral. From their first meeting in San Francisco in 1864, when Harte was nominally working as a private secretary in the U.S. mint but actually spending his time on his own writing and editing (first of *The Californian*, and later the *Overland Monthly*), Twain was impressed by Harte's confident tone, his virtuosity, and his sheer talent. His admiration remained strong enough for Twain to ask Harte in 1868 to edit the manuscript of *The Innocents Abroad*. Perhaps Twain's eventual dislike rose in proportion to his sense of Harte's talent.

The reasons for the eventual falling out between the two remain matters of speculation. Their competition in the literary field, Harte's later borrowing from Twain and freeloading (Harte once so overstayed himself at Twain's home that Twain listed him in the Hartford city directory as his boarder), Harte's suspect moral character, and finally his insult to Livy (for which he apologized rather glibly)—all fed the fires of Twain's annoyance. While the exact cause of the breakup of the friendship remains uncertain, the terms in which Twain denounced Harte are infamous.[2] Notorious as they have become, however, Twain's charges were not generally known at the time. It is important to note that while he fulminated against Harte, Twain confined his outraged criticism for years to his private correspondence, personal notebooks, and unpublished autobiographical dictations. His single published critique—a one-paragraph observation in a sizeable essay, a paragraph about equally divided between criticism and praise—appeared anonymously (see "Reply to a Boston Girl," *MTC1* 742–46). But Twain's private vituperations were often as violent and biased as his public criticism was mild and judicious. Once the decisive break between the two occurred, Twain derided Harte, off and on for almost thirty-five years, with a consistency that suggests settled conviction—and something more. Here are three of Twain's attacks, two from the early, one from the final stages of his rancor, which reveal the keynotes of disliking Harte he struck throughout his life. The first, from a letter to Howells in June 1878, is a sharp but simple assault on Harte's character:

> Harte is a liar, a thief, a swindler, a snob, a sot, a sponge, a coward, a Jeremy Diddler, he is brim full of treachery. . . . How do I know? By the best of all evidence, personal observation. (*MTHL* 235)

The second, recorded in his notebook almost exactly a year later, assails not Harte's character but his immoral subject matter:

> Indignation meeting of Bret Harte's characters for being so misrepresented & required to talk impossible & non-existent "dialects" & change them every ten minutes. Till at last some of the whores & burglars said, "We owe him *one* grace, anyway. We have been the filthiest lot of heartless villains all our lives that ever went unhung—now instead of using the sufferings of the really good & worthy people whom we have robbed & ruined as the basis of his pathos, he hunts out (no, not that,)—he *manufactures* the one good deed possible to each of us, & in this way he has set the whole world to snuffling over us & wanting to hug us. We owe Harte a deep debt of gratitude—the reverence in which gamblers, burglars & whores are held in the upper classes to-day is all due to him, & to him only—for the dime novel circulates only among the lower ranks.["] (*N&J2* 311–12)

Finally, in this famous autobiographical outburst, dictated in June 1906 but not published until 1940, Twain merges the personal and the literary:

> He hadn't a sincere fiber in him. I think he was incapable of emotion, for I think he had nothing to feel with. I think his heart was merely a pump and had no other function. . . . This is the very Bret Harte whose pathetics, imitated from

Dickens, used to be a godsend to the farmers of two hemispheres on account of the freshets of tears they compelled. He said to me once with a cynical chuckle that he thought he had mastered the art of pumping up the tear of sensibility. (*MTE* 265)

How can one account for such strong—and persistent—venom? The usual explanations are that, on the personal side, Twain was offended by Harte's frequent requests to borrow money, by his snide remarks, and by his general air of superiority, and that, on the literary, he found objectionable Harte's want of realism as a writer.[3] These are no doubt true, but there is perhaps even more at work. Hamlin Hill once shrewdly observed that what Twain "attacked and attempted to destroy in his enemies" were "parts of his own personality, traits to which he was himself committed, roles which he had, in part at least, played himself" ("MT and His Enemies" 521). For Hill, in the case of Bret Harte what Twain saw was "a specter image of himself"—a western writer seeking money as much as literary achievement, carefully cultivating the eastern establishment; and further, a writer whose sudden plummet from eminence to mediocrity offered a fear-inducing cautionary tale (521–23).

Hill is almost certainly right in suggesting that in denouncing Harte, Twain contended with himself. In addition to the issues of personal character and probable career, however, we can also locate literary anxieties underlying Twain's vilification. For Twain seems to assail in Harte's work qualities that trouble him about his own.

The notebook entry just cited (the second of the three passages) is a revealing case in point. The passage is especially interesting because it plots a literary representation of Harte's characters. With playful malice, Twain thinks of having Harte's "gamblers, burglars & whores" first complain about their creator's incorrect and inconsistent dialect and then thank him for overlooking the people they have "robbed & ruined" to dramatize instead the "one good deed possible to each" of them. Twain's imagined satire is pointed at Harte's evocation of sympathy for vile and immoral characters ("he has set the whole world to suffering over us"), and it is energized by his annoyance with Harte's faulty diction, his falsification of character, and his contrived pathos. Twain is agitated, however, not only by morality but also by sexual disgust. While he uses the neutral—and precise—"gamblers," he softens "thieves" into the slightly comic "burglars" and hardens "prostitutes" into "whores." His emphasis in the last instance is on debased, commercial sexuality—a reality foreign to Harte's fiction, which always assiduously avoids such explicit naming in favor of genteel circumlocutions. A few pages further on in his notebook Twain focuses his disturbance in this single-line entry: "Bret's saintly wh's & self-sacrificing sons of b's" (*N&J2* 342).

Of course, Harte does people his stories with sexually potent women. Henry Adams was largely right to suggest that besides Whitman only Harte had "insisted on the power of sex," had presented the woman—"as far as the magazines would let him venture"—as "a true force" (Adams 384–85). Harte is archly circumspect about sexual power, however; he delicately suggests its presence in men and women alike as an energy, "intense, erotic and irresistible," one that drives the acts of men and women, one that guides, even compels, their choices (Thomas, "BH and the Power of Sex" 93). But he never explicitly represents sexual desire itself. Though sexually attractive and sexually driven, his women are never, as Twain implies, filthy creatures who ruin men.

As everyone knows, Mark Twain was even more circumspect in print about sexual matters than Harte. In *The Innocents Abroad* he does visit the notorious Cancan, discuss nude art, and moralize over the legendary love of Héloïse and Abelard, and in *A Connecticut Yankee in King Arthur's Court* he both denounces the sexual indelicacy of the aristocracy and creates in Morgan le Fay a sexually potent, emasculating, and finally lethal woman. It was not until the final decades of his career, however, that he began to explore openly what Susan Gillman has termed "tales of sexual identity" (see her chapter 4); and only in the posthumously published *Letters from the Earth* did he talk explicitly about sexual matters in a book. Significantly, at the time he denounced Harte in his notebooks, he was considering, even beginning to write about, sexual issues. In 1876 (just three years before his notebook entry on Harte) he wrote—and circulated among male friends—the bawdy *1601, Conversation as It Was by the Social Fireside in the Time of the Tudors*. While its attention to farting, penis measurement, and sexual prowess makes it seem adolescent, it has been interpreted as an "exhibitionistic substitute for overt sexual aggressiveness" (Cardwell, *The Man Who Was MT* 171). Nothing in Harte's fiction even begins to approach the explicitness of Twain's conversation. Surely, in objecting to what he saw—or imagined he saw—as Harte's inappropriate treatment of sexual figures, Twain betrayed an anxiety over his own proclivities, inclinations that were beginning to find expression in his writings, however carefully he curbed their circulation.

In his biography, *Mr. Clemens and Mark Twain*, Justin Kaplan has argued that in 1879, when Twain was living in France (just when he was denouncing Harte in his notebooks), he began to express "his own intensely troubled, incurably divided concern with sexuality" (222). He finds Twain at this time obsessed with the sexual, and a great deal of the available evidence supports his contention. Viewing Titian's Venus, for instance, Twain describes her, again in his private notebook, as "grossly obscene," the "Goddess of the Beastly," one who is "thinking bestialities." Since statues do not think, it is easy to see in Twain's ruminations his own sexual disturbance. He goes on to note, in terms that reveal unequivocally his own torment of desire and prohibition, that this woman "inflames & disgusts at the same moment" (*N&J2* 319). Setting aside the personal implications of such transparent conflict, the danger for Mark Twain—one he obliquely checks in his remarks on Harte—is that he will begin to sully his writings with expressions of his sexual interests. He cut from the book he was composing in fits and starts at the time, *A Tramp Abroad*, a variety of salacious and scatological passages that range from quips about sex to a disquisition on nudity in art to a tale of bodily smells.[4] To himself he noted, perhaps lamented, "the funniest things are the forbidden" (*N&J2* 304). Significantly, it was at exactly this time that he gave to the all-male Stomach Club in Paris his bawdy speech "Some Thoughts on the Science of Onanism." And at this very time, as he railed against licentious France and complained of Harte's corrupting "whores," he instructed himself, "Make a collection of my profane works," and then added the safeguard that would, at least to his own sense of things, mark him off from Harte, "to be privately printed" (*N&J2* 333).

Untroubled by questions of voice or persona in literature, of the distance between the writer and his creations, Twain tended to link the nature of the literary work with the character of its creator. The criticism of his era generally did so. Even Henry James resolved, at least to his own satisfaction, the vexed question of morality in fiction by asserting as axiom—one that covers "all needful moral ground"—that "the deepest quality of a work of art will always be the quality of the mind of the producer" ("The Art of Fiction" 66). It is not surprising, then, that Twain believed that

Harte's treatment of sexual matters in his fiction was matched by, or, more accurately, was caused by, his flawed character.

Duckett has pointed out that Twain's depiction of Harte in his autobiography is designed to suggest "effeminacy, even homosexuality" (*MT and Bret Harte* 10):

> He was showy, meretricious, insincere; and he constantly advertised these qualities in his dress. He was distinctly pretty. . . . He had good taste in clothes. . . . They always had a single smart little accent, effectively located and that accent would have distinguished Harte from any other of the ultrafashionables. Oftenest it was his necktie. Always it was of a single color, and intense. Most frequently, perhaps, it was crimson—a flash of flame under his chin; or it was indigo blue and hot and vivid as if one of those splendid and luminous Brazilian butterflies had lighted there. Harte's dainty self-complacencies extended to his carriage and gait. His carriage was graceful and easy, his gait was of the mincing sort, but was the right gait for him, for an unaffected one would not have harmonized with the rest of the man and the clothes. (*MTE* 264–65)

While Twain's own attitudes toward homosexuality may have been mixed (see Andrew Hoffman, "MT and Homosexuality"), he certainly knew that it was socially condemned. Here he either deliberately stigmatizes Harte or honestly defines him as he saw him. He faults him further on two other counts, both related to sexuality but contradicting the imputation of homosexuality. He notes first that, in San Francisco, Harte "kept a woman who was twice his age—no, the woman kept him" and that "twenty-five or thirty years later, he was kept, at different times, by a couple of women." To this attribution of impropriety, he adds a second two-pronged charge: that Harte mistreated his wife—a "fine and loveable and lovely" woman— by speaking "sarcastically, not to say sneeringly, of her" and that he happily "deserted" her and his family, never to send them so much as "a dollar" for their support (*MTE* 281–82, 278, 291).[5] From Twain's point of view, this Bret Harte might naturally write of immoral men and fallen women.

Twain attacked Harte even more often—and more stridently—for his sentimentality. And just as he saw (or imagined he saw) the objectionable sexual subject matter in Harte's fiction as the natural result of his flawed morality, so he believed that Harte's sentimentality also arose from his faulty character. Over and over Twain insisted, with a repetition that borders on obsession, that Harte had "no feeling" and "no conscience." Harte had, he says, "no feeling, for the reason that he had no machinery to feel with." And again, this time with self-conscious apology, he points to the same essential flaw: "I have said more than once in these pages that Harte had no heart and no conscience" (*MTE* 272, 288, 289). Harte was, for Twain, insincere—a fake, the "Immortal Bilk" (*MTHL* 326). According to Twain, Harte had no feeling because he had no heart, and hence all the renderings of emotion in his fiction were necessarily spurious. All Harte could do was create false "pathetics" by mechanically "pumping up the tear of sensibility." Lacking the capacity to feel, Harte was incapable of creating true sentiment; he could only be sentimental. But as with the sexual, so with the sentimental: Twain attacked in Harte's writings what he feared in his own.

At the time Harte and Twain emerged as writers, literary emotion itself was a contested issue. The great age of American romance, with its underside of sentimentality, was under attack by a new generation of fictionalists who dismissed the prevailing literary constructions as so many falsifications of reality. Although sentimentality in particular was under assault, the mode persisted and even found new forms. Local-color fiction, for instance, arguably the kind of writing first practiced by both Harte and Twain, continued and extended many of the emotional effects of the sentimental novel, adding the piquant sense that good-heartedness could be found in all parts of the country, in all—diverse—kinds of down-home country folk. Both Harte and Twain took up arms in the ongoing battle between romance and realism, joining passionately—indeed, good-humoredly—in what their mutual friend and sponsor, William Dean Howells, called "banging the babes of romance about" (qtd. in Cady, *The Realist at War* 1). Twain labeled the preceding age "an era of sentimentality & sloppy romantics" (*MTB* 1197), and Harte, somewhat more colorfully, spoke of "the days when literature spread its refreshment table for the weary traveller with indigestible moral pie, sensational hot coffee, sentimental tea, and emotional soda water" (*California Sketches* 91).

Harte made fun of the sentimental mode in his early poems and sketches. In his popular *Condensed Novels* he burlesqued such writers of romantic adventure as James Fenimore Cooper, Alexandre Dumas, and Bulwer-Lytton; at the same time, he mocked the sentimental style practiced by

Charles Dickens and T. S. Arthur. His 1867 spoof of Whittier, "Mrs. Judge Jenkins" (subtitled "The Only Genuine Sequel to 'Maud Muller'"), concludes: "Alas for the maiden! alas for judge! / And the sentimental,—that's one-half 'fudge'" (*Poems* 289).

Early Mark Twain worked the same vein, writing sketches, such as "Love's Bakery" and "The Sentimental Law Student," that satirize sentimental love, and even turning out a few condensed novels of his own—an "Original Novelette" and "Lucretia Smith's Soldier," for instance—which make fun of sensational romances. In the climax to his "Original Novelette," he observes that the "heroine of this history is stricken with grief," and then with a deliberately mocking echo of Susan Warner's best-selling novel, *The Wide, Wide World*, he adds that she is "set adrift upon the wide, wide world, without a rudder" (*ET&S2* 32). Clearly for Twain, as for Harte, sentimental fiction itself, awash in a sea of emotion, is rudderless.

While they sought the real—or their constructions of it—and made fun of the romantic in its various forms, Harte and Twain embroiled themselves in contradictions. Both used humor as a principal weapon in the war against romance, the war for realism, yet both believed that humor depended on pathos. Echoing an idea common in his era, Twain late in his career articulated a belief he had held for most of his creative life. "I maintain," he insisted to an interviewer, "that a man can never be a humorist, in thought or in deed, until he can feel the springs of pathos" ("MT Talks" 11). Ironically, at the near start of Twain's career, in a review of *The Innocents Abroad*, Harte used the same concept to qualify his praise of Twain's achievement in his first travel book. "If he has not that balance of pathos which we deem essential to complete humor," he pontificated, "he has something very like it in that serious eloquence to which we have before alluded" (*CH* 35). Further, both Twain and Harte valued emotion, even the tender emotion of sympathy, for its own sake. But while Harte openly acknowledged the importance of such feeling, Twain most often disguised his interest in it.

For both writers, negotiating between authentic emotion and its sentimental imitation was perilous. For one thing, even in the halcyon days of their apprenticeship in literature, days in which each would write almost anything (though Harte was even then the more fastidious stylist), both understood that they were latecomers to the art of fiction. Despite the posture each assumed as one insufficiently educated, both had read widely through the years before they found themselves as writers. Both knew more than they let on about the great works of English and American literature. And both knew the works of the most important sentimentalist in English fiction, their immediate predecessor, Charles Dickens. Their mutual interest in Dickens bespeaks their interest in emotion-filled writing. Of course, any writer coming of age in the afterglow of the Dickens mania, a paroxysm that seized people on both sides of the Atlantic, had to come to terms with the master. Predictably perhaps, Harte and Twain pay tribute to Dickens and distance themselves from him, responding to their belatedness with a mix of admiration and criticism. Harte is more open and emphatic on both points. His condensed novel parody, "The Haunted Man, By CH-R-S D-CK-N-S, A Christmas Story," makes fun of Dickens's heavy use of atmosphere, his typed characters—the child, the good woman, the wicked lady—his foreshadowing, and his rhetorical style. Harte also mocks Dickensian pathos (the child, "prematurely old and philosophic," dies "in poverty to slow music"), but in the end, as the awakened dreamer of the narrative unconsciously reenacts "A Christmas Carol's" morning of rejuvenation, he exclaims, "What a genius this Dickens has!" (*Writings of BH* 1:188–96). At the time of Dickens's death Harte wrote a memorial tribute, praising his pathos, his vitality, his humor, his poetic prose, and his humanity—a humanity that enabled him to bring "the poor nearer to our hearts" (*Writings of BH* 20:165–67). Despite Harte's early, playfully expressed reservations, Patrick D. Morrow is surely right when he says that Dickens was Harte's "literary hero" (53). With transparent openness, Harte imitated Dickens in his own fiction and more often than not welcomed the comparison he thus prompted.

Not so Mark Twain. In an 1862 letter to his mother from Carson City, Nevada, Twain reports carrying *Dombey and Son* with him on his 350-mile excursion to and back from the Humboldt mining area (*L1* 147), but he would never again acknowledge so dramatically that Dickens's work made a valued—even inspiring—fellow-traveler. Although his letters contain numerous references to Dickens, and although Twain's own writings often have Dickensian echoes, Twain liked to maintain that he did not, indeed could not, read Dickens. To Albert Bigelow Paine, his authorized biographer, he explained, "My brother used to try to get me to read Dickens, long ago. I couldn't do it" (*MTB* 1500–1501). Several explanations have been advanced to account for Twain's deceptive disclaimers. Minnie M. Brashear opined that Twain was filled with "boredom" (a curiously slight term) by "the critics' insistence upon a Dickens influence" (212). Alan Gribben cautiously suggests that Twain felt "envy of Dickens as an artist on the lecture platform" (*MT's Library* 186). Taking a broader view, Joseph H. Gardner sees in Twain's rejection of Dickens an attack on "the genteel cult that lionized him" ("MT and Dickens" 97). Albert E. Stone comes closest, I believe, to the basis of Twain's resistance when he argues that "what put Twain off was the very aspect of Dickens's fiction that made him so successful and invited imitation—his pathos" (15). Certainly, when he reported on the Dickens reading he attended in New York in December 1867, Twain criticized Dickens for his pathos (along with his bad reading): "His pathos is only the beautiful pathos of his language—there is no heart, no feeling in it—it is glittering frostwork" (qtd. in Gardner, "MT and Dickens" 95). Twain's charge here is precisely the one he would level at Harte many years later—no heart, hence no true feeling; and he probably makes it here, as in all likelihood he did against Harte, to cover his own literary tracks, to conceal, perhaps from himself as well as his readers, his own susceptibility to pathos.

Harte, an open sentimentalist. Twain, a covert one. How did two "realists" come to such a state? In his compelling study of sentimentality in the Victorian and modern eras, Howard W. Fulweiler describes the change in collective consciousness that gave rise to sentimentality: "Victorians who were sensitive to the subtle shifts in basic consciousness around them felt themselves increasingly cut off, increasingly bereft of the sense of belonging—not just belonging to a church or to an organic state, but to nature as well. This growing change in perception of the world engendered a search for the remnants of belonging, for the links that might still connect human beings to nature and to the past, in which an organic relationship to nature was felt to have been unbroken" (21). Both Twain and Harte seem to feel such a loss of connection: a sense of "alienation, disorientation, and homelessness" (Fulweiler 5), and their recurrent subjects may well reflect both an acknowledgment of this bereavement and an effort to overcome it through human relationships. Like a typical Victorian, Twain enshrined the holy trinity of the innocent child, the pure woman, and the sacred home-and-family. Harte, too, focuses much of his fiction on the child and the woman, but unlike Twain, his child is often allowed to grow into maturity, often a sexual maturity, and his women are frequently far from pure; stable homes with families, even the partial family of an Aunt Polly, are seldom seen in Harte's fictive world. While both Twain and Harte turn to the figure of the orphan to evoke a lonely, separate human existence, Twain's women and families offer ways to reconnect that are not to be found in Harte's scheme of things. Both Harte and Twain treat subjects that embody their loss and longing, and, despite their differences, both present their subjects sentimentally: that is, with excess emotion conveyed through formula and contrived rhetoric.

Once a nearly universal term of admiration, then an equally widespread term of opprobrium in literary criticism, sentimentality has of course been recuperated in recent years. Its restoration, however, has led to new debate. Jane Tompkins has maintained that sentimental texts function within their culture as instruments of social self-definition that have the power—because of their very sentimentality—to alter social reality (introduction and chapter 6). And Philip Fisher has argued persuasively that from about 1740 to 1860 sentimentality was the key device in the politically radical representation that attempted to bestow personhood, humanity, on repressed or marginalized people—the poor, the insane, women, and slaves, for instance (92, 99–104). However, a provocative recent collection of essays, *The Culture of Sentiment: Race, Gender, and Sentimentality in Nineteenth-Century America*, demonstrates that sentimentality is not always an agent of progressive change; on the contrary, it sometimes operates repressively to maintain an unjust status quo (see Samuels). In short, though currently valued for its cultural power, sentimentality is not inherently liberal or conservative. Socially aware and at least sometimes politically minded as both Twain and Harte were, it is natural that each would exploit one of the most effective literary tactics of their time.

Harte's sentimentality is worth revisiting both for its own sake and for the light it sheds on Twain. However Harte is estimated, it is generally agreed that his early California stories constitute some (if not all) of his finest work. And unmistakable in those tales, as both the early appreciations and later condemnations make clear, is Harte's penchant for sentimental pathos. Virtually ever-present, this pathos assumes several forms. In "The Outcasts of Poker Flat," we join the stoic Oakhurst as witness to a self-sacrifice that entails death:

"I'm going," she said, in a voice of querulous weakness, "but don't say anything about it. Don't waken the kids. Take the bundle from under my head and open it." Mr. Oakhurst did so. It contained Mother Shipton's rations for the last week, untouched. "Give 'em to the child," she said, pointing to the sleeping Piney. "You've starved yourself," said the gambler. "That's what they call it," said the woman, querulously, as she lay down again, and, turning her face to the wall, passed quietly away. (*Selected Stories and Sketches* 26)

In "The Luck of Roaring Camp," Harte's single most famous—and perhaps most representative—tale we are given a beneficent, nurturing, even entertaining Nature that seems to minister to the baby Luck:

Howbeit, whether creeping over the pine-boughs or lying lazily on his back blinking at the leaves above him, to him the birds sang, the squirrels chattered, and the flowers bloomed. Nature was his nurse and playfellow. For him she would let slip between the leaves golden shafts of sunlight that fell just within his grasp; she would send wandering breezes to visit him with the balm of bay and resinous gums; to him the tall red-woods nodded familiarly and sleepily, the bumble-bees buzzed, and rooks cawed a slumbrous accompaniment. (*Selected Stories and Sketches* 15)

And in "Tennessee's Partner," we are given first the dying Partner's final vision of reconciliation and union and then the narrator's apparent confirmation of it:

"It is time to go for Tennessee; I must put 'Jinny' in the cart . . . There, now, steady, 'Jinny,'—steady, old girl. How dark it is! Look out for the ruts,—and look out for him, too, old gal. Sometimes, you know, when he's blind drunk, he drops down right in the trail. Keep on straight up to the pine on the top of the hill, Thar—I told you so!—thar he is,—coming this way, too,—all by himself, sober, and his face a-shining. Tennessee! Pardner!"

And so they met. (*Selected Stories and Sketches* 48–49)

Surely these three passages disclose the Harte that rose so suddenly to near-cosmic popularity, as well as the Harte that found his home (and his considerable income) for so many years in the hearts of English readers. Represented here, arguably at his best, is the sentimental Bret Harte.

Variously defined as an excess of emotion, a falsification of feeling, a manipulation of the reader's responses, or a deliberate evocation of empathy, such sentimentality is often artful, albeit in ways largely foreign to subsequent centuries. In the first instance, Harte's noting of a "tone of querulous weakness" captures a contentiousness that checks somewhat the noble self-sacrifice being registered, making Mother Shipton human even as she seems to become saintly. In the second passage, nature is both caught in familiar cliché (something of an art in itself)—"The birds sang, the squirrels chattered, and the flowers bloomed"—and rendered curiously insubstantial—"sunlight . . . within his grasp." In the third passage, the suggestion of authentic colloquial speech ("There, now, steady, 'Jinny' "), the insistence on realistic detail ("Look out for the ruts"), and the inclusion of irrelevant direction ("Keep on straight up to the pine"), all play against the emerging ecstasy ("Tennessee! Pardner!"). In each case Harte not only evokes tender feeling but also balances it with countervailing notations. In doing so, he simultaneously creates sentimentality and palliates it.

The subjects here are typical of Harte: a noble human, a beneficent nature, a quasi-religious vision of spiritual union between kindred souls. They are all in themselves, apart from their artistic realization, charged with strong affirmative feeling, and they are all notions Harte's era wanted to believe in. But at the same time he entrances his readers with compelling versions of their own predilections, he problematizes them. All three moments of pathos are marked, if not marred, by a play of comic irony. Mother Shipton's laconic remark (still in her querulous mode), in response to Oakhurst's assertion that she has "starved" herself, "That's what they call it," opens the possibility that she takes a different view: that her death is a fulfilling escape rather than a depleting self-destruction. Tommy Luck's seemingly wondrous encounter with nature as "nurse and playfellow" is so carefully and insistently presented as his perception alone— "to him," "for him," "to him"—that it bespeaks a child's egocentric illusion as much as true ministration. And the narrator's concluding remark about the vision of Tennessee's Partner—"And so they met"—far from confirming the imagined reconciliation suggests that such a union is only possible—"so," that is, "in this way"—as delusion.

Harte's sentimentality, at its strongest, is thus fraught with its own ironic undercuttings. His sentimental moments are anything but the simple "pathetics" Mark Twain thought them to be. They reflect something of the contrariety that his San Francisco friend and fellow writer, Charles Warren Stoddard, called attention to in his reminiscence "Early Recollections of Bret Harte." Stoddard identifies as characteristics of Harte's work this notable gathering of oxymoronic qualities: "pathetic humor," "humorous pathos," "tragic fun," and "comic tragedy" (674). While Stoddard pointed to a medley of opposites, William Dean Howells saw something close to complete decentering. Speaking of Harte the man, Howells pinpointed an evasiveness that is actually characteristic of the fiction. "You never could," he said, "be sure of Harte," for "only by chance" could he "be caught in earnest about anything or anybody" (*Literary Friends and Acquaintances* 248). Harte's narrators operate out of just such a refusal to be steady and sincere. Striking one posture after another, only to subvert it, they typically destabilize the fiction, creating a world of emotional and normative indeterminacy. In what seems to be a classic case of "the pot calling the kettle black" Harte once faulted the literary newcomer Rudyard Kipling for writing stories with "a certain smart *attitude*" (*Selected Letters* 366). It is Harte himself, of course, who adopts just such an attitude.

Perhaps, then, Harte cannot be caught in being earnest even when he is, as Twain put it, "pumping up the tear of sensibility." Perhaps Harte is a more ironic writer than we have realized.[6] But if Harte ironizes his sentimentality, what happens when he is treating, either in fiction or essay, a wholly serious subject to which he is committed? Insofar as Harte is alive and well in current literary study, it is not for his once-famous western tales but for his writings of social protest. Recent evaluations of Harte celebrate his social criticism: his attacks on race prejudice, on gender constraints, and on international imperialism. What role does Harte's sentimentality play in such writings? While the sketches and tales in which his social critiques appear are varied, it seems to me that Harte's reform fictions are most successful when he suspends his typical ironic sentimentality, least successful when he indulges it.

The end of the anti-imperial story "Peter Schroeder" poses the key problem. Having first struck it rich in the California gold fields and then volunteered in the name of republican principles on the side of the North during the Civil War, Schroeder is later talked into joining an imperialist venture in South America. That the effort to colonize (only reported in the story), however bathed in republican rhetoric, is morally wrong is brought home by Harte's evocation of the real filibuster, William Walker, who conquered

Nicaragua (and reestablished slavery there), only to be executed in Honduras. (Interestingly, Mark Twain admired Walker as a man of dauntless courage.)[7] Like Walker, Peter Schroeder is executed by a firing squad. Harte ends his story this way: "Peter stepped calmly before the loaded muskets. But his friend saw in dismay that he had changed his clothes, and wore his faded blouse and blue army cap of an American sergeant. . . . The officer's sword waved, there was a crackle of musketry and the rising of pale blue smoke. And on its wings the soul of Peter Schroeder went in quest of his ideal republic" (*Writings of BH* 11:89). To make the scene touching Harte cloaks Schroeder's objectionable imperialism beneath the reminders of his laudable service in the Civil War. Schroeder dies not as a filibuster but as an American patriot. Yet Harte undercuts the pathos he evokes with his final ironic remark: "the soul of Peter Schroeder went in quest of his ideal republic." Harte's "smart attitude" here muddles not only his sentimentality but also his political protest.

On the other hand, when Harte refrains from deploying sentimentality, his protest fiction is often powerful. The early "Wan Lee, the Pagan," though marred by some racist typing, is an effective condemnation of bigotry and racial intolerance. Although the narrator insists on communion with his audience in the end—"Dead, my reverend friends, dead!"—Harte resists his characteristic sentimentality, letting the "facts" speak for themselves, albeit with a dash of affectation: "Stoned to death in the streets of San Francisco, in the year of grace, eighteen hundred and sixty-nine, by a mob of half-grown boys and Christian school-children" (*Selected Stories and Sketches* 209). Harte's most extended treatment of racial prejudice and the imperialism it sanctions is his novella, *The Crusade of the Excelsior.* Harte himself felt that his story was "on new ground" and that it had "an original idea for its foundation" (*Letters* 314). Overall, the story seems to endorse what one critic has called "benign modernization through commercial trade" (Scharnhorst 105), even as it condemns colonial exploitation. Significantly, however, while there are some typical moments of pathos involving personal relations, the novella's politics are largely realized through irony.

In many ways the most intriguing of Harte's fictions of social protest is a short story he published just two years before his death, "Three Vagabonds of Trinidad." Despite its misleading title, the tale is set in an American frontier community in California, a place inhabited by representative

American types: the county newspaper editor; a farmer proud of his large radish; a deacon of the Methodist church; a kindly farmer's wife; some ragtag and bobtail miners; Mr. Parkin Skinner, a prominent citizen; and his son, Master Bob Skinner (most often referred to as "the Boston boy"). Most of these good citizens find themselves first annoyed by and then incensed to violence against two of the vagabonds of Harte's title: Li Tee, a "waif from a Chinese wash-house" charitably employed by the editor, and Jim, a "well-known drunken Indian vagrant of the settlement." Persecuted by the community for the mishaps of their kite (one with a tail made from the clothesline of the farmer's wife, with her personal under-garments still on it), Li Tee and Jim take refuge on a "lonely island" where they make camp and live off of the land and such fish as they can catch. The third vagabond is Jim's dog—a "slinking, rough, wolf-like brute" whose "superior instinct" enables it to "detect the silent presence" of "alien humanity." Skinner's son, Bob, finds the three on their island and joins them for a time before he returns home. Always carrying with him what Harte calls a "consciousness of his superior race," Bob is first a boyish adventurer out for a lark, then a confederate of the two outcasts, weighing the burdens of civilization, and finally their betrayer, for he not only tells the townspeople where the three are but also lies about them (*Writings of BH* 17:187–95).

Midway in the story Harte makes his moral point by exposing, perhaps somewhat too explicitly, the racist vision of Mr. Skinner:

> It's all very well for you to talk sentiment about niggers, Chinamen, and Injins . . . but I kin tell you, gentlemen, that this is a white man's country! Yes, sir, you can't get over it! The nigger of every description—yeller, brown, or black, call him "Chinese," "Injin," or "Kanaka," or what you like—hez got to clar off of God's footstool when the Anglo-Saxon gets started! It stands to reason that they can't live alongside o' printin' presses, M'Cormick's reapers, and the Bible! Yes, sir! The Bible; and Deacon Hornblower kin prove it to you. It's our manifest destiny to clar them out—that's what we was put here for—and it's just the work we've got to do! (*Writings of BH* 17:191–92).

This race hatred clearly infects the young Bob as well as the old Skinner (Harte makes his readers realize that prejudice is taught). The townsmen fulfill their "manifest destiny": Li Tee, cut off from the town, dies of starvation, and Jim is shot to death. In something like poetic justice, as Jim's killer observes the dead body with "the easy air of a conqueror," the jaws of Jim's dog close on the killer's throat (*Writings of BH* 17:200). This grisly ending is anything but sentimental.

"Three Vagabonds of Trinidad" is carefully structured. Its first half, with its report of a kite gone so astray as to deposit a woman's stockings on both the saloon and the church, is lightly comic; its second, focused on starvation and violent death, is darkly tragic. Harte thus creates, somewhat mechanically since the two parts are so sharply separated, a balance between humor and pathos. His pathos is effectively conveyed through largely flat reporting—a narrative devoid of presentational or linguistic excess. "Three Vagabonds of Trinidad" is an effective fictional condemnation of prejudice and its political implications.

"Three Vagabonds of Trinidad" may also be Harte's revisioning of Twain's *Adventures of Huckleberry Finn*. Harte clearly returns to the West he and Twain first shared and then fictionalized. His outcast Indian "Jim" seems to conflate the Injin Joe of *Tom Sawyer* with the slave Jim of *Huck Finn*. Indian Jim's retreat from oppression and persecution to the safety of an island replicates Jim's escape, in *Huck Finn*, from St. Petersburg to Jackson's Island. The addition of Li Tee recuperates Harte's own early attention to the oppressed Chinese. The vagrant Bob Skinner seems a reworking of both of Twain's most famous boys: like Tom Sawyer, Bob is given to transgressive adventure but firmly tied to his community's dubious values; and like Huck Finn, he comes to enjoy a kind of lawless freedom, a liberty significantly realized as illicit company—the ostracized, detested, and hunted racial outcasts. Harte's revisioning—if it is that— of Twain's two most famous fictions defies Twain's fictional rendering of race. For while Twain suggests that racial prejudice can be checked, if not overcome, as it is in Huck, Harte demonstrates that it is not only ineradicable but also lethal. Significantly, Harte makes his moral point astringently, without any trace of the sentimental "pathetics" Twain insisted on seeing as the essence of Harte's fiction.

At the time of Harte's death, the minor poet, distinguished editor, and popular novelist Thomas Bailey Aldrich expressed what was by then a familiar view of Harte. "I dropped reading him," Aldrich wrote, "when I found that he was not going to add anything to those first eight or ten fine stories of his" (qtd. in Scharnhorst 117). Contrary to this conventional view, several cases have been made for Harte's development, most notably

Scharnhorst's perceptive argument that Harte's fiction became darker, more violent, more in tune with what would soon be called naturalistic determinism (78–79, 94). But even within such variation Harte repeated many of his stock plots, characters, and themes, as he himself acknowledged when he complained of dishing up the same "old gruel" (qtd. in Scharnhorst 68). Fulweiler has described sentimentality as "an appeal to emotion which has become conventional rather than fresh, dogmatic rather than imaginative, reductive rather than enlarging" (184). In these terms one might say that the later Harte remained sentimental by copying the formulas of his own most commercially successful early fiction.[8]

In April 1888 Robert Louis Stevenson wrote to Mark Twain to say that his father had laughed himself silly over chapters 32 and 33 of *Roughing It* (*Letters of RLS* 6:162). In those chapters Ollendorff, Ballou, and the narrator become lost in a blizzard at night, fear death, and so reform before meeting their maker, one giving up his whiskey, another his card-playing, and the third his compulsive pipe-smoking. When dawn reveals that the three are "not fifteen steps" from the stage station, all three revert to their wicked ways and agree to "say no more about 'reform'" (*RI* 218–19). This well-known episode may be Twain's most forceful response to Bret Harte: a high-spirited parody of Harte's theme of sudden regeneration. Clearly Twain looked askance at such moral reformation in tried-and-true reprobates. Is he then only the critic of sentimental goodness? Or did he condemn in Harte what he feared in himself?[9]

Twain's condemnations of sentimentality are best understood in terms of the literary culture of his time. Although writing in America had been first a gentlemanly avocation and then a largely male profession, women writers had begun to dominate the marketplace by the middle of the nineteenth century. Women writers were so many in number and so celebrated in popular acclaim that the profession of writing itself became thought of as female (see Baym 13–14). Most of the major women writers, whether of the novel or local-color stories, were sentimental. To enter the literary profession, then, posed a threat for any man—the threat of appearing effeminate. And to write in the sentimental vein of women was to turn the threat into a reality.

This change in the gendering of literary activity vexed male writers throughout the second half of the century. Exploring the impact of the newly feminine literary culture, Alfred Habegger has discussed Howells and Henry James as "sissies" (chapter 7). Michael Davitt Bell has examined in careful, illuminating detail how several male realists negotiated the difficulty of being male in a female occupation *(The Problem of American Realism)*. For several reasons, though, Twain was less challenged by the re-gendering of the literary culture than were Howells and James. For one, he came to writing via the print shop and newspaper journalism, both then still largely male preserves. His early genre of choice, southwestern humor, was equally male-dominated. And Twain, unlike Howells and James, did not aspire, at least not early in his career, to publish in the established high-culture journals where women increasingly commanded space. But Twain was certainly aware of—indeed strongly influenced by—the change from a male to a female literary culture.

Laura E. Skandera-Trombley has argued that Twain was not just influenced by but deeply dependent on a community of women for his creative work *(Mark Twain in the Company of Women)*. Her case is convincing, but his hostility toward the popular women's writing of his time also needs to be taken into account. In the very first extant piece signed "Mark Twain," "Letter from Carson City," Twain makes fun of the well-known poem—turned into a beloved song—"Rock Me to Sleep, Mother," by Elizabeth Ann Allen *(ET&S1* 194–98). Thereafter, Mark Twain was steadily inclined to laugh at, criticize, or parody various forms of women's writing, especially the sentimental ones. He associated palpable feeling in fiction or poetry or song with women. In a letter to his boyhood chum Will Bowen he crystallized his objection to emotional writing: "Sentiment is for girls" *(MTLB* 23).

Twain's frequent attacks on sentimentality may in fact arise from his sense that it is essentially a female mode. His depiction of Harte as an effeminate male links with his sense that sentimentality, Harte's abiding literary flaw, is a woman's way of writing. Twain's condemnations of both Harte and sentimentality (and of Harte as sentimental) probably betray Twain's own gender anxiety, but Twain has a further problem. While he dismisses sentimentality, he also believes in, indeed values, genuine emotion. In the very letter to Bowen in which he says that sentiment—"the maudlin article"—is for girls and announces that he has "not the slightest sympathy with what the world calls Sentiment—not the slightest," he praises true emotion in hyperbolic terms. In fact, he celebrates it in terms we might well call "sentimental." "*Real* sentiment," he tells Bowen, "is a very rare & godlike thing.—You do not know anybody that has it; neither do I" (*MTLB* 24, 23, Twain's emphasis). Twain tries to represent "real sentiment" in his own writings, but the moments of intense feeling he creates often fall well short of the "rare & godlike."

According to Twain himself, Harte "trimmed and trained and schooled" him as a writer, changing him from "an awkward utterer of coarse grotesquenesses" into one whose "paragraphs and chapters" were well received by "some of the very decentest people in the land" (*MTL* 182–83). Harte had in fact gone through the entire manuscript of *The Innocents Abroad,* showing Twain "what passages, paragraphs, & *chapters* to leave out," and Twain claimed to have "followed orders strictly" (*L4* 248). It is more than a little ironic, then, that when he reviewed Twain's book in the *Overland Monthly,* Harte found fault with the writing, pointing out "some mannerism that is only slang" and "some skepticism" that lacks "cultivation." More revealing still, and particularly interesting in the light of Twain's central charge against Harte (and of Harte as imitator of Dickens), is his observation that when he is not feigning annoyance Twain is "*really* sentimental." Harte suggests that the sentimentality shows in "fine writing"—in "sentiment that is only rhetoric" (*CH* 33–35).

Harte is right. Twain's travel narrative is freighted with heavy passages of fancy writing intended to evoke tender emotions. Often Twain expresses his sentiments (or what he takes to be appropriate ones) in an ornate rhetoric that is, as Harte said, sentimental. A single—quite famous—passage will illustrate the general point. During his time in Pisa, Twain describes the effect of an Etruscan tear-jug, a vessel used to receive the tears of those bereaved by a family member's death:

A Pisan antiquarian gave me an ancient tear-jug which he averred was full four thousand years old. It was found among the ruins of one of the oldest of the Etruscan cities. He said it came from a tomb, and was used by some bereaved family in that remote age when even the Pyramids of Egypt were young, Damascus a village, Abraham a prattling infant and ancient Troy not yet dreamt of, to receive the tears wept for some lost idol of a household. It spoke to us in a language of its own; and with a pathos more tender than any words might bring, its mute eloquence swept down the long roll of the centuries with its tale of a vacant chair, a familiar footstep missed from the threshold, a pleasant voice gone from the chorus, a vanished form!—a tale which is always so new to us, so startling, so terrible, so benumbing to the senses, and behold how threadbare and old it is! No shrewdly-worded history could have brought the myths and shadows of that old dreamy age before us clothed with human flesh and warmed with human sympathies so vividly as did this poor unsentient vessel of pottery. (*IA* 197–98)

The object here, the tear-jug, is invisible—undescribed in itself, for what Twain wants to create is only a melancholy reflection on passing time and inevitable human loss. He becomes the translator of the jug's "language of its own," trying to capture in his words "a pathos more tender than any words might bring." But here the sentiment is all sentimental rhetoric.

Twain wrote passages like this one throughout his career. If his expression of such emotion was often sentimental, the feelings themselves were authentic. Famed for his empirical eye, for his ability to create—or recreate—quotidian life, life in its gritty particulars, he was nonetheless a man and writer moved by ideas—by abstractions. Often the conceptions to which he was most alive were moral imperatives. Retrospectively, he would claim that his humorous writings, his bread-and-butter, had lasted as long as they had—thirty years or more—because they were moral. "Humor," he insisted in his autobiography, "must not professedly teach and it must not professedly preach, but it must do both if it would live forever." Although he surely distorts his work and underestimates the uncheckable comic spirit within him, there is also a truth in this self-description: "I have always preached. That is the reason that I have lasted thirty years. If the humor came of its own accord and uninvited I have allowed it a place in my sermon, but I was not writing the sermon for the sake of the humor. I should have written the sermon just the same, whether any humor applied for admission or not" (*AMT* 273).

Setting aside the question of which came first, the preaching or the laughing, Twain did embed in his fictions any number of moral instructions about which he felt passionately—cloaking them in various ways so that they would not "professedly" teach. The medium of this moralizing is often sentimentality, and this, too, he disavowed and disguised when he could. Twain would perhaps naturally resort to sentimentality to make his moral points, since he often (though not always) shared the outlook of the sentimentalists. Camfield describes it as "an anti-authoritarian belief in the innate goodness of each human being and a belief in each person's access to that goodness through intuitive knowledge" (*Sentimental MT* 17). However, unlike Camfield, most critics who take note of sentimental moments in Twain lament them; they write them off as lapses. Everyone familiar with the Twain canon acknowledges that *The Prince and the Pauper* and *Personal Recollections of Joan of Arc* are full-scale sentimental fictions, but they are generally seen as aberrations. And there is general agreement that several of his late tales and sketches, notably "A Dog's Tale," "A Horse's Tale," "Eve's Diary," and "Eve Speaks," to cite a prominent few, are sentimental, but these are overlooked—or forgiven as the atypical effusions of an aging writer. However, to become sentimental in order to drive home a moral point is, for Mark Twain, neither a lapse, nor an aberration, nor a failing of old age; it is a fundamental gesture in his writing. It occurs in his best fiction as well as his strongest polemical essays.

Unlikely as it might seem, *Adventures of Huckleberry Finn* is a case in point. While the novel has stirred up controversy from the time of its first publication to now, amidst the violent tides of contention one dimension of the novel has stood rock solid: its realism. But *Huck Finn* is often as sentimental as it is realistic. In *The Problem of American Realism*, Bell makes an essential point: "The passages in *Huckleberry Finn* that one remembers and rereads with greatest fondness" are "those devoted to sincere description and emotional expression, to the recreation of feeling." "The most memorable accomplishments of Huck's vernacular," he explains, involve "the *evocation* of sentiment" (52). If this does not completely turn Twain's realistic text into a sentimental novel, it at least underscores the fact that the book is rife with emotion. And surely the single most famous—most remembered, cherished, and debated—of the novel's many emotional moments is the long struggle Huck has with his conscience, which culminates in his decision to go to hell.

Brilliant and moving as it is, the entire process of Huck's internal reflection is staged as pure sentimental melodrama. Here is the prelude to Huck's decision, a part of the familiar whole: "And at last, when it hit me all of a sudden that here was the plain hand of Providence slapping me in the face and letting me know my wickedness was being watched all the time from up there in heaven, whilst I was stealing a poor old woman's nigger that hadn't ever done me no harm, and now was showing me there's

One that's always on the lookout, and ain't agoing to allow no such miserable doings to go only just so fur and no further, I most dropped in my tracks I was so scared" (*HF* 268–69).

Henry Nash Smith's formulation of the tensions at play here has become something of a standard reading. Approaching the episode in terms of Twain's own explanation of the novel as a conflict between a "sound heart" and a "deformed conscience," Henry Nash Smith locates in Huck's struggle a clash between "the perverted moral code of a society built on slavery and the vernacular commitment to freedom and spontaneity." For Smith the clash is realized as a dialogue between the conventional voice of authority internalized in Huck and his own deepest self, a conflict registered in the contrast between "the language of the dominant culture" and Huck's "dialect" (122). One thing to observe, though, is that *both* languages here are literary constructs, verbal artifices; Twain's rendering of dialect is no more authentic—no more real—than his version of dominant cultural discourse. He is creating two languages in conflict in order to dramatize his moral point, and as a part of the drama he intensifies Huck's emotional state. Huck's realization reaches an emotional climax that begins to transform the moral moment into melodrama: "I most dropped in my tracks I was so scared." What saves the utterance from rhetorical posturing, what makes it *seem* real, is the vernacular—"most dropped in my tracks." Like Harte's use of the vernacular in the final moment of "Tennessee's Partner," Twain's careful deployment of Huck's natural speech achieves a tempering of emotion.

In a provocative reading of Huck's moral debate, Jonathan Arac finds in it "considerable dialogism between voices," noting the voice of "the schoolmarm" and, especially, the voices of "preacherly exhortation" and of "revival testimony." This leads him to conclude that when Huck declares he will "go to hell," the "religious satire outweighs the experiential pathos" (52–54). Arac therefore contests Toni Morrison's assertion—a graceful summary of the conventional interpretation of the novel—that Huck's decision to go to hell constitutes his "ultimate act of love, in which he accepts the endangerment of his soul" (xxxvi). Arac is surely right about the comedy, but rather than negating the pathos, the comedy actually makes possible—makes acceptable, that is, seemingly genuine and real, not mere rhetoric—Huck's "act of love." As we have seen, Twain— and Harte—believed that humor and pathos were conjoined. Here he uses humor to make the pathos ring true, but it is still pathos. Just as the vernacular certifies Huck's intense fear, so the humor buoys up his pathos.

The counterbalance to Huck's internal voice of conformity, of course, is his recollection of his time with Jim. Stylistically, his remembrance of these things past is very much in the mode of, say, Susan Warner, or Charles Dickens, or even Bret Harte.

> I felt good and all washed clean of sin for the first time I had ever felt so in my life, and I knowed I could pray, now. But I didn't do it straight off, but laid the paper down and set there thinking; thinking how good it was all this happened so, and how near I come to being lost and going to hell. And went on thinking. And got to thinking over our trip down the river; and I see Jim before me, all the time, in the day, and in the night-time, sometimes moonlight, sometimes storms, and we a floating along, talking, and singing, and laughing. But somehow I couldn't seem to strike no places to harden me against him, but only the other kind. I'd see him standing my watch on top of his'n, stead of calling me—so I could go on sleeping; and see him how glad he was when I come back out of the fog; and when I come to him again in the swamp, up there where the feud was; and such-like times; and would always call me honey, and pet me, and do everything he could think of for me, and how good he always was; and at last I struck the time I saved him by telling the men we had smallpox aboard, and he was so grateful, and said I was the best friend old Jim ever had in the world, and the *only* one he's got now; and then I happened to look around, and see that letter. (*HF* 269–70)

What transpires here is enough to wring the heart: a beleaguered innocent boy recalling the goodness of a self-sacrificing slave, remembering their times together "talking, and singing, and laughing." One needn't point out that Huck and Jim never sing together (that's Broadway's "Big River") to see the idealization taking place, for it is registered in the subtle changes in Huck's style, which suddenly turns poetic in its graceful rhythms, its use of antithesis, its triadic structures, and its crafted dramatic climax. The syntax of Huck's narrating betrays, perhaps more than anything else, Twain's urge to drive home the moral point by rendering it in a sentimental style. Conceptually—or more precisely, morally—what Twain strives for through his emotion-laden rendering is, on the one hand, sympathy for Huck in his struggle to resist his conscience, and on the other, empathy for the benevolent, loving Jim whose human relatedness is restricted to one vagabond boy and whose own good-heartedness—his capacity for kindness and gratitude—is denied by the nonpersonhood of chattel slavery. Twain's turn to emotion to bring home a moral point is characteristic of sentimentality. And the moral purposes served by this emotional passage are entirely in keeping with the intent of liberal sentimentality.

A second passage, this one from the much-admired "The Private History of a Campaign that Failed," reveals not only how naturally Twain turned to sentimentality as his means of conveying a moral but also how fraught with aesthetic difficulty his strategy is. "The Private History" is a fictionalized account of Sam Clemens's brief service as a Confederate soldier, a fiction that deploys humor to defeat any potential aspersion of wrong-doing for taking up arms on behalf of the Southern cause. The tale disarms its audience by making the campaigners mere boys—slightly older Tom Sawyers, trapped in history, who nonetheless refuse to follow its dictate, in this case to wage war, preferring instead to wrangle with each other and to play. The story thus exculpates Clemens, but in its climax it furthers the act of exoneration by seriously condemning bloodshed itself. After they actually kill an apparent Northern soldier (the only one they encounter), the "boys" feel not just the wrong of what they have done but the wrongness of all killing:

When we got to him the moon revealed him distinctly. He was lying on his back, with his arms abroad; his mouth was open and his chest heaving with long gasps, and his white shirt-front was all splashed with blood. The thought shot through me that I was a murderer; that I had killed a man—a man who had never done me any harm. That was the coldest sensation that ever went through my marrow. I was down by him in a moment, helplessly stroking his forehead; and I would have given anything then—my own life freely—to make him again what he had been five minutes before. And all the boys seemed to be feeling in the same way; they hung over him, full of pitying interest, and tried all they could to help him, and said all sorts of regretful things. They had forgotten all about the enemy; they thought only of this one forlorn unit of the foe. Once my imagination persuaded me that the dying man gave me a reproachful look out of his shadowy eyes, and it seemed to me that I could rather he had stabbed me than done that. He muttered and mumbled like a dreamer in his sleep, about his wife and his child; and I thought with a new despair, "This thing that I have done does not end with him; it falls upon *them* too, and they never did me any harm, any more than he." (*MTC1* 879)

Twain's narrator goes on to say that "the taking of that unoffending life seemed such a wanton thing," to which he adds what is surely the final moral of the tale: "And it seemed an epitome of war" (*MTC2* 880). Setting aside the possibility of a just war, Twain's moral is as unimpeachable as it is commonplace. Harte might have called it "moral pie." The drama smacks of the very "pathetics" for which Twain lambasted Harte. He resorts to lurid clichés—open mouth, heaving chest, blood-splashed shirt—as well as stylized gestures—"stroking his forehead," "gave me a reproachful look"; and he evokes the stock figures of bereaved wife and fatherless child, thus extending and enlarging the pathos. At the center of this emotional outpouring is an avowal so improbable that it rings as hollow rhetoric: "I would have given anything then—my own life freely." Not relieved by humor, not made fresh by any special turns of a vernacular, the passage, especially when extracted from the story, is problematic in its sentimentality.

In a letter to a friend late in his career, Twain defended an even more egregiously sentimental story of his, "A Horse's Tale," in revealing terms. "I know it is a pity," he wrote, "to wring the poor human heart, and it grieves me to do it; but it is the only way to move some people to reflect"; in further justification of his story, he added that the tale "has a righteous purpose" (qtd. in Gardner, *Dickens in America* 41). Explicitly asserted here is Twain's understanding of the moral power of sentimentality: it provokes new thought, contests prejudice, and enjoins true ethics. He thus not only tolerated in his own work what he objected to in Harte's but even argued for its legitimacy. Perhaps the difference for Twain between his use of sentimentality and that of his one-time mentor lies in the absence of "righteous purpose" in Harte's work. While Twain may well have taken note of the early Harte's defense of the Chinese (see Duckett, chapter 5), there is no evidence that he knew Harte's later attacks on imperialism. Ironically, however, the more committed Twain was to making a moral point, the more inclined he was to become sentimental, while the more Harte had a moral in view, the more he was apt to eschew sentimentality in favor of irony.

As critics have noted, Twain's later stories and personal sketches—of which "A Dog's Tale" and "Eve Speaks" may serve as representative examples—became more laden with sentiment. What has not been taken fully into account, however, is the fact that his later essays are also rife with strong emotion. As William M. Gibson has pointed out, Twain, writing in a variety of forms—speeches, private letters, pamphlets, essays—tackled "an astonishing variety of topics, problems, and people." In what is only a partial reckoning, Gibson lists nearly two pages of different subjects (*Art of MT* 134–35). The range is astounding; so is the welling up of feeling in these pieces. Given his recurrent use of the sentimental on behalf of the moral, it is not surprising that many of his polemical essays contain passages of intense—perhaps excessive—emotion. The same question posed about Harte's reform fiction, then, is worth considering with reference to Twain's: how effective is its mode?

His most famous political essay, "To the Person Sitting in Darkness," affords the best example. In his fine commentary on the essay, William R. Macnaughton calls it Twain's version of "A Modest Proposal," in which he facetiously advocates "perpetuating the misuse of power" (149, 155). Posing as a dismayed observer who wants to promote international imperialism, Twain, often with heavy-handed irony, calls attention to the egregious disparities between national principles and actual practice in foreign countries. He indicts the imperialist actions of England, Germany, Russia, and—most of all—the United States, while exposing the fraudulence of the religious and cultural rationales under which such ventures take place.

He opens the essay by juxtaposing two radically different newspaper accounts of conditions in America. The juxtaposition sets the framework for the ironic contrast to follow and makes the implicit point that Christian missionary efforts might well begin at home. But it is still an odd opening. The first newspaper account proclaims that America is a land of hope, cheer, and contentment, while the second defines it as politically and morally corrupt—a place where (at least in some parts of New York) prostitution is rampant and murder, rape, and robbery go unpunished. Given his usual reticence about the sexual, it is strange that Twain uses corrupt sexuality as his principal example of a debased America: young girls forced into prostitution; small boys turned into pimps *"for the women of disorderly houses"*; and *"naked women"* dancing at night in the streets

(*MTC2* 457, Twain's emphasis). There is no direct connection made between this account of sexual trade and the ensuing revelations of imperialist barbarism, for Twain skirts not only the issue of prostitution in colonial countries but also the fact of rape during their subjugation. His attention to corrupt sexual practices may, however, function on the personal level as an initial empowering. For it enables him to feel pure, and superior in his purity; it strengthens his moral righteousness.

His craftsmanship in the essay is as artful as it is obvious. He creates a morally polarized global picture, exploiting a series of stark contrasts that center on the differences between a true religion and a deceitful one, a true civilization and a sham one. He embeds his fundamental criticism in ironic metaphors: extending the "Blessing of Civilization" is a *trade*, a commercial venture that pays; it is also a *game*, one to be played well or badly. He blends colloquial language alive with touches of slang—it's "a Daisy"; "Sir, it is pie"—with a stately pseudo-biblical rhetoric: "Then they that Sit in Darkness are troubled" (*MTC2* 461–63). He casts religious, political, and military leaders as villains—Ament, Chamberlain, the Kaiser, the Czar, Kitchener, and America's own McKinley—and details some of their nefarious doings, emphasizing sensational events. He depicts a series of innocent victims—"pauper peasants," "simple-minded patriots," "confiding people," "the weak and the friendless." He creates lurid images: "*another* Civilized Power, with its banner of the Prince of Peace in one hand and its loot-basket and its butcher-knife in the other." And he bathes the whole in images of light and darkness. In all these ways—exploiting hyperbolic figures, lurid images, sensational events, villainy persecuting innocence, historical characters masked by their hypocrisy, extreme suffering, and the clash of light and dark—Twain stages his ideas as sentimental melodrama (*MTC2* 457–73).

His style often rises rhetorically to match his melodramatic effects. Here is a representative moment:

> There have been lies; yes, but they were told in a good cause. We have been treacherous; but that was only in order that real good might come out of apparent evil. True, we have crushed a deceived and confiding people; we have turned against the weak and the friendless who trusted us; we have stamped out a just and intelligent and well-ordered republic; we have stabbed an ally in the back and slapped the face of a guest; we have bought a Shadow from an enemy that

hadn't it to sell; we have robbed a trusting friend of his land and his liberty; we have invited our clean young men to shoulder a discredited musket and do bandit's work under a flag which bandits have been accustomed to fear, not to follow; we have debauched America's honor and blackened her face before the world; but each detail was for the best. We know this. (*MTC2* 471)

Although emotionally intense and obviously crafted, this passage is quite different from Twain's early rhetorical sentimentality. When he mourned human loss signified by an Etruscan tear-jug, his lament was not only all fancy language (what Harte objected to as "sentiment that is only rhetoric") but also without any sustaining moral purpose. Here, in contrast, Twain's outpouring is charged with didactic intent. While the passage has nothing of the linguistic ballast provided by Huck's incorrect—and therefore comic—vernacular, it is pretty plain speaking, despite its elaborate syntax. And throughout, the whole is alive with irony. Twain thus combines his pathos, captured in such figures as "confiding people," the "weak and the friendless," a "trusting friend," with his humor. Surely the passage confirms his contention that wringing the human heart as a "way to make people think" is acceptable in a righteous cause.

As the moralist in Twain grew stronger, so did the sentimentalist. As moralist, Twain pits himself against the world, melodramatically imagined as a simple clash of good and evil, and indulges an indignation born of the conviction of absolute rectitude. Whatever he may have been at other times, when he writes as sentimental reformer, Twain writes out of a singleness of feeling that resolves any divisions within himself. Robert Heilman has theorized that melodrama itself is rooted in the individual in what he calls an "innocence neurosis," that is, a need to hold the self guiltless while indignantly blaming others (113–19). Such a neurosis combines self-pity with self-righteousness; it leads one in its grip to seek victimization in personal defeat and to search for justice in personal triumph. This psychic profile fits much of what his biographers have established about Clemens's emotional orientation—and Mark Twain's expressions of it. In his life, as in his writing, he did long to feel guiltless and frequently lashed out at adversaries—like Bret Harte—with a savage vehemence he rationalized as just. Two of Twain's long late texts, *Personal Recollections of Joan of Arc* (1896) and *What Is Man?* (1906), taken together, are especially revealing in this regard. Psychologically, *Joan* is an extended, emotional exercise in imagining victimization, while *What Is Man?* is an equally intense exercise in demonstrating uncontestable individual authority. The first is awash with displaced self-pity; the second is full of aggressive self-justification. Together, the two works seem to disclose a pathology of innocence in Twain.

Yet another spur to sentimentality may also be at work within Twain. Although he consciously used sentimentality within his more or less realistic fiction to impart morality, he may have been moved to do so by an unconscious feeling common to many moral-minded realists of his time. In *The Melodramatic Imagination* Peter Brooks has argued that for some realists, notably Balzac and Henry James, the turn to emotional excess, to melodrama or sentimentality, is prompted by a desire to recover—and express—"the moral occult": a "domain of operative spiritual values which is both indicated within and masked by the surface of reality" (5). As science and rational skepticism challenged the moral order once defined by a God-ordained universe, ethical realists longed for the lost or vanishing moral certainty. Seemingly, on its surface, simply a standard (perhaps even outworn) literary tactic, Twain's sentimentality may disclose not just a strain of his sensibility, not just his didacticism, and not just his moral impulse, but also a fundamental craving for the universe of moral order called into question in his time by secular rationalism. It seems significant that Twain's sentimentality, arguably always present in his writing, becomes notably more prominent in his later work when he was more given to reflecting on a divine order—and more skeptical about it. Bret Harte, on the other hand, seems to have undergone no such philosophical sea change.

After their break in 1877, followed by Harte's appointment as U.S. commercial agent in Krefeld, Prussia, in 1878, Mark Twain and Bret Harte never saw each other again. Twain continued to read Harte now and then, and in 1888 he included—or agreed to include—four of his works (two poems, two stories) in *Mark Twain's Library of Humor*, facetiously defending the inclusions on the ground that the collection needed "some funereal rot" as a "foil" (*MTHL* 396).[10] Twain also continued to blackguard Harte in his private letters and to belittle his writings. On the other hand, Twain occupied no such place in Harte's thought and activities. Once, with a curious sort of ambivalence, Harte explained to his sister that he could not write sketches about German life because if he treated it "with American freshness" he would "only become a Mark Twain" (*Selected Letters* 237). But after that, through more than two decades, Harte seemed to forget Mark Twain.

Harte acknowledged early in his career that he had "little interest" in politics (*Selected Letters* 103), and while his awareness of political problems deepened through the years, he was, an occasional protest piece notwithstanding, never truly absorbed in public issues. He assured his wife in 1887 that he was "an earnest Republican" and a "*just* one," and he said he understood not only "how a man feels" when he is a communist or socialist but also "what makes him one" (*Selected Letters* 345). He had a lively sympathy for the poor—"these terribly famished creatures," he called them (*Letters* 302). But by and large these views did not shape his fiction. Broadly humanitarian in outlook, he avoided public forums on controversial topics. Here, Mark Twain, especially the later Mark Twain, was Harte's opposite, for he loved—and welcomed—notoriety, enjoyed holding forth on the vexed topics of his day, and found something to say about most everything. Equally humanitarian, Twain was more outspoken and more partisan than Harte. In his later essays, he expressed consistently a hatred of tyranny, an outrage at injustice, a sympathy with the oppressed, and an insistence on liberty. While both Harte and Twain opposed imperialism, there is no evidence that Harte joined the Anti-Imperialist League, of which Twain was a prominent vice-president and for which he was an ardent spokesman. Thus while Twain and Harte shared a general, liberal orientation, they differed in temperament and so in conduct: Twain was a political gadfly, Harte a retiring aesthete. One wonders what (had they known it) each would have made of the other's reform fiction, with its informing—and sometimes deforming—sentimentality.

What we can see in the Twain-Harte literary relationship is much clearer. As he began the process of autobiographical dictation that would eventually include his tirade against Harte, Twain first exclaimed in delight over the procedure to Howells—"You will never know how much enjoyment you have lost until you get to dictating your autobiography"—and then, just two months later, confessed that the autobiographical mode consisted "mainly of extinctions" and that its truth could be found only "between the lines, where the author-cat is raking dust upon it" (*MTHL* 278, 782). In his attacks on Harte, Twain—author-cat extraordinaire—piled up a lot of dust. In the posthumously published *Mark Twain in Eruption*,

Twain raked up some thirty-eight pages of dust, covering his own sentimentality by denouncing Harte's. He repeated again and again—as he had already repeated in his personal correspondence and notebooks—the charge that Harte was devoid of heart, given to false pathos, a sentimental poseur.

There are turnings here no doubt lost on Twain. If we recall Fulweiler's point that one aspect of sentimentality is "an appeal to emotion which has become conventional rather than fresh, dogmatic rather than imaginative, reductive rather than enlarging" (184), then in what must be one of the great ironies in our literary history—certainly one of the sharpest ironies in Twain's own various literary relations—one can see that, in the end, Mark Twain became sentimental over Bret Harte.

CREATING HUMOR

# Mark Twain
# & William Dean Howells

*His [Howells's] is a humor which flows softly all around about*
*and over and through the mesh of the page, pervasive, refreshing,*
*health-giving, and makes no more show and no more noise than*
*does the circulation of the blood.*

MARK TWAIN, 1906


William Dean Howells to Mark Twain, March 16, 1878: "The new thing you
send me is perfectly delicious. It went right home every time. What a fancy
you *have* got! And what sense!" Mark Twain to William Dean Howells,
June 22, 1882: "I am in a state of wild enthusiasm over this July instal-
ment of your story. It's perfectly dazzling—it's masterly—incomparable"
(*MTHL* 224, 407). With such exclamations of delight and admiration,
Howells praised Twain, and Twain praised Howells, during the long course
of their forty-year friendship.

Their relationship has been described as a "friendship of equals" (Smith
and Gibson, *MTHL* xiii), and it seems as natural a friendship as it was
warm and long lasting.[1] Both men grew up in western villages that were
at once determinedly literate and largely unlettered; both knew their region's struggle to establish itself as a civilization. Twain's Hannibal was
more southern in its culture than Howells's Ohio homes of Ashtabula and
Jefferson, which bore the imprint of New England culture from the time

the region was Connecticut's Western Reserve, but Howells had gleaned something of the outlook and temper of the South during his earliest years in Martin's Ferry, Hamilton, and Dayton. Both men knew their region, then the West, well enough to realize that the literary culture that interested them was to be found most fully formed in the East, and of course both eventually established themselves near what Oliver Wendell Holmes dubbed the "hub of the universe"—Boston—Howells at the edge of the hub in Cambridge, Twain somewhat farther away in Hartford. They also shared a formative past experience, the significance of which can scarcely be overestimated, as apprentice printers and editors for local newspapers. When Howells wrote of that special world in "The Country Printer," pointing out that the printing office was unquestionably a "school" (297), Twain told him that he thoroughly enjoyed the account and found it all "true" and "intimately recognizable in all its details" (*MTHL* 652). Most importantly, they both eventually committed themselves for life to the profession of writing. Howells would sometimes think of the profession as belles lettres, while Twain liked to call it a "trade," but Howells himself eventually insisted that "the author is, in the last analysis, merely a workingman" ("The Man of Letters as a Man of Business" 307). Once formed, their friendship deepened through their shared interest in writing, in making money as well as books, in home and family, in public events and political affairs, in passing fads and ephemeral notions, in metaphysical questions and moral truths. Together, they explored not only the idle drifts of their time but also its prevailing winds and abiding currents.

For Twain the writer, Howells (1837–1920) became a lifelong literary guide, mentor, and critic, easily supplanting—and surpassing—Bret Harte. "Give me your plain, square advice," he enjoined Howells, "for I propose to follow it" (*MTHL* 248). All the extant evidence indicates that he did follow Howells's advice, with confidence as well as gratitude, for as intensely as Twain came to dislike and contemn Harte, just so intensely did he like and admire Howells. Perhaps because Howells was chiefly committed to being a serious novelist, while Twain pursued humor in a variety of genres, there was never any competition between the two. The rivalry that shaped the Twain-Harte relationship had no place in the long personal and professional relationship between Twain and Howells, and Twain found in Howells no part of himself or his writings that he needed to deny. Further, whereas Twain most often evaluated Harte in the course of their acquaintanceship, in the Twain-Howells connection it was Howells who evaluated Twain. Howells tried, not to reveal the shortcomings of Twain's work—indeed, he often glossed over them—but to make clear its many unnoticed merits. He took Mark Twain seriously. He offered guidance in matters of genteel phrasing, appropriate incident, and vivifying detail, and Twain readily accepted his suggestions. However, the general nature of their long literary relationship is this: each encouraged the other and confirmed the worth of the other's work.

Clearly documented in the two volumes of their published mutual correspondence (the *Mark Twain–Howells Letters,* brought out in 1960), the friendship of Twain and Howells is one of the most familiar and most commented on in American literary history. Their best biographers—Kaplan, Hoffman, on Twain; Cady, Lynn, on Howells—repeatedly illuminate the individual life through Twain's and Howells's joint interests, collaborative schemes, and shared visions. The friendship itself, in all its warmth and rich variety, has been carefully studied by Kenneth E. Eble, who concludes that the two were "as great in their friendship as in their literary abilities" (219). The specifically literary side of the Twain-Howells relationship has been examined chiefly in terms of the two writers' antagonism toward romanticism, their interest in realism, and, to a lesser degree, their shared social vision.[2] There is, however, at least one other area of common ground between the two that remains to be fully explored: their humor.

Given how prolific each writer was, the topic is vast, but three facets of it seem especially worth looking into, not in terms of influence or intertextuality, but in terms of shared comic practice: their travel humor, the humor of their correspondence, and their late satire. These reveal the striking degree to which Twain and Howells had similar comic inclinations.

It is surprising that the similarity between their humors has been generally neglected. Perhaps the neglect is due to the fact that Howells himself, for all his prestige as a critic and interest as a novelist, is not often thought of as a humorist today. But in his own day the critical perception was quite different. As Don L. Cook has pointed out, it was Howells's "humor, his amusing and genial wit" that "earned him a national audience" (69). When he came to write publicly of Howells in one of his rare literary appreciations, Twain singled out his humor. He praised Howells for the gentleness of his humor—"a humor which flows softly all around about and over and through the mesh of the page, pervasive, refreshing, health-giving" ("William Dean Howells," *MTC2* 727).

A humorist himself, as well as a lover of humor, Howells quite naturally undertook to evaluate Twain's. He assessed it off and on for over forty years, from his 1869 review of *The Innocents Abroad* to his final book-length reminiscence, *My Mark Twain*, published in 1910. Howells's first review of Twain is revealing. Unlike most reviewers of Twain's first travel book, Howells did not find fault with its often broad, roughshod humor, which ranged from physical slapstick to verbal buffoonery, often assailing the sacred pieties and proper decorum of the age. Instead, Howells focuses on Twain's understanding of "the realities of human life everywhere," finding in the narrative "a base of excellent sense and good feeling." When he does touch on the humor—in very quick passing—Howells describes it as "ironical drollery," and while noting some "impudence," "sauciness," and "irreverence," he chooses to emphasize not the sometimes combative turns of Twain's humor (the very ones that would eventually make the book infamous) but the "amount of pure human nature in the book" (*CH* 27–29). Howells's review seems a curious recasting of the wild, offensive Twain into a tamer, thoughtful one.

Howells's reformation of Twain in his very first review of Twain's work—a review published before he met Twain personally—is intriguing. On the face of it, one is inclined to see in the review's positive construction of Twain three things: first, Howells's own fastidious appreciation of gentle, not to say genteel, humor, as well as his own moral humanitarianism; second, a curious falsification of *The Innocents Abroad* itself; and third, a clear forecast of the literary relationship between the two, in which Howells would try to tame the Wild Humorist of the Pacific Slope so that he could pass muster within the realm of New England letters. The last point in particular is important, for the accepted view of the Twain-Howells relationship is still that Howells, habituated to the New England tone himself, taught Twain to modulate his writing to fit the lower keys of decorum. However, Howells was in fact less comfortably at ease with the genteel mode than literary history imagines, and Twain, for his part, was surprisingly less at odds with it.

Howells's first assessment of Twain is best understood in terms of his own early comic practice, and that practice is most evident in his first two travel books, *Venetian Life* (1866) and *Italian Journeys* (1867).[3] Both were the result of his residency in Venice from 1861 to 1865. The two books were especially important in Howells's career, for they not only gave him considerable critical attention but also opened to him the heavy doors of editorship, first for *The Nation*, then for the *Atlantic Monthly*.[4] Twain's more famous first travel book, *The Innocents Abroad*, based on his 1867 trip to Europe and the Holy Land, did not appear in print until 1869. Like Howells's two narratives, Twain's travel book was especially important not only because it made a small fortune for him but also because it made him famous in the New England world he would soon seek to enter.

The New England sphere of letters provides the crucial context for examining the early travel humor of both Howells and Twain. Howells became an assistant editor of the *Atlantic* in 1866, and he and his wife settled into a home in Cambridge that same year. Having secured a foothold in New England literary culture, Howells worked to extend and solidify it, partly by adapting his talents to Boston standards. Although, when Twain finally moved to Hartford in 1871, he was farther from the hub than Howells, he located himself at Nook Farm in a literary community that included Charles Dudley Warner, John and Isabella Beecher Hooker, and Harriet Beecher Stowe. Like Howells at Cambridge, Twain was in the thick of a vigorous intellectual community for which literature was the principal means of personal cultivation and social transformation (see Andrews, especially chapter 5). Of the community he entered at Nook Farm Twain said, even before he was settled there, "I desire to have the respect of this sterling old Puritan community, for their respect is well worth having" (*MT to Mrs. Fairbanks* 15). Howells, whose place in New England was more immediately professional than Twain's, acknowledged the same presence of the Puritan past, but while Twain initially sought accommodation, or so he said, Howells was (at least in retrospect) critical. The literature current at the time he went to work for the *Atlantic* was, he said late in his life, "marred by the intense ethicism that pervaded the New England mind for two hundred years" (*Literary Friends* 101).

With Boston as its center, New England exerted in the mid–nineteenth century a hegemonic power in American letters not witnessed before or since. The emerging print culture, whose major publishers were all located in the East, many in New England, furthered the region's control of American literature. Harriet Beecher Stowe was quite right when she called her native New England the "seed-bed of the nation" (qtd. in

Westbrook 9), and some of the transplants were being force-fed. However one defines it, the New England way of writing—no matter what the genre—bore the stamp of the moral climate both Twain and Howells recognized.

Although religion was the origin of the ethical bent characteristic of New England writing, by the time Howells and Twain located themselves in sterling old Puritan communities, the theological foundation that had created the region's habit of mind had shifted, and religious modes of thought had become diverse. The moral tone remained, but it was increasingly guided by something other than divine truth interpreted by the clerisy as well as the clergy. One social historian has described the emerging Boston (we may enlarge this to New England) situation this way: "Its 'culture' was to be achieved by 'education' in 'standards' of critical discrimination among the products of the arts, but also among styles of moral and rational discourse, and models of personal and group behavior. These were not standards derived from theology or philosophy or any structure of theory, but from the co-operative practice of evaluation in a community—'the common pursuit' " (Green, *The Problem of Boston* 26). The term "community" here suggests a wider spread of power than actually existed, for the arbiters of the standards of discrimination tended to be the economic and social elite (see Persons and Kolko). Holmes's Autocrat of the Breakfast-Table is a representative type of those who exerted power in all cultural venues.

Howells described the cultural circumstance with clarity and simplicity and an insistence that may betray—after the fact—annoyance: "The literary theories we accepted were New England theories, the criticism we valued was New England criticism, or, more strictly speaking, Boston theories, Boston criticism" (*Literary Friends* 100). What was the New England, or Boston, theory of humor by which Howells's own *Venetian Life* and *Italian Journeys*—and after them, Twain's *The Innocents Abroad*—might be measured?

The New England mode of humor, whether whimsical or satirical, was invariably decorous. Taking much of its tenor from such eighteenth-century writers as Addison and Steele, it was refined, sophisticated, genteel. It most often arose, as Emerson put it in his 1839 essay on "The Comic," from the "contrast" between "the idea and the false performance"—from the gulf between "the ideal of right and of truth" and the "yawning delinquencies of practice" (*Works* 8:154–55). Knowing, as they believed they did, the right and the true, New England writers were ready with comic measurements of all that fell short of these norms. New England humor tended to be a conservative force, one that endorsed conventions and upheld proprieties. It also insisted upon social hierarchies. Above all it operated out of a moral framework of perception. Even its famous regional types—the Yankees like Haliburton's Sam Slick, Seba Smith's Major Jack Downing, or Lowell's Birdofredom Sawin—were used for moral instruction. They functioned as embodiments of shady ethics, alarming signals of an unsteady social order, or, occasionally, as voices of backwoods innocence raised in unconscious critique of a society that was failing to live up to its ideal. These famous Yankee types were the barbarians at—or, more alarmingly, just within—the gates of the *civitas*, and New England humor fought to maintain its civilization. The theory of its humor was in sum this: that one laughed in one's own voice or through a persona at what was wrong in order to correct it, from a position of moral certitude, social rectitude, and intellectual superiority.

Just as there was a crisis in sentimentality when Twain and Harte entered the literary world, one that marked at its profoundest philosophical reach the gradual displacement of ideality by scientific materialism, so when Twain and Howells fronted the East with their travel books, American humor was in conflict, if not crisis, reflecting this time a social disruption rather than a metaphysical one. New England humor was being challenged by an assortment of heterodox humors that did not axiomatically endorse or uphold either the social order or the idea of a moral universe upon which it depended. Born of the frontier, this new unruly humor had left its place of origin and undergone various transformations. Permutations of it were as common in the urban East as the backwoods. But wherever it cropped up, this unruly humor inclined to extravagance (and sometimes to violence), reveled in linguistic dislocations, honored no stabilizing conventions, indulged the anarchic, and promoted, it seemed, nothing more than wildness set loose for the purpose of sheer comic fun. It has been called "subversive" (Reynolds 443) and, compared to the typical New England variety, it must have seemed so. To write humorously at the time Howells and Twain settled in the East was to enter an arena of significant cultural conflict.[5]

When Howells went to Europe in November 1861, he was not "drifting with the tide of a great popular movement" (*IA* 24), as Twain felt he was when he sailed abroad in 1867. To be sure, the tide of Americans going abroad had risen steadily in the nineteenth century, but the Civil War checked the surge, and it was only after the war had ended that the tide, swelled by postwar prosperity, peaked. As historians have often pointed out, foreign travel, especially travel to Europe, became something of a compulsion for Americans interested in the nation's cultural identity: to take the full measure of the New World, one had to know firsthand the Old. However, the motives that led Americans abroad were various: some went to find high culture, some to create an independent identity, some to confirm an already established one (often by reaffirming their race, class, or gender—or all three), some to advance themselves socially, some to escape a constricting or distasteful home-life (Stowe, *Going Abroad* 3–16).

Howells's motive was quite different. He went abroad—as U.S. consul to Venice—to advance his career, both in terms of money (which he sorely needed) and in terms of writing (which he longed to do). In the year before his appointment and departure, he had failed to find a literary position in New England, though he was graciously received there and had audaciously suggested himself as an assistant editor of the *Atlantic*. He had fared even worse in New York, where he was hardly received at all. (With characteristic honesty, Howells would later describe himself at this time as "a youth whose aims were certainly beyond his achievements" [*Literary Friends* 60].) Howells then actively lobbied for a political appointment abroad, not to escape the battlefields of the irrupting Civil War but to prosecute his own campaign to become a man of letters. Though there were multiple considerations, Howells went abroad above all else to become a recognized writer, to create a literary identity.[6]

The identity he first achieved was carefully defined, with sympathy and sensitivity, in 1868 by Henry James. Commenting chiefly on *Italian Journeys* but also acknowledging *Venetian Life*, James draws a portrait of the artist as an American traveler. He notes that Howells has "an eye for the small things of nature, of art, and of human life, which enables him to extract sweetness and profit from adventures the most prosaic." He describes him as a "sentimental traveller" who is "a moralist,—a gentle moralist, a good deal of a humorist, and most of all a poet." He calls him an observer with a "kindly heart," a "lively fancy," and a "healthy conscience." Howells is alert to "the human element in all that he sees," and he records "the manners and morals of the populace" with a constant "charm of manner." He deals, James says, "gently and tenderly with the foibles and vices of the land, for the sake of its rich and inexhaustible beauty." Above all, Howells is artful, possessing a "charm of style" that is "perfection" and a "faculty for composition" that creates an equal "perfection of form." Given his style and artistry, Howells's two travel books have for James "solid literary merit," and Howells himself is a writer of "taste and culture and imagination" ("Howells's Italian Journeys" 198–202). Somewhat exceptional in its lavish praise and its emphasis on style and form, James's review nonetheless encapsulates the early critical view of Howells.[7]

As James's enthusiastic praise suggests, Howells creates in his two travel books a persona consonant with Bostonian propriety. His traveling self is generally superior in outlook, proper in manners, moral in conduct, and dignified in utterance. He asserts himself with absolute certainty. Indeed, he writes of all things—of history, art, economics, politics, and social customs—with astonishing authority.[8] In keeping with the New England way of writing, Howells often uses his authority for instruction. He is, as James observed, "a moralist—a gentle moralist." However, while adopting the didactic mode familiar to the East, he employs it on behalf of what would become the center of his later campaign for realism—the necessity of seeing things as they are—and he expresses the need through gentle deflationary comedy. He dramatizes, sometimes at his own expense, the need to give up romantic illusions in the face of commonplace realities. He often uses humor to effect such correction. At Genoa, for instance, the statue of Columbus, which seems under the moon bathed in "splendor," proves in the light of common day marred by a "uselessly big head" and tottering "sea-legs."[9] Similarly, in storied Verona, the romance of *Romeo and Juliet* dissolves as her latter-day counterpart appears at "the top of a long, dirty staircase," "dowdily dressed," and Juliet's own tomb, her sacred "sarcophagus," seems to be no more than "a horse-trough roughly hewn out of stone" (*IJ* 306–7). By comically revealing the gap between cultural romance and actuality, Howells strikes an instructional posture that proper Boston could easily applaud. As he says in an aside that is very much in keeping with New England ethicism, "The melodrama is over, friends, and now we have a play of real life, founded on fact and inculcating a moral" (*IJ* 33).

Well before Twain became famous for such revelations, Howells exposed both the fraudulence of some cultural sites and the fakery of the typical tourist. Shown at Padua a well in which "the bones of three thousand Christian martyrs" were said to have been thrown, Howells searches by lantern-light for the remains but finds no bones. He does find "a great number of coins," however, cast into the cistern by the credulous—true cash paid by the dupes of commercial tourism for nonexistent relics (*IJ* 205–6). He reports in another instance that to pay homage to the great poet he visits the alleged prison of Tasso, only to be shown a "coal-cellar" in which, he says, the poet was "never imprisoned" (*IJ* 14). Always mocking his own inclination to wax romantic—"I rioted sentimentally on the picturesque ruin"—he spends a good deal of time exposing the "sentimental errors" fostered by poets, historians, and other travelers.[10]

However, Howells is not a cynical travel writer. Although he never allows false emotion to control his narrative, what he does instead is try to locate something genuinely moving within the real. This intent is gracefully introduced in the account of an evening at the theatre in Padua with which Howells opens *Venetian Life*. Seated by chance in a side-box whose view reveals the machinery of the staging, Howells sees through the illusion of reality crafted by the play's presentation, but within the "sham" he nonetheless finds "much truth and beauty." More often than not, his own discoveries of beauty and truth are made not as he observes the contrived or the rare or wondrous but the commonplace. In an old man roasting coffee, for instance, he sees not merely the "squalor of a beggar" but the "unconscious grandeur of humanity"—a "sublime and hopeless magnificence," and in the figure of a street boy, a seller of Indian meal cakes who whirls into dance whenever music strikes up—despite his rags, the street itself, and an encumbering pair of wooden shoes—Howells imagines even more. He glimpses, he feels, something of the spirit that built Venice itself: "The same genius that combated and vanquished the elements, to build its home upon sea-washed sands in marble structures of airy and stately splendor, and gave to architecture new glories full of eternal surprise" (*VL* 1:10, 44, 45–46). Through such relocations of the grand, the moving, indeed the picturesque within the commonplace, Howells, the nascent realist, celebrates much of what he sees.

The keynote of his first two travel books, though, is a far cry from rapture. Throughout his narratives he insists repeatedly that Venice—indeed Italy itself—is "fallen and forlorn" (*VL* 1:171). He becomes a connoisseur of decay. He finds deterioration in fabled churches (including St. Mark's), in famous art of all kinds, in public events that range from regattas to the storied Carnival, in the theater and the opera, in grand architecture, in international commerce, in genteel social life, in national politics, and in the Italian character. Howells often strikes a melancholy note as he bears witness to decline, but equally often his tone is matter-of-fact. He speaks of "weary, forlorn Venice," yet seems to accept the idea that in Venice "nothing in decay is strange" (*VL* 2:104, 50). Nathalia Wright has observed that in the travel books Howells's own Puritanical morality, disinterest in the past, and imperfect sense of art are clearly apparent (171). More striking than these, however, is simply the dark strain in Howells's envisioning.[11] Well before his future friend Mark Twain went underground into prisons, caves, crypts, morgues, and catacombs to discover the dark underside of Europe's past, Howells testified to the Old World's decay evident everywhere on the face of things.

Despite his deep feeling for decline and the melancholy it often inspires, he is humorous in a variety of ways. Somewhat too coyly he announces at the onset of his journeying that his reader "shall suffer no annoyance from the fleas and bugs which in Latin countries, so often get from travellers' beds into their books." He makes bad jokes, as when he observes Titian's *The Martyrdom of St. Lawrence*, hanging in "the coldest church in Venice," and says, one turns from it "envious of the Saint toasting so comfortably on his gridiron amid all that frigidity." He observes of a fellow stage traveler whom he nicknames "the Mouse" that he disappears, perhaps "down the first hole in the side of a house," and then moving from whimsy to irony he adds: "He might have done much worse, and spent the night at the hotel, as we did" (*VL* 1:12, 57, 187–88). On an eighteenth-century altar he notes "insane and ribald angels flying off at the sides, and poising themselves in the rope-dancing attitudes favored by statues of heavenly persons in the decline of the Renaissance." His irreverence can turn playfully coarse. Faced with broken statues of Venus and Diana on the Lido, he first describes them as headless and handless yet having "swaggering attitudes," then grotesquely suggests that they "extended their mutilated arms toward the sea for pity" (which the sea refuses), and finally says: "We passed before them scoffing at their bad taste, for we were hungry." It is not only the Old World that Howells laughs at—and over—for he also mocks the typical American tourist. He reports on how a "sharp, bustling, go-ahead Yankee" rushes into the Convent San Lazzaro, "rubbing his hands, and demanding, 'Show me all you can in five minutes'" (*VL* 1:238, 226–27, 251).

In such moments as these, in tones that range from gently comic to severely ironic, Howells enlivens his dark travel books with humor. He indulges in his own writing the kind of "impudence," "sauciness," and "irreverence" he later noted—and praised—in Twain's *The Innocents Abroad*. Given his own comedy, it is no wonder he liked Twain's. But in such moments as these he also brings his texts to the border of the strict decorum of New England writing. At other times, he boldly crosses that border, creating moments in which his humor is out of sync with that of the New England culture he was seeking to make his own. He even dares to sport with the moral. Having met early in his journeys what he calls "the only honest man in Italy," he soon finds, he says, the man's "integrity" so "oppressive" that he is "glad to be swindled" later by an overcharge for dinner. He strikes postures and employs tones foreign to the New England mode of humor. Peering at the reputed tomb of Virgil, he says that it looks "like a bake-oven," and he scoffs at his guide's explanations because he is "a singularly dull ass." With shocking coarseness, he bluntly announces, "I do hate a Frenchman," and then makes a joke about the French as fellow ship-passengers, which sounds like the Twain of *The Innocents Abroad* at his crudest: "I could hardly have been happy, had I not seen them horribly sea-sick" (*IJ* 11, 13, 82, 65). And with an insensitivity easily the equal of Twain's, he observes that the Jewish ghetto in Ferrara is "not so foul as one could wish a Ghetto to be" (*IJ* 26). Howells's remark that the cost of his breakfast at Pompeii would make "an ancient Pompeian stir in his urn" (*IJ* 89–90) is hardly disturbing today, but it evokes the dead in an irreverent, grotesque way likely to offend the fastidious of his time. His declaration that he "would like to have the ducal cities of North Italy, such as Mantua, Modena, Parma, and Ferrara, locked up quietly within their walls, and left to crumble" (*IJ* 26, 89–90, 21) not only expresses a shocking indifference toward the cities themselves and their rich pasts but also poses an affront to the very sensibility of the traveler—or travel reader—who cherishes such scenes. At such moments as these Howells's humor teeters out of control.

His most egregious violations of the proprieties of New England humor occur, however, when he depicts himself as a bumpkin or fool or vulgarian, sacrificing for the moment the very superiority and cultivation upon which

New England humor depended. Such moments are relatively infrequent but all the more discordant for their rarity. In Rome, at St. Peter's, Howells begins a panegyric worthy of any sentimental traveler: "I recollect, with a pleasure not to be left unrecorded, the sweetness of the great fountain playing in the square before the church, and the harmony in which the city grew in every direction from it, like an emanation from its music, till the last house sank away into the pathetic solitude of the Campagna, with nothing beyond but the snow-capped mountains lighting up the remotest distance." And then, with a sudden comic impulse that both shatters the scene he has painted and demeans himself, he adds, "At the same moment I experienced a rapture in reflecting that I had underpaid three hackmen during my stay in Rome." When he visits Petrarch's house, he observes with smug superiority that the "passion for allying one's self to the great, by inscribing one's name on places hallowed by them, is certainly very odd," and then coyly notes that he "added our names to the rest" (*IJ* 164, 225). In unexpected moments such as these, Howells undermines his own dignity for the sake of a humor gone slightly awry. He begins to sound rather like Mark Twain.

Two other turns of Howells's humor also anticipate Twain's own antics as a travel writer. Observing two captains whose boats have just bumped into each other on the Grand Canal, Howells gently mocks his own curiosity, playing genteel language off against the vernacular to create a small turn of comedy: "I looked on with that noble interest which the enlightened mind always feels in people about to punch each other's heads." With refined condescension, he coyly describes the ensuing altercation in the arch, indirect language of strict propriety: "Reciprocally questioning the reputation of all their female relatives to the third and fourth cousins, they defied each other as the offspring of assassins and prostitutes." In all this mild humor Howells himself appears properly distant from, and appropriately superior to, the rough barge captains, but then, as one of the two captains gathers a stone to hurl at the other, only to refrain at the last moment from actually throwing it, Howells unexpectedly defines his reaction in a way that aligns him with the low behavior he is amusedly observing from his more civilized perspective. "To my disappointment," he says, "it [the rock] was not fired" (*VL* 1:174–75). To long for violence, even as a joke, is to betray one's standing as a proper gentleman. In this episode Howells violates his usual narrative stance as a refined traveler and assumes instead the posture of common vulgarian thirsting for a good fight. On another occasion, very much like Twain, Howells gives vent to an impulse to vex those who pester one with superiority predicated on a magnificent cultural heritage. In *The Innocents Abroad* Twain torments his guides by asking, with mock innocence, who such people as Columbus are, and then following the dismayed answer with the even more infuriating query: "Is he dead?" (*IA* 239). Howells anticipates Twain's famous tactic, albeit only once, when he disingenuously inquires of his gondolier, who preens over a past that inspired Shakespeare, "Who was Othello?" Howells reports that he asks this "meekly," which is to say, with all the deadpan innocence he can muster (*VI* 2:148).

Howells's non–New England humor plays against the sedate tone of his narratives as a whole. But it also calls into question his moral earnestness, contesting, if not undermining, the authority of his texts—an authority essential to the prevailing seriousness. Put simply, when he plays with unruly humor, he suggests his narrative's unreliability, thus destabilizing his texts. Howells is notably self-conscious within his narratives about his performance as writer, and this, too, sometimes proves destabilizing. Often he invokes a conventional posture, speaking modestly of his insufficient pen or his "poor art," but at other times he calls into question something more than his skill as writer. "It is," he observes at one point, "one of the pleasures of by-way travel in Italy, that you are everywhere introduced in character, that you become fictitious and play a part as in a novel." Howells thus problematizes his identity within his text. And further complicating his narrative presence, he avers, "It will not do to trust travelers in any thing" (*IJ* 308, 280, 313).

Who, then, is this traveling William Dean Howells? When he expanded the second of his initial travel narratives, *Italian Journeys*, by adding a new final chapter in 1872, Howells seems to have answered the query his own texts prompt. If his original texts are punctuated by subversive comic turns, twists of tone, of value, and of narrative persona at odds with gentility, his new ending is carefully constructed to avoid such pitfalls: it is devoid of humor.[12] The chapter is also largely without any on-the-spot record of touring. Howells presents himself more as a chronicler than a traveler, a historian whose aim is to "rehabilitate," on the basis of historical documents, "the ducal state of Mantua" (*Italian Journeys*, 1872 ed., 328). Thus at the end of his expanded narrative Howells becomes a fusty historian, repeating, synthesizing, and moralizing on the accounts of others. He recovers, that is, the posture of rectitude central to the New England ethos—and its sphere of letters. Since final impressions are often lasting ones, it is no wonder that Howells's travel books seemed at the time of their eastern popularity to certify Howells as one of New England's own.

Mark Twain's first travel book earned him no such welcome. Although present-day critics still balk at the idea, the clear fact is that Twain courted eastern respectability. For deep personal reasons, including a need to certify his innate sense of propriety, and for pragmatic ones, including a desire to be near centers of power, he longed to enter the sanctuaries of the literary establishment. But of course he did not want to be caught with his nose on the candy-store window; hence his anger at Bret Harte when Harte announced at an *Atlantic* luncheon with Ralph Keeler, Thomas Baily Aldrich, James T. Fields, and Howells himself all in attendance, "Why, fellows, this is the dream of Mark's life" (*MyMT* 8). As important as Harte's exposure is the fact that Howells, originally from Twain's own West, and lately in exile in Italy, already looms in 1871 as the embodiment of eastern culture. If, however, Twain was initially drawn to Howells as a figure of power and respectability, he soon came to like the man himself. Although Twain's dream of acceptance by the East took a long time to become real, his recognition by Howells started, as we've seen, with the review of *The Innocents Abroad*.

More generous than most, Howells's notice was not alone in liking the book. The reviews were in fact mixed. Many of them praised Twain's vigorous and graceful prose, his enjoyable humor, his fine descriptions, and his general originality. What creates the impression today (and probably at the time) of an overwhelmingly negative response, however, is just the fact that so many reviews, including the positive ones, seized on the same single feature to criticize. They disliked, as the *Hartford Courant* put it with genteel indirection, Twain's "not always refined humor." His unruly humor seemed a sure sign of his unconventional, perhaps even subversive, outlook: "Mr. Clemens has an abominable irreverence for tradition and authority,—which sometimes unfortunately degenerates into an offensive irreverence for things which other men hold sacred,—and makes not the slightest hesitation at expressing his opinions in the very plainest possible language, no matter how unorthodox they may be" (Budd, *Mark Twain: The Contemporary Reviews* 36, 49). Such reviews were not entirely off the mark, to be sure. They were responding to such moments of rowdiness as these:

> The great altar of the cathedral, and also three or four minor ones, are a perfect mass of gilt gimcracks and gingerbread. And they have a swarm of rusty, dusty, battered apostles standing around the filagree work, some on one leg and some with one eye out but a gamey look in the other, and some with two or three fingers gone, and some with not enough nose left to blow—all of them crippled and discouraged, and fitter subjects for the hospital than the cathedral. (*IA* 46)

> Here, in Milan, in an ancient tumble-down ruin of a church, is the mournful wreck of the most celebrated painting in the world—"The Last Supper," by Leonardo da Vinci. (*IA* 150)

> Look at the grand Duomo of Florence—a vast pile that has been sapping the purses of her citizens for five hundred years, and is not nearly finished yet. Like all other men, I fell down and worshipped it, but when the filthy beggars swarmed around me the contrast was too striking, too suggestive, and I said, "O, sons of classic Italy, *is* the spirit of enterprise, of self-reliance, of noble endeavor, utterly dead within ye? Curse your indolent worthlessness, why don't you rob your church?" (*IA* 203)

Here we have a paradox of sorts. Despite his bouts of unruly humor, his violations of New England decorum, Howells was accepted as a genteel writer, while Twain was attacked or at least held suspect for his similar comic performances.[13] What was overlooked—or forgiven—in Howells was singled out and condemned in Twain.

Clearly, all the varieties of unruly humor evident in Howells's first two travel books can also be found in *The Innocents Abroad.* Like Howells, Twain creates humor through sharp, indecorous tones, through contrived irreverence and calculated grotesquerie, through posing as bumpkin, fool, or vulgarian, and through flippant complaints about travelers as well as the sites they visit. To see these similarities is to see a slightly different Howells but a very familiar Twain. What we need to see anew about Twain are not the torques of his unruly humor but his unexpected ties to the New England mode of letters.

Some time ago, in what is still a provocative account, James M. Cox argued that when Twain first entered the East he was in disguise. For

Cox, Twain was "a complete outlaw" who chose to appear law-abiding and amiable, and who emerged in New England as a westerner when he was truly a southerner, schooled in the humor—the unruly humor, we might add—of the old Southwest ("Humor and America" 595–96). It seems to me, however, that his disguise was somewhat different: Twain presented himself, especially in *The Innocents Abroad*, principally as a disruptive humorist, when in fact he was also a serious moralist. His humor concealed his moral bent.

Twain's prefatory emphasis on "seeing" in *The Innocents Abroad* would have been particularly resonant for New Englanders shocked—or inspired—by the recent transcendentalists. For "seeing" was arguably at the heart of their cultural enterprise. With a curiously prescient sense that he should defend himself, Twain announces that he has "seen with impartial eyes" and "written at least honestly, whether wisely or not." To these disarming claims he adds a surprising didactic intent: his book "has a purpose, which is, to suggest to the reader how *he* would be likely to see Europe and the East if he looked at them with his own eyes" (*IA* 3). To those readers acquainted with Emerson's lectures and essays or Thoreau's *Walden*, Twain's remarks would have struck a familiar chord. One may want to object at once that what Twain is interested in seeing is different from what Emerson and Thoreau wanted to see, and indeed it is. Of the next generation, Twain looked at new things (one is reminded of Gertrude Stein's observation that "each generation has something different at which they are all looking" [513]), but at least in his first travel book Twain also looked at some things that had already captured the gaze of New Englanders—from society to nature to spiritual truths. And like the New Englanders, he not only looked anew but also reflected on the process of perception itself.

Twain, or the Mark Twain persona, in *The Innocents Abroad*, is seldom accorded such seriousness. Some of his very best critics insist on his playful unreliability. Cox, for instance, defines Twain's narrative stance as a "fusion of burlesque and mock innocence" (*Fate* 48), and Michelson calls it "paidiac make-believe"—a "fictive, improvisatory play" ("Mark Twain the Tourist" 395). While these postures are certainly discernible in the book, they disguise Mark Twain as much as they reveal him. For Twain is a serious as well as a comic traveler. As he tries to see with his own eyes, he fixes his gaze on three things: first, he looks at the world of travel—that is, travel books, travelers, and travel destinations; second, he examines the Old World in terms of the New; and third, he looks beyond such immediacies to the seemingly timeless sphere of morality and human existence itself. Scrutinizing these disparate realms, he discovers precisely what Emerson defined as the comic: the "contrast" between the "ideal of right and truth" and the "delinquencies of practice."

Twain's exposé of travel—of its practitioners and paraphernalia—is trenchant. Travel itself is, in his view, undertaken largely for self-aggrandizement; travel books—"incendiary" ones (*IA* 297)—are often falsifications of both place and experience; travelers are hypocrites, or fools, or romantic frauds who see what isn't there; and the sites of travel are frequently, though not always, commercial shams. Twain has most fun, of course, spoofing the pretensions of his fellow pilgrims. He faults them—not all at once, but slowly along the way—for affectation, undue gravity, censoriousness, hypocrisy, stupidity, false piety, chauvinism, sentimentality, materialism, and minor criminality, all ironically capped by smug self-complacency. He finds—or rather, invents—their analogue in the Zoological Gardens at Marseilles in the figure of a silly, long-legged, ungainly bird whose demeanor proclaims, "Defile not Heaven's anointed," despite his ludicrous incongruities—the manifest disparities between his actual physique and his seeming self-importance. Twain's criticisms of the pilgrims are registered in ways that range from direct statement—they are "image-breakers and tomb-desecraters"—to whimsical conceit: they will "dig" up a "pit" and "carry it away with them." But his principal, most strongly felt charge against them is a significantly moral one: they lack "gentleness," "charity," and "tender mercy"—in contrast to and in failed imitation of their savior, who was "so gentle and so merciful toward all" (*IA* 81–82, 390, 356, 217).

Paradoxically, as he sees through Americans abroad, creating a general moral and social critique, Twain celebrates America itself. He lauds its landscape, its urban order, its technology, its democratic polity, its prosperity, and its general achievement of and commitment to progress in all its forms. Years, indeed decades, before Howells said so, Twain found the "more smiling aspects of life" the "more American" (*Criticism and Fiction* 62). He uses these qualities to measure the backwardness, shortcomings, and insufficiencies of the Old World.

Twain most often views the Old World as a moralist, and his morality is thoroughly conventional—more conventional, to be sure, than that of those before him who, in Emily Dickinson's phrase, saw "New Englandly" (*Complete Poems* 132). He judges people, cultural sites, and traditional information by standards of honesty and authenticity established by his own immediate experience. Often in an Emersonian frame of mind, he will accept nothing at second-hand but seeks to know it directly for himself, to see it, as he says, with his "own eyes." As much as Thoreau, he strains to penetrate "the mud and slush of opinion, and prejudice, and tradition, and delusion, and appearance," the "alluvion which covers the globe, through Paris and London, through New York and Boston and Concord, through church and state, through poetry and philosophy and religion" (*Walden*, chapter 2). "Why," Twain asks, sounding like a New England sage, "should not the truth be spoken in this region?" Ironically, however, while he exposes sham, challenges ordinary opinion, explodes prejudices, and contests tradition, when he comes to assert his own positive values, they prove not only familiar but highly conventional. He extols "charity," "purity," and "unselfishness." He celebrates generosity and hospitality. An apostle of self-help, he asks how the indolent—and the "unthinking"—can call "themselves men" and "consent to be so degraded" (*IA* 406, 205, 477–80, 164). At one moment he invents a visitor to America, returned to his native Italy, who speaks to his countrymen of the wonders of the New World, noting everything from hygiene to housing to dress to governance to landscape to social equality to religion, but stressing several times over the importance of independent thinking and learning: "The common people there know a great deal." When he retells the legend of Abelard and Héloïse, Twain not only attacks "nauseous sentimentality" but also upholds traditional sexual standards: Abelard is denounced as "a dastardly seducer," while Héloïse is commiserated with as a "misused, faithful girl." Visiting the national burial ground of France, Twain risks sentimentality himself to laud not the royalty of blood but a "nobler royalty"—the "royalty of heart and brain" (*IA* 212, 117, 111).

Naturally enough, given his moral inclinations, Twain finds numerous occasions to reflect on the most traditional truth of all: the vanity of human achievement. Viewing the encoffined body of St. Charles Borromeo, bedecked with "costly habiliments," "scintillating gems," and a "crown sown thick with flashing brilliants," Twain draws a moral: "You that worship the vanities of earth—you that long for worldly honor, worldly wealth, worldly fame—behold their worth!" (*IA* 140–41). Having just visited Rome,

Baise, and Pompeii, studying especially the ruins in all three places, Twain again waxes moral, becomes preacherly: "One thing strikes me with a force it never had before: the unsubstantial, unlasting character of fame." Reflecting on all human endeavor, he asks, "What is left of these things?" His answer is stark: a "crazy inscription on a block of stone," a "bare name." But he then adds one further observation that raises a different perspective even as it, too, drives home the point of human insignificance: "No history, no tradition, no poetry—nothing that can give it even a passing interest" (*IA* 266). In the face of time's inevitable annihilation of the human, Twain thus locates a curious, fragile counterpoint to sure obliteration: the records of humankind—its self-stories, cultural practices, and literary creations. It is perhaps no wonder then that the climax to Twain's traveling should come as he sees with his own eyes the Sphynx, and interprets its inscrutable visage as a "type of an attribute of man—of a faculty of his heart and brain": "MEMORY—RETROSPECTION" (*IA* 140–41, 266, 502).

Twain thus valorizes the human impulse that, one might argue, underlies the cultural and religious tour he has taken. The monuments of the past, whether secular or religious, exist because of humankind's urge to memorialize. Famed for his ability to strip away the haze of illusions that clusters about the relics of the past, to insist on seeing clearly, Twain also likes to see through a lens of association so thick that at times it distorts. At some moments Twain becomes—or longs to become—the very type of inspired, romantic traveler he most often burlesques.

Using the familiar contrast, one Howells exploits to an opposite end, between seeing by daylight and seeing by moonlight, Twain often opts for what he calls the "charitable moon." He prefers to see Venice by moonlight, to see Athens and the Acropolis by moonlight, to see the sea of Galilee by moonlight (*IA* 173–74, 274–76, 407). Such visions enable Twain to tap—to remember, to feel, to reflect upon—precisely those things that endow the blank stones of human existence with some meaning: history, tradition, poetry. What Twain employs in these moments, indeed what he endorses, is another way of "seeing," an alternative to knowing through rational observation. Usually a skeptic, Twain even extends this notion of envisioning to spiritual truth. In the holy land, near the village of Banis, he ponders the fact that he is "standing on ground that was once actually pressed by the feet of the Saviour." He finds the reality of the place—its "tangibility"—at odds with his conception of a divine redeemer. A god, he observes, should be apprehended through "vagueness and mystery and ghostliness." And then, returning to the cosmic imagery he has used to "see" historical sites aright, he observes, "the gods of my understanding have always been hidden in clouds" (*IA* 374). Mystery calls forth spiritual insight; intuition—or faith—becomes the medium through which one "sees," or understands, spiritual presence. It is a notion not unknown to those of his time who saw New Englandly.

Looked at in terms of its moralizing, *The Innocents Abroad* instills standards of critical discrimination, utilizes moral and rational discourse, and affirms models of personal and group behavior. That is to say, it fits the paradigm of the New England way of thinking (and writing) cited at the beginning of this chapter. (Even the epistemology Twain eventually entertains matches the earlier New England way of knowing.) But of course few of Twain's readers looked at his book in terms of its moralizing; most saw only—or chiefly—its comic play. Just as Howells's first two travel books contained bits of unruly humor that were overlooked, so Twain's *The Innocents Abroad* offered up strong doses of moralizing (more than enough to please any old Puritan community) that were largely ignored. Howells, an unruly humorist, posing as a genteel one. Twain, a conventional moralist, masquerading as an unruly humorist. It's no wonder the two became close friends for life.

The best record of that friendship is forty-one years of correspondence—wonderful letters full of information, plans, criticisms, affection, and fun—letters that range from cockamamie schemes to cool-headed calculations, from tender reflections to angry condemnations, from contrived performances to spontaneous revelations. If Howells was a genteel writer, given to an occasional flight of subversive play, and Twain a free-flying humorist, given to treading moral ground, each man grasped the full nature of the other. For whatever was secret or concealed or just hard to discern in their published works is quite visible in their personal letters. One finds, for instance, the decorous Howells employing taboo words: "I want to see you, and will come as soon as we can get out of this hell of noises" (*MTHL* 821). Although he would shy at Twain's "Elizabethan breadth of parlance" (*MyMT* 5), he approached it himself at times in all but orthography: " 'Try to *do* a G—— d—— man a G—— d—— kindness'—and you know how it turns out." He plays—obliquely—with God: "For the creature of the

Presbyterian deity who did make you, you are very well," but "I could have improved you." He sports with the language of nudity and sex: "Couldn't I reduce the number of selections from you so as to sort of fig-leaf over your editorial nakedness?" He indulges in a grotesque humor of physical disability—to get a consul's post for their friend Charles Warren Stoddard: "Epilepsy or softening of the brain is requisite: a game arm will not do. He should be bedridden." Howells even stoops to scatological humor: "I'm *not* coming, till heaven knows when. My bowels of compassion have broken loose in the wrong direction, and if I came now I should have to pass my visit in your bath-room" (*MTHL* 177, 707, 541, 155, 840).

Twain, for his part, decorates his letters with the marvelous panoply of his varied humors. Any of his many public expressions of comedy can be matched, albeit in miniature, in his letters to Howells. But overall what one finds is that Twain chooses most often to be soft, gentle, whimsical. In a now-famous letter, written as he was crafting "Old Times on the Mississippi" for the supremely genteel *Atlantic Monthly*, Twain assured Howells, who had solicited the work from him, that the *Atlantic* audience was "the only audience" he sat down before "in perfect serenity" for the "simple reason that it don't require a 'humorist' to paint himself striped & stand on his head every fifteen minutes." Howells—the audience for Mark Twain who truly evoked "perfect serenity"—did not require such buffoonery either, and in his letters to him Twain avoids creating the hearty horselaugh. He generally eschews the outlandish, the bumptious, even the grotesque, preferring instead the more civilized. He more often sounds like Oliver Wendell Holmes than Artemus Ward. "Haven't you," he asks Howells at one point, with all the coyness and assurance of Holmes's Autocrat, "had reviewers *talk* Alps to you, & then print potato hills?" (*MTHL* 49, 586).

What transpires in this private correspondence is a release from public image and general expectation. Each writer finds himself—to borrow Huck Finn's famous terms for idyllic time on a raft—free and easy and comfortable enough to indulge a fundamental, if seldom seen, aspect of his sensibility. Writing to his intimate friend, Howells, the proper Victorian, is free and easy and comfortable enough to be a bit coarse and crude. And Twain, the sometimes raucous humorist, is free and easy and comfortable enough to express his own gentility.

In his final memoir about Twain, Howells recalled that much of the fun of his correspondence with him resided in what he calls their "rapping" and "rapping back" at each other (*MyMT* 42). The letters are peppered with such good-natured ribbing. Howells often teases Twain by alleging that he is an unprincipled person, an out-and-out "miscreant." "I don't know," he wryly observes, "how you've escaped arrest up to this time. It shows you were always right about the inefficiency of our detective system" (*MTHL* 772, 823). He raps Twain for being an inferior—hardly creative—writer: "Here I am, painfully clawing a few tattered dollars together from a colossal work of the imagination, and you from a few paltry compilations of facts are able to roll in wealth." Twain raps back about Howells's work: "You will be old yourself some day. Yes, & neglected, too, if *I*'m any judge of literature" (*MTHL* 57, 327). Twain's favorite maneuver in this friendly epistolary skirmishing, however, is to feign delight in disturbing Howells. He pretends to enjoy imposing on him for editorial help, distracting him with wild schemes and extravagant suggestions, burdening him with charitable activities—all ways, he tells him, of "taking the tuck" out of "one of your junketing days." Twain also gives Howells no end of playful moral instruction, aimed, he says, at checking Howells's "debauching" (*MTHL* 325, 327).

These "rappings" constitute simple comic inversion: each writer attacks the other for faults he doesn't possess, accuses the other of harboring attitudes foreign to him, denounces his friend for activities never contemplated, let alone undertaken. Or, turning the play in the other direction, each ascribes to himself intentions the other knows do not exist. Their accusations, their aggressive jibes, are really compliments; their bantering, a cordial means of affectionate praise as well as humorous fun. [14]

The sheer pleasure each finds in humor is most often evident in their mutual zaniness. They become silly or whimsical for no end other than comic joy. Howells announces that, having read at a benefit from "an unpublished novel" of his on one day, he plans to read from "an unwritten one" on the next. Planning a visit to Twain's Hartford home, Howells asks, with an absurdity worthy of Twain's own fame as an inspired idiot, "As Mrs. H. and Mrs. Clemens are both tearing invalids, don't you think it would be better not to give that ball *this* visit?" And when he starts to work on an essay on Twain, he dashes off this lunatic query: "When and why were you born?" (*MTHL* 528, 67, 404). But Howells is no match for Twain when it comes to sheer silliness. Twain sends him this wonderful piece of wild whimsy:

My Dear Howells:

The box came yesterday, & I enclose check—at least I *mean* to, though one of the hardest things in this life to remember is to enclose a thing—even a dog—in the letter one is writing. It most always goes in another envelope, half an hour later, tottering under a load of profanity which runs it aground at the postoffice for insufficient postage. (*MTHL* 319)

After the Howellses spend several days at Hartford, Twain couches an apology for having given them a "villainously hard bed" in whimsical personification: "We did not know," he says, its "abandoned character," only to have Howells respond with his own comic conceit: "I don't wonder you found that bed hard: we got all the sleep out of it, and left it a mere husk or skeleton of the luxurious couch it had been." Always intrigued by machines and mechanical gadgets, Twain bought a typewriter when they were new, found that he was not adept at using it, and so first traded it to Elisha Bliss for a saddle, "cheating him outrageously," and then pledged it to Howells. The typewriter, Twain tells him, will be at Bliss's for a while longer, "grimly pursuing its appointed mission, slowly & implacably rotting away another man's chances for salvation." He assures Howells of its eventual arrival: "You just wait a couple of weeks & if you don't see the Type-Writer come tilting along toward Cambridge with the raging hell of an unsatisfied appetite in its eye, I lose my guess." After Howells receives the machine he reports back to Twain: "The type-writer came Wednesday night, and is already beginning to have its effect on me. Of course it doesn't work. . . . It's fascinating . . . and it wastes my time like an old friend" (*MTHL* 78–79, 89, 109).

Although various types of humorous play recur in the correspondence, domestic comedy appears with such frequency as to constitute an on-going drama. Snippets of the drama emerge naturally enough as each man describes comic events in his home-life. Howells, for instance, reports that his son Johnny protests against God's having allowed him to suffer a bad dream: "I *told* him . . . that I hadn't *sworn* that day!" And in the same vein Twain tells the story of how his daughter Susy, trapped in tight-fitting shoes, replies to her mother's nighttime injunction—"Now, Susie—think about God"—by declaring, "Momma, I can't, with these shoes" (*MTHL* 146, 143). But apart from family incidents, the letters create a plot of sorts out of the domestic comedy Twain and Howells report to each other: both men play the role of wayward homebody, kept precariously in check by their right-thinking wives.

Both Twain and Howells depict themselves as bad boys, harum-scarum souls, in need of steadying, guidance, and correction. Twain strikes the note in full melodramatic key:

> O dear! I came home jubilant, thinking that for once I had gone through a two-day trip & come out without a crime on my soul: but it was all a delusion, nothing but a delusion—as I soon found out. . . . There has been administered to me punishment enough for ten crimes; & I have punished myself enough for fifty, just in tossing, in impotent regret & humiliation, over one shameful detail after another, pointed out by Mrs. Clemens; & which cause me just as real anguish as if I could see, *myself*, that they were brutalities & stupidities & crimes, & *how* they are & *why* they are; & it makes me wish, in the bottom of my broken heart, that this might be a lesson to me, & so burnt in & *comprehended*, that I could depend on going right back there tomorrow & not only not duplicate the whole performance, but not get up another one, by inspiration, a thundering sight worse. —But oh, hell, there is no hope for a person who is built like me;— because there is no cure, no cure. (*MTHL* 401)

Always ready to poach on another literary estate, Twain snares here the language and emotional posturing dear to the heart of the sentimental domestic novel and turns it into comedy through palpable excess, transparent insincerity, and discordant phrases. He caps his parody of plaintive self-laceration by adding, "If I could only *know* when I have committed a crime: then I could conceal it." Without Twain's comic exuberance but with a sense of similar miscue, Howells reports an even more egregious blunder, one he absentmindedly makes at his wife's expense: "Some time when we have got a whole Saturday, I want to tell you how I forgot that Mrs. Howells was to go to a tea-party with me, went alone, excused her according to custom, and involved myself in domestic and social consequences without end." He adds a sentiment certain to meet with Twain's approval: "The worst of these things is that you never can keep them secret" (*MTHL* 400–401, 360).

Playing bad boy, Twain delights in telling Howells of narrowly escaping Livy's corrective wrath. He often casts his misdeeds in the slang of a boy tangling with his mother. Suspected by Livy of putting profanity into one manuscript but leaving it out of his reading to her, he reports that "nothing but almost inspired lying got me out of this scrape with my scalp," and then he asks, not so much to solicit any answer as to allow Howells the pleasure of sympathetic identification: "Does your wife give you rats, like this, when you go a little one-sided?" Howells often goes "one-sided," and he defines his wife, Elinor, as the person who sets him on keel again, the preceptor "who has charge of my sense of decency" (*MTHL* 54, 360). Pretending to suffer petticoat tyranny, both men gently make fun of their wives. Howells accuses his of bragging about her management of him, and with a touch of Twain's own exaggeration, he says at one point that she "will start the universe on the right basis again in a few days" (*MTHL* 361). He laughs at her when she declines to accompany the two adventure-seeking men on a trip down the Mississippi to New Orleans. She says, he writes, "in the noblest way, 'Well, *go* to New Orleans, if you want to so *much*,'" and then he adds for Twain's henpecked ear, "You know the tone" (*MTHL* 61). Twain makes repeated fun of Livy for swearing, which of course she not only never did but also strenuously objected to his doing. He claims that when vexed she says "O, hellfire," but he outdoes himself when he reports to Howells that she is given to *silent* swearing. "To get this woman," he says, "to give up the baneful habit of underhanded swearing, is one of those things which I have long ago been obliged to give up, as being among those things which cannot be accomplished." And then he adds, in gleeful burlesque of a concerned moral father, "But the poor children don't suspect, I thank God for that" (*MTHL* 773, 295).

In this domestic comedy both Twain and Howells use the gender stereotypes of their time, depicting themselves as males in need of social tutelage and moral guidance, their wives as custodians of propriety as well as morality. Both men also, quite naturally, make use of the two spheres: the public arena as the man's field of strife, the home as the woman's citadel. They thus present themselves through the narrow, conventional lens of domestic ideology. In his brilliant and provocative study, *Necessary Madness*, Greg Camfield has examined the comedy of this ideology in the nineteenth century and suggested that men and women alike often used it "to manage their ambivalent feelings" about these genderings (*Necessary Madness* x). In their correspondence, however, Twain and Howells seem completely satisfied with the traditional roles.[15] Despite their gentle mocking of their wives, the domestic comedy they create does not seem to function to release conflicted feelings but only to provide an easy outlet for comic joy.

Not all of the humor of their correspondence is lighthearted, however. Both men comment freely on the often sorry spectacle of the Gilded Age. As they shift attention from themselves, their homes and families, their humor darkens. Both men are animated by what Howells, reviewing Twain's *A Tramp Abroad*, called "a passionate love of justice, and a generous scorn of what is petty and mean"; both write out of, again in Howells's words, "the grimness of a reformer" (*CH* 82). They turn Juvenalian, unleashing bitter contempt. Each, as Swift said of himself, "lashed the vice" ("Verses on the Death of Dr. Swift"). Howells to Twain: "I have just heated myself up with your righteous wrath about our indifference to the Brazilian Republic. But it seems to me that you ignore the real reason for it which is that there is no longer an American Republic, but an aristocracy-loving oligarchy in place of it. Why should our Money-bags rejoice in the explosion of a Wind-bag? They know at the bottom of the hole where their souls ought to be that if such an event finally means anything it means *their* ruin next; and so they *don't* rejoice; and as *they* mostly inspire the people's voice, the press, the press is dumb." Twain to Howells: "I have been reading the morning paper. I do it every morning—well knowing that I shall find in it the usual depravities and basenesses & hypocrisies & cruelties that make up Civilization, & cause me to put in the rest of the day pleading for the damnation of the human race. I cannot seem to get my prayers answered, yet I do not despair" (*MTHL* 626–27, 691). Howells complains of "the greed, solemn selfishness and cruel dullness of society," while Twain insists that "human nature" itself is "the most consummate sham & lie" ever "invented" (*MTHL* 359, 501). Both men grow increasingly disgusted with their time, with its political, economic, and social systems, and even with life at large. Both question individual identity, suspecting that each person conceals what Howells terms "the black heart's-truth." Howells tends to focus on specific social problems, while Twain takes a broader view that enfolds human nature in general and existence at large. Twain sometimes turns their common distress into crude comedy: "Isn't man," he asks Howells, "a creature to be ashamed of in pretty much all his aspects? Is he really fit for anything but to be stood up on the street corner as a convenience for dogs?" (*MTHL* 781, 501).

Twain and Howells also laugh with increasing grimness about their health and inevitable death. Early on, Twain revels in being sick—for the first time, he says, in twenty-one years—because it enables him to "take my meals in bed, neglect all business without a pang, & smoke 18 cigars a day." And early on, Howells tells him: "If you had got sick in our house, Mrs. Howells would have . . . killed *you*" (*MTHL* 62, 469). In their salad days death is just a joke. Canceling a plan for a trip together, Howells writes to Twain, "Forgive my having led you on to fix a time; I never thought it would come to that, I supposed you would die or something" (*MTHL* 58). Not having heard from him for a while, Twain asks Howells, "Are you *dead*—or only sleepeth?" and the line becomes a comic refrain sounded in other letters: "Say—are you dead again?"; "I reckon you are dead again, but no matter, I will heave a line at the corpse" (*MTHL* 268, 288, 290). However, as they aged, laughing at growing infirmities and the certainty of death became a survival tactic. Up from a protracted illness, Howells assures his friend, "I am at least out of bed, and so far on a par with that branch of the human race which is being tried for matricide." Setting affairs in order as if for a vacation, Twain informs Howells, "I have retired from New York for good, I have retired from labor for good, I have discharged my stenographer, & have entered upon a holiday whose other end is in the cemetery." Both men reach a point at which aging is a trial. "This curse of growing old!" Howells exclaims, "The joke is all out of *that*" (*MTHL* 822, 833, 701). And yet they laugh.[16]

They pen imaginary postmortem tributes to each other. With comic self-deprecation, Twain tells Howells—years before the event: "Possibly you will not be a fully accepted classic until you have been dead a hundred years,—it is the fate of the Shakespeares & of all genuine prophets, but *then* your books will be as common as Bibles, I believe. . . . In that day *I* shall still be in the Cyclopedias, too, thus: 'Mark Twain; history & occupation unknown—but he was personally acquainted with Howells.'" And with equal—and equally humorous—self-effacement, Howells writes Twain, "I shall feel it honor enough if they put on my tombstone, 'He was born in the same Century and general Section of middle western Country with Dr. S. L. Clemens, Oxon., and had his Degree three years before him through a Mistake of the University" (*MTHL* 245–46, 851). Their tributes capture not only their great admiration for each other, not only their equally great affection, but also the shared comic spirit that links them together and animates their letters.

In 1901, after having known him for some thirty-two years, and after having read all his major works as well as many minor ones, Howells published "Mark Twain: An Inquiry" in the prestigious *North American Review*. As its title suggests, the essay is a searching exploration of Twain—of his origins, his aesthetics, his accomplishments, his fame, and his humor. It is Howells's most penetrating commentary on the writer he admired (and reviewed with constant approval) and the friend he delighted in corresponding with. Especially significant is his attempt to comprehend the source of Twain's humor. He had described that humor for years—and enjoyed it in their letters, but here for the first time he tries to fathom its very source. His account is doubly interesting because it adumbrates a causal circumstance experienced not just by Twain but by Howells himself. Despite the differences between Howells's Ohio and Twain's Missouri, both writers felt they had once shared common ground—in countryside, town, home, and print shop, and Howells said as much in metaphors that open themselves suggestively: "We were natives of the same vast Mississippi Valley; and Missouri was not so far from Ohio but that we were akin in our first knowledge of woods and fields as we were in our early parlance" (*MyMT* 15). Landscape and language, the immediate encounter with physical reality and the mediating constructions of culture, these commonalities shaped both men.

In Howells's account the overwhelming force of their region was grim: "Any one who has really known the West (and really to know it one must have lived it) is aware of the profoundly serious, the almost tragical strain which is the fundamental tone in the movement of such music as it has." Howells posits that as the West, or more exactly, the western mind, confronts life, it "trusts and hopes and laughs" up to a point, and after such engagement, it "doubts and fears." Then, transcending its own anxiety, it "laughs again." This second laughter (the first being with joy and hope) is both a sign of "disillusion," the "grim second-mind" of the region, and the means by which loss is endured. He suggests two other impulses to laughter characteristic of the region: first, he says, the westerner laughs skeptically as he encounters not only the "modern world" but through it himself, questioning "all his prepossessions, of equality, of humanity, of representative government, and revealed religion"; and second, the westerner laughs acceptingly as a way of bearing the failure of his own convictions as well as the uncertainty of life ("MT: An Inquiry" 148–49). Howells's explanation of the regional humor that engendered Twain's thus divides into three kinds of laughter: laughing in joy, laughing in doubt and challenge, and laughing to endure. (The humor of the correspondence between Twain and Howells expresses all three.)

Howells's fundamental argument is that Twain's humor is dark in its first formation, a result of the "tragical strain" of his region's life. Howells's own humor seems to well up from the same deep spring. Certainly the early humor of each writer's travel narratives reveals an arrestingly grim side: Howells insists on—and sometimes laughs at—Venice in decay; Twain moralizes over—and sometimes laughs at—human insignificance. They are both attuned from the first to the bleak side of human life and often find it cause for laughter, or as Howells put it elsewhere, their "despair" seems to break "in laughter" (*MyMT* 31). As they developed as writers, as they progressed as thinkers—as they aged—their humor revealed more of its dark origins. Their "humorous" works become grim and angry assaults on the ills, wrongs, and injustices they learned to see in life in the very beginning. Howells might well have spoken for both writers when he insisted to Twain in their correspondence that he knew "what a bottom of fury there is to your fun" (*MTHL* 338).

To vent their common fury, their long-felt disgust with the arrangements of life, both Howells and Twain create late in their careers fictions centered on a Mysterious Stranger who is both sage and comic device.

Twain's Mysterious Stranger is now so famous that he is anything but mysterious. Howells's, on the other hand, is still relatively obscure. Beginning in 1897, Twain spent eleven years—off and on—struggling to give fictional form to his Stranger, creating three different versions (and a fragment of a fourth), never completing or publishing one. All have been recovered, however, carefully edited, and printed by modern scholars (see Gibson *MTMS*). Howells's Stranger—a Traveler from Altruria—has been visible since he first appeared in 1894 in the romance named for him. The two Strangers reveal the final dark turnings of the humor of Howells and Twain.

Succinctly expressing in Pudd'nhead Wilson's New Calendar the same idea Howells elaborated in "Mark Twain: An Inquiry," Twain observes, "Everything human is pathetic. The secret source of Humor itself is not joy but sorrow" (*FE* 119). While the late Twain was most moved to laughter by the sense that "everything human is pathetic," the late Howells was impelled to laugh out of "sorrow." What saddened him were the manifold inequities of American life—its economic disparities, backed by a profound indifference of the more privileged classes toward the sufferings of the underclass. The problem gnawed at him. In a well-known letter to Henry James, Howells articulated his growing despair: "After fifty years of optimistic content with 'civilization' and its ability to come out all right in the end, I now abhor it, and feel that it is coming out all wrong in the end" (*Life in Letters* 1:417). His solution was for a time Christian socialism, and he dramatized both the need for it and its potential benefits in *A Traveler from Altruria.*

Although *A Traveler from Altruria* is a deeply serious book, Howells presents his critique of American life comically. His increasing disgust with, indeed his angry hatred of, civilization in America is muted by his careful use of humor. In this book he creates a triad of voices to articulate his criticism: Mr. Twelvemough, the first-person narrator; the members of an elite community of which he is a part; and the Traveler from Altruria (sometimes too pointedly called Mr. Homos), a distant utopian country. The conversations between these figures form a kind of neo-Platonic symposium on the American way.

Mr. Twelvemough, the representative American, and the Mysterious Stranger from Altruria are Howells's versions of the classical *alazon*, the self-satisfied, sometimes smug and preening figure who lays claim to more than he is, and *eiron*, the self-deprecating, often deflating and understating figure who underplays what he is. Like their creator, however, Howells's *alazon* and *eiron* are particularly mild versions of the conventionally extravagant types. Mr. Twelvemough (the pun on *twelvemo* in his name, a variant of duodecimo that signifies the size of a printed volume as approximately 5"x 7½", marks him at once as a writer of somewhat diminutive works) is complacent, indeed prideful, about American life, and it is the function of the Stranger to shake that complacency. As *eiron* the Stranger tries to puncture the inflated *alazon*.

Howells works to make his Stranger mysterious. Beyond the bare facts that he is from Altruria, an isolated country in the Aegean Sea, seeking information about the United States, the "most advanced country of its time," there is no explanation of the Stranger's background.[17] His behavior is strange in that it is actively and indiscriminately altruistic, but his character, his habits, his profession are all left unexplained. Mr. Twelvemough, on the other hand, is presented in full detail. Howells fleshes him out as a fastidious gentleman who punctiliously upholds social decorum, a superficial writer of frothy popular romances, a sentimental admirer of pink sunsets, a smug Christian who trusts that inequities are providentially ordained, a humane man of good will and moral sense whose conscience is stagnant—in short, a thoroughly conventional nineteenth-century man whose only difference from the majority is the dubious one of his profession.

What makes him comic is his witless utterance of self-indicting commonplaces. "America," he happily announces, "is a republic where every man is for himself, and you cannot help others as you do at home; it is dangerous—it is ridiculous" (*TFA* 74). After extolling the superior intellect and culture of American women, he observes with equanimity that in America "women have no influence in public affairs" (*TFA* 26). Howells multiplies this comedy of self-incrimination by adding to Mr. Twelvemough's remarks those of a chorus of like-minded men—a banker, an industrialist, a lawyer, a professor, a minister, a doctor—and one woman, a socialite. These characters are as uncritically pleased with America as Mr. Twelvemough is; they are in fact apologists for the American way. Since they are meant to express from their different vocational perspectives the shared body of American belief, Howells gives them little individuality. In the broadest terms, the issues they raise constitute, as Edwin H. Cady has observed, "the American Dream" itself (*The Realist at War* 198). A brief sampling of their statements demonstrates not only the outlook that Howells is attacking but also the way he transmutes his bitterness into irony simply by letting his typical Americans condemn themselves through their uncharitable pronouncements:

We consider the pinch of poverty the highest incentive that a man can have. (*TFA* 50)

That question of what would become of people thrown out of work by a given improvement, is something that capital cannot consider. (*TFA* 113)

The poverty of some and the wealth of others, isn't that what forms the great tie of human brotherhood? (*TFA* 88)

No, the American ideal is not to change the conditions for all, but for each to rise above the rest if he can. (*TFA* 41)

The spur and counterpoint to these complacencies is the Mysterious Stranger. He explains his intentions early in the book as a desire to "penetrate the fact of American life" (*TFA* 28), and to this apparent end he provokes explanations like the ones just cited. The Stranger both puzzles and unsettles everyone he encounters. He seems to suspend all personal judgment in the objective pursuit of information, yet he leaves those he talks to disquieted. They cannot quite make him out. Howells very carefully makes the question of the Stranger's outlook a central part of the plot. The Stranger is neither self-deprecating nor obviously superior. His manner is always open and friendly, always earnest and sincere, always sweet and innocent. He insists that he is not a "humorist," and he seems to those around him to take everything "in dead earnest" (*TFA* 25, 112). Yet his remarks and questions are at times so pointed that even Mr. Twelvemough begins to suspect "something ironical in the man"; he finds that he does not wholly trust "such innocence" (*TFA* 25, 29). Indeed, Howells's Stranger is a mock innocent, his earnest and simple manner merely the deadpan traditional in western humor.

Concealing his own unhappy and critical spirit beneath the Stranger's mask of innocence, Howells exposes in his romance the social indifference, corruption, and cruelty at the heart of the American system. The Stranger's deadpan queries reveal the absurdities as well as the inhumanities of American life. Told that working-class women are kept healthy by their brutal work, for instance, the Stranger asks, "Do you suppose that they are aware of the sacrifices which the ladies of the upper classes make in leaving all the work to them, and suffering from the nervous debility which seems to be the outcome of your society life?" When he learns that all work is valued in America but that no one wants to be a domestic, he sums up the situation with an irony worthy of George Orwell: "So it seems that while all honest work is honored among you, there are some kinds of honest work that are not honored so much as others." Most often his pose of innocence is carefully maintained. Nothing could appear more guileless, for instance, or be more devastating, than his polite, childlike query, "May I ask what the use of your society life is?" (*TFA* 68, 15, 63). But at some moments, the Stranger's irony becomes so palpable as to undermine his innocence: "Am I right in supposing that the effect of your economy is to establish insuperable inequalities among you, and to forbid the hope of the brotherhood which your polity proclaims?" And again: "Then, in your conditions, a kindly impulse to aid one who needs your help, is something to be guarded against as possibly pernicious?" (*TFA* 59, 87). In questions like these the Stranger's deadpan begins to give way to a sardonic grin.

For the most part, however, Howells keeps the Stranger's mask of innocence firmly in place. The result is an exposé of American life conducted with the quiet and solemnity of a church service. Howells's critique is as clear as it is subdued. While the Stranger remains always unmoved, if always questioning, those about him laugh in revealing ways: they joke competitively, putting down others to advance themselves, and they joke dismissively, subjecting their economic and social inferiors to ridicule aimed at putting—or rather keeping—them in their place. Humor itself thus becomes a reflection of the divisive American system. Although Howells lets his Stranger lecture in the end about the ideal world of Altruria and about the changes in human nature it creates (simply put: from egoism to altruism), the Stranger's message is generally dismissed by those in power as humbug (the underclass, on the other hand, often applauds his analysis), and the Stranger himself is considered a fraud. Howells's utopian satire thus ends in paradoxes: the reality of an alternate system seems a fantasy, and authentic altruism appears fictitious. At the end, Howells's Stranger is said to be visiting other places, but he is clearly in exile from representative America. Howells's text also seems to suggest a loss of faith in humor itself, for, on the one hand, circumstances in America are too dire to laugh lightly about, and on the other, corrective, satiric humor—the dark vein Howells turns to—goes unheard.

Twain's more famous Mysterious Stranger makes an interesting comparison. Although the three versions, "The Chronicle of Young Satan," "Schoolhouse Hill," and "No. 44, The Mysterious Stranger" (the fragment of a fourth version was incorporated into "The Chronicle"), differ in setting, time, plot, and, most importantly, in the nature of the Stranger himself, they all seem to arise from the same impulse. In a long letter to Howells, written from Vienna after he had been working on his Stranger tale for over a year and a half, Twain explained his enterprise: "What I have been wanting was a chance to write a book without reserves—a book which should take account of no one's feelings, no one's prejudices, opinions, beliefs, hopes, illusions, delusions; a book which should say my say, right out of my heart, in the plainest language & without a limitation of any sort." What he wanted to say through his Stranger was "what I think of Man, & how he is constructed, & what a shabby poor ridiculous thing he is, & how mistaken he is in his estimate of his character & powers & qualities & his place among the animals." With characteristic enthusiasm he found his creative work "an intellectual drunk," and delighted in Livy's declaration that it was "perfectly horrible—and perfectly beautiful" (*MTHL* 698–99).

Like Howells, Twain clearly designed his Stranger as the agent of critique. But just as Howells's satiric outbursts in their correspondence tended to focus on specific civic arrangements—the economic order, class cleavage, and the principles underpinning these—while Twain concerned himself more broadly with the nature of human nature and the construction of life itself, so in their Stranger fictions they target different objects for ridicule. The later Twain did, of course, attend to public polity in such works as *Following the Equator*, "To the Person Sitting in Darkness," and other essays, but in his Stranger texts he concentrates morally on humankind and philosophically on existence. (The imbalance between moralist and humorist in the early travel narratives, in which the latter outweighs the former, is reversed in the Stranger texts.) Twain's complaints are now familiar: humanity is base and selfish; the moral sense is corrupt; history is the record of cruelty and inhumanity; the separate self is controlled by the forces of heredity and environment; human identity is multiple; God is malign or nonexistent; and existence itself is only an expression of individual consciousness. All this is the late Twain's grim litany.

He recites it—via his Stranger—with special ferocity. A single, not unrepresentative, example: "Man is a museum of disgusting diseases, a home of impurities; he comes to-day and is gone to-morrow, he begins as dirt and departs as a stench" (*MTMS* 55). Besides containing Twain's energizing—and sometimes deforming—didactic impulse, the various Stranger texts have one central trait in common: in all three versions, Twain's Stranger is a pseudo-innocent. Like Howells's Traveler from Altruria, Twain's

Stranger is a mask through which he utters his dark convictions. In creating his Stranger, Howells jettisons all the unruly turnings of his humor that occasionally crop up in his travel narratives and seizes on the deadpan, seldom used before, as his preferred, ironic mode. Twain's Stranger, on the other hand, though always a mock innocent, assumes several different comic postures.

In "The Chronicle of Young Satan," besides being a superior being with omniscience, supernatural power, and no feeling whatsoever, the Stranger has the familiar impassivity of the deadpan pose. "He was bent," Twain's youthful narrator says, "on putting us at ease, and he had the right art . . . so earnest and simple and gentle" (*MTMS* 45). But his mode is not the irony of Howells's Stranger, which exploits discrepancies between behavior and principle, but rather cool, straightforward denunciation. He is in fact so dispassionate that his attacks on humanity lack the traditional sting of Juvenalian satire. Although Twain sometimes gets off a good comic line (Young Satan says he has "an uncle in business down in the tropics"), his Stranger in this version is not much of a vehicle for humor. It is not surprising, then, that the Stranger should, in a now famous passage, define laughter itself as a "weapon" that can destroy its object: "blow it to rags and atoms at a blast"; nor, given this sort of humor in the story itself, is it surprising that the narrator, the Stranger's audience, Theodore Fischer, is often "too much hurt to laugh" (*MTMS* 68, 165–67).

To a degree, Twain's next Stranger text, "Schoolhouse Hill," redeems the character of his supernatural figure by making him more humanly childlike. This Stranger becomes the schoolmate of Tom Sawyer and Becky Thatcher, and he is not only more innocent, in that he knows less of humanity and human history than in Twain's first version, but also more kindly disposed toward people in general. (He rescues several from an annihilating snowstorm.) Further, this Stranger's announced intention in visiting Earth is to help humankind recover from the consequences of the fall it suffered at the instigation of his uncle Satan. Narrating in the third person (unlike the first of the other two versions), Twain creates, as he always had, considerable schoolroom comedy. He also generates humor from the encounters between the Stranger, his hosts the Hotchkiss family, together with their slaves and a gathering of village folk. But, for the most part, these humorous moments of childhood high jinks and village caricature occur largely apart from the Stranger himself or, at most, with the

Stranger as the occasion (rather than the medium) of the humor. Twain raised the mask of innocence to let his first Stranger vent sardonic condemnation, but with his second, he keeps the mask so securely in place that the innocence seems more real than mock and hardly comic at all.

Twain's final attempt to have his "say, right out of [his] heart," "No. 44, The Mysterious Stranger" suggests an attempt to merge the unfeeling, contemptuous nature of the first Stranger with the boyish pleasantness of the second. No. 44 has the transcendent knowledge and the power of the first Stranger, but he is not much given to savage denunciation, and, like the second Stranger, he is often kind and childlike. Twain makes him sprightly and playful. He is said to be "capricious, unstable," "forever flitting and sampling here and there and yonder, like a bee" (*MTMS* 313). He is given to comic frolics—to circus antics that rival, he himself says, Barnum and Bailey. He attempts to entertain both himself and his interlocutor August Feldner by zany acts: he plays a Jew's harp and dances to his own tune, parades like a prince doing a cakewalk, and performs a minstrel show (*MTMS* 299, 303, 354–56). He is in fact more comic showman than cynical critic, so much so that Twain imparts to other characters many of the dark messages usually voiced by his Mysterious Stranger. This Stranger is, as various critics have observed, a representation of the creative imagination (e.g., see Cox, *Fate* 275), but he is more than that. He embodies the comic spirit itself. In the end, of course, he proclaims himself merely a subjective expression of his auditor Feldner—nothing more than "a dream" of his "imagination" (*MTMS* 404).

Interestingly, Howells too flirts with such solipsism. Mr. Twelvemough wonders at one moment if the Stranger from Altruria is "really a man" and speculates at another that he is a "celestial angel"; at times the Stranger seems to him to be "entirely subjective" (*TFA* 99, 112, 92). But although the Strangers of Howells and Twain have similar functions, they are quite different. In the end, while Howells reports that his wanders off to another part of America, Twain has his Stranger announce that he is "but a dream" (*MTMS* 404). Whether dream or exiled reformer, insofar as these Strangers embody the late humor of their creators, dark and critical as it is, their ultimate fates suggest a kind of giving up on the comic itself. First shaped, if Howells is right, by the bleak, often tragic, certainly disillusioning aspects of their regional homeland, the humor of Twain and Howells shifted from the unbridled subversions of their early travel narratives to the sheer comic joy of their correspondence to their final satiric probings of not just America but of human existence. In the end, both writers all but despair of humor itself, silencing their Mysterious Strangers.

There is no indication that Twain read Howells's *Traveler from Altruria*. When it appeared in 1894, he was not only embroiled in bankruptcy proceedings but also living abroad to save money. The halcyon days at Hartford, which saw so many extended visits between the two writers, were at an end. Since Twain never completed, let alone published, any of his Stranger texts, Howells could not have known them. The final, similar turn of their humor toward corrective satire was visible to each writer in glimpses in their correspondence but not in their Stranger texts. And this similar turn in their humor was largely lost on their public. In the closing years of his life Twain was celebrated as much for his humanity and philosophy as his humor (in one sense readers and critics now saw clearly the seriousness Howells had pointed to in his very first review of Twain). Howells, who would live twenty years longer than Twain, was widely honored as a novelist but not as a humorist, and while he received many accolades—chief among them perhaps his election in 1908 as the first president of the newly formed American Academy of Arts and Letters— there was a countercurrent of negative commentary that pilloried Howells as the embodiment of a timid and repressive Victorianism.

The publication of Howells's *My Mark Twain* in 1910, shortly after Twain's death, signaled the importance of their long friendship. Howells ends his affectionate account by repeating the idea he had adumbrated in 1901 in "Mark Twain: An Inquiry": Twain's "tragical seriousness broke in the laughter" that made him famous (*MyMT* 84). Ironically, however, early-twentieth-century critics refused to see that Howells saw—and honored—Twain's dark seriousness. From the pinnacle of the Nobel Prize podium, Sinclair Lewis said to the world what other critics in America had been saying less resoundingly: Howells "was actually able to tame Mark Twain, perhaps the greatest of our writers, and to put that fiery old savage into an intellectual frock coat and top hat" (15). This surely misreads the past. It misconstrues the literary relationship in which Howells and Twain shared an unruly humor as well as a stabilizing morality, shared all manner of comic fun in their correspondence, and shared a final lashing of the vice in their dark Stranger texts. It misses the comic kinship at the heart of their long friendship.

# Mark Twain
# & Harriet Beecher Stowe

*He snatched the child from her, and then made the men slaves*
*who were chained before and behind her throw her on the ground*
*and hold her there and expose her body; and then he laid on with*
*his lash like a madman till her back was flayed, she shrieking and*
*struggling the while, piteously.*

MARK TWAIN, 1889

In "Tom Sawyer's Conspiracy," a sequel to *Huckleberry Finn* once again featuring Tom, Huck, and Jim—which Twain began in 1897 and worked on intermittently until 1901—Tom worries over how to have a thrill-filled summer until he hits upon the idea of instigating a "civil war." After Jim learns what a civil war is, he begs Tom not to start one, and eventually Tom agrees. Full of admiration, Huck explains what has transpired:

> So Tom done it. . . . It shows what a good heart he had; he had been just dead set on getting up a civil war, and had even planned out the preparations for it on the biggest scale, and yet he throwed it all aside and give it up to accommodate a nigger. . . . But he give up the civil war, and it is one of the brightest things to his credit. And he could a had it easy enough if he had sejested it, anybody can see it now. And it don't seem right and fair that Harriet Beecher Stow [*sic*] and

all them other second-handers gets all the credit of starting that war and you never hear Tom Sawyer mentioned in the histories ransack them how you will, and yet he was the first that thought of it. (*Huck Finn and Tom Sawyer Among the Indians* 137–38)

Huck's comments here—unexpectedly, uncharacteristically learned—reveal Mark Twain's uneasiness about one of his literary progenitors, Harriet Beecher Stowe. In this passage, never published in his lifetime, he laughs chiefly at Tom's fantastic scheming and Huck's numskull innocence, but he also plays gently with Stowe. From time to time Twain had, through the years, recorded in his notebooks, with mild but unmistakable aggression, Harriet Beecher Stowe jokes—one example: "Mrs. S. 'Ever read *Uncle Tom?*' Tried to" (*N&J3* 356). Yet he never mocked her openly in print. What troubled him most deeply, however, may be disclosed in Huck's curious remarks. For through Huck, Twain imparts to Tom what he could never achieve in his own literary relation to Stowe: priority.

Whatever genre Twain turned to as a writer, Stowe had already written in. Before he recorded his travels in *The Innocents Abroad* (1869), Stowe had remembered hers in *Sunny Memories of Foreign Lands* (1854). Before he and Charles Dudley Warner satirized public life, including its sexual politics, in *The Gilded Age* (1873), Stowe had exposed love and marriage in high society in *Pink and White Tyranny* (1871). Before Twain captured boy-life in *Tom Sawyer* (1876) and *Huckleberry Finn* (1884–85), Stowe had dealt with children in *Queer Little People* (1867) and *Little Pussy Willow* (1870). (Her later *Poganuc People*—published in 1878—reversed the flow, for it is probably indebted to *Tom Sawyer*.) Before Twain tried his hand at historical romance in *The Prince and the Pauper* (1881) and later *A Connecticut Yankee in King Arthur's Court* (1889), Stowe had created her fictive version of history in *Agnes of Sorrento* (1862). Before Twain created extended treatments of regional comic types in *Tom Sawyer* (1876), *Huckleberry Finn* (1884–85), and "The Man That Corrupted Hadleyburg" (1899), Stowe had depicted both regional life and its comic figures in *Oldtown Folks* (1869) and *Sam Lawson's Oldtown Fireside Stories* (1872). And before Twain wrote his complex novels of race in the slaveholding South, *Huckleberry Finn* (1884–85) and *Pudd'nhead Wilson* (1894), Stowe had become famous for *Uncle Tom's Cabin* (1852) and *Dred* (1856). In short, in many literary matters it was Mark Twain who was, as Huck put it, one of the "second-handers."

Although he eventually owned fourteen of Stowe's books, Twain did not necessarily recognize the range of her works that anticipated his (see Gribben, *MT's Library* 669–73). He did, however, acknowledge—and seek to match—her enormous popular success. The sales of *Uncle Tom's Cabin* became a benchmark for his own books. In December 1869, for instance, he wrote to his fiancée, Olivia Langdon, about the sales of *The Innocents Abroad:* "Twelve thousand copies of the book sold *this month.* This is perfectly enormous. Nothing like it since Uncle Tom's Cabin, I guess" (*L3* 440). And a year later he bragged to Horace Bixby, the pilot who had taught him the river: *The Innocents Abroad* "has met with a greater sale than any book ever published except Uncle Tom's Cabin" (*L4* 58). When he later published *Mark Twain's Library of Humor,* he tried to capitalize on Stowe's selling-power by including in his anthology her sketch "The Parson's Horse-Race." It is clear that Twain was generally conscious of Stowe as a predecessor in some areas. In "The Man That Corrupted Hadleyburg," to cite a single famous instance of acknowledged indebtedness, Twain defines his small-town jester, Jack Halliday, as the "loafing, good-natured, no-account, irreverent fisherman, hunter, boys' friend, stray-dogs' friend, typical 'Sam Lawson' of the town," fully expecting his readers to recognize that Sam Lawson was Stowe's comic figure in *Oldtown Folks* (*MTC2* 402). Like a ghost from the recent past, she haunted his creative work.

Harriet Beecher Stowe (1811–1896) was a formidable figure—a cultural force—for Twain's era. After the publication of *Uncle Tom's Cabin* in 1852, she quickly became not just the most famous woman writer in America but one of the most famous in the English-speaking world. Even today her sales figures are astounding (see Mott 114–22), as first thousands, then millions, of readers responded very much as Howells did: "The book that moved me most . . . was then beginning to move the whole world more than any other book has moved it. I read it as it came out week after week in the old National Era, and I broke my heart over Uncle Tom's Cabin, as every one else did. . . . I felt its greatness when I read it first, and as often as I have read it since, I have seen more and more clearly that it is a very great novel" (*My Literary Passions* 63). In his autobiography, Henry James called *Uncle Tom's Cabin* his "first experiment in grown-up fiction" and confessed that "we lived and moved at that time, with great intensity, in Mrs. Stowe's novel." He groped to describe its extraordinary effect on the public:

There was, however, I think, for that triumphant work no classified condition; it was for no sort of reader as distinct from any other sort, save indeed for Northern as differing from Southern: it knew the large felicity of gathering in alike the small and the simple and the big and the wise, and had above all the extraordinary fortune of finding itself, for an immense number of people, much less a book than a state of vision, of feeling and of consciousness, in which they didn't sit and read and appraise and pass the time, but walked and talked and laughed and cried and, in a manner of which Mrs. Stowe was the irresistible cause, generally conducted themselves. (*A Small Boy and Others* 158–60)

There is no record of when Twain first read *Uncle Tom's Cabin* or of how he responded. However, in 1853 he noted that the play based on the novel was "in full blast" in New York, and observed that everyone "cried over Tom's griefs" (*Mark Twain's Travels with Mr. Brown* 84).

He met Stowe at a dinner given by her brother Henry Ward Beecher in January of 1868. When Twain went east after journalistic work in Nevada and his informal apprenticeship under Bret Harte in California, he carried with him letters of introduction to several prominent clergymen, including Beecher. He found preachers "gay," he told his mother, and said he wanted to run with "the fast nags of the cloth." Twain reported nothing about Harriet Beecher Stowe at the time of this first encounter, but he enjoyed the dinner immensely—"a tip-top" time at which he claimed to have "told more lies" than he had "told before in a month" (*L1* 368, *L2* 144–45). With a playful irreverence intended to horrify his mother, he wrote home that "Henry Ward is a brick" (*L2* 144–45).

Twain's real friendship with Mrs. Stowe began when he moved to the Nook Farm community at Hartford (that "sterling old Puritan" one), where she was already a celebrated denizen. Twain lived first at her brother-in-law John Hooker's home, renting it from October 1871 to September 1874, and then moved into his own newly built house at 351 Farmington Avenue, a home he poeticized—or at least versified:

. . . cozy, sunny and snug retreat,
At once both city and country seat,
Made up of bricks of various hue

And shape and position, straight and askew,

With nooks and angles and gables too,

The curious house that Mark built. (qtd. in Comfort, "Nook Farm" 545)

Stowe herself first built in 1864 at the southern edge of Nook Farm a sumptuous house, Oakholm—a house, she liked to point out, with eight gables, one more than Hawthorne's seven (she disapproved of Hawthorne's friendship with and support of Franklin Pierce). Then in 1870, when her dream home proved too expensive to keep up, she moved to a smaller house on Forest Avenue—a house that eventually perched just behind Twain's, making them backyard neighbors. For twenty years, then, from 1871 to 1891, when Twain, facing multiple financial difficulties, closed up his house, Mark Twain and Harriet Beecher Stowe were not only close neighbors but also active members of the same social, intellectual, and literary community. That community was for its time both notably creative and unusually casual. John Hooker remembered its conviviality this way: "Each of us made free of the others' houses . . . each keeping open house, and all of us frequently gathering for a social evening or to welcome some friendly visitor, often some person distinguished in political, literary, or philanthropic life, who had come to some of our houses" (170–71).

All the evidence indicates that Twain loved his life at Nook Farm.[1] Kaplan points out that he "shared the group's faith in a dynamic aristocracy, their high respectability, their earnest idealism, and their intellectual dedication" (*Mr. Clemens and MT* 141). Twain was a good neighbor to Stowe. He invited her to dinners and private theatricals. He had her speak at the Saturday Morning Club, a club he organized around 1875 as a cultural and social aid to the young women of Hartford. (The Monday Evening Club, a twenty-member discussion group restricted to men, to which Twain was elected in 1873, had been founded by Stowe's husband, Calvin Stowe, and two other Hartford luminaries, Horace Bushnell and James Hammond Trumbull.) Twain and Stowe sent each other their books, suitably inscribed. Twain went out of his way—or, more precisely, across his backyard—to entertain Stowe. He paid visits, sent flowers, and even arranged unexpected, sometimes elaborate, entertainments. Moncure Conway, Twain's informal literary agent in England, remembered accompanying Twain to Stowe's house for what he thought was a casual visit, only to discover that Twain had designed a small pageant for her: costumed characters suddenly appeared, one after another, entering her house, as Twain provided explanatory remarks about their nature and achievements (Paine, *MTB* 570). Twain also joined Stowe at public events that ranged from Hartford charity fundraisers to *Atlantic Monthly* lunches and dinners to honor the magazine's famous contributors. It's no wonder that Twain's daughter Clara once listed Harriet Beecher Stowe as one of the world's most notable women (*MTHL* 424), or that his daughter Jean, at age nine, would proudly announce at dinner one night when a guest mentioned *Tom Sawyer*, "I know who wrote that book—Harriet Beecher Stowe!" (qtd. in Hoffman, *Inventing MT* 352).

In her later years, especially after the death of her husband in 1886, Mrs. Stowe began to behave oddly. She wandered in and out of Nook Farm homes without any purpose, and her conversations were not always coherent. Annie Fields recalled Stowe's later years this way: "She endured . . . some years of existence when the motive power of the mind almost ceased to act. She became 'like a little child,' wandering about, pleased with flowers, fresh air, the sound of a piano, or a voice singing hymns, but the busy, inspiring spirit was asleep" (*Life and Letters of HBS* 392). However, she somehow continued to supervise her son Charles Edward's official biography of her and to keep an eye on her emerging collected works, *The Writings of Harriet Beecher Stowe*, in sixteen volumes.

In his autobiography, Twain recalled Stowe's late, erratic behavior: "Her mind had decayed and she was a pathetic figure. She wandered about all the day long in the care of a muscular Irishwoman. Among the colonists of our neighborhood the doors always stood open in pleasant weather. Mrs. Stowe entered them at her own free will, and as she was always softly slippered and generally full of animal spirits, she was able to deal in surprises, and she liked to do it. She would slip up behind a person who was deep in dreams and musings and fetch a war whoop that would jump that person out of his clothes" (*MTA* 2:242–43). In his notebook, Twain also recorded plans to fictionalize Stowe's escapades, noting again her knack for slipping up behind people: "She escapes daily & suddenly appears softly in people's houses letting off her hideous gobblings in their ears—a terror to women great with child" (*N&J3* 627). At times, ghostlike, she would glide unseen into Twain's home and play the piano: "Sometimes we would hear gentle music in the drawing-room and would find her there at the piano singing ancient and melancholy songs with infinitely touching effect" (*MTA* 2:243). The remembered scenes are richly suggestive. Just as Twain's creative life transpired with the shade of Stowe's literary work hovering just behind him, so in the late 1880s and early '90s her ghostly presence literally haunted him.

There have been few extended commentaries on the purely literary connections between Twain and Stowe. The two have been linked—usually quite briefly—in terms of their exploitation of regional material, their interest in dialect (Turner, "Comedy and Reality"), their recreation of childhood (Stone), and, most of all, their representation of race. Indeed, comparing the treatment of race in *Uncle Tom's Cabin* and *Huckleberry Finn* has become something of a standard stratagem in various kinds of critical commentary (see Arac, chapter 4). Occasionally, rather than finding similarities, critics have cited significant differences. James M. Cox, for instance, has paired Stowe and Twain as representatives of two fundamentally antithetical modes of writing: Stowe, the sentimental; Twain, the humorous ("Humor and America"). (Though seldom commented on, Stowe has her own kind of humor, and as the first chapter of this study suggests, Twain himself is often a sentimentalist.) There remains one further, largely unexplored ground that is common to both writers: the Gothic, especially what has come to be known as the Gothic body.[2]

Stowe evokes the Gothic from time to time in her short stories, and it emerges in her regional novels on dark nights around flaming hearths. She uses the Gothic most extensively, however—and most tellingly—in her two famous novels of social protest, *Uncle Tom's Cabin* and *Dred*. As Karen Halttunen has explained, "Stowe chose the Gothic mode to represent the worst evils of the social sin she attacked because its characteristic atmosphere of evil and brooding terror provided her with an excellent device for engaging readers in her cause" ("Gothic Imagination and Social Reform" 118). Twain, as Roger Salomon has pointed out, "incorporates many Gothic elements piecemeal into his works" ("Gothic" 332). Twain's fictions, early and late, are littered with twisted corpses, crisscrossed by subterranean passageways, peopled by demonic figures, demarcated by haunted houses, filled with yawning graves, and shrouded by ghosts. Sorcerers, fortune-tellers, magicians, spiritualists, mesmerists, and wizards pass fleetingly through his fictive world, and a malign supernatural force often seems to hover over it. Most often, however, such manifestations of the Gothic are dismissed as mere trappings, designed to titillate, thrill, or even—if the paraphernalia is all in good working order—terrify. Few critics take seriously the Gothic Mark Twain. And even when it is recognized, Twain's Gothicism is accorded nothing like the serious function, not to mention the personal importance, given to Stowe's.

That Twain as well as Stowe should use the Gothic mode is hardly surprising. For as Joel Porte has argued, the American Gothic tradition was in large measure rooted in Calvinism, with its dark, terror-inducing drama of sin, guilt, and damnation, and both Twain and Stowe were brought up within versions of Calvinism ("In the Hands of an Angry God" 42–64). As the daughter of famed theologian and evangelist Lyman Beecher, Stowe grew up in an atmosphere of intense religiosity. Though in many ways a kind and loving man, her father forced his children to scrutinize their consciences to discover sin and, if possible, conversion, and he regularly brought home to them the likelihood as well as the horror of eternal damnation at the hands of a just God.[3] Though far less intensely religious, Twain's childhood was also dominated by Calvinist doctrine, in his case a frontier Presbyterianism that left its mark on him as surely as Lyman's fathering did on Harriet.[4] In his autobiographical remembrances Twain testifies repeatedly to the power and persistence of his early religious training, noting in particular his belief—"educated as I had been"— in the controlling force of a retributive Providence (*MTOA* 155). Angrily, in a rhetoric derived from the peculiar institution of chattel slavery, he explained "mine was a trained Presbyterian conscience and knew but the one duty—to hunt and harry its slave upon all pretexts and on all occasions, particularly when there was no sense nor reason in it" (*AMT* 41). Like Stowe's, Twain's imagination was haunted by the prospect of divine reckoning.

Twain and Stowe also lived during a time in which their culture became obsessed with manifestations of the occult.[5] As with sentimentality and humor, the Gothic mode was generated by a dis-ease in American culture. While sentimentality, especially the belated sentimentality that arose in the age of realism, reflected a desperate attempt to ground morality in a time of ethical uncertainty, and while the clash between conventional and unruly humor expressed dramatic shifts in the social order, the popularity of the Gothic in the mid– to late nineteenth century stemmed from the steady waning of religious faith. The Gothic assumes many forms and has multiple dimensions, but it is predicated in the main on a belief in the supernatural. Peter Brooks has linked the rise of the Gothic to the "process of desacralization that was set in motion at the Renaissance, passed through the momentary compromise of Christian humanism, and gathered momentum during the Enlightenment." In the face of the loss of the sacred, whether mythic or doctrinal, the Gothic reasserts "spiritual forces and occult issues" (*Melodramatic Imagination* 15, 17). It has been defined as a "quest for the numinous" (Varma 211).[6] As conventional religious faith eroded in America, the supernatural was frantically sought after. Interest in the Gothic increased in proportion to the loss of traditional religion, for the Gothic was an attempt to recover ties to something beyond—something above—the human. The fact of mortality forced the issue. While death is always with every society, the high infant-mortality rate in America made death in families a frequent occurrence. The mass slaughter of the Civil War not only brought death home to the living but also magnified its reality. Living under the shadow of death, people worried about their individual immortality. To borrow a phrase from Elizabeth Stuart Phelps's best-selling novel of 1869, Americans longed to discover "gates ajar" into another life after this one.[7]

All manner of cultural figures—from true believers to charlatans to philosophers and scientists—offered to help. Mesmerists, phrenologists, and clairvoyants commanded not only attention but often credence. Even before (and certainly after) the Fox sisters reported spirit-rappers and caused a clamor, mediums abounded. Séances became a fad. Ghosts and specters hovered, if not in the actual air, at least in the minds of many earnest people. The culture seemed to hold its breath for the next manifestation of the unknown. The obsession with mysterious realms was not the expression of a passing fad but an abiding fascination with, first, the spiritual dimension of human life and, second, the relation of the material to the spiritual. Toward the end of the century the quest for the supernatural, the seedbed of Gothicism, even acquired a rational sanction as scientific societies were formed to conduct psychical research. The personal and cultural stakes involved in the various seeming confrontations with another, more permanent world were large, for they ultimately called into question the constitution of the human itself. The interest in the supernatural was so widespread that, as several cultural historians have pointed out, "almost every American writer of note had some direct experience with the popular spiritualisms of the nineteenth century" (Kerr, Crowley, and Crowe 4). Certainly Twain and Stowe did.

Though most often thought of as a rational skeptic, Twain was in fact intrigued throughout his life by the possibility of paranormal human powers and supranatural phenomena. Along with the rigid strictures and horrifying visions of Presbyterianism, Twain grew up in an atmosphere rife with superstition. And he grew up hearing—and loving—ghost stories. In his autobiography, in the midst of his reminiscent tour de force about idyllic life at his uncle John Quarles's farm, he recalls "the creepy joy" that "quivered" through him when, gathered about the hearth at night, it was time to hear "the ghost-story of the 'Golden Arm' " (*MTOA* 122). Twain's childhood was shrouded by the spirit-world, and he sought for signs of it throughout his adult life.[8] The range of his exploration is impressive: hypnotism, palmistry, phrenology, fortune-telling, clairvoyance, mental telepathy, spiritualist communication, dream vision, mind-healing, materialization, de-materialization, and in the broadest terms, scientific research into the psychical. (He belonged to the Society for Psychical Research from 1884 to 1902.) What to make of such curiosity is almost as mysterious as the subject under investigation. Howard Kerr sees Twain predominantly as a skeptic who makes fun of the supernatural in the manner of the literary comedians (*Mediums, and Spirit-Rappers* 188). Alan Gribben, on the other hand, suggests that Twain would endorse "whatever occult art could withstand his rational scrutiny." In a precise (and lovely) phrase he describes Twain's attitude as "wishful interest" ("When Other Amusements Fail" 175, 179). Recognizing Twain's combination of skepticism and hope, William M. Gibson has defined him as having a bifurcated vision: as taking "a rational and satiric view and a speculative and psychological view" (*MTMS* 27).

Stowe, on the other hand, is generally seen as a confirmed believer, as a person—and writer—whose fundamental religious faith was pliant enough to include all manner of the marvelous. Her father, Lyman Beecher, witnessed the presence of his deceased first wife in his bedroom one day, and Harriet's husband, Calvin Stowe, had throughout his life more or less regular psychic visions of the living and the dead. Stowe herself once suggested that she had had conversations with the spirit of the dead Charlotte Brontë (Rourke, *Trumpets* 119). And famously or, perhaps more accurately, infamously, Stowe maintained that God wrote *Uncle Tom's Cabin*. After the death of her son Henry, she tried to commune with him through mediums. Her sister Isabella Hooker, a committed spiritualist, a friend and follower of Victoria Woodhull—herself a leading spiritualist as well as a feminist and sometime advocate of free love—lived as neighbor to both Twain and Stowe at Nook Farm. Annie Fields, her close friend and the wife of one of her publishers, avowed that Stowe always believed in spiritualism, recalling that "she affirmed her entire belief in possible manifestations of the nearness and individual life of those who had passed to the unseen world" (*Life and Letters* 306–7). To George Eliot Stowe wrote, "In regard to the subject of Spiritualism I am of the opinion of Goethe that 'it is just as absurd to deny the facts of Spiritualism now as it was in the middle ages to ascribe them to the devil,'" but she stopped short of believing that spiritualist manifestations were "a supplement or continuation of the revelations of Christianity," preferring instead to see them as "an interesting and curious study in psychology." She proposed an article for the *Atlantic* on the planchette, a board by which spirits were believed to communicate with the living, claiming that her "materials" for the piece were "really very extraordinary" (*Life and Letters* 336, 317).

However, her commitment to spiritualism seems to have remained provisional, tempered by her confidence in biblical revelation as superior—incontrovertible—truth and checked by her awareness of charlatans. In a statement Annie Fields said was intended for Stowe's children, Stowe attributed the interest in spiritualism chiefly to the desire of the living to be reunited with their beloved dead. She identified with their longing: "Ah, *were* it true! Were it indeed so that the wall between the spiritual and material is growing thin, and a new dispensation germinating in which communion with the departed blest shall be among the privileges and possibilities of this our mortal state!" But she insisted that only God could effect such a reunion, and she doubted whether the spirits of the dead would express themselves in the fashion popularized by current mediums:

And when we look at what is offered to us, ah! who that has friends in heaven could wish them to return in such wise as this? The very instinct of a sacred sorrow seems to forbid that our beautiful, our glorified ones should stoop lower than even to the medium of their cast-off bodies, to juggle, and rap, and squeak, and perform mountebank tricks with tables and chairs; to recite over in weary sameness harmless truisms, which we were wise enough to say for ourselves;

to trifle, and banter, and jest, or to lead us through endless moonshiny mazes. Sadly and soberly we say that, if this be communion with the dead, we had rather be without it. (*Life and Letters* 308–9)

Here, securely ensconced within the framework of her traditional faith, Stowe unleashes a skepticism worthy of Twain in one of his moments of satire.

Stowe's skepticism shapes her use of the Gothic in *Uncle Tom's Cabin*. She distances her narrative from the Gothic devices she employs, and like Poe before her and Henry James after, she locates the Gothic not in some momentary rending of the veil between the material and spiritual but in the fissures of the human psyche. Although she exploits the Gothic only briefly in the final sequence of events at Simon Legree's plantation, the events themselves form the dramatic climax to Stowe's melodrama, the last act in her morality play. The Gothic functions to evoke the ultimate horror of slavery, to define the threat of predacious sexuality, and to limn the hideous character of a soul damned to eternal perdition.

Stowe slowly envelops her tale in the atmosphere of horror. Having made what she pointedly calls the "middle passage" up the Red River, Legree's entourage of new slaves enters an ever-darkening wilderness, marked with portents of evil: "It was a wild, forsaken road, now winding through dreary pine barrens, where the wind whispered mournfully, and now over log causeways, through long cypress swamps, the doleful trees rising out of the slimy, spongy ground, hung with long wreaths of funeral black moss, while ever and anon the loathsome form of the moccasin snake might be seen sliding among broken stumps and shattered branches that lay here and there, rotting in the water."[9] Legree's home, once a "large and handsome" mansion, has slipped into "utter decay"—its grounds "ragged, forlorn," littered with "broken pails, cobs of corn, and other slovenly remains," all "grown over with weeds"; the house itself a ruin—its windows "shattered panes" or "stopped up with boards," its "shutters hanging by a single hinge," all "desolate and uncomfortable." Stowe suggests, perhaps too clearly, that Legree's home is fast returning to the wilderness that surrounds it, as its owner becomes more bestial than human, more demon than man. The most ominous—and horrifying—feature of the Red River plantation, however, is a stark, lightning-struck tree under which, as

Cassy intimates to Emmeline, slaves have been burned to death: "There's a place way out down by the quarters, where you can see a black, blasted tree, and the ground all covered with black ashes. Ask anyone what was done there, and see if they will dare tell you" (*UTC* 491–92, 534).

In creating this landscape of nightmare, Stowe works effectively within the tradition of literary Gothicism. But when she turns from depicting hell on earth, the abode of demonic evil and a place of unspeakable torture, to describe supernatural, or perhaps infernal, visitations, her skepticism informs the narrative. She begins the chapter in which she relates Legree's terrified visions of otherworldly presences with a passage from Byron's *Childe Harold:*

> And slight, withal, may be the things that bring
> Back on the heart the weight which it would fling
> Aside forever; it may be a sound,
> A flower, the wind, the ocean, which shall wound,—
> Striking the electric chain wherewith we're darkly bound.

Stowe then insists that Legree is "superstitious" because he is a "godless and cruel" man; he is susceptible to dream-visions and seeming spectral visitations because he is an "unbelieving" reprobate who lives (and sleeps) "in superstitious dread" (*UTC* 524, 527, 540). The "electric chain," in Byron's phrase, "wherewith we're darkly bound," does not connect this world to some other but rather links the depraved soul to its past transgressions. The "Authentic Ghost Story," as Stowe entitles the chapter in which it occurs, is a story of a mind haunted to terror by its own dark sins and crimes. The ghost that torments Legree is never for even a moment presented as a possible reality. Stowe not only makes it plain that Cassy creates the horrors Legree perceives but also makes fun in general of those who think they see ghosts, noting that they usually respond to an apparition by "shutting the eyes, and covering up heads under blankets," and pointing out with considerable humor that the "ghost tribe," as envisioned by the superstitious, have a "family peculiarity"—the "wearing of a *white sheet*" (*UTC* 594). Rationally debunking the ghostly, she relocates it from the haunted house to the haunted mind.

Laughing at the Gothic even as she uses it, Stowe links the moral crime of slavery to traditional Gothic horror, letting the latter envelop and define the former. For Stowe, given her Christian ideology, only a depraved soul like Legree's could sanction and sustain slavery, especially in its most brutal practices. In Uncle Tom, Stowe creates Legree's antithesis, her ideal of a perfect Christian: loving, long-suffering, self-sacrificing, compassionate, firm in belief, and forgiving. (Tom is the ideal victim for a sadist.) Stowe also makes Tom the embodiment of conventional domestic virtue—he has, she says, "to the full, the gentle, domestic heart"—which emerges in the novel as a principal, indeed redemptive, norm (*UTC* 162).[10] However one values Tom, however one measures his acts as responses, adequate or inadequate, to slavery (or to oppression in general), he emerges as noble to the point of heroic in Stowe's telling. And correspondingly, Legree, the representative of the moral and spiritual degradation at the heart of slavery, emerges as cruel to the point of fiendish.

Stowe claimed that the origin of *Uncle Tom's Cabin* was a vision she had one Sunday morning in church of a pious Christian slave being flogged to death. When she wrote the vision into words and read them to her children, they wept, and one exclaimed, "Oh, mamma! slavery is the most cruel thing in the world" (Wilson, *Crusader in Crinoline* 256–57). Whatever its authenticity, the recollection points accurately to one of the major strategies Stowe employs to convey the horror of slavery: she evokes the bodily pain it occasions. Stowe herself was well acquainted with the pains of the body. She not only gave birth to seven children but also suffered on-going eye problems, chronic fatigue, and recurrent neuralgia in addition to an array of intermittent illnesses (she eventually sought relief in hydrotherapy). To turn to the body in pain was in a sense quite natural for Stowe.[11]

She is not graphic in her depiction; rather, she suggests the violence, often describing its effects in evocative ways. Thus she reports the aftermath of Tom's flogging—"Tom lay groaning and bleeding," tortured by "his wounds." He is so "stiff with wounds and bruises," Stowe says, he can hardly roll over. She relates Legree's death-blow to Tom—"foaming with rage, [Legree] smote his victim to the ground"—but she shuns any actual description of Tom's body in pain. In fact, she immediately explains her circumspection: "Scenes of blood and cruelty are shocking to our ear and heart. What man has nerve to do, man has not nerve to hear" (*UTC* 510, 511, 583).

Violence to the body, whether threatened, reported, or depicted, is a staple of Gothic fiction, but Stowe's evocation of the suffering body has special significance, for such representation was one of the most recurrent—and effective—tropes in antislavery discourse. Slave narratives, as well as antislavery essays and fictions, acquired persuasive force by representing the body in pain—a vivid means of revealing the brutality at the heart of the slave system. As various critics have recently pointed out, abolitionist *and* feminist writers began from about 1820 on to embody the victims of abusive oppression, giving corporeal identity to figures—the slave, the woman—most often left as abstractions in political and legal discourse. This constituted nothing less than a major shift in the nineteenth-century discourse of reform (see Sanchez-Eppler). Stowe's deployment of the body in pain is so pervasive that Richard Brodhead has called *Uncle Tom's Cabin* a "meditation" on the issue of "corporal correction" that vexed the North as well as the South in the antebellum period. Focusing on Topsy, he locates in the novel a debate between two kinds of discipline used to exercise authority and to establish control: corporal punishment versus gentle nurturing (35–42). Ironically, in the Gothic sequence in which Legree first brutalizes Uncle Tom and finally kills him, Tom himself, acting on the principle of love, eventually asserts more authority over the slaves, including Quimbo and Sambo, than Legree does. Religious love and domestic sentiment prove more powerful than the lash.

Stowe also focuses on the body in her representation of slavewomen, and here her need for indirection is even stronger. As she observes in *A Key to Uncle Tom's Cabin*, "slavery, in some of its workings, is too dreadful for the purposes of art" (5). One of the aspects of slavery too dreadful for art is the sexual exploitation of slavewomen. While Legree looms as a physical threat to Tom, he is a sexual threat to his female slaves, first Cassy, then Emmeline. While observing the decorum that limited a woman's freedom to discuss sexual matters, Stowe nonetheless makes it unmistakable that Legree is a sexual predator. Legree and the other plantation owners she depicts purchasing slaves look with lascivious care at the women, not only eyeing them as sexual objects but even touching and fondling them (see chapter 30, "The Slave Warehouse"). In the face of inevitable sexual violation, slave mothers, Stowe says, wish their daughters were "not handsome and attractive" (*UTC* 473). Legree clearly buys Emmeline to make her his forced concubine, as he has previously done with Cassy. As demonic in lust as in rage, Legree destroys tokens of female purity, first his mother's lock of hair, then the innocent Little Eva's—just as he violates the actual women within his power. Though the victims of his sexual desire are slaves, the text enfolds slavery and the abuse of women in general, making it, as critics have pointed out, a protest against the subjugation of both women and African Americans as well as a call for female empowerment (see Ammons, "Heroines," and Tompkins).

Insofar as Stowe embodies Cassy, she makes her a figure of beauty, refinement, and gentility. She is, Stowe says, "tall and slenderly formed, with remarkably delicate hands and feet"; she has a high "forehead," eyebrows "marked with beautiful clearness," a "straight, well-formed nose," a "finely-cut mouth," and a "head and neck" of "graceful contour." Once lovely, still striking, Cassy is emaciated, and her face reveals her suffering: "deeply wrinkled with lines of pain." Despite her degraded condition and the marks of her bodily suffering, Tom instinctively recognizes from her "air and bearing" that she is a "refined, and cultivated" woman (*UTC* 501–2). Her history, the rather stock tale of the tragic mulatto, is the record of a woman's betrayal by men: the daughter of a white man and a black slave, Cassy is raised in a convent as a gentlewoman, a lady, only to be bought after the death of her father by a handsome young man who promises to be her friend and protector. He becomes her lover—and the father of her first two children—only to sell her and her children to pay off gambling debts. Thereafter she is used by one owner after another, losing her first two children through slave sales and finally killing her third to save him from the horror of slavery. Her experience drives Cassy somewhat mad, the sign of which for Stowe is her loss of faith in God, a faith Tom restores through the example of Christian forbearance, compassion, and suffering. Forced to serve Legree's sexual appetite, Cassy becomes first his adversary and then his just tormentor.

Cassy clearly has a double function: most obviously, she is used by Stowe to reveal the plight of women in slavery, but she is also used to suggest the predicament of women in bondage to men. As a symbol of womanhood as well as slavery, Cassy is twice-bound. She frees herself (and Emmeline) by manipulating the Gothic: arranging mysterious sounds, suggesting ghostly presences, and even flitting about in a white sheet. In short, she plays with Legree's fear and creates for him stock but terrifying Gothic horror. As Gilbert and Gubar have pointed out, she also exploits the Gothic tale of "the madwoman in the attic" (534). As she does so, she seems to reveal herself as the antithesis of the proper woman, as that figure was defined by the cult of true womanhood (Halttunen, "Gothic Imagination and So-

cial Reform" 122), and certainly her condition as slave has forced her beyond the norms of purity, propriety, domesticity, and submissiveness.[12]
Casting Cassy as a figure whose tragic history is a travesty of true womanhood, Stowe seeks to arouse the sympathies—and perhaps the anger—of
her female readers. But Stowe herself was a believer in true womanhood,
conventionally defined, and to a degree she restores Cassy to the ideal by
having her performance as ghost mistaken for the return of a pious, proper,
domestic woman—Legree's mother. Her masquerade takes on special significance: it symbolically reclaims true womanhood for her by figuring her
as a ghost, that is, a bodiless being devoid of sexuality.

Late in 1869 or early in 1870 Mark Twain created a ghost of his own. He
wrote the start of a sketch—unfinished and unpublished, as many of his
were—in which the shade of Lord Byron appears. Byron's ghost says he
would like to hear about "the Byron-Scandal lately stirred up on earth by
Mrs. Harriet Beecher Stowe" (qtd. in Gribben, *MT's Library* 670). Twain
himself was deeply interested in the scandal, and he wrote several newspaper pieces about it. The Byron scandal forms an illuminating intersection
in the lives of Twain and Stowe, one that marks significant similarities and
differences between the two writers.

The uproar broke out in late summer 1869, when Stowe published in
the *Atlantic Monthly* "The True Story of Lady Byron's Life."[13] Claiming
to have heard the truth from Lady Byron herself in 1856, Stowe explained
that Lady Byron separated from her husband because of his incestuous
affair with his half-sister, Mrs. Augusta Leigh. Stowe pressed her charge
circumspectly—Lord Byron "fell into the depths of a secret adulterous in-
trigue with a blood relation"—but surrounded it with contentious attacks
on Lord Byron's intimates, with angry biographical readings of his poems,
and with crabbed discussions of the events of Byron's life that often ob-
fuscated as much as they clarified.[14] Her exposition is anything but lucid,
yet it was understood well enough to provoke "howls of rejection from almost every side where a critical dog is kept" (Howells, *Life in Letters* I:147;
Howells had struggled as *Atlantic* editor to improve the essay). Such dogs
were kenneled on both sides of the Atlantic, and they attacked Stowe for
having facts wrong, for lacking substantiating evidence, for misconstru-
ing the poetry, for making dubious evaluations of the participants, and for
relying on hearsay and conjecture. Ironically, Stowe's critics protested on

behalf of quite different causes: Lord Byron himself, of course, but also Lady Byron, Mrs. Leigh, and, beyond the participants, great poetry, the feeling of the English people, the relations between the sexes in society, the public weal, and general Christian principles. Almost apart from the validity or falsity of Stowe's charge, reviewers found that it was "an offense against morals to tell such a story as Mrs. Stowe has told" (McCarthy 172). Refined people, especially women, were not supposed to talk about such things.

What caused Stowe to write her essay—to speak the truth as she saw it— remains complex and conjectural. In a detailed and convincing account, Alice C. Crozier has argued that Stowe, like many writers and readers of her generation, had a lifelong infatuation with, and uneasiness about, Lord Byron that reflected nothing less than a crisis in religious belief. The religious perceived Byron as a flamboyant example of their own wavering faith, a grand personage whose anguish suggested their own and whose life therefore evoked pity as well as censure (194–217). (It makes perfect sense, then, that Stowe would use Byron's poetry in describing Legree.) Stowe's interest in defending Lady Byron as a wronged woman also reflects both her loyalty to a friend and her growing involvement in contemporary women's issues. Stowe had for some time celebrated domestic feminism, but through reading and through personal acquaintanceships, she had gradually moved toward the militant contingent of the Woman's Movement (Hendrick 353–79). In her representation of Lord and Lady Byron, however, she employs highly conventional tropes. The portraits she creates of the two are unmistakably flat, familiar pictures of stereotypical gender types: Lord Byron is a self-indulgent male governed by his animal passion, while Lady Byron is a self-sacrificing female devoted to morality derived from spiritual truth. She is a wife and mother full of "faith" and the "power of love"—the angel in the household; he is a dissolute libertine moved by unchecked "brutality" and licentious desire—the unregenerate man of the world. At stake for Stowe in the Byron scandal, then, is nothing less than "reverence for pure womanhood" (445, 436, 450).

Mark Twain added his voice to the Byron tumult by writing for the *Buffalo Express* six editorial notices and one humorous sketch about the scandal (he was at the time part owner and managing editor of the paper). Though he occasionally gives her detractors their due—"We wish all sides to have a hearing" (*MTBE* 43)—he generally sides with Stowe and often accuses her critics of harboring a prejudice against her as the author of *Uncle Tom's Cabin*. Most significantly, he, too, employs the gender types of his time—the pure woman, the bestial man—to describe Lady and Lord Byron. If anything, Twain is more confident of their applicability than Stowe. Stepping outside of his usual, largely objective report of the controversy, he says in his own voice, on his own authority, that Byron was "a bad man; as bad perhaps, as a man with a great intellect, a passionate animal nature, intense egotism and selfishness and little or no moral principle to restrain or govern either of these, could be." He calls Lady Byron "a woman, not only of remarkable loveliness, both in person and disposition, but of remarkable mental gifts," and praises her "sweetness of temper, her charitableness and her womanliness." While upholding culturally sanctioned gender roles, Twain defends Stowe's exposé—"there is no question that it was her duty to set it before the world"—and expresses his conviction that all "who respect literature" have a just interest in the determination of whether or not Lord Byron was "the most unspeakably infamous of wretches" (*MTBE* 20–21, 30). Twain's position in his notices reveals starkly his conventional ideas about men and women, his traditional morality, and his conception of literature itself as subject to ethical scrutiny.

In his humorous sketch, however, he comes close to violating the standards of propriety he defends in his editorial pieces; at the same time, he introduces a view of the Byron affair skirted in other commentaries. His sketch is an extravagant burlesque of those who write—or talk—about the affair out of ignorance. The sketch is a report of a conversation he pretends to have overheard between two women, his landlady, Mrs. Peasely, and her guest, Miss Grace De Griddle. Both are benighted gossips who hold forth with a self-importance exceeded only by their stupidity. (A celebrant of true womanhood in his other essays on the scandal, Twain doesn't mind inventing petty, foolish women interested in a salacious topic for his comedy.) Mrs. Peasely laments the blackening of a name "long gleaming there in bright and glorious concupiscence," while Miss De Griddle expresses amazement that this could have been done by "Harriet Beecher's toe." With, it seems, the kind of reliability characteristic of Stowe's detractors, Mrs. Peasely explains that the glorious poet has been defamed by "Harriet Beecher Stowe," not "toe," but then defines her as the author of " 'Uncle Tom's Cabin,' the Emancipation Proclamation, the Dred Scott

Decision, and I believe several other colored works" (*MTBE* 48–49). While thus mocking Stowe's critics, Twain also attacks Lord Byron, having Mrs. Peasely attribute to him these "wonderful" lines:

> Your nose is red,
> I feel quite blue,
> I've got the [acne]
> And so have you. (*MTBE* 50)

As the editors of Twain's *Buffalo Express* writings point out, "acne" is in all likelihood used here as a slang term for the pox or syphilis (*MTBE* 291, n. 72). Earlier in the sketch, Twain starts the outlandish dialogue between the two gossips by having Miss De Griddle ask, "What it means this 'Byron's Candle' they're talking about so much?" (*MTBE* 48). The ludicrous verse pillories the woman who admires it, while the illiterate question, with its malapropism—Candle, a slang term for penis, for scandal—mocks its asker. But these two bawdy moments in Twain's comedy also do something more. They expose what all the polite essays on the Byron scandal avoided (or approached euphemistically): the bodily nature of Lord Byron's transgressions. Twain's burlesque introduces the physical into the genteel discussion of "incestuous affairs."[15]

Although it has many forms, Twain's Gothicism often centers significantly on the body. Just as his comic sketch about the Byron scandal introduces a penis—and its syphilitic consequences—into the generally circuitous, genteel discourse inaugurated by Stowe, so his Gothicism attends to the body in his representation of slavery. In fact, as he repeats and extends his critique of slavery from *Huckleberry Finn* on, he increases his depiction of embodied slaves.

That Twain should focus on the body is no surprise, for his interest in it is rooted in both literary tradition and personal fixation. As early as 1852 Twain, who was then just sixteen- (almost seventeen-) year-old Sam Clemens, published in the *Hannibal Journal* a short sketch that plays with the body. Entitled "Historical Exhibition—A No. 1 Ruse," the comic sketch (his seventh printed piece) reports in deadpan on one local store's pay-per-view exhibition of "Bonaparte Crossing the Rhine." After collecting cash from the curious, the local entrepreneurs proudly display a small bone, announcing that it is "the 'bony-part' of a hog's leg," which they then rub back and forth over a piece of skin, a "hog's rind." Having thus provided their performance of Bonaparte, or bony part, crossing the Rhine, or rind, the showmen laugh at the audience of rubes, ironically maintaining that they have provided "a valuable lesson" by duping them (*ET&S1* 80–81). Slight as it is, the sketch reveals the nascent writer's interest in fraudulent diddles, outrageous puns, and crude sexual innuendo. It also discloses a curious fascination with dismembered but manipulable bodily parts.

Eleven years and half a world away in the Nevada Territory, Mark Twain (he had by then sported his pen name for some eight months) published in the *Virginia City Territorial Enterprise*—again in deadpan style—what purported to be a factual news story about "A Bloody Massacre near Carson." This now well-known piece reported the slaughter of a family (a wife and nine children) by a deranged husband and father, a respectable man driven mad by his failure in the stock market. Twain records the slaughter in grotesque detail: six of the nine children dead on the bedroom floor, battered by a "blunt instrument," their brains "dashed out with a club"; two more collapsed askew in the kitchen, "bruised and insensible"; and the last dead in the garret, her body "frightfully mutilated," the knife with which her "wounds had been inflicted" still "sticking in her side." The mother also lies dead and mutilated: "scalpless," her head "split open," and her right hand "almost severed from the wrist" (*ET&S1* 324–25). The news report was of course a hoax, one aimed at exposing shady stock dealing, but it was taken seriously by the western press and widely reprinted as a true account. Avidly read, it got Twain into trouble when its bogus nature was finally discovered. While the response to the hoax reveals a general interest in sensationalism, especially its more horrifying versions, the episode also exposes the inclination of Mark Twain to imagine, as young Sam Clemens had, dismemberment, mutilation, and death. It discloses a fundamental strain in his sensibility and points toward what would become a lifelong fascination: the deformation of corporeal identity.

The frontier humor in which Twain was schooled exploited the physical in ways that ranged from jokes about bodily discomfort to grotesque scenes of physical violence. In contrast, the traditions of polite domestic fiction, sentimental romance, children's tales, and moralized character sketches in which Stowe first practiced writing all eschewed the physical in everything but rosy cheeks. Twain learned the stock routines of southwestern humor, but in using them he seems to have satisfied something in himself as he wrote to form within a literary tradition. For as various critics have pointed out, there is a macabre streak in Twain (see especially Lynn, *MT and Southwestern Humor* 157–59; and Bridgman, *Traveling in MT* 14–29). The dark strain in his sensibility no doubt accounts for the curious presence— in the writings of America's greatest humorist—of the Gothic.

He experimented with the Gothic from his apprentice pieces to his final unpublished fragments, often, as in the 1859 tale of "The Mysterious Murders in Risse," displaying more interest in Gothic effects than skill at creating them. Like Stowe, he frequently distances himself from the Gothic even as he uses it. In his early journalism he makes fun of the very foundation of the Gothic, laughing at those who believe in the supernatural and look for a return of the spirit from the dead. In a spate of articles published in *The Golden Era* he mocks stories of ghost-haunted houses ("spirits tramp, tramp, tramp about the house at dead of night," and "disorderly corpses shy old boots" at the terrified owner); sports with spirit-rapping (" 'Is the spirit of John Smith present?' Whack! whack! whack! whack!"); caricatures mediums ("she left off a blast which was so terrific that I half expected to see young Ollendorf shoot up through the roof"); and generally spoofs spiritualism, "a wildcat religion" that drives people to "madness" (*Washoe Giant* 121, 123, 127, 133). He has most fun, however, imagining the ontology of spirits communing with the living: "He said he had no tangible body; a bullet could pass through him and never make a hole; rain could pass through him as through vapor, and not discommode him in the least (wherefore I suppose he don't know enough to come in when it rains—or don't care enough); says heaven and hell are simply mental conditions— spirits in the former have happy and contented minds; those in the latter are torn by remorse of conscience; says as far as he is concerned, he is all right—he is happy; would not say whether he was a very good or a very bad man on earth (the shrewd old water-proof nonentity!)" (*Washoe Giant* 128).

The book that made Twain famous, *The Innocents Abroad*, might well be called a Gothic travel narrative, for in it Twain goes out of his way to visit the kinds of sites enshrined in the Gothic mode. He seeks out fabled ruins, of course (like the castle-keep that imprisoned Dumas's man in the iron mask), but also cemeteries, caves, grottoes, catacombs, and morgues. He is preoccupied with jails, prisons, and torture chambers, discovering in them the horrors of history wrought upon the human body. While the rapping spirits he spoofed in his early sketches proclaimed themselves joyful in their bodiless state, Twain locates on his tour through Europe the reality of corporeal extinction. His visit to the crypt of the Capuchin Convent in Rome is typical of his macabre traveling into Gothic darkness. There he witnesses the full spectacle of the unburied dead:

> Here and there, in ornamental alcoves, stretched upon beds of bones, lay dead and dried-up monks, with lank frames dressed in the black robes one sees ordinarily upon priests. We examined one closely. The skinny hands were clasped upon the breast; two lusterless tufts of hair stuck to the skull; the skin was brown and sunken; it stretched tightly over the cheekbones and made them stand out sharply; the crisp, dead eyes were deep in the sockets; the nostrils were painfully prominent, the end of the nose being gone; the lips had shriveled away from the yellow teeth: and brought down to us through the circling years, and petrified there, was a weird laugh a full century old! (*IA* 238–39)

Having lingered over the ruination of the human here, he tries to deflect its ghastliness by suggesting that the "weird laugh" on the disintegrated face was caused by a "joke" so "extraordinary" that the corpse "has not got done laughing at it yet" (*IA* 239).

Twain's obsession with the dead is no doubt rooted in his past, and at one moment in *The Innocents Abroad* he all but says so. Observing the sculpture of a skinned man, he recalls a night of horror from his past: a night on which he slips into his father's office where he senses in the dark "a long, dusky, shapeless thing stretched upon the floor," and soon glimpses by moonlight first a "white human hand," then "a naked arm," and finally "the pallid face of a man . . . with the corners of the mouth drawn down, and the eyes fixed and glassy in death!" (*IA* 139). Recorded with the same part-by-part precision with which he observes cadavers abroad, the incident marks the indelible hold death—death of the body—has on Sam Clemens's mind and Mark Twain's imagination. The young Sam was repeatedly exposed to death: he saw murder on the streets of Hannibal; he saw killing feuds along the river; he saw steamboat explosions; he saw a man burn himself to death in the town jail (with matches provided by Sam himself); he even saw—through a keyhole—the autopsy performed in the family parlor on the body of his own father.

It is not surprising, then, that when Twain writes of boy-life in *Tom Sawyer* and *Huckleberry Finn*, he shrouds it with Gothic horror. Like Stowe in *Uncle Tom's Cabin*, however, he uses the Gothic skeptically, but he distances himself from the mode in a different way. He does not locate the Gothic in a deranged mind and damned soul but in an innocent mind and pure soul. In both *Tom Sawyer* and *Huckleberry Finn* he evokes as backdrop for a world of terror the web of superstition that entangles not only the mind of the young Tom and Huck but also the consciousness of the oppressed slave, Jim. By often making the superstitions palpably silly, the stuff of the untutored, he creates an ironic perspective through which to view all manifestations of the Gothic except one: the indubitable fact that the body suffers pain and is vulnerable to extinction. Thus in *Tom Sawyer*, one of two gateways to *Huckleberry Finn* (the other being *Life on the Mississippi*, which also has its Gothic moments), while the haunted house in which Tom and Huck seek buried treasure is only haunted by "witches and ghosts a-fluttering around" in their imaginations, the grave-yard they visit with Huck's dead cat ends up revealing not some feared but only fancied "spirits of the dead," but two very real corpses (*TS* 179, 93). The cemetery on a hill just above St. Petersburg and the cave in the riverbank just below it mark the physical—and psychological—landscape of the novel. Both eventually yield up dead bodies, which Tom, in danger himself, observes with horror.

Even in this benign fiction (Twain called *Tom Sawyer* a "hymn, put into prose form to give it a worldly air" [*MTL* 2:477]), in which Gothic horror is largely imagined by superstitious boys, Twain begins to give the body special significance, especially as a marker of race—and racial abuse. Hovering over *Tom Sawyer* from first to last is the threat of violence to the body: Aunt Polly gives corrective whacks; the schoolteacher, Dobbins, inflicts sadistic whippings; and Injun Joe commits murder and threatens mutilation. Injun Joe bears the stigmata of his bodily difference from the white community that ostracizes him as a half-breed. (Twain's name for Joe is itself racist but in keeping with the community whose perspective he is representing.) Injun Joe is embodied as a demonic source of evil, but Twain uses him to signify two other important aspects of his tale (both more latent than overt): Tom's potential for criminality and the commu-nity's prejudice. As readers have often noticed, Twain makes Injun Joe a dark twin to Tom. What Tom plays at—stealing, killing, living in lawless freedom, amassing treasure, getting revenge—Injun Joe actually does. And while Tom imagines hurting Becky by disappearing or even dying, Injun Joe sets out to attack the Widow Douglas—to "go for her looks," to "slit her nostrils," to "notch her ears" (*TS* 198). If Joe reveals Tom's dark side, however, he exposes even more about Tom's hometown. For inscribed on his body is the racial prejudice concealed beneath St. Petersburg's façade of democratic equality, religious morality, and social propriety. Injun Joe, we learn, has gone begging door to door "for something to eat," only to be first jailed as a "vagrant" and then, as he explains, "*horsewhipped*!— horsewhipped in front of the jail, like a nigger!" (*TS* 95, 198). He thus receives an extreme form of the physical punishment that perpetually threatens Tom, and he receives it for a "crime"—vagrancy—that is a virtual definition of Tom's life. But Tom is loved, while Injun Joe is condemned and whipped in public, leaving the markings on his body to disclose most fully the town's racial prejudice.

In the end Joe dies in a cave of Gothic horror. He is accidentally killed when Judge Thatcher, acting in response to Tom's misadventures (Tom is thus indirectly the killer), has the cave closed with boiler iron, thus turning it first into a place of torture as Joe starves to death and then into a tomb that holds his corpse. Twain in a sense re-stages on his home ground the horrors he witnessed in *The Innocents Abroad.* Just as he had gone underground to see the body in extinction, so—perhaps projecting and mocking his own fascination—he has the townspeople and the country people "from all the farms and hamlets for seven miles around" come with "their children" to stare at the site of Joe's death, to watch his funeral, and to witness his interment "near the mouth of the cave" (*TS* 221). In killing off Tom's nemesis—and alter ego—Twain brings his summertime story of boy-life to its necessary close: he confirms Tom's absolute innocence.

Twain's imagination plunges into the darkness of the cave—his fictional version of the real one near Hannibal—to kill Injun Joe, to evoke the threat of death for Tom and Becky (and then save them from it), and to restore unequivocal innocence to Tom. (One remembers Stowe's symbolic restoration of purity to Cassy.) In doing all this, he returns stability to St. Petersburg (and no doubt ease to his own psyche), as evil on the loose is destroyed and death is escaped. Twain ends his tale happily: the hero gets the girl, the gold, and the glory. What Twain's fantasy of boyhood cannot accomplish, however, is any permanent purgation of his abiding awareness of bodily extinction. And it's no wonder. Looming in Twain's consciousness, as he himself acknowledged, is the horrifying image of the body's end. In his autobiography, he lingers over McDowell's cave, the real-life cave he fictionalized in *Tom Sawyer*, and recalls its Gothic horror: "The cave was an uncanny place, for it contained a corpse—the corpse of a young girl of fourteen. It was in a glass cylinder inclosed in a copper one which was suspended from a rail which bridged a narrow passage. The body was preserved in alcohol and it was said that loafers and rowdies used to drag it up by the hair and look at the dead face" (*AMT* 9). This dead body, a grotesque image of death in life, hangs in Twain's imagination as fixedly as it did in McDowell's cave: a sign of the fate of corporeal being. The image haunts him and shapes his later fictions, just as it informs his first significant one.

Although he began *Huckleberry Finn* as he finished *Tom Sawyer*, the novel took some seven years for Twain to complete. In between, he turned out for children (his own, in the first instance) a historical romance, *The Prince and the Pauper*. Coyly subtitled *A Tale for Young People of All Ages*, Twain's costume fiction catered to the young through its exciting and touching plot of switched identities and through its melodramatic scenes of peril, suffering, injustice, and eventual triumph; it satisfied older readers at the time by its stylistic elegance, its general tone of propriety, and its conventional morality. As reviewers in Twain's time and critics in ours have recognized, it is a genteel literary work, but within its gentility Twain uses the body in pain as a form of protest, and in doing so, he sometimes approaches the boundaries of propriety.

As Twain explained to Howells, the tale was intended to give "a realizing sense of the exceeding severity of the laws of that day by inflicting some of their penalties upon the king himself & allowing him a chance to see the rest of them applied to others" (*MTHL* 291). Twain records for the king to learn that under his law murderers are slowly boiled to death, beggars are whipped, put into the stocks, or mutilated by having an ear cut off, thieves are executed for petty offenses, poachers are hanged for killing the king's deer, believers in another faith (Baptists, for instance) are burned at the stake, and suspected witches are burned alive before crowds as instructive examples. One down-and-out, starving commoner (turned petty criminal) recounts a history that replays Injun Joe's:

I begged, from house to house—I and the wife—bearing with us the hungry kids—but it was crime to be hungry in England—so they stripped us and lashed us through three towns. Drink ye all again to the merciful English law! . . . I begged again—begged for a crust, and got the stocks and lost an ear—see, here bides the stump; I begged again, and here is the stump of the other to keep me minded of it. And still I begged again, and was sold for a slave—here on my cheek under this stain, if I washed it off, ye might see the red S the branding-iron left there! A SLAVE! Do ye understand that word! An English SLAVE!—that is he that stands before ye. I have run from my master, and when I am found—the heavy curse of heaven fall on the law and the land that hath commanded it!—I shall hang! (*Prince and the Pauper* 196–97)

What keeps the physical violence, mutilation, and carnage of Twain's tale from violating genteel decorum is the way Twain renders it: it is all reported rather than depicted. Nothing is graphically represented. His attention to the body in distress is very much like Stowe's in *Uncle Tom's Cabin*. He evokes the *idea* of bodily suffering rather than its reality, creating moral outrage through the conception of brutality. And the idea of such suffering is horrifying to adults as well as children. Harriet Beecher Stowe liked *The Prince and the Pauper*. "I am reading your Prince and Pauper for the *fourth* time," Twain remembered her saying to him, "and I *know* it's the best book for young people that was ever written!" (*MTLP* 216).

In writing *Huckleberry Finn* Twain was free from the genteel constraints that delimited *The Prince and the Pauper*. However, he faced an aspect of form that set its own limits on his use of Gothic bodies in pain: he was writing a humorous book. Anything too grisly would jar. He sometimes sports with the body in trifling, wholly comic ways. In the manner of frontier humor, for instance, he has Huck tell—his gullible innocence serving as deadpan—the tall tale of Old Hank Bunker, who once defied the rules of bad luck by looking at the new moon over his left shoulder and ended up (after he "got drunk") falling off a "shot tower"—his body so flattened it was "just a kind of a layer," so his friends "slid him edgeways between two barn doors for a coffin, and buried him so." At times Twain maintains the comedy of bodily distress while making it serve a significant function. His famous description of Pap with his "long and tangled and greasy" hair hanging down so "you could see his eyes shining through like he was behind vines" and his white face, "not like another man's white, but a white to make a body sick, a white to make a body's flesh crawl—a tree-toad white, a fish-belly white," is a case in point, as its metaphors define Pap as both a savage and poor white trash. And as he exposes Pap's racism, Twain has him climax his tirade against a government that would allow a black man to be free with a farcical kick at a tub of salt: "He raised a howl that fairly made a body's hair raise, and down he went in the dirt, and rolled there, and held his toes" (*HF* 65, 23, 34).

As he did throughout *Tom Sawyer*, Twain saturates *Huckleberry Finn* with superstition, and his treatment of black and white magic is most often comic.[16] The supernatural Gothic is still silly stuff. Although superstition sometimes empowers Jim—when he is right about omens, for instance— and though it sometimes enables him to fashion a compelling identity well beyond that of slave, as telling his tale of being ridden by witches does (Smith, "Huck, Jim, and American Racial Discourse"), for the most part Twain laughs at any discernment of the supernatural. When Jim first sees Huck, who is presumed dead, on Jackson's Island, he mistakes him for an apparition: "Doan' hurt me—don't! I hain't ever done no harm to a ghos'. I awluz liked dead people, en done all I could for 'em." And later on the river Huck and Jim think they hear "spirits carrying on . . . in the air" until Huck realizes that spirits wouldn't say "dern the dern fog." Nonetheless, they feel "crawly," for what Twain laughs at they suffer. Huck and Jim— and Tom—believe that they are at the mercy of dark forces beyond their control, and they read signs and perform rituals to appease the powers they believe in and to ward off bad luck (*HF* 51, 157). They live in fear.

Hamlin Hill has observed that fear was the "controlling emotion" in Twain's life (*MT: God's Fool* 269), and whatever the truth of this for Twain, fear is the most recurrent emotion in Huck's adventures. And what he is most afraid of is death. At the beginning of his story he senses death in the stillness of a house, and, in the end, in the thrum of a spinning wheel— "the lonesomest sound in the whole world"—he hears the threatening yet attractive beckoning of death: "I wished I was dead," he tells us (*HF* 5, 276). Thus, like Mark Twain in his travels abroad and Tom Sawyer in his adventures, Huck is both terrified by death and drawn toward it.

He confronts death in Pap's cabin, a backwoods equivalent of the tra- ditional Gothic dungeon. Haunted by supernatural visions, as terrifying— and as unreal—as Legree's, Pap seeks to avoid the Angel of Death by killing Huck. Huck's fear then becomes a possible reality, but he escapes by staging his fake death, demonstrating as he does so an impressive awareness of body parts, movements, and traces. His respite is brief, however, for when he and Jim explore the wrecked steamboat, another Gothic moment replete with dark night, storm, lightning, and two murderous thieves, Huck is again in danger of being killed. He is enveloped by killing during the Grangerford-Shepherdson feud, and he is at risk once more in the Wilks episode. The Wilks interlude has been seen as a pivotal moment, an emotional, thematic, and normative center of the novel (Towers, "Love and Power"). Huck seems to learn during this episode not only to act— to overcome his characteristic passivity—on behalf of others but also to put kindness above all else, to value love above principle, thus acquiring the attitude that will lead to his decision to steal Jim out of slavery, even if he goes to hell for it. But the Wilks sequence is also one in which Twain broadens, however slightly, his representation of slavery, for in it he records, very much in the manner of Stowe, the tragic breakup of slave families, in particular the separation of the mother from her children (see chapters 27 and 28). There are no actual slavewomen depicted (their sale is just reported), so Twain does not face the problem that confronted Stowe: the representation of violated, yet cherished, slavewomen in the face of the culture's conception of true womanhood. Twain's white women are all down-home, river-world versions of the ideal enshrined by the cult of true womanhood.

While deepening the protest against slavery and skirting the difficulty of affirming a sexually violated woman, the Wilks episode is also the most death-ridden, in some ways forming a climax to Huck's Gothic adventures. Precipitated by the death of the real Peter Wilks, highlighted by his funeral, the events turn on the attempt of the Duke and the King to pass themselves off as kin to the deceased, a claim they pretend to certify by explaining the markings on the body of the dead Peter Wilks. Their ruse is challenged by the mob of townspeople determined to exhume the Wilks corpse and so discover on it the marks that will prove identities true or false. Reading the dead body thus becomes a central signifying activity in Twain's narrative. As all this transpires, Huck himself feels "this was the most awful trouble and most dangersome I ever was in," having, he believes, just the marks on the body "betwixt me and sudden death." He bolts, as Gothic lightning flashes over the grave, escaping the sight of death as well as the possibility of his own, only to be confronted by what appears to be a standing cadaver, "all over a dead dull solid blue, like a man that's been drownded nine days" (*HF* 257, 203). Escaping one corpse, he seems to face another, for Twain's text keeps discovering real—or imagined—dead bodies.

In this case it is just Jim. The newly recovered manuscript of the first half of *Huckleberry Finn* reveals that Twain's obsession with bodies originally led him to create one especially grisly episode, tinged with racist comedy. In the episode Jim tells Huck how once, following the instructions of a Mars William, he entered the "dissectin' room" of a local college to "warm up a dead man dat was dah on de table, en git him soft" so that William "can cut him up." He uncovers the "carcass," upends it on a table, "laigs" drawn "apart," "knees" somewhat "cocked up," and "toes stickin' up," only to have the body first open "his eyes" and then lurch toward him: "*down he comes*, right a-straddle er my neck wid his cold laigs" (*HF*, comprehensive ed. 62, 63–64). Embraced by the dead in a grotesque gesture of sexual encounter, Jim flees. And having thus represented his own horrified attraction to the dead, Twain canceled the passage. Despite the fact that the cadaver in this excised part of the text is white, what Jim encounters in this dead body is a form of himself. For historically, as Twain acknowledged in *The Gilded Age*, bodies dissected for medical knowledge were often black.

Long read as an attack on slavery, *Huckleberry Finn* has recently been interpreted as Twain's critique of post-Reconstruction practices in the South. One of the earliest and most suggestive of such commentaries is Louis J. Budd's 1959 essay, "The Southward Currents under Huck Finn's Raft." Budd argues that Twain's novel "took on fresh meaning as a judgment of the South's conduct after the withdrawal of federal troops had paroled it to its own conscience," and he identifies these aspects of the Southern Question in the text: the problem of poor white trash, the proclivity to violence, the resurgence of mob-law, the resistance to intellectual advancement, the antiquated economic system, the persistence of racial bigotry, the bogus southern chivalric gentry, and the general backwardness of vicious ignorance (227–37). What Budd's persuasive analysis does not fully account for—the final abjection of Jim by Tom, with the acquiescence of Huck, in the Great Evasion—has been convincingly explained by Victor Doyno, who argues that what Twain is about in that final sequence is a critical depiction of the postbellum convict lease system (*Writ-*

*ing "Huck Finn"* chapter 10, part 2). What Twain uses as the critical foil in his synergized story of the pre- and postbellum South is the body of the slave. For in his tale of racism in both slave and post-Reconstruction times, he makes violence loom over Jim's body as surely as death stalks Huck's.

The danger to Jim underpins the final, problematical series of events at the Phelps farm. Although Tom Sawyer says, in Twain's early comic chapters, that ransoming women means "that you bring them to the cave" and keep them "till they're dead" (*HF* 10–11), in the end he tries to keep not women but Jim, a freed slave, imprisoned in the cabin on the Phelps farm. There he invents escape maneuvers for him tantamount to dissection. Guided by his reading of Gothic romances, Tom turns the cabin into a veritable torture chamber.[17] He fills it with rats, spiders, and snakes, with chains and stones; he plans to have Jim scrawl messages in his "own blood"; and he contemplates sawing off Jim's "leg" or cutting off his "hand" (*HF* 299–302). In all this Tom is a grotesque rendering of both the cruel slavemaster and the post-Reconstruction white Southerner intent on re-enslaving the freedman (Nilon 62–76). Twain's burlesque, often objected to as thematically compromising or aesthetically mistaken, has multiple functions: it mocks Tom as a Gothic adventurer; it echoes slave narratives, which often found in Gothic horror a useful means of expressing authentic suffering; and it protests against not only slavery but also post-Reconstruction practices. It does all this largely by embodying Jim and by suggesting the threats to his physical well-being, thus revealing the violence at the heart of both slavery and white schemes in the post-Reconstruction South. Pointing to bodily suffering, Twain extends one of Stowe's strategies for condemning slavery to the postbellum era. On the personal level, he thematizes in his finest work his obsessive preoccupation with imprisoned and brutalized bodies. Although he is no more graphic than Stowe in depicting the body in pain—his comic form dictates gentle representation—like her, he makes the body a key weapon in the attack on the consequences of race prejudice.

In her post–*Uncle Tom's Cabin* protest novel, *Dred, A Tale of the Dismal Swamp*, Stowe herself deepened her attention to the body in pain as a spur to the eradication of slavery, but at the same time she deployed a new tactic in her crusade, one that Twain would subsequently employ. *Dred* is constructed, however haphazardly, as a novel of debates: staunchly maintaining slavery versus gradually eliminating it, armed rebellion versus passive submission, the legal codes of a region versus the dictates of a higher morality, the rule of law versus control by violence, militant revenge versus Christian forgiveness, and religion as relinquishment of earthly affairs versus religion as an imperative to social reform. These dialectical arguments are most often expressed by representative characters—contemporary types—engaged in heated conversation. But running along with this ongoing extrapolation of ideas from events are Stowe's depictions of physicality. From the pale refinement of her genteel heroine to the sallow complexioning of poor white trash, Stowe colors her narrative with the hues of the body. And at the center—visually and thematically—of her representation is the depiction of Dred himself: the abused, escaped, and now rebellious slave who threatens the existence not just of individual slaveowners but of the peculiar institution itself.

Stowe describes Dred in his first appearance as a powerful, enticing, and ominous bodily figure:

> He was a tall black man, of magnificent stature and proportions. His skin was intensely black, and polished like marble. A loose shirt of red flannel, which opened very wide at the breast, gave a display of a neck and chest of herculean strength. The sleeves of the shirt, rolled up nearly to the shoulders, showed the muscles of a gladiator. The head, which rose with an imperial air from the broad shoulders, was large and massive and developed with equal force both in the reflective and perceptive department. The perceptive organs jutted like dark ridges over the eyes, while that part of the head which phrenologists attribute to the moral and intellectual sentiments, rose like an ample dome above them. The large eyes had that peculiar and solemn effect of unfathomable blackness and darkness which is often a striking characteristic of the African eye. But there burned in them, like tongues of flame in a black pool of naphtha, a subtle and restless fire, that betokened habitual excitement to the verge of insanity. If any organs were predominant in the head, they were those of ideality, wonder, veneration, and firmness; and the whole combination was such as might have formed one of the wild old warrior prophets of the heroic ages.[18]

The rhetorical effort here is, on the one hand, to make Dred powerful, both physically and mentally, and to elevate him as a classical figure—

"a gladiator" or one of the "old warrior prophets"—and, on the other, to make him both exotic—"unfathomable blackness"—and threatening: his eyes flame with a "restless fire" that burns on the "verge of insanity." Dred is thus racialized, mythologized, and demonized all at once.

As her subtitle, *A Tale of the Dismal Swamp*, suggests, Stowe's story is partly about the influence of the wild upon the human. Stowe, who had never seen an actual swamp, relies on its traditional Gothic associations as the "domain of sin, death, and decay; the stage for witchcraft; the habitat of weird and ferocious creatures" (Miller, *Dark Eden* 3). She describes the swamp as a region of "hopeless disorder, where the abundant growth and vegetation of nature, sucking up its forces from the humid soil, seems to rejoice in a savage exuberance." Dred is the product of this wildness, "completely," Stowe says, in "sympathy and communion" with it. Shaped by "the singularly unnatural and wildly stimulating properties" of the swamp's "slimy depths," he is himself a figure of disorder and savagery, a man, as Stowe says over and over again, whose mind borders on madness (*Dred* 275, 354, 616). If Dred is driven by his experience of slavery, angered by his father's execution (Stowe imagines him to be the son of Denmark Vesey), and inspired by visions (she patterns his character on that of the visionary Nat Turner), he is also dominated by the swamp's unchecked wildness. And for all of her sympathy for Dred and sponsorship of his moral condemnations of slavery, Stowe warns against his warped outlook—what she calls the "darkly struggling, wildly vegetating swamp of human souls, cut off . . . from the usages and improvements of cultivated life" (*Dred* 616). While Cassy impersonates the dark forces of the unknown to terrify Legree and ultimately free herself, Dred actually participates in such Gothic darkness.

In contrast to Dred's wild call to violent insurrection, the slave Milly, a female Uncle Tom, is the advocate of forbearance, long-suffering, and Christ-like forgiveness, and she is often interpreted as winning out over the militant Dred (see Newman 24–25 and Crozier 45–50). Indeed, late in the tale she speaks directly against Dred's position, and he acquiesces: "Woman, thy prayers have prevailed for this time! . . . The hour is not yet come" (*Dred* 577).

But Stowe goes much further toward crediting Dred's outraged call for vengeful rebellion than is generally acknowledged.[19] She cannot let him succeed outright, for she is constrained by history: there was no successful slave rebellion in the United States. What she does do, however, is create in Dred a figure whose message transcends the plot of the novel. His death—itself an instance of white violence that justifies Dred's call to arms—is endowed with myth. Shot by slave hunters, Dred reappears before his people in the swamp, with "a wound in his breast, from which the blood was welling." The awful violence to the body is matched by Dred's final act. As he dies, Dred makes a gesture that simultaneously curses the land, as well as the people on it who have first enslaved and finally destroyed him, and posits an enduring sign of the violation that requires violent retribution: "He put his hand calmly to his side, and felt the gushing blood. He took some in his hand and threw it upward, crying out, with wild energy, in the words of an ancient prophet. 'O, earth, earth! Cover thou not my blood.' " As she eulogizes Dred, Stowe does not linger over the physical power with which she has endowed him, that colossal strength that has made him a threat to the southerners wed to the system of slavery, though she acknowledges it—the "splendid, athletic form," the "powerful arm"; instead, what she dwells on is the loss of Dred as a "prophet": "The grand and solemn voice hushed, and all the splendid poetry of olden time, the inspiring symbols and prophetic dreams, which had so wrought upon his own soul, and with which he had wrought upon the souls of others, seemed to pass away with him, and to recede into the distance and become unsubstantial, like the remembered sounds of mighty winds, or solemn visions of evening clouds, in times long departed" (*Dred* 636–37). While Stowe makes Dred something of a demonic force inhabiting the Gothic dark of the great swamp and threatening violent rebellion, she also casts him throughout as a righteous voice crying in the wilderness for the destruction of his people's oppressors.

Mysterious voices sound throughout Gothic fiction, of course, but Stowe's use of the familiar device to condemn and threaten the slaveholding South is stunning. The power of her novel resides neither in its instances of violence, compelling as they are, nor in its abstract debates, provocative as they are, but in Dred's voice—heard from treetops, from the recesses of the swamp, from darkness—sounding doom. Dred's voice dominates the novel. Madly mixing the biblical and the political, such outcries as this are arresting:

Wilt thou not visit for these things, O Lord? Shall not thy soul be avenged on such a nation as this? How long wilt thou endure? Behold under the altar the souls of those they have slain! They cry unto thee continually. How long, O Lord, doest thou not judge and avenge? Is there any that stirreth himself up for justice? Is there any that regardeth our blood? We are sold for silver; the price of our blood is in thy treasury; the price of our blood is on thine altars! Behold, they build their churches with the price of our hire! Behold, the stone doth cry out of the wall, and the timber doth answer it. Because they build their towns with blood, and establish their cities by iniquity. They have all gone one way. There is none that careth for the spoilings of the poor. Art thou a just God? When wilt thou arise to shake terribly the earth, that the desire of all nations may come? Overturn, overturn, and overturn, till *he* whose right it is shall come! (*Dred* 619)

Such orations—and the novel is full of them—finally give Dred's call for violent resistance more power than Milly's plea for passivity. In fact, they overwhelm all else in the novel. Garbled and repetitive as they are, no single one of Dred's declamations stands out by itself (Dred is no Ahab on the Quarterdeck or even Colonel Sherburn before the crowd), but they resound beyond the text, leaving the sense of powerful preachment—of a voice, incoherent, hysterical, yet commanding, righteous, just, and perhaps even fateful. If Stowe attacked slavery in her first novel chiefly by embodying slaves and depicting their physical violations (and separations), in her second she does so by creating a single eloquent, ominous, haunting voice proclaiming injustice and prophesying vengeance. Her Gothicism brilliantly serves her moral purpose.

There is no record that Twain heard Dred's dark voice (he does not seem to have owned the novel in which it sounds so forcefully), but in 1901 he wrote to his sister-in-law Sue Crane, asking her for a slave narrative that recorded the kind of horror Stowe evoked in *Dred.* "You have," he wrote, "a small book by a negro named Ball, which tells of terrible things in the Dismal Swamp in slavery times. Won't you send it to me—for use?" (qtd. in *MT's Library* 43).

Twain had already made use of Ball's book for his own condemnation of slavery in *A Connecticut Yankee in King Arthur's Court.*[20] Although in his original preface to *A Connecticut Yankee* he described his "object" as the depiction of some of "the most odious laws which have had vogue in the Christian countries" in "the past eight or ten centuries," it is clear that his text is double-sided, commenting not only on the past but also on nineteenth-century America (Appendix S, *MTB* 1656). To represent some of the horrors of his own time, Twain, like Stowe before him, turns again to the Gothic body. And given his skepticism, in order to use the Gothic at all, Twain once again surrounds it with mockery. Twain's medieval setting almost inevitably leads him to Gothic situations, involving, as it does, a range of Gothic props such as omens, magicians, credulous people, necromancers, dark queens, dungeons, and torture chambers. But Twain satirizes all this. His rational hero sets himself up as the adversary of superstition in all its forms and attempts to laugh every manifestation of dark otherness out of existence. *A Connecticut Yankee* might well be termed Twain's most anti-Gothic text.

Paradoxically, however, even as he distances himself from the Gothic, Twain also employs it—lavishly, in fact. He creates scene after scene of the body in pain, not only exempting such Gothic extremity from his satire but even intensifying and magnifying it until it reaches lurid proportions. To bring home the horror of slavery, he makes the body the site of suffering more fully and explicitly than he ever had before. Drawing on Ball's accounts of actual slave life in the Dismal Swamp (the very Swamp later inhabited by Stowe's fictive Dred), he shows slaves chained "collar to collar," driven by the "knotted" whip that rakes skin from their bodies; he shows them stripped and lashed until their bodies are "flayed" raw. Like Stowe, he depicts the body in such pain to promote sympathy and stir outrage. Here, for instance, is his melodramatic representation of a slave trader's treatment of a mother and her child: "He snatched the child from her, and then made the men slaves who were chained before and behind her throw her on the ground and hold her there and expose her body; and then he laid on with his lash like a madman till her back was flayed, she shrieking and struggling the while, piteously" (*CY* 243–46). Using the body in pain, Twain extends his protest beyond slavery to a variety of unjust laws and human cruelties. His representation of bodily maiming is so intense in this text that the protest is sometimes all but lost in the sensationalism.

For something besides protest is transpiring in Twain's tale. The carnage exceeds its moral function. *A Connecticut Yankee* simply reeks with the destruction of the corporeal: bodies are hacked, carved, maimed; bodies are racked, whipped, burned; bodies are stabbed, dismembered, blown up. The damage to the body is pervasive to the point of obsessive. What seems to be occurring in this blood-drenched tale is that Twain is taking revenge on the very fact of physical vulnerability that has haunted him—attracted and repulsed him—throughout his writing. It is no wonder, then, that the destruction of the body becomes gratuitous. When Hank encounters a band of twenty-four knights who race toward him in fluttering array, he calmly throws a bomb into their midst and coolly observes "a neat thing, very neat and pretty to see. It resembled a steamboat explosion on the Mississippi; and during the next fifteen minutes we stood under a steady drizzle of microscopic fragments of knights." This rain of human flesh pleases Hank and, it seems, Twain himself. His hostility toward the body creates the famous cataclysm of the novel's close in which Hank gleefully dynamites, drowns, machine guns, torpedoes, and electrocutes twenty-five thousand knights, creating a ring of standing dead men. This circle of the dead traps Hank himself and even threatens to kill him as he is enveloped by "the poisonous air bred by those dead thousands." Thus even as he takes revenge on the body, Twain betrays his fear of it. He creates one final emblem of corporeal death, one that recalls, some twenty years later, the dead face he found staring at him in the crypt of the Capuchin Convent in Rome. Merlin, having cast a spell on Hank, reels, laughing in delirium, and touches one of Hank's electrified wires: "His mouth is spread open yet; apparently he is still laughing. I suppose the face will retain that petrified laugh until the corpse turns to dust" (*CY* 318, 489). Merlin, a laughing corpse: this is Twain's ultimate symbol of the body's joke on human being.

*A Connecticut Yankee* moves from using the suffering body to condemn slavery and a range of unjust laws to an all-out attack on corporeality itself. Hank dies in the end, suffering the fate he has inflicted on so many others, but what Twain emphasizes is not the extinction of Hank's body but the cessation of his voice; he dies "talking brokenly," "muttering incoherently," issuing at the last a final command: "Man the battlements—turn out the—" (*CY* 491–93). Like Dred's, Hank's is a resounding voice, and while it is silenced in the end, it lives on in Hank's manuscript narrative. Hank's voice does not have the biblical assurance and prophetic mystification of Dred's, but like his, it resonates with moral outrage and righteous indignation. As many critics have observed, often to condemn *A Connecticut Yankee* as a failure, Hank's voice is radically inconsistent. Sentimental one moment, callous the next, it veers from lofty pronouncements to burly horse-laughs. But whatever its tone, sentiment, or principle, it is clear that Twain himself is fascinated by Hank's voice. He likes holding forth through him as moral critic, universal sage, and prophet of doom.

The impulse to propound, to moralize, to philosophize dominates Twain's writing as well as his public speaking in the last two decades of his life. It infiltrates *Pudd'nhead Wilson*, his most significant late attempt to revisit the issues of slavery and race that had so long preoccupied him, creating the famous calendar headings, Wilson's maxims, that transcend the text that contains them. It leads to the sentimental moralizing of *Joan of Arc* (interestingly, a liberator inspired by voices) and to the ponderous arguments of Twain's "bible": *What Is Man?* As he entered "the kingdom of personality" (Cox, *MT: The Fate of Humor* 297), he voiced through his characters his own varied beliefs, heretical ideas, and conventional notions. The more his fictional characters—Pudd'nhead Wilson, Joan of Arc, and the Old Man of *What Is Man?*—give voice to his views, however, the less they are represented in his texts as actual physical presences. Having used the body in *A Connecticut Yankee*, only to discover the irresistible attraction of abstract articulation, Twain stayed with the power of speech.

There is, then, a logic to his obsession with the figure of the Mysterious Stranger—a bodiless being, or rather, a being who can assume any physical form he chooses. The Stranger is primarily a voice. As William Gibson puts it, he is "a truth-speaker momentarily banished from heaven" (*MTMS* 15). In his Stranger texts, which he worked on sporadically for almost eleven years, Twain's lifelong obsession with the corporeal reaches its climax. On the one hand, the body is denounced: "It is these bonds . . . oh, free me from *them*; these bonds of flesh—this decaying vile matter, this foul weight, and clog, and burden, this loathsome sack of corruption in which my spirit is imprisoned, her white wings bruised and soiled."[21] And on the other hand, it is proclaimed unreal: "Nothing exists but You. And You are but a *Thought*—a vagrant Thought, a useless Thought, a homeless Thought, wandering forlorn among the empty eternities!" (*MTMS* 369, 405). Twain has abandoned the body in pain, the Gothic tactic he shared in his protests against slavery with Stowe, to long for—and even to insist on—the nonexistence of human flesh. There is a final, quite natural, turn to this bent. In several late unpublished, indeed unfinished, dream-tales, he creates new imaginings of corporeal being itself. In "Three Thousand Years among the Microbes," for instance, he creates a version of the human turned into a cholera-germ, one that lives in the bloodstream of a tramp and makes his way there—his living, really—by singing "Buffalo Gals Can't You Come out To-night" to the other microbes. And in "The Great Dark" he imagines humanlike beings existing within a drop of water, irretrievably lost, unable to certify the reality of their existence, prey at all times to devouring sea monsters. In such fragments he explores the construction of the human body itself, and in so doing he joins, albeit unknowingly, a significant turn-of-the-century movement. Kelly Hurley has defined this cultural discourse as one that envisions the "ruination of the human subject" and a concomitant reconstruction of it in new forms (*The Gothic Body*, chapter 1). But Twain was anxious about the body from the inception of his career. The fate of the body was something like a felt horror for him, one that returned from every repression until it was finally embraced as the ultimate escape from the travail of human life itself. In the end, what he once dreaded, he finally longed for.

Harriet Beecher Stowe reached no such conclusion. Buoyed throughout her life by her Christian faith, she bore the difficulties of existence, including the bodily pain she knew so well, with fortitude and the consoling expectation of spiritual immortality. She simply awaited the separation of body and soul—or as the Apostles' Creed has it, "the resurrection of the body." (Stowe was an Episcopalian in her later years.) As she awaited such a glorious transformation, she acknowledged the decay not only of her body but of her mind as well. In a moving letter written during her decline toward death, she described her mental condition as "nomadic" and figured her physical being as "a moored boat, rising and falling on the water, with loosened cordage and flapping sail." She was content, however, believing that she had arrived, as she said, at "heaven's borderland" (qtd. in Wilson, *Crusader* 636).

Close neighbors, and kindred spirits in their fictions' assault on slavery, Stowe and Twain arrived at opposite poles: she accepted the body—and its pains—in anticipation of the spirit's release from corporeality; he denounced the body—and its manifold ills—in the desperate belief that consciousness was all or, failing that, in the forlorn hope of oblivion. But they arrived at such antithetical positions only after having shared and fictionalized the dark sense that the body in pain, a Gothic horror to be reckoned with, was a useful tactic in the long struggle to promote the light of moral reform.

# Mark Twain
# & Matthew Arnold

*I bring you the stately matron named Christendom, returning bedraggled, besmirched and dishonored from pirate-raids in Kiao-Chow, Manchuria, South Africa and the Philippines, with her soul full of meanness, her pocket full of boodle, and the mouth full of pious hypocrisies. Give her soap and a towel, but hide the looking-glass.*

MARK TWAIN, 1900

Wild oats are often sown in very different places, among the verdant hills of Oxfordshire, England, for instance, or in the flat, dusty streets of the sagebrush community of Virginia City, Nevada Territory. Matthew Arnold (1822–1888) wandered the hills, and Mark Twain roamed the streets. Their worlds were antipodal. Oxford was devoted to the intellectual life of the mind and the moral life of the spirit; Virginia City was committed to the strenuous search for wealth and the material life of the self. The one, Oxford, was encumbered with traditions, while the other, Virginia City, was largely without established practice or custom or belief. Yet both offered latitude to their inhabitants. More than an ocean apart, separated by vastly different histories, and having completely dissimilar modes of living, these disparate places saw Matthew Arnold and Mark Twain live out their salad days in curiously parallel ways. Their personal circumstances were radically different. Having matriculated from Rugby, Arnold was an undergraduate at Oxford. Having graduated from the print shop—the poor boy's college, as Howells once called it—and been driven off the Mississippi by the coming of war, Twain was a fledgling newspaper reporter. But despite the enormous variance in cultural situation and the manifold difference in personal activity, both pursued a common pattern of youthful behavior: both indulged wayward impulses and made themselves conspicuous in society. Both conducted themselves flamboyantly in speech, action, and dress; both adopted extravagant styles contrived to impress the public. At the same time they captured notice they also tested out uncertain interests. Each performed not only as a way of commanding attention but also as a way of exploring facets of a nascent personality.

To the dismay of his family (and the amusement of his friends), Arnold became something of a dandy. He affected an arch, knowing tone, one rife with irony; he dressed somewhat dashingly in clothes that stretched his budget; and he lived self-indulgently, enjoying fine food and drink, leisurely walks, fishing, and French novels. Twain put on somewhat different airs, but they were equally affected. At times he adopted the dress of the West—coarse cotton shirt, open at the collar, baggy denim pants, and leather boots—but more often he dressed as something of a gentleman— white shirt, tie, coat, and polished shoes—an attire that stood out more. Like Arnold's, his tone was knowing, though what he knew was a question, and it was backed up by a sharp tongue. If Arnold was smugly ironic, Twain was boldly cheeky.[1] Twain lived as comfortably as he could, frequenting fine hotels, health spas, first-class restaurants, and entertainment spots that ranged from hurdy-gurdies to opera houses. He had a fondness for oysters on the half-shell, washed down with champagne. Like Arnold, he drank convivially and socialized acerbically. Although he complained of Bret Harte's effete dandyism, he was at ease with his own version of a stylish, bohemian gentleman.

Arnold at Oxford, Twain first on the Comstock, then on the California coast, both sought satisfaction as well as notoriety in flamboyant personal display and privileged living. Both humored themselves and turned their humor against others. However, in time each became, as Arnold phrases it in the title poem of his first volume of poetry, a "Strayed Reveller."[2] Each strayed at a different pace, but both eventually forswore their youthful lifestyles. (When Twain went west at twenty-five, he was almost eight years older than Arnold was when he entered Oxford.) Arguably, they both initially embraced their early revels for the same reason that they later left them: because they saw the vanity of life. Each first made merry in the face of emptiness, then later tried to fill the void of human existence with some meaning.

At first glance, the initial—and now somewhat famous—meeting between Arnold and Twain hardly supports the similarity briefly suggested here. When Arnold arrived in Boston in 1883 for an American lecture tour, he sought out Howells at his home (a clear measure of Howells's stature), only to learn that he was in Hartford visiting Mark Twain. Arnold then said to Howells's wife, "Oh, but he doesn't like *that* sort of thing, does he?" To which Mrs. Howells replied, "He likes Mr. Clemens very much, and he thinks him one of the greatest men he ever knew." At a subsequent Hartford reception for the distinguished English critic, Arnold noticed a man across the room and asked Howells, who was this time with him, "Who—who in the world is that?" The answer was: "Oh, that is Mark Twain" (*MyMT* 25). The encounter becomes even more intriguing when Arnold dines at Twain's home the next day, feels the full force of his personality, and, leaving with another guest, the Reverend Edwin P. Parker, asks, "And is he *never* serious?" To which Parker, who knew Twain well from the Monday Evening Club, answered emphatically, "Mr. Arnold, he is the most serious man in the world" (*MTB* 758–59). The episode evokes stock images: the solemn—and very serious—Arnold, the ebullient—and irrepressibly humorous—Twain.

At the time Arnold was in America lecturing Americans on the need for culture, observing their civilization, and accidentally meeting Mark Twain, Henry James was in England writing about Arnold. As a young man James had fallen under the spell of Arnold. Along with Oliver Wendell Holmes Jr. and John Chipman Gray, James had read—and reveled in—Arnold's poetry and early essays. Arnold became for him, as he later explained, "in prose and verse" the "idol" of his early years (*Wetmore Story* 2:208), and in 1865 he had reviewed Arnold's *Essays in Criticism* for the *North American Review*. (Not knowing the author of the review at the time, for it was unsigned, Arnold was quite pleased by it, writing to his sister, "I like [it] as well as anything I have seen" [*Letters* 2:471].) Arnold's high seriousness and catholic perspective, no less than his ideas, created in

James "the liberation and justification" of his own "critical and creative energies" (Stone, *Communications* 13). In his 1876 study of Hawthorne, James had taken up the Arnoldian idea of culture, and in what has become one of the most famous passages in American letters, he itemized the elements of civilization *missing* in American life (*Hawthorne* 34–35), an infamous listing that Arnold would later echo in "Civilization in the United States."

James's effort in 1884, however, was a general assessment of Arnold as critic. More appreciation than evaluation, the essay, published in the *English Illustrated Magazine*, offers little criticism and much praise (James later called it a "puff" [qtd. in Dawson 1]). Nevertheless, he caught in the delicate web of his own sensibility many ideas then floating in the literary atmosphere. He lauds Arnold's analyses of English life. Placing Arnold as a critic between Sainte-Beuve and Ernest Renan, James admires his "love of letters, of beauty, of all liberal things," and praises him for setting standards of "literary feeling" and "good manners." Above all, however, he insists upon Arnold's humor. He sees multiple kinds of humor in Arnold's writing, and so he describes his humor variously as a "bantering way," "lightness of form," "jauntiness," "wit," "irony," and "satire." Though some of these turns of humor have a decided bite, James proclaims Arnold a "charming humourist." Unknowingly reversing the now familiar configurations of Arnold and Twain that were at that very moment emerging from Arnold's encounters with Twain, James notes that Arnold is so humorous as to appear to his critics "not serious" ("Matthew Arnold" 276–86).

Matthew Arnold, a "charming humourist"? Mark Twain, the "most serious man in the world"?

Although Arnold and Twain had quite different personal experiences, cultural circumstances, sensibilities, and temperaments, there is a striking similarity in the pattern of their emotional and intellectual lives. Both men remembered—or imagined—an idyllic past associated with childhood, family, and friends and with a natural world of beauty and enchantment. For Twain, that past transpired most indelibly at his uncle John Quarles's farm, which he frequently visited during his boyhood (the pleasures of his time at the farm radiated out to touch Hannibal). Arnold's golden past occurred first during his family's visits to the Lake District and then, from the time he was ten, at Fox How, a vacation house his parents built there and to which they escaped whenever they could (Arnold's joy in life at Fox How eventually spread to his time at Rugby). Both men carried the imprint of their idyllic times with them for life, and it gave shape and direction to their writings. Both found occasion to celebrate versions of that cherished past, Arnold in his poetry, Twain in his fiction.

As each writer aged and drew further from his past, however, each felt the loss of that more perfect moment. Each became nostalgic and struck an elegiac chord in his writing. It was, then, against a vanished, idealized past that each began to measure the present—and find it wanting. (Of course, such a pattern was not uncommon in the troubled second half of the nineteenth century.) In the face of a diminished present, each writer became a critic of his times. And as critic, each was not only highly serious but also stridently comic. The forms of their literary expression differed, of course, but the final stance assumed by each was the same. Each in time became a sage. Arnold shifted from poet to academic to sage;[3] Twain, from comic journalist to novelist to sage. Foreshortening the journey each made, it is worth looking briefly at their common point of departure on their way to becoming sages who would hold up the looking glass to their age.

In 1870, at the still young age of thirty-four, Twain was already nostalgic about his past. To his childhood chum Will Bowen, he wrote, "The old life has swept before me like a panorama; the old days have trooped by in their old glory, again; the old faces have looked out of the mists of the past; old footsteps have sounded in my listening ears; old hands have clasped mine, old voices have greeted me, & the songs I loved ages & ages ago have come wailing down the centuries!" (*MTL4* 50). Twain turned his "old life" into significant fiction first with *Tom Sawyer* and then with *Huckleberry Finn.* His well of reminiscence would never quite run dry, but these two early works encapsulate his "old days" in all their "old glory." His fictionalization of those times past (his own not-so-innocent real-life youth) is perhaps the most familiar dimension of his writing. From Tom Sawyer's idyllic playground—"Away off in the flaming sunshine, Cardiff Hill lifted its soft green sides through a shimmering veil of heat, tinted with the purple of distance; a few birds floated on lazy wing high in the air; no other living thing was visible but some cows, and they were asleep" (*TS* 81)—to Huck's gloomy but alert feeling for nighttime—"The stars was shining, and the leaves rustled in the woods ever so mournful; and I heard an owl, away off, who-whooing"—and his now famous, affectionate account of watching "the daylight come" slowly over the river until everything is "smiling in the sun, and the song-birds just going it!" (*HF* 4, 156–57), Twain celebrates the child's responsiveness to the natural world. He employs what Susan K. Harris has perceptively examined as "the imagery of unity" (*MT's Escape from Time*, chapter 6). Through such imagery, Twain evokes a feeling of psychic wholeness, a sense of some fundamental tie to the elemental world, and a suggestion of suspended—or endless, mythic—time. He creates a pristine, innocent realm—what Arnold would call in "Memorial Verses" the "freshness of the early world."

This world is one of sensuous experience of nature, of lightsome play, of serenity, delight, and joy. It is Twain's fond recreation of his times at the Quarles farm—"a heavenly place for a boy"—which he recalls in his autobiographical dictations with an abundance of specific detail in a kind of incantation, or litany, intoned by the repeated phrases "I can call it all back," "I can see," "I know," "I know how." He evokes this idyllic time and place with romantic intensity, realistic detail, and personal consecration: "I can call it all back and make it as real as it ever was, and as blessed" (*MTOA* 113, 120–21). Recalling that time, he rejuvenates himself—and also discloses something of the psychic and emotional center of his being. To be sure, this sunshine world has its dark underside, and *Huck Finn* is surcharged with a bitter irony foreign to the indulgent good humor of *Tom Sawyer*. But both books bear the imprint of Twain's deepest feeling. There are manifold, multiple differences between the two books, of course. Still, for all their differences, both books record the time Twain described fondly in "Villagers of 1840–3" as "an intensely sentimental age," one that, in contrast to his present, "took no sordid form," for it lacked "the lust for money which is the rule of life to-day, and the hardness and cynicism which is the spirit of to-day" (*Huck Finn and Tom Sawyer Among the Indians* 100).

Arnold's poetry is shot through with images of "the freshness of the early world."[4] It is charged with brief, luminescent moments that register Arnold's delight in the beauty, vitality, and serenity afforded by nature, for as he says in "Lines, Written in Kensington Gardens," "in my helpless cradle I / Was breathed on by the rural Pan." Even Arnold's Empedocles—a despondent thinker overmastered by the "devouring flame of thought," which strips the world of meaning and deadens him to "Joy and the outward world"—even this doubt-torn, strife-ridden prisoner of consciousness, who finds life no longer worth living, acknowledges the indelible power of past times: "When we were young," we felt "a pure natural joy" and had "delightful commerce of the world." As he trudges to the top of Etna to find oblivion in its fiery void, he recalls, much as Arnold himself does throughout his poetry, past moments of unalloyed delight:

> The smallest thing could give us pleasure then—
> The sports of the country-people,
> A flute-note from the woods,
> Sunset over the sea;
> Seed-time and harvest,
> The reapers in the corn,
> The vinedresser in his vineyard,
> The village-girl at her wheel.

As Empedocles' list of lost joys suggests, Arnold frequently evokes the innocent bygone time in stylized, even conventional, images. His poetry often seems somewhat attenuated from the physical world, or, to put it more precisely, he realizes his feelings for that world in stock images, metaphors, and tropes. This sometimes creates the sense that his poetry is contrived, abstract, cerebral. There is, of course, a calm tantamount to coolness about many of his poems (perhaps he is, as he says in "A Summer Night," "Never by passion quite possess'd / And never quite benumb'd by the world's sway"). He resists the impassioned, personal mode of Romantic poetry, the sign of which is the all-pervading "I," but he also stops well short of exploiting fully the ironic, fictive monologue, made famous by Browning, which opened the way to the modernist insistence on complete impersonality. If he captures the "early world" in conventional figures, however, they are nonetheless often moving. In "Resignation," for instance, a poem sometimes compared to Wordsworth's "Tintern Abbey" (see Knoepflmacher), the landscape he revisits is quite generalized:

> Once more we tread this self-same road,
> Fausta, which ten years since we trod;
> Along we tread it, you and I,
> Ghosts of that boisterous company.

Here, where the brook shines, near its head,
In its clear, shallow, turf-fringed bed;
Here, whence the eye first sees, far down,
Capp'd with faint smoke, the noisy town;
Here sit we, and again unroll,
Though slowly, the familiar whole.
The solemn wastes of heathy hill
Sleep in the July sunshine still;
The self-same shadows now, as then,
Play through this grassy upland glen;
The loose dark stones on the green way
Lie strewn, it seems, where then they lay;
On this mild bank above the stream,
(You crush them!) the blue gentians gleam.
Still this wild brook, the rushes cool,
The sailing foam, the shining pool!

The stock quality of a "grassy upland glen," "dark stones," "this mild bank above the stream," a "wild brook," and a "shining pool" does not keep these images from being evocative emblems of a treasured place first visited in youth. Twain recalls his idyllic early world in vivifying specific detail, while Arnold summons his in familiar poetic figures, but both writers feel keenly the hold of such enchanted realms of time past.

In Arnold's poems only a mythic figure like the Scholar-Gipsy, someone who roams the hillsides "in spring," the "lone wheatfields" in autumn, and the "wide grass meadows which the sunshine fills" in summer, who visits moors and "fields of breezy grass / Where black-wing'd swallows haunt the glittering Thames," and upland "hills" where stray the "feeding kine," only such a figure can live as "a truant boy," and so living, know "unclouded joy." And only such an idealized, mythic figure can preserve "glad perennial youth." For again and again in Arnold's poetry the golden world of innocent youth—of integrated being and restful ease—is darkened by "this strange disease of modern life, / With its sick hurry, its divided aims, / Its heads o'ertax'd, its palsied hearts." The freshness of the early world gives way fatally to what Arnold calls "the iron age" ("Memorial Verses").

Confronting the "iron age," Arnold gives up writing poetry, turns to essays, and eventually functions as a sage. Facing the "sordid" "hardness" of his day, Twain ceases writing hymns to boyhood, turns from lighthearted humor to ever darkening satire, and eventually performs as a sage. Both men come to feel, as Arnold puts it in his most famous poem, that the world which seems "So various, so beautiful, so new, / Hath really neither joy, nor love, nor light, / Nor certitude, nor peace, nor help for pain" ("Dover Beach"). Both feel trapped on "a darkling plain," and both try as sages to bring some light to that darkness.

Although the figure of the sage is as ancient as traditional wisdom literature and the Hebrew prophets (Landow 17–40), the Victorian sage is somewhat distinct. For the Victorian sage was engendered by the times. In his seminal study of the Victorian sage, John Holloway has described the predisposition of the sage as an "interest of a general or speculative kind in what the world is like, where man stands in it, and how he should live" (1). While these are timeless questions, what activated the inquisitive, philosophical, and moral intelligence characteristic of the Victorian sage was change, which of course shook first Victorian England and then its trans-Atlantic offshoot, America. That Victorian England experienced unprecedented, multitudinous, ever-accelerating change by now no longer needs illustrating; it only needs recalling. The lay of the land and the work of the people on it shifted from rural-agricultural to urban-industrial. Transformations tantamount to explosions occurred in manufacturing, trade, finance, energy, technology, transport, communication, and political organization, and these shifts in material conditions called into question traditional social ideas, intellectual explanations, and moral systems. These changes altered both the fabric of individual life and the patterns by which it was understood. Although such change came a bit later in the United States, and though the specific manifestations were different, the general pattern of radical change that generated conceptual challenge was the same.

There was, in short, on both sides of the Atlantic during the long period to which Victoria lent her name, a crisis in culture. Put simply, the pervasive problem, in England and America alike, was that vertiginous change undermined traditional authorities, making their explanations seem dubious or just irrelevant to the altered conditions of life.[5] Some Victorian writers then undertook, as Richard Ohmann has put it, "to overcome doubt and confusion in a period when the avenue to truth" was "far from broad, straight, or public" (303). The age itself "looked to its writers for help in understanding the universe as it was then being found to be" (Tillotson 90), and writers began to assume the function of prophet or sage.

Both Arnold and Twain were equipped by temperament to play the role of sage. Arnold's early letters to his friend Arthur Hugh Clough reveal a disposition to challenge his time, to question why things were as they were, and to ask whether they should be as they were. From the first, his probing intelligence manifests itself in his criticism, no matter what its object. By the time he had published *Essays in Criticism* (first series), *Culture and Anarchy*, and *Literature and Dogma*, he had not only commanded attention and stirred controversy but also revealed the range of his critical interests: he was a critic of literature, a critic of culture, and a critic of religion. In the essays and lectures that he collected into his books Arnold often invoked the wise man, saint, or prophet, thereby suggesting the tradition in which he saw himself as well as the role he hoped to play, and his design was not lost on his audience. His role as sage was often no more welcome than his ideas, however. Ironically, some of Arnold's most diligent readers attacked him as "the elegant Jeremiah," a "high-priest of the kid-gloved persuasion," a "literary coxcomb," more "fop" than "prophet" (Dawson and Pfordresher 163–66). At the least, such vituperation took the measure of Arnold's aspirations even as it pronounced him a fraud and a failure. Throughout his career, Arnold was inclined to do what, in the formulation of George P. Landow, every sage hoped to accomplish: to save the community "by comprehending the nature of man" (43).

Mark Twain had a similar impulse. Although there is something disconcerting about his emphatic declaration in his autobiography—"I have always preached" (*AMT* 273)—there is also something true about it. From the beginning there was a moralist inside the humorist, and there was as well a mind that took nothing for granted, a questioning intellect that liked to think things through on its own. As much as Arnold, Twain had the sage's "interest of a general or speculative kind in what the world is like, where man stands in it, and how he ought to live." Two things have impeded the recognition of Twain as sage. First, even as sage, he is often a lively humorist, and it is sometimes hard to take seriously what is rendered humorously. This was especially true in Twain's own era, which most often conceived of humor as antithetical to seriousness. Second, Twain lacked formal higher education (he had nothing like Arnold's rigorous training at Rugby and classical education at Oxford), and this deprived him of one of the sage's most accepted sources of authority. Yet as Howells observed, Twain was "always reading some vital book," and he always had not only an opinion about it but also critiques of its ideas. These formed the core of those endless conversations that Howells enjoyed in their long friendship and testified to in *My Mark Twain:* "We both talked and talked and talked, of everything in the heavens and on the earth, and the waters under the earth," reasoning "high" " 'Of Providence, foreknowledge, will and fate, / Fixed fate, free will, foreknowledge absolute.' " Like other sages, Twain, again in the words of Howells, "pierced to the heart of life" and "tried for the reason of things" (*MyMT* 15, 10, 83).

From his first collection of essays on, it was evident that Arnold was inclined to analyze his age, to reveal what was wrong with it, to reawaken it to fundamental, timeless concerns, and to guide it toward better values. He was from the first a sage, and the reviews of his work acknowledged that fact (see Dawson and Pfordresher). Nothing of the kind can be said of Twain—far from it. Although he himself would claim, three years before his death, that "everything" he had written had "a serious philosophy or truth as its basis" (qtd. in Budd, *Our MT* 220), few readers in his time (and, to be fair, in ours) discerned the sage at work in Twain's writings and speeches. Late in his career, however, the serious Twain made himself more visible. Most critics see the sagely Twain as emerging in 1900, when he returned to the United States after living abroad for some nine years; indeed, William R. Macnaughton speculates that just before his celebrated return, Twain determined to solidify his standing as a writer with a serious side by "becoming a moralist and a reformer" (143). Examining Twain's whole career, however, Arthur L. Scott sees the serious turn taking place somewhat earlier, as Twain began to speak out as America's ambassador-at-large from the time he went into exile in 1891 (162–223). The sage in Twain may actually have emerged even earlier, in the 1880s, for during that decade Twain was exuberantly confident of his ideas, active in politics, ready to give instructive speeches as well as write corrective essays, and anxious to insert his ideas into his fictions (see Krauth, chapter 7). Apparently, all that curtailed his functioning full blast as a sage was time; he was too busy with business schemes to critique his age in any steady way. Perhaps the most accurate thing to say is simply that from 1880 on Twain was increasingly ready to speak as a sage on a variety of topics.

Twain's stance as sage is a curious replay of postures he initially imparted to his fictional characters Tom and Huck. Like Huck he is often alienated from the world he addresses, discontented with it, disgusted and repulsed by it. Unlike Huck, however, he feels superior to it. Like Tom, Twain as sage attempts to control his society, or if control is too strong a term, he at least strives to manipulate it. Thus the psychic extensions of Twain into his most famous characters are recuperated in his role as sage. In a now-famous letter to Howells, written just after the completion of his most didactic fiction, *A Connecticut Yankee*, Twain disclosed the impulse that governed his work as a sage: "Well, my book is written—let it go. But if it were only to write over again there wouldn't be so many things left out. They burn in me; & they keep multiplying & multiplying; but now they can't ever be said. And besides, they would require a library—& a pen warmed-up in hell" (*MTHL* 613). Characteristically, Twain overstates and miscalculates here; not all of the things he burned to say needed a pen hot with hellfire, and he would find ways to say them (even though his morally instructive novel was finished). Perhaps the most revealing thing here is just the enormous urge Twain had to instruct. Joe B. Fulton has argued (correctly, I believe) that the "point" of Twain's writing was "to provoke thought and ethical rejuvenation among his readers" (*MT in the Margins* 96). While Arnold held forth as sage in formal lectures, essays, and full-length books, Twain expressed himself as sage in more varied forms—and forums. He delivered numerous speeches (shorter than Arnold's lectures and often given in casual settings); published essays, some in popular magazines, some in elite journals; and gave, especially during the final two decades of his life, countless interviews to the newspapers. As sage, he even brought out one full-scale book, albeit in an unsigned, limited edition, *What Is Man?* In short, he vented the fiery convictions that multiplied in him with such force.

But even as sage or enraged prophet Twain was not solely serious even when he was serious. Although his utterances as sage, spoken and written (and written but unpublished), increasingly dominated the work of his later years, he continued to spin off comic pieces ranging from complete silliness, to his always-favorite burlesque, to prickly satire. He was a humorist as well as a sage. It is especially notable that during the thirty years or so in which Twain was most visible as sage, the last three decades of his life, he wrote works at odds with his own effort. His posture as sage is marked by didactic intent, moral concern, relentless seriousness, and corrective fervor. Yet in "Advice to Youth" he spoofs the didactic; in "On the Decay of the Art of Lying" he twits morality; and in "Traveling with a Reformer" he makes fun of moral reform itself. Which is to say, he played with the very impulses that informed his posture as sage.

Arnold, too, had fun with his role. In the underrated *Friendship's Garland*, in which he pretends to be the editor of letters from the famous Arminius Von-Thunder-ten-Tronckh, he laughs at himself. Arminius, Arnold's fictive Prussian philosopher, says at one point, "I love to proceed with the stringency of a philosopher, and Mr. Matthew Arnold with his shillyshallying spoils the ideas I confide to him" (5:44). Arnold twists his own tail throughout the *Garland*, but unlike Twain, he does not undermine, even in jesting fun, the very premises of the sage.

Because it is central to virtually all his prose writings, Arnold's role as a sage has often been analyzed and explicated. In comparison, Twain's similar role has received scant attention and almost no extended analysis. Critics, especially those concerned with his last two decades, have noted Twain's propensity to speak out as a wise man, and they have attended to many of his ideas, especially his political ones, but there has been relatively little consideration of his modes of presentation as a Victorian sage. Critics of Arnold have sometimes complained that he lacks a coherent philosophy or system of ideas. Arnold himself acknowledged his lack of coherent view: "From a man without a philosophy no one can expect philosophical completeness" (*Culture and Anarchy* 5:137), and it is true that he comments variously, sometimes contradictorily. The same, of course, holds true for Twain. Indeed, he is most often—and most appropriately, given his chosen pen name, which invites us to take note of two—described in terms of dualities. These contraries may be said to describe *both* Twain and Arnold: democrat and elitist, optimist and pessimist, revolutionary and conservative, idealist and empiricist. Such tensions within each writer may account for their varied self-positioning, and they may give rise in both writers to what Lionel Trilling, writing of Arnold, has called an "eclectic and dialectical method" (13). Twain and Arnold are also at one on some fundamental ideas. Both share a belief, as Arnold puts it in "The Function of Criticism at the Present Time," in the value of "the free play of the mind upon all subjects" (3:268); both are inclined to "try and approach truth on one side after another" (preface to *Essays in Criticism* 3:286).

To see how each of these similarly disposed writers functions as sage, it is useful to consider the foundations of their thought and moral judgment, the discourse of civilization each characteristically employs, and their styles. These constitute key strategies by which each sage expresses his sense of what the world is like, where man stands in it, and how he ought to live. And having seen these strategies, we can look anew at the specific disagreements between the two.

In his illuminating study of two acknowledged American sages, Emerson and Thoreau, Sam McGuire Worley raises the question of the source of the sage's authority. He posits two possibilities: a belief in a higher law or an immersion in contemporaneous culture. Contrary to most interpretations of Emerson and Thoreau, he argues that both base their critiques on their command of culture, not on their transcendental visions (see vii–xv, and especially chapter 1). If we ask the same question—what is the foundation of their authority?—of Arnold and Twain, the answer is different for each.

For all his attention to the social conditions of his time, Arnold often gives his ideas a spiritual underpinning. The final shift in his career to the analysis of religion only discloses clearly what was latent in his writing from the first: his criticism of society and culture is precipitated by his belief in transcendent truth. Sinewing through his arguments against anarchy, for culture, against materialism, for sweetness and light, against practical action, for the humanizing of the individual in society, against party policy, for seeing straight and clear, against collective enterprises, for the perfection of the individual, is a sense of a higher truth framing human affairs. Critics disagree over the nature and importance of Arnold's religious outlook. Basil Willey has argued that Arnold's religious writings are his "centre of gravity," the very "corner-stone" of all his work (252–53), whereas J. Hillis Miller sees Arnold as working in the grip of "the true emptiness of consciousness," which is its "infinite distance from the buried self and from the divine transcendence" (259).[6] But, it seems to me, as early as "The Function of Criticism at the Present Time" Arnold laid out the moral grounding of his thought: "It is because criticism has so little kept in the pure intellectual sphere, has so little detached itself from practice, has been so directly polemical and controversial, that it has so ill accomplished, in this country, its best spiritual work; which is to keep man from a self-satisfaction which is retarding and vulgarizing, to lead him towards perfection, by making his mind dwell upon what is excellent in itself, and the absolute beauty and fitness of things" (3:271).

Arnold himself wants to accomplish "spiritual work," and for him the absolute beauty and fitness of things are not accidental. The spiritual is not so much directly invoked as a standard for criticism as it is insinuated into his criticism as a perspective that posits importance. As David J. DeLaura puts it, "Arnold persistently appeals to a covert supernaturalism" (xvii). Arnold calls upon people to exercise their powers of conduct, of intellect and knowledge, of beauty, and of social life and manners with such insistence because he sees significance in life above and beyond the material. A sense of a higher realm hovers over—informs and directs—Arnold's trenchant criticism of society, but it appears somewhat elusively in his analysis, usually in unexplained phrases such as the following (all from *Culture and Anarchy*): "feeling after the universal order," "a perfect spiritual condition," *"an inward spiritual activity."* Occasionally, Arnold is explicit in his invocation of a divine order mixed in human affairs: "He who works for sweetness and light, works to make reason and the will of God prevail" (5:165, 98, 108, 112; he is using Bishop Wilson's phrase). While the moral force of his criticism at least implicitly derives from his sense of spiritual things, Arnold not only brings the spiritual—or perhaps more precisely, the significance the spiritual endows—to bear on the human but also uses the human to grasp the spiritual. In this wise, he has been described as an ethical idealist who grounds "religion itself in ethics"—believing that God must be what humanity's moral insight says he is (Robbins, *Ethical Idealism* 173). Whether thinking from the top down or the bottom up, to use familiar spatial metaphors, Arnold proceeds as critic by presenting "the ideal and eternal in reciprocal relation to the pragmatic and historical" (Robbins, *Ethical Idealism* 173, 163).

Though nearly obsessed with such relations, Twain made no such application. He had, as Everett Emerson has put it, a lifelong "quarrel with God" ("MT's Quarrel with God"). Yet even as he vacillated in belief, he generally refrained from publicly expressing his doubt, not wanting to tarnish his public image (or diminish his book sales). If Arnold conceived of God by construing him in terms of the best of human ethics, Twain defined him by attributing to him the worst of human attributes. In his later years, especially, Twain imagines God as little more than a human monster, maliciously inflicting on humankind all the ills of existence. God

and his spiritual realm are most often wholly absent from Twain's social and political criticism. When he writes as sage, then, Twain usually
avoids using any conception of divine eternal law as a basis for his criticisms. He has nothing like Arnold's insistent, if often nebulous, evocation
of the spiritual. (When he does invoke God or some higher law, Twain does
so briefly, usually as a condemnatory counterpoint to misguided human
action, for he likes to turn religion against the religious.) While the underpinning of Arnold's critiques is ultimately spiritual, Twain—like Emerson
and Thoreau before him—derives his critiques from "his place in a shared
culture" (Worley xiii, in reference to Emerson and Thoreau). What Twain
extracts from that culture is a very general scheme of ethics, a set of values
so commonly accepted as to seem self-evident. But just as Arnold employs
the ideal or eternal to generate personal authority as well as moral force in
his writings, so Twain uses commonplace ethical notions to create personal
authority as well as moral force in his.

The grounding of Twain's criteria for judgment in the general culture
is nicely revealed in "Edmund Burke on Croker and Tammany," a speech
he gave in 1901. In some ways it is a curious performance, for it is somewhat longer than his typical speech and is pointedly topical, having for
its occasion the New York City municipal election in which the newly
formed Fusion party advanced a slate of candidates to unseat the minions
of Tammany hall. Twain first gave the speech to a group of newspapermen,
calling themselves the Order of Acorns, who supported the Fusion candidates, and then quickly published it in *Harper's Weekly* (19 October 1901).
With ingenuity as well as contrivance, he uses Burke's famous 1788 speech
impeaching Warren Hastings, one of the chief administrators of the East
India Company, to condemn Richard Croker in particular and Tammany
in general. He sets up what he calls "parallels"—"exact and complete"
ones—that turn Croker into Hastings and Tammany into the East India
company. What is remarkable, besides the feat of historical prestidigi-
tation, are the terms, the criteria, borrowed from Burke for judgment—
and Twain's delight and confidence in them. One of the most sweeping
is "whether millions of mankind shall be made miserable or happy." He
employs abstractions such as "honor, justice, and humanity," and the "national character" is invoked, along with the "credit and honor" and "trust"
of the nation. And he uses, as if they were self-evident, the "eternal laws
of justice" and "human nature itself" as his standards (*MTSpk* 404–12).

Throughout his utterances as sage, Twain employs such terms as these, ignoring for his moral purposes his awareness of the relativity, the arbitrariness, indeed the insubstantiality of them as social constructs variable in time and place. Although he cannot and does not appeal to a divine order, he invokes its equivalent in the deployment of seemingly universal moral standards.

"What is civilization?" Arnold asked in 1888, and then provided this answer: "It is the humanization of man in society, the satisfaction for him, in society, of the true law of human nature" ("Civilization in the United States" II:352). In *Following the Equator*, Twain faced the same question in a different way. Noting that many indigenous natives went from surrounding islands to the Queensland plantations, he explained why: "He goes to acquire *civilization.*" What he receives, Twain says, are "a hat, an umbrella, a belt, a neckerchief" (*FE* 85–86). Twain's remarks are meant to expose exploitation, but he half believes what he comically suggests: Western civilization consists principally of frangible goods (the finery Shakespeare's Trinculo revels in). While Arnold writes magisterially and Twain comically, they are both responding to a regnant idea in the nineteenth century: the centrality of civilization. From the early modern period on, spurred by rising nationalism and colonial expansion, the idea of civilization—of the merits or demerits of one's own and of one's own in comparison to those of other countries—became a dominant element in the self-conceiving of Western nations. There emerged in England and then in its colonies what has come to be called a discourse of civilization. By the nineteenth century such a discourse was not just familiar but standard, and the global expansion and material prosperity that occurred during that century, even with its concomitant intellectual unrest, intensified the discourse of civilization. It is no wonder, then, that both Arnold and Twain made use of a discourse of civilization in their pronouncements as sage.

John Stuart Mill's 1836 essay, entitled simply "Civilization," signals the importance of this discourse and provides in brief a glimpse of how it was constructed. Mill explains at the outset that civilization "sometimes stands for human improvement in general, and sometimes for certain kinds of improvement in particular." "We are accustomed," he says first of all, "to call a country more civilized if we think it more improved; more eminent in the best characteristics of Man and Society; farther advanced in the road to perfection; happier, nobler, wiser." He then acknowledges that a second, equally common sense of the term civilization is that which "distinguishes a wealthy and powerful nation from savages or barbarians" (18:119). This version of civilization arises from the then commonplace view of human development as an evolutionary process in which mankind moves from a relatively simple or primitive state to a more complex state of individual and social existence. "Whatever be the characteristics of what we call savage life," Mill argues, "the contrary of these, or the qualities which society puts on as it throws off these, constitute civilization" (18:120). He creates a short taxonomy: dense population, cities, agriculture, manufacturing, commerce, wealth, government by social consent, a system of law, a concern for justice, and an attention to the "arts of life" (18:119–21). This definition of civilization as not only the opposite of the barbarous but also its superior was of course used to rationalize all manner of colonial ventures and imperialist intrusions. But Mill's first definition construes civilization quite differently—and its analytical use is accordingly different—for in it "improvement" lies not in the altered material conditions of a society but in the transformation of human character within society; it points to a human character made "happier, nobler, wiser." Although Mill tries to separate them, these two strands are inextricably intertwined (in the rest of his essay he takes up, most prominently, cooperation, knowledge, intelligence, education, and literature as shapers of character and morality). Twain's joke—clothes make civilization—points to the material, while Arnold's description—the humanization of man—points to the shaping of character. As sages, Arnold and Twain use both notions, but they often differ in their emphasis.

In *The Innocents Abroad*, the best-seller that made him truly famous as well as rich, Twain creates a striking tableau that encapsulates his own early view of the superiority of Western civilization. Watching an official review of troops at the Arc de l'Etoile by Napoleon III and Abdul-Aziz, Lord of the Ottoman Empire, Twain reflects on the contrast between the two empires in terms perfectly congruent with Mill's: "Napoleon III., the representative of the highest modern civilization, progress, and refinement; Abdul-Aziz, the representative of a people by nature and training filthy, brutish, ignorant, unprogressive, superstitious—and a government whose Three Graces are Tyranny, Rapacity, Blood. Here in brilliant Paris, under this majestic Arch of Triumph, the First Century greets the Nineteenth!" (*IA* 101). On the whole, Twain's enthusiasm for Western civilization remained in place—and entered variously into his writings—at least until his around-the-world lecture tour of 1895–96. Though he was, to be sure, often a critic of Western civilization before 1896, he tended to criticize it from within as someone who supported it even as he tried to improve it. After his tour, however, his outlook shifted decisively.

In 1900, thinking about the Boer War and his account of the Boers in *Following the Equator,* he wrote to his friend and pastor Joseph Twichell: "He [the Boer] is popularly called uncivilized, I do not know why. Happiness, food, shelter, clothing, wholesale labor, modest and rational ambitions, honesty, kindliness, hospitality, love of freedom and limitless courage to fight for it, composure and fortitude in time of disaster, patience in time of hardship and privation, absence of noise and brag in time of victory, contentment with a humble and peaceful life void of insane excitements— if there is a higher and better form of civilization than this, I am not aware of it and do not know where to look for it" (*MTL* 2:694–95). Twain is not, as it may seem, endorsing the Boers over the English, the savage over the civilized, as they were conventionally construed; rather, he is locating within the descendants of the Dutch colonists the conditions and qualities he believes should comprise civilization. Unmistakably, the emphasis here in his long catalog of what constitutes civilization falls on human attributes. While touching on the material—food, clothing, shelter—he virtually equates a true civilization with strong character. Twain thinks here not as a political analyst or economist or advocate of either intellectual growth or social refinement, but as a moralist. And it is as a moralist that he goes on in his letter to Twichell to say, "My idea of our civilization is that it is a shabby poor thing and full of cruelties, vanities, arrogancies, meannesses, and hypocrisies" (*MTL* 2:695). Clearly he is thinking of civilization in terms more appropriately applied to people. He conceives of it—anticipating the universal standards he would later invoke via Burke to condemn Tammany hall—as a set of sound moral values. He no longer believes, however, as he had for over three decades, that Western civilization is a superior one. In his letter to Twichell he suddenly roils with indignation: "As for the word"—civilization—"I hate the sound of it, for it conveys a lie; and as for the thing itself, I wish it was in hell, where it belongs" (*MTL* 2:695). He detests civilization not because its constitutive moral elements are wrong but because they are not upheld in practice. Failing to live in accord with its professed values, civilization becomes for Twain a complete sham, a lived falsehood.

As sage, Twain often employs his discourse of civilization to attack civilization itself. Thinking most often of the civilized as the moral, he assails the various Western societies (sometimes lumping them together) by turning against them the very values they nominally espouse. Perhaps the most famous of such moral reboundings, certainly one of the most trenchant, is "To the Person Sitting in Darkness." Ironically defining the extension of Western civilization to the underdeveloped countries as a "trade," Twain itemizes the "goods" intended for export:

| | |
|---|---|
| love, | law and order, |
| justice, | liberty, |
| gentleness, | equality, |
| christianity, | honorable dealing, |
| protection to the weak, | mercy, |
| temperance, | education, |

—and so on. (*MTC2* 462)

Improved material conditions are as notably absent here as moral attributes are present. Twain's point is that while such "goods" are desirable enough, they are not what the imperial powers actually deliver. Instead, they trade in invasion, bloodshed, conquest, exploitation, control, and dehumanization—"harryings and burnings and desert-makings." In short, the "civilized" powers fail to enact the human and moral imperatives that constitute their claim to civilization. They fail to demonstrate, Twain insists, "gentleness and charity and loving kindness," and fail to conduct themselves with "magnanimity, forbearance, love, gentleness, mercy" (*MTC2* 463, 459, 463). The terms are striking. Whatever his quarrel with God, whatever his dislike of organized religion, Twain as sage often speaks in the language of spiritual righteousness with the fervor of a backwoods, camp-meeting preacher.

Arnold's tone is as different as his concept of civilization. No less than Twain, he employs a discourse of civilization, but his notion of it is not a cluster of moral traits and beneficent human attributes. As everyone who reads Arnold knows, the center of his conception of civilization is culture. In his analysis, it is culture that creates the humanization of man in society. In *Culture and Anarchy*, he defines culture precisely (at least to his own way of thinking): "Culture is then properly described not as having its origin in curiosity, but as having its origin in the love of perfection;

it is *a study of perfection.*" And perfection itself is defined as "the pursuit of sweetness and light," that is, beauty and intellectual illumination. Paradoxically—and this adumbrates a tension throughout Arnold's writing—culture is thus imagined as an individual pursuit, but one to which he wants to impart larger collective force. He confidently asserts, "There is a view in which all the love of our neighbour, the impulses towards action, help, and beneficence, the desire for removing human error, clearing human confusion, and diminishing human misery, the noble aspiration to leave the world better and happier than we found it,— motives eminently such as are called social,—come in as part of the grounds of culture, and the main and pre-eminent part" (5:91, 112, 91). Arnold's concept of culture as the centerpiece of civilization thus totters between cloistered learning and social endeavor. In his discourse of civilization, culture, the very core of civilization, is both an inward state of being and an outward striving.

Though it clearly has moral implications, Arnold's sense of civilization as culture does not foreground right behavior; it posits learning "the best that has been thought and known" as an end in itself and as a good that may yield appropriate individual and social conduct (*Culture and Anarchy* 5:113). But exactly what the "best" is—however seductive its sound, however striking its appeal—is left largely unspecified by Arnold. It looms as an abstract ideal toward which one should aspire. He is emphatic in his belief that culture can ameliorate the ill conditions of society, but how this will happen is unexplained.[7] Arnold's injunction to become cultured in order to further true civilization floats lightly—and beautifully—in the ethereal air of his argument. (Henry James might have called it a "romance," "disengaged, disembroiled, disencumbered" from the "inconvenience of a *related*, a measurable state, a state subject to all our vulgar communities" [*The Art of the Novel* 33].) For Arnold, culture is a matter of knowing and therefore doing, but there is meager attention to the practical in Arnold, as he himself was aware. Paradoxically, he advocates disinterest at the same time he envisions consequent action.

Arnold's notion of civilization as humanization through culture poses a problem that Twain's conception of civilization as familiar morality solves. In Arnold's scheme culture is so elevated as to seem almost inaccessible; certainly it does not seem readily available to all. He insists on the contrary: "It [culture] does not try to teach down to the level of the inferior classes;

it does not try to win them for this or that sect of its own, with ready-made judgments and watchwords. It seeks to do away with classes; to make the best that has been thought and known in the world current everywhere; to make all men live in an atmosphere of sweetness and light, where they may use ideas, as it uses them itself, freely,—nourished, and not bound by them" (*Culture and Anarchy* 5:113).

But how all men can come to live in sweetness and light is left in the dark, as opaque as the terms themselves. Oddly perhaps, Twain's generalized, free-floating, universal morality is—in contrast to Arnold's culture—both more specific and more accessible. Its very ordinariness makes it available to anyone, of whatever condition in society, who wants to pursue it. And it is equally available to any well-disposed country. Arnold's culture seems restricted to an enlightened elite, and, as we shall see, this aspect of his discourse of civilization bothered Twain.

In his writings as sage, Arnold employs his idea of culture as the lynchpin of civilization with great insistence. He describes—and redescribes—it with sharp clarity, uses it to analyze a myriad of social ills, and urges it as the solution to nothing less than the human problem of living well. Curiously, in his fervid advocacy, he sometimes turns the idea rhetorically into a near entity; it becomes an almost live, independent protagonist. He speaks of culture as "always assigning to system-makers and systems a smaller share in the bent of human destiny than their friends like"; culture is said "to deal" with the men of a system; it can confer a "boon"; and it "shows its single-minded love of perfection" (*Culture and Anarchy* 5:109, 111, 127, 104). Although he does not quite personify culture, Arnold turns it from an abstraction into an almost animate figure. In his discourse of civilization he uses culture above all as the basis for adjudication. He is explicit about its function: "Now culture, with its disinterested pursuit of perfection, culture, simply trying to see things as they are in order to seize on the best and to make it prevail, is surely well fitted to help us judge rightly" (*Culture and Anarchy* 5:124). What generalized morality does in Twain's discourse of civilization, culture does in Arnold's. And if Twain's tone is often that of the impassioned preacher, Arnold's is frequently that of the overbearing, sometimes pedantic schoolmaster.

"Style," the youthful Arnold assured Clough, is "the saying in the best way *what you have to say.*" He then added, "The *what you have to say* depends on your age" (*Letters to Clough* 65). Notable here is his emphasis on "what you have to say"—twice italicized for emphasis—on the ideas to be conveyed in writing, no matter what one's age. Clearly for Arnold, determined conviction supersedes or, perhaps more accurately, dictates expression; this is the key to Arnold's style as sage. He is one of the most distinctive stylists of his era, and his mode as sage has often been analyzed, so often in fact that its main features are by now familiar. His prose is of course pellucid, always pushing toward greater and greater clarity. Although modern taste in style might find his elongated syntax encumbered, he controls it perfectly. Plain in its way, certainly direct, Arnold's prose is above all lucid and forceful. Lucidity and force are conjoined to persuade, for persuasion is central to Arnold's writing, but lucidity and force when used to express controversial notions also create provocation, and through provocation they promote, whether by assent or resistance, thoughtful response. To precipitate such reaction is generally seen as the achievement of Arnold as a writer. There is, however, something of a paradox about his stylistic presentation of "what you have to say," for on the one hand he is stridently confident about his ideas, while on the other he invites—indeed ignites—disagreement.

As a sage intent upon directing his age, Arnold is masterful in saying what he has to say. Unlike some of his contemporaries, he eschews florid rhetoric. Although at least one critic has insisted that "all the great Victorian prose writers are rhetoricians, practicing at one time or another every mode of rhetoric" (Svaglic 271), Arnold is most frequently straightforward to the point of blunt. One "endeavors," he explained to Clough, "to write deliberately out of what is in one's mind, without any veils or flippancy levity metaphor or demi-mot" (*Letters to Clough* 129–30). His exposition of ideas unfolds steadily and for the most part without linguistic flourish or rhetorical embellishment. He makes such sparse use of the figurative that when it appears it is especially striking, its force being proportional to its rarity. Numerous critics have praised him for the reasonableness, the equanimity, of his tone, and he did in fact like a calm rather than contentious presentation, despite the fact that he enjoyed intellectual combat. Writing to his mother in 1864, he averred: "In the long run one makes enemies by having one's brilliancy and ability praised; one can only get oneself really accepted by men by making oneself forgotten in the people and doctrines one recommends. I have had this much before my mind in doing the second part of my French Eton. I really want to *persuade* on this subject, and I have felt how necessary it was to keep down many and many sharp and telling things that rise to one's lips, and which one would gladly utter if one's object was to show one's own abilities" (*Letters of MA* 2:266). Arnold focuses here on how to enable his abiding didacticism. While his avowed interest in self-effacement is sometimes cited as proof of his congenial spirit (see, for instance, Robbins, *The Arnoldian Principle of Flexibility* 28), what the letter actually discloses is how naturally Arnold was inclined to say "sharp and telling things."[8] Insofar as his arguments seem sensible and are presented in an even tone, they are carefully muted, cleverly controlled expressions of what he felt passionately and had an impulse to assert with acerbity.

In one of the best accounts of Arnold's style, Geoffrey Tillotson has called attention to these salient features: paragraphs opening with abrupt monosyllables, unusual word order, personal interpolations, conversational intensities, vivid slang words and homely expressions, deliberate clumsiness, syntactical inversions, smooth gentle phrasing, sharp awkward phrasing ("spikiness"), and ever-present repetition. Tillotson sees the style as "both suave and obstructed, smooth and attitudinizing, flowing and striking, urbane and barbarous." He concludes that Arnold alternates "long stretches of the gentleman with a flash here and there of the *enfant terrible*" (91–93). John Holloway, on the other hand, sees only the gentleman at work in Arnold's prose—an "intelligent, modest, urbane" writer and thinker. For Holloway such a posture is at the very center of Arnold's work as both style and content, medium and message. He sees Arnold as conducting argumentation through careful distinctions, concessions, polite irony, slanted evaluations, definitions and redefinitions, quotation of authority, and the coinage of memorable catchphrases. He argues that the overall import of this kind of writing is to bring home to the reader, by representing it, the value of "a gentle critical reasonableness." "He mediates," Holloway says, "not a view of the world, but a habit of mind" (*Victorian Sage* 209, 206–7). While this interpretation undervalues the very ideas Arnold himself cherished (the what he had to say in the best way he could), it does capture one of the essential achievements of Arnold's prose.

In "The Function of Criticism at the Present Time," Arnold praises Edmund Burke for bringing "thought to bear upon politics" (precisely what Arnold himself was to do), and he cites Burke's relinquishment of his position on the French Revolution as the epitome of sound thought:

That return of Burke upon himself has always seemed to me one of the finest things in English literature, or indeed in any literature. That is what I call living by ideas: when one side of a question has long had your earnest support, when all your feelings are engaged, when you hear all round you no language but one, when your party talks this language like a steam-engine and can imagine no other,—still to be able to think, still to be irresistibly carried, if so it be, by the current of thought to the opposite side of the question, and, like Balaam, to be unable to speak anything *but what the Lord has put in your mouth.* (3:266–68)

Critics have seen this capacity to return upon oneself as typical of Arnold himself. Without question Arnold became an advocate of the free play of thought. He championed "openness and flexibility of mind" as "the first of virtues" ("Democracy" 2:29), but in many cases there is little such openness and flexibility evident in an individual Arnold essay. Arnold demonstrated these qualities in the overall course of his career, as he expanded, modified, and even changed his ideas. But when he writes a single piece as sage, he rather closes down than opens up; he imposes—often through his famed repetition—rigidity rather than flexibility. For all of his celebrated reasonableness, there is still an unmistakable feel of dogmatism in his individual utterances as sage.[9]

Unlike Arnold's, Twain's style as sage has received little critical attention. What are the sources of power in Twain's sagely pieces? In very general terms, one can say that he employs all three of the tactics of persuasion outlined by Aristotle in his *Rhetoric:* the ethical, the rational, and the emotional. The ethical pervades all of Twain's work as a sage. He really has, then, two modes, each surcharged with moral imperative: a style of close reasoning and logical analysis, and a style of dramatic spectacle and emotional evocation.

Only Twain's rational mode approximates Arnold's, of course. As a rational sage, Twain deals directly with ideas—articulates them, redefines them, places them in the context of current affairs, and measures them against timeless first principles. (His essay "Consistency," in which he argues the virtue of inconsistency, is a good example of his rational mode.) He yokes the local and topical to the universal and historical. He marshals facts and invokes common experience. Often he assaults conventional thinking, dismantles the language used to embody it, and exposes (indeed, sometimes exaggerates) what he takes to be errors of thought. He

deploys blatant rhetorical structures, exploiting the balance of antithesis, for instance, or simply compounding his point—and thereby creating
heavy-handed emphasis—through parallel structures. He is far more figurative than Arnold, yet in his predominantly rational arguments the figurative turns are relatively infrequent and always subordinate to the ideas
he is attacking or defending. He employs syllogistic reasoning to trap the
ideas he is assailing or to confirm those he is upholding. In such exposition
he assaults fiercely opposing positions on the one hand, while, on the other,
he drives home the rightness of his own ideas. His style of dismissal and
assertion, though never as elaborately pursued as Arnold's, is nonetheless similar. And like Arnold, Twain achieves near-perfect clarity. He is
always briefer than Arnold (this sometimes reflects his form—an after-
dinner speech, for instance); he lacks Arnold's complex working out of
ideas and their contraventions; and, even in his most rational arguments,
he indulges in sudden appeals to emotion largely foreign to Arnold.

Where Arnold creates the impression of the rational mind strenuously
conveying the results of careful rumination, Twain imparts the sense of the
rational mind ardently insisting on firmly held convictions. Arnold seems
reflective and analytical; Twain appears thoughtful and contentious.

Twain's other style of dramatic and emotional appeal is almost completely foreign to Arnold.[10] ("The New Dynasty," in which Twain celebrates the emergence of united workers, is a prime example.) Commentators on Twain's late polemical pieces—usually responding to his
anti-imperialist essays—have exclaimed over the sharpness of his writing,
over its satiric barbs and bite (e.g., see Geismar, chapter 5). But Twain's
second style as a sage is far more emotional than critical. In this mode he
usually offers some generality—in "The New Dynasty," for instance, the
notion that power always oppresses—and then gives examples cast in lurid
rhetoric. He describes past or present circumstances in adjectival or verbal terms that are extreme, and he piles one upon another, heaping them
up to create an avalanche of feeling. Even more striking is his insistent
use of heartrending situations—people tortured grotesquely, or mothers
suffering for their children, or a whole nation persecuted with bloody violence. To reach the hearts of his audience, Twain in this mode resorts
to the creation of moving spectacle, to sensational panoramas of history
that illustrate the point of his argument. His presentation reflects, indeed
imitates, what he praised as Macaulay's "glittering pageantry" (*L3* 26), the

"march of his stately sentences" (*IA* 389).[11] (Arnold denigrated Macaulay for not striving "to utter the real truth about his object" and described his style as "wrapping in a robe of rhetoric the thing it represents" ["A French Critic on Milton" 8:165–66].) Twain unleashes plenty of invective toward his antagonists (real or straw) as he strings derogatory terms together to describe his opponents or those who have erred in the past, and the effect of such compounding is emotional intensification rather than real definition. He is highly metaphoric, and his metaphors, like the rest of this style of discourse, are usually extreme and emotion-laden. There is sometimes a note of prophecy, for in this mode as sage Twain is as certain about the future as he is about the past and present. All in all, he declaims far more than he reasons, and he vivifies his ideas in every way he can until they gleam, and he charges them with feeling until they rend the heart.

Needless to say, in his style of emotional appeal Twain shows none of the open-mindedness or flexibility celebrated by Arnold. Like Arnold, however, he believes in both. He was in fact a lifelong champion of independent thinking, and he upheld the idea of change as basic to free thought (sometimes he did so to defend himself against his critics' charge of mercurial positions). In both his styles as sage, the rational and the emotional, there are no Burkean turns back upon himself; instead, he pushes straight on with his central idea, defending it with all the logic he can muster, in the one case, or all the emotion he can generate, in the other.

Sages are not expected to be comedians, and most are far from it, but both Arnold and Twain use humor in their utterances as sage. Humor is a basic part of their style. (James was, I believe, right to praise Arnold for his varied humor.) As one might expect, beyond passing mention of irony, most commentaries skirt the presence of humor in what are overwhelmingly serious social critiques. Even as sages, however, both Arnold and Twain have moments of play, sudden turns to sheer frolic. The giddiest of such moments tend to occur when each writer unexpectedly introduces himself as a character in one of his essays, an exemplary figure of one sort or another from whom one is invited to learn something, whether positive or negative. Two of these comic pirouettes, one from *Culture and Anarchy*, one from Twain's essay "Does the Race of Man Love a Lord?", may represent this odd comic inclination in each sage.

For all its high seriousness, *Culture and Anarchy* is alive with humor, light as well as heavy, and it takes on something of a comic sheen in the famous chapter 3, "Barbarians, Philistines, Populace." The chapter often has a jaunty tone as Arnold speaks tongue-in-cheek of the Barbarians "to whom we all owe so much" and describes with palpable sarcasm the anticipated union of the working class with the middle class to "carry forward" the liberals' "great works, go in a body to their tea-meetings, and, in short, enable them to bring about their millennium." Having set forth his invidious categories—Barbarians, Philistines, Populace—he says coyly that he hopes his classification will provide a "convenient division of English society." Arnold's play ranges from whimsical phrasing to forceful banter—so forceful at times as to become battering—and cutting ridicule, but the most striking comic moment comes when Arnold proffers himself as an example: "I again take myself as a sort of *corpus vile* to serve for illustration in a matter where serving for illustration may not by everyone be thought agreeable." Confessionally, he explains, "I myself am properly a Philistine." He has, he points out, the Barbarian's fondness for "field-sports" and often takes "a gun or fishing-rod" into his hands, and like the Populace, he sometimes cherishes "a vehement opinion in ignorance and passion" and longs "to crush an adversary by sheer violence," but he is most fully, most illustratively, a Philistine—and to be a Philistine, he says, is to be "something particularly stiff-necked and perverse" (5:140–44). Arnold thus mocks his own occasional pomposity. Besides leavening his argument with the yeast of humor, Arnold's inclusion of himself as an example of one of the three classes he is excoriating serves to check his autocratic tone. In one sense his self-inclusion as a *corpus vile* is perverse, but in another it is a charming ploy to disarm his adversaries before they can even take the field against him.

Twain's similar moment of comic self-inclusion has a kindred function. Occasioned by the visit of Prince Heinrich of Germany to the United States, "Does the Race of Man Love a Lord?" is a serious disquisition on the common propensity to establish rank and then respect its higher echelons. Probing for the fundamental, trying to get at something elemental, universal, and true about all people, Twain locates the infatuation with rank in what he describes as the dual desire for Power and Conspicuousness. He holds forth with a certitude, born of superiority, which is born in turn of his assurance that he comprehends unchanging human nature. ("There is no variety," he observes, "in the human race.") He declares, "To worship rank and distinction is the dear and valued privilege of all the human race, and it is freely and joyfully exercised in democracies as well as monarchies—and even, to some extent, among those creatures whom we impertinently call the Lower Animals." Amidst his declamations, Twain suddenly tells an anecdote about being cordoned off by the police "with fifty others" from a street in Vienna down which "the Emperor" was about to pass until "the captain of the squad turned and saw the situation and said indignantly to the guard: 'Can't you see it is the Herr Mark Twain? Let him through.'" With disarming candor, he then says of himself, "It was four years ago; but it will be four hundred before I forget the wind of self-complacency that rose in me, and strained my buttons when I marked the deference for me evoked in the faces of my fellow-rabble, and noted, mingled with it, a puzzled and resentful expression" (*MTC2* 512–23). By comically exposing his own share of the vanity he has been proclaiming common to all, Twain dispels the danger of arrogance, heals the breech between himself as sage and his audience of lesser mortals. And the self-deflating drama of the scene is matched by the sudden intrusion of homely image and colloquial speech—"strained my buttons."

There are some acerbic observations in the essay and more than a few ironic comments. Twain even becomes darkly comic: "We do confess in public that we are the noblest work of God . . . but deep down in the secret places of our souls we recognize that, if we *are* the noblest work, the less said about it the better." For the most part, however, the humor is gentle. It seems to arise from the familiar perspective that sighs "what fools we mortals be," or as Twain puts the idea in slightly different terms, "We are all children" (*MTC2* 520–21). His phrasing insinuates the general acceptance that informs the essay as a whole. (It is far from being a satiric piece.) When he includes himself in the lists of the vain, Twain not only relinquishes for a moment his stance of sagely superiority but also discloses his own childishness, a gesture so winning that it removes any sting from his stern strictures and any haughtiness from his pronouncements.

Humor, at least humor of the more corrective kinds, is a natural weapon for a sage to wield when holding up the looking glass to society. Satire, invective, ridicule, and irony all weave smoothly into the fabric of Arnold's and Twain's arguments. When they sport more lightly, however, especially when they mock themselves, they further their cause in somewhat unusual ways. They generate good will, acceptance, and perhaps even acquiescence; they persuade by being charming. What happens to their discourse in such moments is well described by Twain in another context: "Well, humor is the great thing, the saving thing, after all. The minute it crops up, all our hardnesses yield, all our irritations and resentments flit away, and a sunny spirit takes their place" ("What Paul Bourget Thinks of Us," *MTC2* 178).

Beginning in 1882 and continuing off and on until the early 1890s, Arnold and Twain had a direct, running quarrel with each other, or more precisely with each other's ideas. No "sunny spirit" guided it. Arnold commented on America—and on one of its famous leaders—in a series of lectures and essays: "A Word about America" (May 1882), "Numbers" (November 1883), "A Word More about America" (February 1885), "General Grant" (in two parts, January and February 1887), and "Civilization in the United States" (April 1888). Twain probably heard Arnold give his "Numbers" lecture in Hartford, though it is unlikely that he heard the other two of the three lectures Arnold gave while on tour in America, "Literature and Science" and "Emerson." Twain may not have read the first publication of each of Arnold's essays in English journals, but he almost certainly read American reprintings of the two pieces on Grant and probably read one of two American reprintings of "Civilization in the United States." In any case, he owned an apparently unauthorized volume collecting Arnold's essays on America printed in Boston under the general title *Civilization in the United States, First and Last Impressions,* which contained all the essays noted here except "Numbers." Having taken in Arnold's remarks, one way or another, Twain found himself at odds with the English sage over a General and a Civilization.

He replied, in varying degrees of directness, both publicly and privately. Privately, he began to ruminate and, more often, to fulminate in his notebooks about Arnold and his notions. Publicly, he addressed Arnold or his ideas four times: in an after-dinner speech given in April 1887; in a letter to Yale University accepting an honorary Master of Arts in June 1888; in a speech "On Foreign Critics" given in April 1890 at a dinner to honor the French humorist Leon Paul Blouet (who wrote under the pseudonym Max O'Rell); and in his 1894 novel, *The American Claimant.* He was invited by the editor of the *Forum* to write a rebuttal to Arnold's "Civilization in the United States," and apparently intended to do so until he was distracted by illness in the family, the ongoing struggle with the Paige typesetter, and his push to complete *A Connecticut Yankee* (*N&J3* 383, n. 280). However, he planned to answer Arnold in a full-scale book; he piled up notes; he started a half-dozen essays, totaling some one hundred manuscript pages; and he even concocted a title for his imagined volume: "English Criticism on America. Letters to an English Friend" (*N&J3* 391; Baetzhold, "Matthew Arnold"). (He thus unwittingly considered the epistolary mode Arnold himself had used in *Friendship's Garland.*) What agitated Twain so?[12]

The lecture "Numbers" could not have bothered him much, for in it Arnold undertakes to assess "the prospects of society in the United States" by analyzing the majority. He criticizes the majority for its want of principle, inconsistent morality, and faulty judgment—all criticisms Twain could endorse. Despite his severe reservations, Arnold insists that the majority in society must continue to act for itself since "the exercise of power by the people tends to educate the people." Arnold's solution to the problem of an unreliable majority would also have met with Twain's approval. Arnold argues that "States are saved by their righteous remnant"—that is, those who "love righteousness" and are "convinced of the unprofitableness of iniquity," provided that their numbers—hence Arnold's title—increase (10:143–51). Twain himself expressed misgivings about the majority throughout the 1870s and 1880s, and in his 1875 sketch of a utopia, "The Curious Republic of Gondour," he advanced his own remedy. In all seriousness (he published the sketch anonymously to insure that it would be taken seriously), he argues that the franchise should be expanded by giving additional votes to those who own property and those who are highly educated (*MTC1* 634–38). While Arnold dismisses control by people of "property and intelligence" (10:145), Twain seeks to empower exactly these elite. Both leave democracy in place of course, but Twain alters it profoundly—and, one might add, conservatively—by changing the constitutional structure to give more votes to what he conceives of as "the best men" (neither sage urges that the franchise be extended to women). To be sure, Twain assumes that the best men, identified by their property and education, will be ethical—the equivalent of Arnold's righteous remnant, but his notion is notably less democratic than Arnold's.[13] While their solutions differ, both sages share the conviction that, as Arnold puts it, "the majority is and must be in general unsound" (10:162).

On the question of General Grant, the disagreements between the two are clear, and this time Twain responded directly to Arnold. Arnold's decision to review Grant's *Memoirs* was itself somewhat odd since military history was decidedly out of his normal field of interest (though he was a lifelong admirer of the Duke of Wellington). When he first arrived in America, Arnold met Grant at a reception hosted by Andrew Carnegie, and Grant attended Arnold's inaugural lecture, only to leave, as many in the audience did, when he could not hear Arnold. "Well, wife, we have paid to see the British lion," he said, "but we cannot hear him roar, so we had better go home" (qtd. in Honan 398). Nevertheless, Grant was gracious about the failure and went out of his way to congratulate the *New York Tribune* on its report of the lecture (for Arnold's tour and the American response to it, see Raleigh). Arnold's motive in reviewing Grant's book seems likewise prompted by kindness. When first asked to contribute an article to *Murray's Magazine,* he replied: "I think I shall do Genl. Grant's Memoirs. . . . The Americans will like it, the book has hardly been noticed in England, and Grant is shown by this book to be one of the most solid men they have had; I prefer him to Lincoln; except Franklin, I hardly know anyone so *selbst-standig,* so broad and strong-sighted, as well as firm-charactered, that they have had" (qtd. in II :429).

The review itself, though offering some criticisms of Grant—he is "dull and silent" and not "interesting"—creates an unmistakably positive portrait. The first half of Arnold's two-part essay is largely devoted to recounting Grant's life up to the time of the war; the second provides information and anecdotes about his role in the war. Each half lauds Grant: he is celebrated as "a man of sterling good-sense as well as of the firmest resolution; a man, withal, humane, simple, modest," a man who was able "to see straight and to see clear"; and he is compared favorably to the Duke of Wellington as a man "free from show, parade, and pomposity; sensible and sagacious; scanning closely the situation, seeing things as they actually were, then making up his mind as to the right thing to be done under the circumstance, and doing it; never flurried, never vacillating . . . resolutely and tenaciously persevering." All this praise of the man is tempered somewhat by objections to the style of the *Memoirs.* Arnold says Grant's grammar is "all astray in its use of *will* and *shall, should* and *would,*" and his language marred by offensive colloquialisms; it is, Arnold observes, "an English without charm and without high breeding." Yet even on the point of writing, Arnold concedes much: "I found a language straightforward, nervous, firm, possessing in general the high merit of saying clearly in the fewest possible words what had to be said, and saying it, frequently, with shrewd and unexpected turns of expression" (II:145–58). Given the encomiums to Grant's character and even the eventual praise of his prose, it is hard to find the review objectionable.

But Twain did object. He was, as his biographers have pointed out, deeply invested, both financially and emotionally, in the *Memoirs*. He knew Grant personally and admired him greatly. He had secured the publication of the *Memoirs* for his own publishing firm, Charles L. Webster and Company, and he had promised Grant handsome profits from subscription publishing—a promise he eventually met, paying Grant's heirs over $400,000 (and earning about half that for his own firm). Sales were spurred on by incessant marketing, by patriotic admiration for the general who finally won the war, and by sympathy for Grant, who raced against death from throat cancer to complete his story. Newspapers reported simultaneously on his health and his progress in writing. Twain's involvement with Grant ran deeper than money, however. Kaplan has suggested that their relationship was multilayered: rebel son to powerful father, preening antihero to modest hero, aggressive humorist to vulnerable victim (Kaplan, *Mr. Clemens and MT* 275; Daniel Aaron feels that Twain acquired "derived honor" from his association with Grant [139]). Whatever the complexity of Twain's relationship with Grant, in this case, faced with Arnold's mild criticisms, Twain rose up to defend an American hero, a Goliath pelted by a lesser David.

He made his counterattack in a speech delivered in April 1887, two months after Arnold's essay first appeared in England, one month after it was republished in Boston. Guilefully, Twain selected an audience sure to respond favorably to what he said—the members of the Army and Navy Club of Connecticut. Furthermore, the occasion was nothing less than a banquet to commemorate Grant on his birthday. Twain began graciously, "Lately a great and honored author, Matthew Arnold, has been finding fault with General Grant's English." However, he immediately follows his tribute with the bold assertion that "examples of imperfect English" are more frequent per page in Arnold's critique than in Grant's *Memoirs*. Citing *Modern English Literature: Its Blemishes and Defects*, he tallies no fewer than thirty English and American authors, including Shakespeare, Milton, and Dr. Johnson, whose works contain "examples of bad grammar and slovenly English." Then he avers that Arnold's essay itself contains "a couple of grammatical crimes and more than several examples of very crude and slovenly English." To make his point, he quotes this passage from Arnold's review: "Meade suggested to Grant that he might wish to have immediately under him, Sherman, who had been serving with Grant in the West. *He* begged *him* not to hesitate if *he* thought it for the good of the service. Grant assured *him* that *he* had no thought of moving *him*, and in *his* memoirs, after relating what had passed, *he* adds, etc."[14] With devastating humor, Twain says: "To read that passage a couple of times would make a man dizzy; to read it four times would make him drunk."

More gently, he suggests that Arnold was not "quite wise," for he "well knew" that "the man never lived whose English was flawless." Perhaps the most telling turn in his rebuttal of Arnold is his suggestion that questions of grammar are trivial given Grant's profession and his monumental achievements. Twice he makes the point in vivid metaphors: "If you should climb the mighty Matterhorn to look out over the kingdoms of the earth, it might be a pleasant incident to find strawberries up there. But, great Scott! you don't climb the Matterhorn for strawberries!" And again: "There is that about the sun which makes us forget his spots; and when we think of General Grant our pulses quicken and his grammar vanishes."

Twain insists that the style of Grant's *Memoirs* is "flawless," and he observes that "great books are weighed and measured by their style and matter, not by the trimmings and shadings of their grammar." He clinches his case for Grant by quoting four memorable—indeed, he believes, indelible—phrases of Grant's that have "an art surpassing the art of the schools": "Unconditional and immediate surrender!"; "I propose to move immediately upon your works!"; "I propose to fight it out on this line if it takes all summer!"; and, finally, "Let us have peace" (*MTSpk* 225–27). Interestingly, Twain likes best (three of his four examples are of this kind) utterances of Grant's that ring with power, determination, and command—the same sort of preemptory certitude that Twain himself exerts in his writings as sage.

The final and most significant disagreements between Twain and Arnold all turned on the question of civilization in America. Arnold's three essays, "A Word about America," "A Word More about America," and "Civilization in the United States," probe the nature of American civilization and find it wanting in crucial ways. Twain's replies hammer back at Arnold's arguments. There is also a personal dimension to their disagreements, however, for in his first essay Arnold singles Twain out by name as a sign of what is wrong in America, and, in his last, he attacks American humorists in general. Relying curiously on an unspecified French critic (he is using the observations of André Theurist), Arnold asserts in "A Word about America" that the "Quinionian humour of Mr. Mark Twain" appeals to the "Philistine of the more gay and light type." (Quinion was a minor comic character in *David Copperfield.*) Arnold had not even read Twain at the time, but he does not hesitate to say that he wants "to deliver" America (as well as England) from Quinion (10:14–15). When he attacks American humorists in "Civilization in the United States," Arnold at least draws on the firsthand experience of his 1883–84 lecture tour in America. His complaint is that the American humorists as well as the newspapers "kill" the "discipline of respect" and the "feeling for what is elevated." He calls America's "addiction to the 'funny man'" a "national misfortune" (11:361).

Twain replied forcibly. In June 1888 he accepted his honorary degree from Yale on behalf of "the guild of American 'funny men'" lately "rebuked" by Matthew Arnold. "A friendly word," he wrote to Yale's president, "was needed in our defense, & you have said it, & it is sufficient." He then defended the "trade" of the humorist as having "one serious purpose, one aim, one specialty": "the deriding of shams, the exposure of pretentious falsities, the laughing of stupid superstitions out of existence." "Whoso is by instinct engaged in this sort of warfare," he added, "is the natural enemy of royalties, nobilities, privileges & all kindred swindles" and is "the natural friend of human rights & human liberties."[15] Twain thus not only countered Arnold's complaints by giving humorists (including, by implication, himself) the salutary function of destroying the spurious, but he also took the attack onto Arnold's home ground where royalty, nobility, and privilege (including, by implication, Arnold's own) reigned.

Arnold's three essays on America represent both his mode of thought and his means of presentation as sage. Taken together, they create a coherent, largely critical assessment of civilization in the United States. To begin with, he considers the very formation of the United States to have been shaped by the historical moment in which it occurred—a period he calls, using one of his standard historical categories, "an epoch of expansion." Coming into existence in this "modern age," America is unlike the older European countries from which it derives. Its egalitarian spirit, democratic institutions, and general prosperity all give it a distinct order, enabling it to solve "the political problem" and "the social problem" ("A Word More" 10:200, 198). Arnold imagines the United States to be free from class distinctions, to have a relatively homogeneous population, and to suffer few divisions, certainly no deep ones, between the rich and the poor ("Civilization" 11:351). In the first segment of what would become his three-part analysis, Arnold launches his argument in an ingenious way. Keying off a Boston newspaper article ("Novelists and Critics of American Manners," *Boston Daily Advertiser*, 18 November 1879, p. 2, col. 2) and a review in the *Atlantic Monthly* (vol. 44, November 1879, 675–78), he first creates a kind of dialogue between the two essays on the general topic of American manners—the Boston article usually praising them, the *Atlantic* one being more critical—and then turns the terms of their discussion—"good taste, good manners, good education," the "best books," the "best music," "mutual courtesy"—into his own discourse of civilization ("A Word" 10:1–5). Once he has effected this conversion, his arguments flow along familiar lines.

The human problem in America is, he asserts, the problem of creating a true civilization. He is at pains to point out what a true civilization is not: it is not "comforts and conveniences"; it is not the "greatest happiness of the greatest number"; it is not "equality"; it is not "industry, commerce, and wealth"; it is not numerous "churches and schools, libraries and newspapers." True civilization is, instead, "the humanization of man in society" ("Civilization" 11:355–57, 352). And the key to this is, as always for Arnold, culture, the study of "perfection," the pursuit of "sweetness and light," an absorption in "the best that has been thought and written." He longs to find in America "lovers of the humane life, lovers of perfection," and "centres of sweetness and light," but feels that such lovers, such centers, are "not yet numerous enough" ("A Word" 10:5–6, 7).

To this indictment he adds in "Civilization in the United States" a new, wholly compatible element: human nature "demands" of a civilization that it be *"interesting,"* and the sources of the interesting are, he argues, "distinction and beauty": that "which is elevated, and that which is beautiful." With what one might call his vise of the interesting firmly in place, Arnold twists its two jaws, distinction and beauty, tightly against American life. Beauty is nowhere to be found—not in American landscapes, or cityscapes, not in its houses and buildings, not in its place names (Arnold mockingly provides a long list and calls them all "hideous"), and not in its "arts, and in literature." Nor can distinction be found because of the "glorification of the 'average man,'" because of the "addiction to the 'funny man,'" and because of the "sensation-mongering" newspapers. Arnold concludes that "a great void exists in the civilization over there: a want of what is elevated and beautiful, of what is interesting," and with one of those poetic figures so effective in his writing because so rare, he observes that the person who seeks to fill that void "will feel the sky over his head to be of brass and iron." Perhaps hoping to palliate the sting of his criticisms of America, Arnold points in closing toward the English as well as Americans: "That the common and ignoble is human nature's enemy, that, of true human nature, distinction and beauty are needs, that a civilization is insufficient where these needs are not satisfied, faulty where they are thwarted, is an instruction of which we, as well as the Americans, may greatly require to take fast hold, and not to let go" ("Civilization" II:357–61, 368).

Twain took fast hold of Arnold's critique of civilization in America, and he did not let go for over six years. His most direct, coherent, complete rebuttal was a speech he gave in Boston, "On Foreign Critics," in April 1890, over two years after Arnold's death. Like Arnold he asks, "What is a 'real' civilization?" His first playful, comic reply is, "Nobody can answer that conundrum." He undertakes instead to define what civilization is not: "Let us say, then, in broad terms, that any system which has in it any one of these things, to wit, human slavery, despotic government, inequality, numerous and brutal punishments for crimes, superstition almost universal, ignorance almost universal, and dirt and poverty almost universal— is not a real civilization, and any system which has none of them, is." Having thus explained what civilization isn't, he reviews the "partial civilizations" of Europe, past and present, suggesting that they owe their existence to the seeds of "liberty" and "intelligence" planted by the American Revolution. He then repeats some of Arnold's concessions about America: "Mr. Arnold granted that our whole people . . . have liberty, equality, plenty to eat, plenty to wear, comfortable shelter, high pay, abundance of churches, newspapers, libraries, charities, and a good education for everybody's child for nothing." Twain is pointedly claiming as crucial ingredients of civilization precisely those things that Arnold said could not be taken as its measure. He concludes sarcastically, "Yes, it is conceded that we furnish the greatest good to the greatest number; and so all we lack is a civilization." Most interestingly, he echoes—without acknowledging it—Arnold's own definition of civilization, "the humanization of man in society," but significantly alters it to "the humanizing of a people, not a class." He thus lays the groundwork for his most fundamental criticism of Arnold, his sense of the central flaw in Arnold's thinking: Arnold's "civilization" seems to Twain "to be restricted, by its narrow lines and difficult requirements, to a class—the top class—as in tropical countries snow is restricted to the mountain summits." Building on his metaphor, Twain adds that Arnold's civilization is, like snow itself, "peculiarly hard, and glittering, and bloodless, and unattainable," while America's civilization is, like circulating blood, one that "nourishes and refreshes" the whole body, "delivering its rich streams of life and health impartially to the imperial brain and the meanest extremity" (*MTC1* 942–44).

Twain's rebuttal is a curious performance, for while he uses, with a crucial modification, Arnold's own definition of civilization, he ignores it. Overlooking "the humanizing of a people," he extols precisely those elements of society that Arnold sets aside. It is revealing that to refute Arnold, he suspends his characteristic emphasis on civilization as morality and celebrates instead material conditions, democratic equality, and human liberty. Seizing on the very real tension in Arnold's thought between individual perfection and the collective good, Twain brings to bear on Arnold's discussion of civilization, cautiously to be sure, the idea that it is undemocratic because it is available only to the upper class. His speech is less a rebuttal that proves Arnold wrong by argument and evidence than a flat-out contradiction that refutes through contrary definition.

Twain's final, extended public attack on Arnold is once again a speech, but this one is fictional. In his 1892 novel, *The American Claimant*, he creates a scene in which the English Lord Berkeley visits an American Mechanics' Club, where he hears a speaker read an essay about the American press, using as his point of departure two quotations from Arnold's "Civilization in the United States," the first of which celebrates "reverence," the second of which decries American newspapers for destroying "the discipline of respect." The speaker's position is summarized by Twain's narrator: "The essayist thought that Mr. Arnold, with his trained eye and intelligent observation, ought to have perceived that the very quality which he so regretfully missed from our press—respectfulness, reverence—was exactly the thing which would make our press useless to us if it had it—rob it of the very thing that differentiates it from all other journalism in the world and makes it distinctly and preciously American, its frank and cheerful irreverence being by all odds the most valuable of all its qualities." In the words of Twain's fictive speaker, "a discriminating irreverence is the creator and protector of human liberty" as it derides shams, exposes injustice, and promotes equality, while undue reverence is the "steadfast protector of all forms of human slavery, bodily and mental." Twain's English lord is persuaded, indeed converted (what right, he now wonders, has Arnold to say what irreverence is—and who and what are entitled to reverence). He stays at the meeting long enough to hear several more papers read, including a final one that sets forth in numerical detail America's material prosperity. Twain's visiting lord marvels to himself: "What a civilization it is, and what prodigious results these are! and brought about almost wholly by common men, not some Oxford-trained aristocrats" (*American Claimant* 79–85).

Arnold, the Oxford-trained sage, had of course died some four years before *The American Claimant* was published. Twain was haunted by a ghost, jousting with a dead man. Nevertheless, his thrust at Arnold does reveal one of the bedrocks of his thinking as sage: those "common men" he praises as creating America's civilization. Although he had his share (perhaps at times more than his share) of racism, sexism, and elitism—not to mention jingoism—Twain also had, especially in his later performances as sage, a deep—and honest—concern for common people. Much of his commentary as sage is fired by his passion for humanity at large (always contrary, he at the same time liked to denounce "the damned human race"). Just as his morality is highly generalized, so too is his concern for people. Even when they are Boers or Cubans or South Africans or Chinese or Russians or Filipinos or Congolese, he tends to think of them not as a specific people but as humankind in general. Whether addressing local politics or international affairs, he takes a broad view; he thinks of the common lot, and the common nature, of humankind. (This way of thinking finds its philosophical counterpart in his late preoccupation with cosmology and its fictive complement in his imaginings of other worlds—comets hurtling through space toward heaven or vast new realms contained in a water drop or a microbe.) Without slipping into sentimentality, we can add to this bedrock conception of humanity at large his hatred of all forms of oppression, political, racial, economic, and, eventually, even those that are gender-driven. And the counterpoint to his hatred of oppression, of course, is his celebration of freedom. He spoke out on an astonishing number of issues, large ones, small ones, international ones, backyard ones,[16] but his approach to them flowed along familiar channels of thought.

His contretemps with Arnold (and his ghost) is just one extended moment in his work as sage, a moment in which he turns the looking glass away from society toward a single man. What strikes one most, perhaps, is Twain's sheer confidence. He dares to take on England's most eminent man of letters, its preeminent sage. As I've suggested, Twain's assurance springs in large measure from his embrace of what he takes to be incontestable, universal, moral principles. It battens also on the many books he has published, the recognition he has received, the fame he has acquired. And in the case of Arnold, it is further strengthened by patriotism and Anglophobia (for his growing Anglophobia, see Baetzhold, chapter 6). Surely in some deep cell of his being it is also nurtured by pride of birth, humble birth that can show itself the equal of a more privileged one.

Twain was most scurrilous about Arnold in his private notebooks. There, he railed: "Matthew Arnold's civilization is *superficial polish*"; "Yours is the civilization of slave-making ants"; "If you cross a king with a prostitute the resulting mongrel—perfectly satisfies the Eng idea of 'nobility'"; "A monarchy is a perpetual piracy"; "That worm-eaten & dilapidated social structure in England which Mr. Arnold regarded as a 'civilization'" (*N&J3* 383, 398, 400, 401, 406). Yet even as he raged so freely, he could pause, take stock, reconsider. In the very midst of his angry jottings against Arnold, he effected nothing less than a Burkean return upon himself. Writing to Robert Louis Stevenson in April 1888, he denounced not Arnold but the "heedless" American press for distorting "Poor Matthew Arnold," for misunderstanding his comments on civilization in America. He even praised Arnold for his "appreciative and valuable compliments" about America and for his "kind interest."[17] Twain's remarks to Stevenson, however brief, however fleeting, constitute a return upon himself that Arnold himself, a lifelong admirer of Burke's reversal, could well have appreciated, even if Twain's return was followed—as in fact it was—by yet another return to rancor.

# Mark Twain & Robert Louis Stevenson

*I know that in genuine* manliness *they [pilots] assay away above the multitude.*

MARK TWAIN, 1866

In April 1888 Mark Twain jotted down the following entry in his personal notebook: "Robert Louis Stevenson. Apl 19 to 26<sup>th</sup> St. Stephen's Hotel East 11th" (*N&J3* 301). He made his note in response to a cordial letter he had received from Stevenson a week earlier. Stevenson, who had never met Twain or even corresponded with him up to this time, began his letter to him arrestingly: "My dear Mark Twain, I should have written a great while ago to the author of *Huckleberry Finn*—a book which I have read four times, and am quite ready to begin again tomorrow." He went on to tell Twain that some years earlier, when he was having his portrait painted at Bournemouth by a "very refined" painter who was "privately French," he had insisted "that *Huckleberry Finn* was to be read aloud at the sittings." The painter, Stevenson reported, *"wilted,"* but the reading went on, and, Stevenson slyly concluded, "I believe it did him good." He also told Twain that when his father read *Roughing It* he confessed, "I was positively frightened; it cannot be safe for a man of my time of life to laugh so much." Having thus surrounded Twain with praise for his work, Stevenson expressed his desire to meet him in New York, if it was convenient for Twain—"I should be rejoiced to see you"—or if that would not be easy, he offered to "push as far as Hartford just to behold Huckleberry's grandfather." Huck's father, he observed, "is in the tale, and we know him already, thank you!" (*Letters of RLS* 6:161–62).

Stevenson's enthusiasm for Twain's writings was matched by Twain's for Stevenson's. By the time of this correspondence, Twain already owned *Travels with a Donkey in the Cevennes, Treasure Island, Prince Otto: A Romance, The Strange Story of Doctor Jekyll and Mr. Hyde*, and *Kidnapped*. (He would in time buy four more of Stevenson's works.) Twain responded excitedly to Stevenson's overture, inviting him to Hartford but also expressing his willingness to travel to New York to "see you & thank you for writing Kidnapped and Treasure Island . . . Those two great books!"[1]

As Twain recalled in his autobiography, the two met in New York and spent an afternoon on a bench in Washington Square. Stevenson's "business" there, Twain said, was "to absorb the sunshine." Like so many of Stevenson's friends and admirers, Twain was struck by his appearance and touched by the pathos of his condition. He created this memorable vignette: "He was most scantily furnished with flesh, his clothes seemed to fall into hollows as if there might be nothing inside but the frame for a sculptor's statue. His long face and lank hair and dark complexion and musing and melancholy expression seemed to fit these details justly and harmoniously, and the altogether of it seemed especially planned to gather the rags of your observation and focalize them upon Stevenson's special distinction and commanding feature, his splendid eyes. They burned with a smoldering rich fire under the penthouse of his brows and they made him beautiful" (*MTA* 288).

Their talk was literary, and Twain for his part trotted out two of his pet ideas: that Bret Harte was "a thin but pleasant talker . . . never brilliant" (a much milder criticism than his usual one of Harte), and that Thomas Bailey Aldrich was "always witty, always brilliant"—a "fire opal set round with rose diamonds." He assured Stevenson again and again that Aldrich was "always brilliant," that he would "always be brilliant"—he "couldn't help it"—that he would "be brilliant in hell," and he playfully added, "you will see." Stevenson replied, "I hope not," and then having some fun of his own, he asked, "Can you name the American author whose fame and acceptance stretch widest and furthest in the States?" When Twain hesitated, too "modest" to give his real answer, Stevenson said, "Save your delicacy for another time—you are not the one." His candidate was an author—unknown to either of them—named Davis (first name forgotten) whose works filled the shelves of a bookshop in Albany. Stevenson and Twain, basking in the sun, then played with the idea of the famous-but-unknown and coined to their joint amusement the definitive term "submerged renown" (*MTA* 289). Twain's recollections end on this note, but Stevenson was later to recall their time with the same warm affection that colored Twain's remembrance. He wrote to Twain of "that very pleasant afternoon we spent together in Washington Square among the nursemaids like a couple of characters out of a story by Henry James" (qtd. in *N&J3* 301).

Rarely, one imagines, has a first meeting between two famous authors been so cordial. Clearly the two enjoyed themselves, enjoyed each other, enjoyed chatting about other writers, enjoyed joking about fame, fleeting and lasting, acknowledged and covert. Certainly by 1888 both Stevenson and Twain had achieved a wide readership, a popularity that was anything but "submerged renown." Stevenson's evocation of their time together on that bench in Washington Square is especially suggestive, for he places them at leisure in a female world—"among the nursemaids"—and likens them to characters from the refined social fictions of James. What makes the description so striking is its incongruity. For while both Stevenson and Twain were in their own persons quite proper gentlemen (at least by this time in their lives, despite earlier bohemian antics), their fictions, for the most part, treat worlds—and characters—remote from the polite sphere of domestic tranquility conjured up by nursemaids, babies, and sophisticated Jamesian ladies and gentlemen. Their imaginations were fired by quite different things: by dreams of adventure away from hearth and home into exotic, liminal worlds. The fictions created from such fantasies—*Tom Sawyer, Treasure Island, Huckleberry Finn*, and *Kidnapped*—constitute the core of their greatness.

Before their imaginations moved their fictive heroes away from home into realms of adventure, Twain and Stevenson both undertook real-life adventures of their own—they traveled. Rather like Thoreau, who bragged of having traveled much in Concord, Stevenson (1850–1894) traveled more than a little in his beloved Scotland, especially in his home city of Edin-burgh. (The result of his traveling much at home was *Edinburgh: Pic-turesque Notes.*) For his health's sake, he went twice to the French Med-iterranean, first to Menton, then Campagne Defli, and twice to Davos in Switzerland, as his doctors' recommendations vacillated between warm and cold climates. For his health, he also wintered in Saranac, New York. But he traveled to other places as well, and for more than his health. Both Stevenson and Twain were seized by what Twain called in an early let-ter to his friend Dan De Quille (otherwise known as William Wright) the "Gypsy" (*L1* 304); both had, especially in their early years, the impulse to be off from where they were to someplace else. Waiting for his first voy-age to Europe to get under way in 1867, Twain told his family, "All I do know or feel, is, that I am wild with impatience to move—move—Move!" (*L2* 49–50). And in *Roughing It* he confessed, "The vagabond instinct was strong upon me" (*RI* 421). No less than Twain, Stevenson suffered from the "Gypsy" and wanted to "move—move—Move." With his characteris-tically elegant nonchalance he explained his inclinations: "For my part, I travel not to go anywhere, but to go. I travel for travel's sake. The great affair is to move."[2]

And move they both did. Stevenson, adventuring for both excitement and literary material, undertook two taxing excursions—the first in 1876 into northeastern France, traveling by canoe from Antwerp to Pontoise, which gave him the experience he turned into *An Inland Voyage;* the sec-ond in 1878 into the Cévennes, which enabled him to write *Travels with a Donkey in the Cevennes.* These were highly personal trips—outings off on his own (though in the first case, he canoed with Walter Simpson). In 1880, however, he undertook a curious journey of love, traveling second cabin from England to America in a ship full of emigrants, then crossing the United States to California in a crowded emigrant train, to be with his former lover and future wife, Fanny Osbourne. These journeys, po-litely shorn of their true motive, he shaped into two essays, "The Amateur Emigrant" and "Across the Plains" (both were bowdlerized when they appeared in the Edinburgh edition of his works).[3]

Twain's early travels were somewhat different. Setting aside his youth-ful venture (a kind of running away from home) to New York and Phila-delphia when he was seventeen, and his up-and-down-river professional voyages as first a cub and then a licensed Mississippi riverboat pilot from

1858–61, his first real travel adventure was to the Nevada Territory in 1861, and from there, off and on, to California. Finally, after two years of cross-mountain stagecoaching, he sailed to the Sandwich Islands in 1866. And in 1867 he joined the first organized pleasure excursion from America to the Old World, shipping on the *Quaker City* to Europe and the Holy Land. Like Stevenson in his canoe and with his donkey, Twain turned his earliest travels into literature—or journalism—creating first sketches, then a series of letters from the Sandwich Islands, then his best-selling *The Innocents Abroad,* and finally, *Roughing It.*

The impulse that drove each to travel was not solely restlessness or even the need for literary material; both responded to what Stevenson described as "the great affair"—"to move; to feel the needs and hitches of our life more nearly; to come down off this feather-bed of civilization, and find the globe granite underfoot and strewn with cutting flints" (*TWD* 194). To be sure, Twain's excursion to Europe and the Holy Land was an institutional one, an organized pleasure excursion unlike Stevenson's boating and walking trips, but, like Stevenson, he had times in the wild—in the Nevada Territory, camping at the then unsettled Lake Tahoe, for instance, or in the Sandwich Islands, climbing in the Kilauea volcano district, or riding a horse through the Waipio valley. He, too, savored (though one feels to a lesser degree) the thrill of adventure into the little known. "I have been after an adventure," Stevenson proclaimed, "all my life [he was just twenty-eight at the time], a pure dispassionate adventure, such as befell early and heroic voyagers." He longed, he said, to find himself "by morning in a random woodside nook . . . not knowing north from south, as strange to my surroundings as the first man upon the earth, an inland castaway" (*TWD* 189). Here Stevenson characteristically overstates the lure of travel that gripped both writers. Perhaps the bedrock of that appeal is disclosed, however, by an unlikely conjunction of Matthew Arnold, Stevenson, and Twain.

Traveling in the Cévennes, Stevenson visited the Trappist monastery of Our Lady of the Sorrows, and in his book about the journey he devotes three chapters to his time there, introducing the first with these lines from Arnold's "Stanzas from the Grande Chartreuse": "I behold / The House, the Brotherhood austere / —And what am I, that I am here?" Arnold's famous answer is that, "Wandering between two worlds, one dead, / The other powerless to be born," he waits on earth "forlorn." Stevenson responds quite differently in the face of the cloistered life devoted to God. Acknowledging no intellectual doubt, he dismisses the monks as "the dead in life" and revels in the fact that he is "free to wander, free to hope, and free to love" (*TWD* 196, 210). Some seventeen years later, recording his visit to a Trappist monastery in South Africa during his following-the-equator lecture tour, Twain considered citing Stevenson's response to Our Lady of the Sorrows to bolster his own feelings (Baetzhold, *MT and John Bull* 205). In the final version of his encounter, he did not in fact use Stevenson, but his sense of the monastery is exactly like Stevenson's. He sees life there as "an extinction of the man" and creates a page-long litany of the things humanity "likes," things that constitute life itself, all of which are "absent from that place" (*FE* 650–51). Travel, for Twain as well as for Stevenson, revitalized the sense of life, for as Stevenson explained in a letter to his friend Charles Baxter, "If we didn't travel now and then, we would forget what the feeling of life is" (*Selected Letters of RLS* 19).

The more or less youthful travels of Stevenson and Twain, driven by the inveterate impulse to move as well as the need to turn wayfaring into literary capital, were followed by other—notably different—ventures. After the 1867 Quaker City excursion from which Twain created *The Inno-cents Abroad*, he later toured quite comfortably in Europe, principally in Germany and Italy in 1878–79 to create his ironically entitled *A Tramp Abroad*, and then later still, in 1895, he went to lecture in Australia, New Zealand, India, and South Africa, fashioning from this lecture tour *Follow-ing the Equator*. These two excursions were not solo adventures into un-known regions but curiously familial journeys—the first undertaken with his wife, Livy; their two daughters, Susy and Clara; Livy's friend Clara Spaulding; a nursemaid, Rosina Hay; a valet; and a baggage agent; the second, again with his wife and this time only one daughter, Clara, and his booking agent. Very much like Twain's, Stevenson's later voyaging was a domestic affair. Paradoxically, his most famous—and exotic—travel, his voyage in 1888 from San Francisco on the chartered schooner *Casco* first to the Marquesas, then to Tahiti, and finally to Honolulu, was a trip *en famille*. He sailed not as the free spirit in a canoe in France or as the blithe one behind a donkey in the Cévennes but as a married man, taking with him his wife, Fanny, and his stepson, Lloyd, along with a maid, Valentine Roch, and, as a dutiful son, accompanied by his widowed mother. Thus Twain and Stevenson shifted from adventurous solo travelers to domestic ones, seeking not the thrills of individual encounter but the satisfaction of movement with an entourage. While each initially sought to escape what Stevenson called the "Bastille of civilization" (*TWD* 224), both finally traveled with the microcosm of Victorian civilization itself alongside—the family (enlarged by servants)—not so much to escape or to discover as to arrive.

When Stevenson and Twain wrote their famous boy adventures, they recreated for themselves, at some unfathomable level of desire, their early travel adventures (but not, I would argue, their later domestic ones). In their four books of adventure they return to a boyhood past to recuperate some of the psychic and emotional experience of their early travel, but they do so in a paradoxical way. In an illuminating essay on childhood in Victorian literature, Roger B. Salomon locates a profoundly divided impulse in writers who turn to the past. He describes a conflict between the desire to recreate a lost past and the need to acknowledge the lostness, the inaccessibility, of that past. Writers who return to the past in the grip of these two contraries write, on the one hand, out of the "nostalgic sense," that is, "the need to remember that which we know we can no longer have"; and, on the other hand, they write with "nostalgic irony," that is, the sense of "the absurdity of what we find most emotionally compelling" ("MT and Victorian Nostalgia" 75, 76). In their boy adventure fantasies, it seems to me that both Stevenson and Twain write out of exactly this double vision. It creates, in the case of Stevenson, both his sympathetic identification and his cool, detached tone, and in the case of Twain, both his affectionate representation and his ever-present, estranging humor.

If on the personal level the adventure fictions of Stevenson and Twain recuperate, with nostalgia and irony, some of their experience of travel, on the cultural level these fictions do something quite different.

The Anglo-American Victorian culture was the most domestic in Western history; it was virtually defined by the rise and solidification of the nuclear family.[4] Earlier family formations, especially those in rural, agricultural economies, tended to be extended ones, often multigenerational, sometimes enlarged by work associations as well as by blood ties and kinship. However, the steady increase in urbanization, industrialization, and commerce in the Victorian period not only reduced the need for the extended family as an economic unit but also precipitated the enclosure of the family within itself. The home became the center of family life, and family life became a refuge from the harsh, competitive, commercial world. Varieties of religious piety, from traditional to evangelical, also enshrined the home as the sanctuary of morality; it became for many the bulwark of the true and the good against the shifting norms, quixotic ethics, and profit-driven practices of the world at large.

For the Victorian woman, domestic life was both empowering and confining, empowering insofar as it made her the central actor in the formative moral sphere, confining insofar as it denied her access to and significant influence in any realms beyond the home. As recent social history has made amply clear, the doctrine of two spheres—the domestic for the female, the commercial and political for the male—confined the woman economically and socially, while the Cult of True Womanhood, with its insistence on piety, purity, submissiveness, and domesticity, imposed additional moral constraints. The male in this paradigm seems to have it both ways: power in the public sphere, solace in the private. But even as a refuge of serenity, love, and security, the home could—and did—seem to many Victorian men as constricting as it was nurturing. Hence the attraction for men, as well as boys, of adventure fiction: it provided, imaginatively at least, an escape from snug domesticity, with its predictable comforts, its repetitive customs, its sure respectability, its reliable morals, its restricted agency, and its conventional pieties—in short, its dullness. When Twain loosed Tom Sawyer in St. Petersburg and sent Huck Finn downriver, when Stevenson rushed Jim Hawkins off toward Treasure Island and sent David Balfour into the highland moors, they slipped the traces of domesticity, or to put it even more strongly, they unfettered themselves and their readers from the shackles of home and family.

The significance of adventure fiction runs even deeper, however. In "A Humble Remonstrance," his reply to Henry James's "The Art of Fiction," Stevenson defines the "novel of adventure" (the first of three main classes of novel, along with the "novel of character" and the "dramatic novel"). He suggests that adventure appeals "to certain almost sensual and quite illogical tendencies in man," and defends it, indeed celebrates it, as the expression of "desire"—of "those things" that the writer has "wished to do," which constitute for writer and reader alike the satisfaction of "dream" ("A Humble Remonstrance" 196–97). Elsewhere Stevenson maintains, with a certitude bordering on dogmatism, that "the great creative writer shows us the realization and apotheosis of the day-dreams of common men" ("A Gossip on Romance" 175).

Always reticent about his art, about his work in the guild of writers, Twain only jokes about adventure. In his humorously exaggerated opening to *Roughing It*, for instance, he itemizes the desires, the boyish dreams, of his "young and innocent" narrator. The narrator envies his brother's chance, heading west, to "see buffaloes and Indians, and prairie dogs, and antelopes, and have all kinds of adventures, and maybe get hanged or scalped, and have ever such a fine time, and write home and tell us all about it, and be a hero" (*RI* 1–2). Impersonating a romantic naïf here, Twain nonetheless ticks off, with the obvious exception of getting "hanged or scalped," a few of the things that he himself had experienced in his early western days. And Twain did write home about it all in fevered, self-vaunting letters to his mother, sister, and sister-in-law (see *L1*). His comic narrator concludes, "What I suffered in contemplating his [his brother's] happiness, pen cannot describe" (*RI* 2). Twain describes such imagined happiness (and often its concomitant unhappiness) not only in *Roughing It* but also in *Tom Sawyer* and *Huckleberry Finn*.

Despite the announcement of Twain's titles—*The Adventures of Tom Sawyer* and *Adventures of Huckleberry Finn*—there has been little critical attention to Twain's two books as works within the genre of adventure (an exception is Spengemann). And while critics repeatedly mention Stevenson's fictions as boy adventures, they nonetheless tend to overlook the adventure in them in the pursuit of other issues (an exception is Kiely). Stevenson and Twain all but invited this relative neglect, as both were inclined to dismiss the thrilling aspects of their novels. Stevenson sometimes spoke of adventure as "Tushery" (*Letters of RLS* 4:129), while Twain not only joked about it, as we've seen, but also denigrated it as "perishable dream-stuff" (*MTLP* 140).[5] Readers and critics alike, from their time to ours, have patronized adventure fictions precisely because of what they are: for kids and full of adventure. To be sure, both *Treasure Island* and *Huckleberry Finn* have become "classics," but such status has been achieved in each case not because of the adventure but in spite of it. No one has argued that *Huck Finn* is important because it is chock-full of thrilling adventures, or that *Treasure Island* is significant because it deals with a boy, some pirates, and a buried treasure.

If one were to construct even a rudimentary poetics of adventure, one would compile a curious list of aesthetic qualities. Such a taxonomy would include the rendering of danger, suspense, fear, surprise, uncertainty, hazard, thrill, risk, peril, and conflict, to name only an obvious few. These traits provide the pleasure of adventure fiction—they do not seem to signal high art but, rather, something more like sensational journalism. On the scale of human emotions, adventure fiction seems to cater to the low end. That such emotions are not only powerful but also pleasurable, at least when experienced vicariously, seems indubitable, but just as we may blush to acknowledge the sexual, so we blanch to recognize our susceptibility to the other primal emotions aroused by adventure fiction. One can, of course, escape or set aside culturally induced hierarchical aesthetic thinking, and the lover of pure adventure fiction probably does. But to what end?

In *The Adventurer: The Fate of Adventure in the Western World*, Paul Zweig links the outlandish in adventure to the ordinary in life. "Haven't all of us," he wonders, "now and then, experienced moments of abrupt intensity, when our lives seemed paralyzed by risk: a ball clicking around a roulette wheel; a car sliding across an icy road; the excruciating uncertainty of a lover's response; perhaps merely a walk through the streets of a strange city?" In such moments the "cat's paw of chance hovers tantalizingly, and suddenly the simplest outcome seems unpredictable. For a brief moment, we are like warriors, charged with the energies of survival, reading every detail of the scene as if it were a sign revealing what was to come." The "gleams of intensity" that irradiate such moments in real life are a sudden "plunge into essential experience." What adventure stories do, then, is to "transpose our dalliance with risk into a sustained vision" (3–4).

Thinking primarily of real-life adventurers, the sociologist Georg Simmel has, on the other hand, stressed the disconnection between adventure and quotidian existence. For him, the adventurer drops "out of the continuity of life" to experience the "accidental," something remote from "life's more narrowly rational aspects." Insofar as there is one, the tie between ordinary life and adventure lies, for Simmel, in the nature of the adventurer. He is "the extreme example of the a-historical individual," someone who "lives in the present," for whom the future does not exist, a "fatalist" who risks all, a "skeptic" who believes in nothing except "what is least believable." Paradoxically, however, the chance circumstances embraced by the adventurer arise in part from who he is, for despite its "accidental nature," the adventure "connects with the character and identity" of the adventurer. For Simmel, no less than for Zweig, an adventure beckons one into the mysterious, the unknown, which the adventurer's nature compels him to pursue. To begin an adventure is to give oneself over to forces both within the self and beyond it, even if it seems that it is "just on hovering chance, on fate, on the more-or-less that we risk all, burn our bridges, and step into the mist, as if the road will lead us on, no matter what" (187–98).

Propounders of adventure theory seem to divide generally into two camps: those who locate the significance of adventure in universal or archetypal patterns, and those who find it in social configurations. The first group, fairly represented by Joseph Campbell and Marcel Detienne, sees in adventure fiction a re-working (or a working out) of myths. For Campbell an adventure reenacts an archetypal pattern: the hero, a young man, leaves home, separating himself from his community, wanders at large in the world for a time, undergoes a series of trials or tests, masters them, earns a boon, and then returns home, a transformed person, finally bestowing upon the community he initially left the boon he has garnered (Campbell, *The Hero with a Thousand Faces*). Looking, like Campbell, at classical materials but focusing on the hunter adventurer, Marcel Detienne finds in them a fundamental rite of initiation. He suggests that the adventurer leaves "the farmer's fields" and the "enclosed space of the home" to enter a domain open "exclusively to the male sex," a space situated "at the intersection of the powers of life and the forces of death," where he may not only shed blood in the hunt, thereby preparing himself for the male acts of war, but also engage in "deviant forms of sexuality"—all of which introduce this kind of adventurer into "the realm of manhood" (24–26).

The critics of the second group ignore myth in favor of social "realities." They tend to see the importance of adventure in its seeming deviance. For them the adventurer is moved neither to fulfill some cosmic destiny nor to undergo a cultural rite of initiation; instead, he is a person fundamentally at odds with conventional society, whose experience removes him from the familiar world and so allows him, indeed often forces him, to exercise powers normally repressed in ordinary life. Although he is not directly concerned with adventure, Georges Bataille lays out the key opposition between conventional life and adventurous action, between the world of work and reason, which creates taboo, and the realm of violence and desire, which violates it (chapters 2 and 5). Building on these ideas in a full-scale study of adventure fiction, Martin Green offers a succinct definition of adventure construed in social terms: an adventure is "a series of events that outrage civilized or domestic morality and that challenge those to whom those events happen to make use of powers that civil life forbids to the ordinary citizen" (*The Adventurous Male* 4). This formulation crystallizes the approach of those who view adventure primarily as a social phenomenon. It captures the tension between the adventurer and the community, acknowledges his indulgence of the repressed, and points to his arena of action as a liminal space.[6]

There is perhaps something slightly grandiose about adventure theory. It seems to overcorrect the impulse to dismiss adventure fiction as flimsy work—"tushery" or "perishable dream-stuff"—by making it profoundly significant: an embodiment of the universal motions of life or a reflection of the basic tension inherent in social living. Such analyses create something of a felt disparity between what one reads and what it is said to mean. Yet surely this timeless form means something. It seems to me that both mythic and sociological approaches to adventure have one important thing in common: both tend to see adventure as action that leads the adventurer toward maturity. Certainly for Stevenson and Twain, who cast boys as their adventurers, the overall pattern common to the fiction of both is the movement from boyhood toward adulthood. In their fictions the venture away from home, whatever else it may entail, is an adventuring toward— or into—manhood.

*The Adventures of Tom Sawyer* is appealing in elusive ways. Part of its graceful magic comes from the fact that Twain creates precisely the sense of enticing, perhaps dangerous departures that mark all adventure fiction. Tom is always beginning anew, stepping off into the "mist," as Simmel would have it, or, more accurately in this case, into the sunlight or moonlight, venturing he knows not what for the sake of adventure itself. The romance is punctuated with moments like these, irresistible beckonings whose accumulation creates the sense that the possibility of renewal is perpetual:

> Saturday morning was come, and all the summer world was bright and fresh, brimming with life. There was a song in every heart; and if the heart was young the music issued at the lips. There was cheer in every face and a spring in every step. The locust trees were in bloom and the fragrance of the blossoms filled the

air. Cardiff Hill, beyond the village and above it, was green with vegetation, and it lay just far enough away to seem a Delectable Land, dreamy, reposeful and inviting. (*TS* 46)

The sun rose upon a tranquil world, and beamed down upon the peaceful village like a benediction. (*TS* 57)

It was the cool gray dawn, and there was a delicious sense of repose and peace in the deep pervading calm and silence of the woods. Not a leaf stirred; not a sound obtruded upon great Nature's meditation. Beaded dew-drips stood upon the leaves and grasses. (*TS* 121)

Tom does not always get to enter this world that looms so enticingly, or at least not at once, and so its attraction is deepened by prohibition; forbidden adventures become the most alluring.

Stevenson's *Treasure Island* does not have the same luminous beckonings, for the Bristol coastline along which Jim Hawkins lives is foggy, harsh, and cold. His adventures, after a tumultuous beginning at home, will occur on a far-off unspecified ocean island. Stevenson suggests as much at the opening of chapter 2: "It was one January morning, very early—a pinching, frosty morning—the cove all grey with hoar-frost, the ripple lapping softly on the stones, the sun still low and only touching the hilltops and shining far to seaward."[7] The attractive, sunlit, unknown world lies "far to seaward," where Jim will soon go, but before he can venture forth, he is enveloped in mystery. From the first Stevenson evokes the dark side of adventure: mystery, threat, and danger. Who is Billy Bones? What or whom is he afraid of? Who is Black Dog? What is the Black Spot? And above all, who is the one-legged man and why is he so forbidding? Adventure (like the Sublime) is clearly double-sided: on the one hand, as Twain suggests, it is delectable; and on the other, as Stevenson intimates, it is terrifying.

The union of attraction and terror in adventure accounts for its irresistible power. When the old sea-dog Billy Bones establishes himself by the force of his personality at the Admiral Benbow Inn (without paying his keep) and begins to torment the local patrons with drunken, railing tales of "hanging, and walking the plank, and storms at sea, and the Dry Tortugas, and wild deeds and places on the Spanish Main," Jim

Hawkins's father fears that he will drive away the trade with his drunken tyranny and terrifying stories. But Jim finally surmises that the inn's patrons, though "frightened at the time," in the end enjoy their encounters with the overbearing bearer of horrors: "It was fine excitement in a quiet country life" (*TI* 14). Such is the attraction of adventure, whether delectable or horrifying—or both.

Stevenson's novel is a purer adventure tale than Twain's. Stevenson gives his story straight through the altogether serious (though often excited) retrospective narrative of Jim Hawkins, while Twain tells his tale of Tom's adventures obliquely through a third-person narrator who is alternately—perhaps at times confusedly—serious and comic, approving and disapproving, nostalgic and caustic. Much as Twain covers his sentimentality with a burlesque of it—as we saw in considering the relations between Twain and Harte—and his genteel outlook with a raucous spoof of things genteel—as we saw in examining the relations between Twain and Howells—so he guards his delight in adventure with a patronizing, often critical narrative mode. The chief way in which he both indulges his romantic fantasies and hedges against them—and this is true of Stevenson as well—is to cast them as a boy's ventures. Unlike, say, Ouida's *Under Two Flags*, or Haggard's *King Solomon's Mines*, or even Burroughs's later Tarzan stories, *Tom Sawyer* and *Treasure Island* are presented as tales of experience sought not by men but boys.

Books about boys, whether adventure fictions or autobiographical reminiscences, were increasingly popular in the trans-Atlantic culture of the nineteenth century's closing decades. Their appeal has traditionally been described as rooted in four things the second half of the nineteenth century desperately wanted: (1) an escape from anxiety over modernization, (2) a chance to recover a sense of a stable self in the face of an increasingly divided one, (3) a reassertion of hegemonic social control within a multicultural society, and (4) a release from the contradictions of culturally defined manhood.[8] No doubt many boy adventures satisfy all these longings, but in the case of Stevenson and Twain, far from providing an escape from the contradictions of manhood, their adventure fictions dramatize the central conflicts at work in the nineteenth century's evolving concept of what it means to be a man.

Both Twain and Stevenson guide their boy heroes toward maturity and manliness. For each author, the acquisition of these qualities depends in large measure on an escape from domesticity. While Tom slips away from home, from Aunt Polly, Sid, Mary, again and again, Jim makes one decisive break from the conventional life he leads as serving boy at the Admiral Benbow Inn. Tom fusses repeatedly over the constraints of home life, while Jim laments leaving it—at least for one moment. Saying good-bye to his mother and to the cove where he has lived since he was born, he has an "attack of tears" (*TI* 51). But the world he leaves behind—a place, a way of living, and an ethical code of being—is defined for him, perhaps, by one of his two male mentors, Squire Trelawney, who remarks on Long John Silver's reason for giving up his inn and shipping with them. Writing to Dr. Livesey, he says: "He leaves his wife to manage the inn; and as she is a woman of colour, a pair of old bachelors like you and I may be excused for guessing that it is the wife, quite as much as the health, that sends him back to roving" (*TI* 50). The aversion he posits is not just to "a woman of colour" but to the whole world of home, domestic order, and convention. For Jim Hawkins, for whom the squire may speak here, the exciting ideal is "roving."

Jim Hawkins roams with, indeed is guided and constrained by, no fewer than three significant male companions, who represent differing aspects of the maturity and manhood toward which his ventures drive him. Jim's real father dies, and his death frees Jim to pursue the quest for treasure without paternal hindrance. Curiously, while he is nothing like a father, Billy Bones—a prefiguring of the more complex and commanding Long John Silver—has a more significant emotional impact on Jim than his real father. Jim reports his father's death dispassionately (he has been in a steady state of decline so there is no surprise about it), but when Billy Bones dies, he says, "I burst into a flood of tears" (*TI* 29). (He adds that some of them spring from the well of pain over his true father's death.) Bones embodies all the dark, violent ways of pirating as well as the lure of adventure such ways evoke. With the weak real father—he is timid to the point of unmanly—gone, and a strong, domineering substitute dispatched as well, Jim is immediately taken up by Squire Trelawney and Dr. Livesey, two men of power and consequence who have, it seems, only one thing in common: a lust for riches—"money to eat, to roll in, to play duck and drake with ever after" (*TI* 46).

Livesey is a man of learning, rectitude, and courage. He is a magistrate who upholds the law, but he is also a brave man (early on, he stares down and silences the armed, drunken Billy Bones). As a doctor, he is a man who compassionately cares for the sick, regardless of their moral character. By virtue of his class standing, Squire Trelawney is a confident, formidable citizen, who proves in the course of events to be a stalwart man in a fight (perhaps from his idle days of hunting, he is a crack shot with a rifle). But Trelawney lacks Livesey's self-control. Trelawney is an impulsive man, an enthusiast whose passions sometimes override his judgment; he needs—and receives—checking by the disciplined Dr. Livesey. Both Squire Trelawney and Dr. Livesey are gentlemen, and for Stevenson their standing as gentlemen certifies them not only as men of refinement but also as moral models. The two true gentlemen are pitted against the gentlemen of fortune—the pirates. The pirates, of course, lack any semblance of morality. In fact, they flaunt their immorality; they pride themselves on violence and deception, on physical strength and agility, on plundering and killing. In their desire for treasure, however, they are the dark counterparts to the squire and the doctor. Stevenson's representation of manhood thus seems to follow highly conventional Victorian lines, which value certain physical talents while emphasizing the need for morality. He seems to uphold the Victorian distinction between the manly, which denotes physical prowess, and manliness, which is defined by moral character (for the distinction see Buckley, *William Ernest Henley* 14–15).

In his depiction of Long John Silver, however, Stevenson confounds these distinctions. Silver is far and away the most memorable character in the book—and the most morally ambiguous. He is a typical pirate, at least as Stevenson imagines pirates, but besides his greed, his violence, his daring, and his will to power, Silver is also intelligent, charming, and clever. He has wit as well as courage, and he uses both. Above all, he has a gift for speaking—graciously, convincingly—and an all but mesmerizing ability to command.

The character of Long John Silver was, as Stevenson acknowledged, based on William Ernest Henley. In May 1888, while the book version of *Treasure Island* was being arranged (it had been published serially from October 1881 to January 1882 in the magazine *Young Folks*, under the pseudonym Captain George North), Stevenson wrote to Henley: "It was the sight of your maimed strength and masterfulness that begot John Silver in *Treasure Island*. Of course, he is not in any other quality or feature the least like you; but the idea of the maimed man, ruling and dreaded by the sound, was entirely taken from you" (*Letters of RLS* 4:129). Henley did not mind the attribution. He was at the time not only Stevenson's close friend, someone with whom Stevenson had coauthored several (bad) plays, but also an active promoter of his career. As an influential editor of several Victorian journals, a popular poet, and a prolific critic, Henley himself wielded power in literary circles. He had lost one foot—hence Stevenson's "maimed"—from tuberculosis of the bone, and was widely admired for his fortitude. Shortly after its publication, he reviewed *Treasure Island* and praised above all Long John Silver, a muted reflection of himself. He called him "one of the most remarkable pirates in fiction" and described him as "smooth-spoken," "clever," "powerful and charming." Henley went so far as to say that the book should have been entitled "John Silver, Pirate." He especially liked Silver's knack of rising above adversity. Seeing in Silver exactly the posture he would celebrate some five years later in what was to become his most famous poem, "Invictus," he interpreted Stevenson's figure as a man who "maintains a magnificent intellectual superiority" in "victory and defeat alike" (Maixner, *RLS* 131–36). This is precisely the attitude Henley would poeticize so memorably:

> Out of the night that covers me,
>   Black as the Pit from pole to pole,
> I thank whatever gods may be
>   For my unconquerable soul.
>
> In the fell clutch of circumstance
>   I have not winced or cried aloud.
> Under the bludgeonings of chance
>   My head is bloody, but unbowed. ("Invictus")

Silver is unbowed throughout Stevenson's adventure tale, no matter what befalls him, for he has an unconquerable spirit. But it coexists with guile, duplicity, violence, and a readiness for betrayal. Despite his moral shortcomings, though, he remains appealing. All the main characters are at one time or another duped by Silver, but only Captain Smollett is impervious to his beguiling talk and winning insouciance.

Realizing Silver's appeal, Stevenson created a delightful bagatelle entitled "A Fable," in which he has Captain Smollett and Silver step out of *Treasure Island* (just after chapter 32) and debate which of them the "Author" likes best. Smollett disapproves of Silver, but Silver says, "Now, Cap'n Smollett . . . dooty is dooty, as I knows, and none better; but we're off dooty now; and I can't see no call to keep up the morality business." Denounced by the captain as a "damned rogue," Silver observes, "I'm on'y a chara'ter in a sea story. I don't really exist," and since that does not quiet the captain, he adds, "But I'm the villain of this tale, I am." Far from being demeaned by the role, however, Silver insists that he is the Author's "favourite chara'ter." He explains, "He does me fathoms better'n he does you—fathoms, he does. And he likes doing me. He keeps me on deck mostly all the time, crutch and all; and he leaves you measling in the hold, where nobody can't see you, nor wants to, and you may lay to that." Pushed in the argument, Smollett concedes that he is "not a very popular man," but he returns to the moral difference between them, insisting, "I know the Author's on the side of good. . . . Well, that's all I need to know; I'll take my chance upon the rest." But Silver complicates the moral issue: "I'm a man that keeps company very easy; even by your own account, you ain't, and to my certain knowledge, you're a devil to haze." The hard-pressed captain then says lamely, "We're none of us perfect." Smollett reasserts that the author is "on the right side" and warns Silver that "there's trouble coming for you." But Silver stands by his notion of the admixture of good and bad in both of them, asking, "Which is which? Which is good, and which bad?" Silver remains confident that he will come out all right in the end, and Smollett remains content to be himself. The fable closes as the author resumes writing ("A Fable" 223–25).

Self-reflexively, Stevenson plays here with the fictionality of fiction and the illusion of conscious authorial control (postmodernists would love his sketch), but he also underscores the moral dilemma generated by his story. For he does like John Silver, and so does the reader. The villain in some sense becomes the hero, and Jim Hawkins, the protagonist, is stranded between manhood represented by dull virtue in Trelawney and Livesey and manhood embodied in John Silver's unconquerable, albeit amoral, spirit. Stevenson's ambivalence is perhaps registered in Jim's actions. Safety, not to say success, for the respectable men is in the end created by what Jim calls his "mad notions" (*TI* 85), what we might call his breaches of strict moral behavior. There are three: Jim violates the ship's routine, sneaks off to get an apple, and so learns of the incipient mutiny; Jim breaks ranks with the cabin party, dashes ashore with the pirates, and so finds Ben Gunn; and most reprehensibly of all, Jim deserts the beleaguered defenders of the stockade, revisits the ship, and so manages to retake it from the pirates.

The rite of passage into manhood that Jim undergoes is as interesting—and as ambivalent—as these departures from discipline and duty. He shoots and kills Israel Hands (in dire self-defense, of course), thereby participating in the violence that the gentlemen seldom use but the pirates revel in, and when recaptured by the pirates in the stockade, facing death himself, he boasts of having bested them, exercising the power of speech most fully possessed by Silver. To be sure, *what* Jim says is more or less what Dr. Livesey says elsewhere in his own terms about helping miscreants, but Jim says his say with a braggadocio foreign to the doctor. The speech signals Jim's emergence into manhood. Though somewhat long, it is worth listening to in full:

> "Well," said I, "I am not such a fool but I know pretty well what I have to look for. Let the worst come to the worst, it's little I care. I've seen too many die since I fell in with you. But there's a thing or two I have to tell you," I said, and by this time I was quite excited; "and the first is this: here you are, in a bad way—ship lost, treasure lost, men lost, your whole business gone to wreck; and if you want to know who did it—it was I! I was in the apple barrel the night we sighted land, and I heard you, John, and you, Dick Johnson, and Hands, who is now at the bottom of the sea, and told every word you said before the hour was out. And as for the schooner, it was I who cut her cable, and it was I that killed the men you had aboard of her, and it was I who brought her where you'll never see her more, not one of you. The laugh's on my side; I've had the top of this business from the first; I no more fear you than I fear a fly. Kill me, if you please, or spare me. But one thing I'll say, and no more; if you spare me, bygones are bygones, and when you fellows are in court for piracy, I'll save you all I can. It is for you to choose. Kill another and do yourselves no good, or spare me and keep a witness to save you from the gallows." (*TI* 170–71)

Some of the language here—"bygones be bygones," for instance, "the laugh's on my side," or "had the top of this business"—and most of the syntax reflect not the polite phrasing and the measured cadences of Dr. Livesey (or even the enthusiastic outbursts of Trelawney) but the sharp, self-assertive, riveting speech of Silver. (Interestingly, Silver's response to Jim's speech is, like the man himself, equivocal: "I could not," Jim says, "for the life of me decide whether he were laughing at my request or had been favorably affected by my courage" [171].) Jim expresses his newfound manhood in moral terms typical of the two gentlemen; he demonstrates a bravery common to the gentlemen and sometimes to the gentlemen of fortune as well; but he asserts himself with a bold fluency and engaging power typical only of John Silver. While he has absorbed the manliness of the moral character of Livesey and Trelawney, he has also acquired the manful power of speech commanded by Silver. Possessing the two, he has what Stevenson praised in Henley: "masterfulness." Jim's manhood is thus a curious compound that amalgamates differing traits, and Stevenson approves of it. Surely on the side of the good, as Captain Smollett averred in his contretemps with Silver, Stevenson nonetheless lets the pirate escape in the end. Silver slips away like a bad dream best forgotten.

Stevenson was lauded in his time, and has continued to be right down to ours, for his narrative skill. *Treasure Island* is still a treasure to read. Stevenson unfolds his romance with perfect pacing, absorbing plot, finely crafted drama, and stylistic grace; his art is, of course, to appear artless.

Twain's power in *Tom Sawyer* is quite different. His story, as the title makes clear, is really a series of adventures: Tom's tribulations in love, Tom's troubles with communal institutions (home, church, Sunday school, school), Tom's excitement running away from home (and returning triumphantly to attend his own funeral), Tom's life-or-death struggle to risk the vengeance of Injun Joe and save Muff Potter, Tom's trials lost in the cave, and, of course, Tom's recurrent search for buried treasure. Unlike Stevenson, Twain does not have a single line of plot to follow through to its end. Besides being discontinuous, Tom's exploits are not as "real" as Jim Hawkins's. What Jim Hawkins undergoes, Tom Sawyer only plays at. Tom imagines—dreams of—being a clown, a soldier, and an Indian chief, but what he spends most time at is playing pirate. On Jackson's Island he and Huck and Joe Harper—self-denominated the Black Avenger of the Spanish Main, the Red-Handed, and the Terror of the Seas—envision a pirate's life that is remarkably like the pirate's life Jim Hawkins encounters: they "take ships, and burn them, and get the money and bury it in awful places in their island where there's ghosts and things to watch it, and kill everybody in the ships—make 'em walk a plank" (*TS* 119). Having imagined such a life of illicit adventure, Tom then plays it out, creating his boyish version of a dark, morally suspect reality. In contrast, Jim Hawkins does not invent a particle of his adventures (though he dreams some of their dark aspects before they envelop him); his adventures befall him and only after they have come to him does he become an active agent in them. Tom seems in comparison to Jim a mere child toying with the imaginative, while Jim is forced by events to live through for a long time what Tom only fashions at playtime.

What Twain's boy book of adventures achieves, however, that Stevenson's skirts, is insight into the psychology of adventure. Where Stevenson captures the sheer dash and thrill of the adventure genre, Twain reveals the assortment of desires that give rise to adventure in the first place. Tom is animated by, driven to adventure by, a loathing of routine and a longing for unfettered action, by a self-pity that seeks satisfaction in self-destruction (or at least the risk of it), by a contrary self-love that looks for validation in public recognition, by an interest in mystery and a desire to confront the unknown, and by a deep need to find an arena in which he can assert control and take command. Twain often presents these emotional states through burlesque, mocking them even as he depicts them, but his burlesque does not invalidate its objects; it only perceives them from a different perspective, rendering them comic without destroying their authenticity. However silly, for instance, Tom's inner turmoil, his excessive fear, or feelings of slight seem, they are still credible as a boy's suffering, despite the narrator's knowing wink at them. Tom is caught in what one critic has called the "predicament of the man-child" (Cady, *The Road to Realism* 12): he is between two states of being, the boy's restricted, naïve, powerless, yet imaginatively unbounded one, and the man's more flexible, informed, powerful, yet socially constrained one. In his adventurous play Tom manipulates the conditions of the boy to seize the circumstance of the man.

Tom's world has been defined as a "matriarchy," as a "world that holds small boys in bondage" (Wolff 151), and certainly the mothers, real or surrogate, are present not only as nurturers but also, at least from the boys' perspective, as adversaries. They correct, punish, lecture, guide, restrain, and control the boys, striving to instill in them what they take to be the true and the good, which is usually nothing more than the conventional. But the real power structure of St. Petersburg is patriarchal. With the single, and admittedly important, exception of the home, all the institutions of the town—church, school, court—are controlled by men. (Twain's social structure obviously reflects the prevailing doctrine of the two spheres.) While Aunt Polly and Mrs. Harper, mothers to the bone, wash, dress, and instruct the boys, it is in fact Judge Thatcher who has the power to bestow ultimate approval or blame on them. The controlling men are most often out of sight, however, emerging only on grand occasions, on a Sunday with distinguished visitors, on Examination Day, or on a day in court. Not a single father actually appears in the text other than the judge (Mr. Harper is mentioned as attending the gathering at the Widow Douglas's, but we never see or hear him). If Stevenson killed off Jim Hawkins's father, first to free Jim, then to provide more fitting—that is, stronger—male substitutes, Twain seems to clear the deck of fathers altogether. Ironically, the absent Pap Finn is the most present father in the book, for Huck repeatedly cites Pap as an authority, but Twain makes him a travesty of fatherhood. All the information he gives Huck is wrong, his actions are those of a bumbling drunk, and his guidance is misguided. Paradoxically, then, St. Petersburg is a patriarchy virtually without patriarchs.

The one male who is a part of Tom's adventures is Injun Joe. Twain uses him, much as Stevenson does Long John Silver, to reveal the dark side of both adventure and manhood. As many critics have observed, Joe is a kind of shadow self or mirror image of Tom, one that reflects the dire aspects of his character and activities. The tie has been summed up this way: "Tom plays pariah, Injun Joe is a true outcast; Tom feigns bloody deeds, Injun Joe commits them; Tom dreams of treasure, Injun Joe steals it; Tom fantasizes a life of crime, Injun Joe lives one; Tom longs for revenge, Injun Joe murders for it. Even Tom's possessive puppy love has its dark counterpart in Joe's talk of mutilating and violating the Widow Douglas" (Krauth 145). Joe links the world of play to the world of reality, suggesting what adventure, unchecked by morality, might lead to. Though Joe has some justification for anger at his mistreatment by the community (Lowry 100–107), he has none of Long John Silver's winning, not to say redeeming, qualities. He haunts Tom's dreams, filling them with blood and horror, just as the one-legged Silver brings Jim Hawkins nightmares of pursuit by a "monstrous kind of creature" (*TI* 13). But where Jim acts with a disregard for duty not entirely unlike Silver's, and where in the end he acquires and uses something like Silver's command of speech, Tom rejects all that Joe stands for and in the end is at least indirectly responsible for his death. He purges himself of his nightmare, while Jim's remains to be confronted, and not entirely banished, in the act of writing a book about it.

Quite naturally, all the future occupations Tom imagines are commonplace: he thinks of becoming a clown, soldier, Indian chief, or pirate. With the exception of clown, who paradoxically works to create as an adult the child's act of play, Tom's dream-roles are not only stock boyhood fantasies but also traditional male ones that call for manly prowess and, with significantly differing degrees of justification, involve violence. Tom plays at all four, and while there is no possibility of his ever becoming any of them (except perhaps a soldier), his play is a rehearsal for manhood; for all of their childishness, his adventures are training grounds for maturity. Tom Sawyer's adventuring into manhood is of a peculiar sort, however, one quite different from Jim Hawkins's. The most obvious difference is that there is no male guide to Tom's maturation—no Livesey or Trelawney. (His guides, insofar as he has any, are derived from his reading of dime novels and penny-dreadfuls.) Those critics who have attended to Tom's growth in the course of his adventures have seen him acquiring chiefly those adult male attributes that will equip him to function in the economic sphere as an entrepreneurial capitalist: aggression, manipulation, competition, self-possession, risk-taking, and domination, to mention a significant few. Looked at this way, Tom becomes not only a "proto-capitalist" but also a "confidence man" who represents the "dominant values of an emergent capitalist culture" (Messent 73). He practices skills that will qualify him for male adulthood in a society uneasily shifting its values toward an acceptance of what was once morally condemned (for the shift, see Halttunen). Such a reading of Twain's "hymn," as he once called *Tom Sawyer* (*MTL* 2:477), is plausible, but it ignores another dimension of the book that is equally present and that runs counter to Tom's growth into a manhood defined by powerful but shady business acumen.

In chapter 6 Tom happily arranges to be banished to the girls' side of the classroom, where he can pass notes and whisper to Becky Thatcher. He draws a house, and after pretending not to want to, he proudly shows it to her. "It's nice," Becky tells him, and then asks him to "make a man." He does one that resembles "a derrick," but the figure enthralls Becky: "It's a beautiful man," she tells Tom (*TS* 79). This scene in the schoolroom, with Tom on the girls' side of the classroom, drawing pictures of home and homebodies (he quickly adds a picture of Becky to his drawing), an idyllic vision of domesticity with a gigantic man overlooking it all, prefigures the true shape of Tom's manhood. For, ironically, what Tom learns on his adventures away from home are the values enshrined in the home. What Aunt Polly preaches to Tom at home he learns while off on his adventures.

Mothering Tom, Aunt Polly goads him toward respectability. She urges upon him cleanliness, punctuality, proper dress, manners, and conventional morals. But beyond or, perhaps more accurately, beneath her insistence on what sometimes seem like narrow proprieties lies a large, humane moral: she wants him to take others into account and treat them with compassion, with fellow feeling. Chiding him for his "selfishness," she often sounds both injured and sentimental—"O, child you never think," never "think to pity us and save us from sorrow" (*TS* 150), but what she wants to instill in Tom is nothing less than the principle of consideration for others. Tom's self-centeredness is virtually a definition of his childishness, of his boy's estate, and what Aunt Polly calls for is a re-centering: a tempering of self-absorption and a concomitant strengthening of concern for others. Ironically, this is what happens to Tom during his adventures. Time and again his adventuring leads him to think—and to feel—beyond himself on behalf of others: as a runaway on Jackson's Island, he learns to set aside play and consider the worry (and pain) he is inflicting on Aunt Polly; as nocturnal witness to a graveyard murder, he learns to put his own safety aside and swear to the truth to save Muff Potter; as a lost cave-explorer, he learns to sacrifice himself to comfort and care for Becky. (He even ends up, somewhat shockingly, pitying his dark nemesis, Injun Joe.)

Tom's ultimate adventure into the depths of the cave is surely a rite of passage, an initiation into manhood, but it is a manhood of caring, of compassion, of concern for others. It is no wonder that the village patriarch, Judge Thatcher, has in the end (and the end is a long way from the opening humiliation of Tom before the judge in church when all Tom sought was to be the center of attention) "a great opinion of Tom" and envisions his manly future as "a great lawyer or a great soldier" (*TS* 232–33), both, one might argue, professions in which one serves others. Troubling to many readers and critics because they seem to mark a sellout to the conventional world he has run from throughout his adventures, Tom's final efforts to bring Huck Finn back to the widow's are also acts undertaken not for himself but for others—for the good of the widow and even of Huck. His use of the robber gang to win Huck over suggests that he is still a boy, but his effort itself signals that he is a boy at the edge of manhood. As Twain says in his conclusion, his story "could not go much further without becoming the history of a *man*" (*TS* 237).

Besides empathy—and glory, and a girl—Tom does in the end also get the gold, and this too seems to mark him for manhood. He does not, however, acquire it through any activity even vaguely like—or preparatory for—capitalist enterprise. He gets it by luck and pluck through his adventures. His acquisition of wealth matches that of Jim Hawkins. Confessing that he is "rich," the half-mad Ben Gunn says to Jim, "And I'll tell you what: I'll make a man of you, Jim," implying that he will make him a man by making him rich (*TI* 95). Some such feeling informs the closing of *Tom Sawyer*. Both adventure tales, while emphasizing the moral dimension of manhood, also link manliness with wealth. Wealth is an ethically neutral position (though there were endless warnings against its dangers in the nineteenth century), neither moral nor immoral, but it is still a far cry from principle. One could perhaps reconcile some of the different aspects of manhood dramatized in these two books of boy adventure—physical prowess, morality, and money, for instance, and perhaps even compassion—by seeing them all as forms of power. But Stevenson and Twain leave these as unreconciled in their fictions as they were in their culture.

To return to Stevenson's formulation in defense of the romance, if adventure fiction embodies boyish dreams and desires, then it must have been hard for a boy coming of age after, say, 1850 to dream a clear dream of manhood, however much he may have desired it. For during the second half of the nineteenth century, there was in Britain as well as America a growing uncertainty about the meaning of manhood. As one critic has put it, manhood had become "problematic" (Curtis 67). The traditional Victorian concept of masculinity, which emphasized moral character, the repression of desire, the postponement of gratification, and the need for hard work to produce economic competency, was challenged by a host of new forces. What emerged were competing "styles of masculinity" (Griffen 185), and the collision between these styles was often extreme enough to be seen as an out-and-out conflict: "A war of sorts was waged over male identity in the nineteenth century" (Griswold 97). Different subgroups within the trans-Atlantic culture, the working class, the landed gentry, the military, the aristocracy, the merchants, the civil servants, the emigrants and immigrants, the educators, and the entrepreneurs, to cite a few, often developed divergent notions of manhood. However, if one samples the now extensive body of scholarship on nineteenth-century masculinity, one can discern a series of contraries at work.

The traditional male model for success (celebrated in America as the self-made man), which had emphasized such attributes as diligence, hard work, submission to authority, and reliability, was giving way to a new one, which valued daring, aggression, challenges to authority, and a readiness to seize the main chance (Burns; Cawelti, *Apostles;* and Wyllie). The manhood required in the workplace—a matter of seriousness, rationality, and constraint, of necessary cooperation, imposed harmony, and ordered behavior—was at odds with the manhood practiced outside the workplace in recreational activities, in fraternal clubs, and in athletics, for these indulged frivolity, spontaneity, release, and valorized conflict, hostility, and unruliness (Grossberg, Carnes). The so-called cult of masculinity, with its celebration of such traits as ruggedness, brawn, force, and the stiff upper lip, collided with what has been termed "masculine domesticity" (March 112), which called for tenderness, sensitivity, nurturance, and affection. In the broadest terms, as Gail Bederman has argued in *Manliness and Civilization*, the discourse of civilization itself, which guided (or misguided) international politics in general and imperialist ventures in particular, reflected conflicted ideals of manhood: on the one hand, the primitive man or savage, with his force, violence, strong emotions, and animal spirits, provided a provocative image; on the other, the civilized man, with his rationality, civility, knowledge, and analytical intelligence formed a contrasting ideal (Bederman 1–44). Men were drawn to both. Given all the contraries at work in the social construction of manhood, perhaps it is no exaggeration to say that the nineteenth century experienced a "confusing 'crisis of masculinity' " (Griffen 183). Certainly, then, it is not surprising that when Stevenson and Twain wrote fictions in which the boy was separated from home to discover a kind of manhood in his adventures, they inscribed in them some of the age's unresolved conflicts over masculinity.

The moral dimension of manliness was instilled in Stevenson and Twain in their childhoods. Both Twain and Stevenson grew up in stern, strict, true-believing Calvinist homes, and while both in time left behind the faith of their fathers (and mothers), the imprint of their religious upbringing was with them for life. In both cases it manifested itself most strongly in an ever-active conscience. After Bohemian interludes—Twain's in the West, first in the Nevada Territory and then in California; Stevenson's first in Edinburgh, then in France in Fontainebleau, Grez, and Paris—both sought, if not stability, at least some means of attaining economic sufficiency. Stevenson's parents first intended for him to pursue the paternal—and quite manly—occupation of civil engineer, specializing, as his father and grandfather had, in lighthouse building. ("I . . . was at the building of harbours and lighthouses," Stevenson later recalled, "and worked in a carpenter's shop and a brass foundry, and hung about wood yards and the like" [*Letters of RLS* 6:47].) Then, when he resisted, his parents urged upon him the equally manly profession of the law. He defaulted on that, too (though he was admitted to the bar), and turned instead, with copious apologies, to writing, an art which he sometimes denigrated as unmasculine (see "My First Book"). His father having died when he was eleven, Twain (of course he was Clemens then) was freer to find his own way, but he was also forced to pay his own way. (Stevenson received parental support until the death of his father in 1887, at which time he got a considerable inheritance.) Twain pursued the manly occupations of printer, pilot, prospector, and journalist, before he turned more completely to writing and lecturing. When he made that turn, the mode he practiced—humor—was, unlike Stevenson's belletristic essays, firmly rooted in male literary traditions. Marriage brought some stability to each writer (and some money), though Stevenson's life remained nomadic and exotic while Twain's became settled and more or less conventional. As young men growing into manhood, however, they both witnessed and experienced the age's conflicting notions of what constituted a man.

Both Stevenson and Twain were inclined to perform versions of themselves. Such posturing was no doubt deeply linked to their creativity; it was also a way of not only testing out roles but also concealing an often insecure self. Both writers played with male gender roles. Twain often mocked the roles he assumed, including manly ones. Writing to his mother in 1864, for instance, he informed her that he belonged to "the San F. Olympic Club," a men's gymnasium that offered classes in gymnastics, boxing, and fencing, and he assured her that going there had been "a great blessing" to him. He elaborated: "I feel like a new man. I sleep better, I have a healthier appetite, my intellect is clearer, & I have become so strong & hearty that I fully believe twenty years have been added to my life." And then having seemed to extol the benefits of manly exercise at the club, he added that he was "well satisfied" with the result of belonging to it, since he had only been in the gymnasium "once"—and that was "over three months ago" (*LI* 305–6). Thus teasing his mother over her concern for his health, Twain also dismisses the ideal of the physically fit male and makes fun of the pursuit of such manly sports as boxing and fencing. He was, however, more serious about another aspect of manhood, conventionally conceived. He subscribed to the ideal of manliness as moral character, insisting to his family that he avoided "dissipation," that he knew the "value of a good name," and that he was "man enough to have a good character and keep it" (*LI* 262).

Perhaps his deepest feelings about what constituted manhood are revealed in an 1861 letter to his brother and sister-in-law, a letter in which he reports, by means of approximate quotation, on what a New Orleans clairvoyant or fortune-teller had said to him. The secondhand nature of this account, the fact that he is ostensibly reporting the fortune-teller's analysis, seems to have freed him to define himself as he liked to see himself. Here are the key observations pertaining to manhood he says the fortune-teller made: "you are the best sheep in your flock"; "there is more unswerving strength of will, & set purpose, and determination and energy in you than in all the balance of your family put together"; "you never brought all your energies to bear upon an object, but what you accomplished it—for instance, you are self-made, self-educated" (*LI* 109). And then as if to prove that he actually possessed the qualities she assigned him, the fortune-teller told him, he says, of how he attained his present occupation (he was a licensed riverboat pilot at the time): "When you sought your present occupation, you found a thousand obstacles in your way— obstacles which would have deterred nineteen out of any twenty men— obstacles unknown,—not even suspected by any save you and I, since you keep such matters to yourself,—but you fought your way through them, during a weary, weary length of time, and never flinched, or quailed, or never once wished to give over the battle—and hid the long struggle under a mask of cheerfulness, which saved your friends anxiety on your account" (*LI* 109). As Twain must have realized, this reads like a summarizing passage from a sentimental novel. Yet it is reasonable to believe that the account captures Twain's true sense of himself. Clearly the emphasis is on effort, fortitude, persistence, stoic endurance, and the concealment of personal anguish.

The account is a virtual model (or at least one model) of what the nineteenth century thought of as appropriate behavior for a man, and the very terms employed celebrate heroic manliness: "fought your way through," "never flinched or quailed," "never once wished to give over the battle." Twain figures his professional achievement in metaphors of warfare, associating his effort to become a pilot with the soldier, a highly valorized image of what constituted a man. Only under the guise of a clairvoyant's vision could Twain so laud himself for the qualities he believed he possessed as a man: strength, purposefulness, courage, stoicism. To be sure, having reported the fortune-teller's words, he undercuts her reliability—visiting her was, he says, "just as good as going to the Opera." But even at the time, he felt that she had "said some very startling things, and made some wonderful guesses" (*LI* III–I2), and some forty-six years later in his autobiographical dictations, he attested to her accuracy (see *LI* II6, n. I4).

Twain's much-heralded struggle to recover from bankruptcy—to pay off his creditors dollar for dollar and reestablish financial security for himself and his family—may be seen as a repetition, in his sixties, of his youthful efforts to rise in the world. To be sure, he was by then not only a well-established writer but also a famous humorist. He did not have to find a congenial profession, as he had in his youth, only to practice the ones he had already been successful in, and he had the help and support of shrewd men of business, notably Henry Huttleston Rogers. But he worked with the strength, purposefulness, and courage—if not the same stoicism (he complained a lot to his friends)—that he felt he had exerted in becoming a pilot. It is not too much to say that the manly qualities Twain claimed for himself in his youth remained with him throughout his life.

Ever lively and elusive in his personal relationships—and in the letters that cemented his friendships—Stevenson often postured in antithetical ways. One minute he was the perennial child, the next the struggling adult writer, then the suffering but stoic invalid, and then again the swaggering male who could talk of dying with his boots on. (These postures are all evident in his correspondence. For his wish to die with his boots on, see *Letters of RLS* 7:287.) In his letters to Henley, perhaps naturally enough, given Henley's own stance as a man of defiant will, Stevenson sometimes adopted a tone of belligerent manliness. Where Twain at times mocked muscular manhood, Stevenson occasionally made fun of its opposite: effeminate masculinity. One of his targets was none other than Matthew Arnold. When he wrote to Henley praising Beethoven's *Eroica* symphony, Henley replied with bluster: "You are right about the Eroica. It is with celestial vigour armed, if ever anything was in the world. It makes one hate Matthew Arnold to think of it. He is a man with an Eyeglass. How I wish that Bunyan had met him by the way! How I wish that you'd do a little dialogue between John and the Man with the Eyeglass. He is the worst Philistine of all. Culture is only an intelligent apology for emasculatedness; for lack of manly vigour, Sir!" (qtd. in *Letters of RLS* 209, n. 6). Stevenson had read Arnold with interest, but he seems to share Henley's view of him as lacking "manly vigour."[9] Stevenson and Henley collaborated on a satire called "Diogenes," and while they never finished it, one fragment, "Diogenes in London," done by Stevenson, makes fun of Arnold along the lines of Henley's vituperative outburst.

Stevenson has Diogenes lose his lantern in front of Scotland Yard (part of the satire is directed at the Yard), where he happens to meet Arnold. Arnold says to the cynical philosopher, "Chipe? You surprise me. The loss, however, might have been . . . [m]ore light, perhaps, than sweetness." Arnold takes Diogenes to Howard Vincent (the first head of the Yard), who records the number of the crime—"3,566,783"—and tells the philosopher that the men of Scotland Yard "do not cope with crime: we investigate it." When Arnold learns that the Yard's system is based on the French, he is beside himself with enthusiasm. " 'Lucidity, levity, clarity, classicality,' cried Mr. Arnold in a rapture. 'French is irresistible.' " The popular author of frothy romances Mary Elizabeth Braddon shows up, and she and Arnold launch into "a gay impromptu dance" to a "sweet melody" piped on a "penny whistle," each "bounding and tripping like a kid." Stevenson intensifies the absurd scene: " 'You now behold me happy,' said the poet. 'Quite the Greek, you see. Ah!' he cried, still leaping to the air, 'if the clergy of England were but here! What a lesson they would receive from this—this is worship.' " Each sings in turn—"With French and Greek in fit proportions / I write my classical abortions," Arnold intones— and then both perform a "Grand Dance & Finale," in which they sing together, "Our names can never die, huzza, / Our names can never die"

(*Works* 5:189–95). Stevenson thus turns Arnold into a vain, silly, egotistical, effeminate fop.

Twain and Stevenson both knew, in friends and public figures alike, extremes of male types. In his autobiography, Twain records his encounter with two quite different men whose dissimilarity is highlighted by their juxtaposition. One was George Dolby, his lecture agent, the other Charles Warren Stoddard, a poet and professor of English literature.[10] Twain begins by recalling that during his lecture tour in England in 1873 he hired Stoddard to be his "private secretary" even though there was "nothing for him to do" except to be his "comrade." He had in fact hired him "in order to have his company." He then presents this vignette:

> He was good company when he was awake. He was refined, sensitive, charming, gentle, generous, honest himself and unsuspicious of other people's honesty, and I think he was the purest male I have known, in mind and speech. George Dolby was something of a contrast to him, but the two were very friendly and sociable together, nevertheless. Dolby was large and ruddy, full of life and strength and spirits, a tireless and energetic talker, and always overflowing with good-nature and bursting with jollity. It was a choice and satisfactory menagerie, this pensive poet and this gladsome gorilla. An indelicate story was a sharp distress to Stoddard; Dolby told him twenty-five a day. Dolby always came home with us after the lecture, and entertained Stoddard till midnight. Me too.
> (*MTOA* 159)

Just as Twain enjoyed Stoddard and Dolby, so Stevenson liked Stoddard and Henley. Stevenson met Stoddard in 1880 in San Francisco, where Stoddard was active in the Bohemian Club, and the two corresponded for a time, expressing affection for each other and admiration of each other's work. In December 1880 Stevenson wrote a playful poem, largely in Scottish, "To C. W. Stoddard," that ends with these lines: "Far had I rode an' muckle seen, / But ne'er was fairly doddered / Till I was trystit as a fren' / Wi' Charlie Warren Stoddard!" (*Letters of RLS* 3:139). In Stoddard and Dolby, Stoddard and Henley, Twain and Stevenson had friends who were radically different men—to use Twain's invidious but affectionate terms, a "pensive poet" and a "gladsome gorilla." The fact that Twain and Stevenson were fond of both kinds of men may suggest something of the complexity of their own makeup as men. It certainly reveals that, whatever their mockery of male types, both Twain and Stevenson were freed from the homophobia common in their time.

It seems safe to say that Twain and Stevenson each combined some of the contrary aspects of manliness common in their time, overcoming most notably the notion that the hard is manly, the soft feminine. They shared the conventional sense that a true man was a man of moral character, however. They also shared one further feeling about manhood: they believed that a man should live life vigorously, to the full, for the very core of manhood was a vital expenditure of self, whether the self were hard or soft or both, in the engagement of life. They felt that a man should exert himself with force, no matter what the endeavor. "And what" Twain exclaimed, "is *a man* without energy? Nothing—nothing at all" (*LI* 96). And Stevenson avowed that he could not rest: "I have a goad in my flesh continually, pushing me to work, work, work" (*Letters of RLS* 2:218). Good Victorians both, Twain and Stevenson could subscribe to the idea that a man should be "strong in will / To strive, to seek, to find, and not to yield" (Tennyson, "Ulysses").

Ironically, their most important boy adventurers, after Jim Hawkins and Tom Sawyer, Huck Finn and David Balfour, do not set out "to seek, to find, and not to yield," for they are, rather clearly, reluctant adventurers. Huck's adventures do not really begin until he escapes from his confinement in Pap's cabin, and he frees himself from Pap not to undertake an adventure but to avoid his increasingly violent abuse. After thinking up two slightly different plans to gain his freedom, he finally decides just to live on Jackson's Island and to "paddle over to town, nights, and slink around and pick up things" (*HF* 41), a far cry from seeking adventures. It is not until Huck and Jim are on the river and encounter the wrecked steamboat, the *Walter Scott* (the name is Twain's joke on Sir Walter), that Huck considers having an adventure: "Well, it being away in the night, and stormy, and all so mysterious-like, I felt just the way any other boy would a felt, when I see that wreck laying there so mournful and lonesome in the middle of the river: I wanted to get aboard of her and slink around a little, and see what there was there." The language in which Twain casts the spur to Huck's desire—"away in the night, and stormy" and "all so mysterious-like"—borders on parody, and he makes Huck's one self-conscious attempt at what he says Tom Sawyer would call "an adventure" turn terrifying, as Huck finds himself first eavesdropping on thieves planning murder and then in danger of their discovering him (*HF* 80–81). After this, Huck never again seeks adventures; they just befall him, and he deals with them reluctantly, as best he can. But they also fit Huck insofar as he lives come-what-may, always curious, open to experience even as he tries to evade it, caught, as Simmel defined the quintessential adventurer, between the connection of the "accidental" nature of life and the "character and identity" of the adventurer who lives it out.

David Balfour, orphaned by the death of his father, first seeks his rich uncle as a source of support, an undertaking that is a necessity rather than an adventure. But before long he imagines that he is in fact having, as he says, an "adventure," and he considers giving it up and returning to his home village (*K* 18). David feels the real excitement and attraction of adventure only when he longs for "a nearer view of the sea and ships," and he succumbs to it as he lets himself be taken, against his judicious suspicions, on board the brig *Covenant* because he longs "to see the inside of a ship" (*K* 41, 48). But after he is bludgeoned aboard it and kidnapped, he, like Huck, ceases to seek out adventure. Indeed, thereafter, as catastrophic events befall him—ones that befit his character—he yearns to "be home" from all his adventures (*K* 152). Both Huck and David undertake adventures reluctantly, and both find in the first throes of chance and hazard a dire reality from which they long to be released. Both are, then, only ironically adventurers, for they both end up undergoing what they would prefer to elude. But like Twain's and Stevenson's earlier boy adventurers, Tom Sawyer and Jim Hawkins, Huck and David experience a series of adventures that move them from boyhood toward manhood.

Although it has generally been ignored, one of the central concerns of *Huckleberry Finn* is manhood. Perhaps inevitably, as he tapped the deep well of his boyhood past, Twain confronted the question of what it is to be a man. He depicts types of manhood throughout his novel and, at the exact center of the book, in chapter 22 of 43, he has the cold-blooded murderer—and aristocratic southern gentleman—Colonel Sherburn give a lecture on manliness. Confronted by a lynch mob, he defiantly tells them that they haven't "pluck enough to lynch a *man*!" He then expatiates on manhood, declaring that the "average man's a coward," that "the average man don't like trouble and danger," and that a "mob" of men is just like an "army"—a unit that does not fight with "courage that's born in them, but with courage that's borrowed from their mass, and from their officers" (*HF* 190–91). Sherburn (sometimes taken as a spokesperson for Twain's own ideas) is himself a wanton killer, but his speech, along with his own "manly" killing, calls attention to the issue at the very heart of *Huck Finn:* what makes a man?

Twain presents manhood in this text in two complementary ways. First, he satirizes spurious forms of manhood; and second, he creates in place of the false varieties his own version of true manhood. All the men Twain creates in *Huckleberry Finn* are inadequate. At one extreme they are confused and ineffectual, like the kindly, addlepated Silas Phelps; at the other, they are fierce and lethal, like the proud Colonel Sherburn. From Pap, the degenerate poor white trash, to the foolish new judge, who decides he will "make a man" of Pap only to have his guest bedroom destroyed by Pap's drunken carousing (the judge concludes that the only way to reform him is "with a shot-gun" [*HF* 26, 28]), Twain creates flawed men. In his still provocative *Studies in Classic American Literature*, D. H. Lawrence long ago described the essential American as "hard, isolate, stoic, and a killer" (73), and while his pejorative terms hardly do justice to the varieties of Americans, they fit remarkably well the men Twain depicts in *Huck Finn*. They are hard in their demeanor and conduct, isolated in their pride, indifferent to others, and often violent to the point of murderous.

In the famous raftsmen's passage, now restored to chapter 16 in the definitive California edition of *Huck Finn*, Twain furthers his attack on specious manliness. In Bob and the Child of Calamity, he brilliantly depicts two swaggering, tall-talking, ring-tailed roarers who boast of their physical might and their propensity for destruction in cosmic hyperbole: "I'm the man they call Sudden Death and General Desolation! . . . I split the everlasting rocks with my glance, and I squench the thunder when I speak! Whoo-oop!" To make it clear that their claims to brawny backwoods manliness are all bluster, Twain has the spindly Little Davy not only denounce them as a "couple of chicken-livered cowards" but also thrash them until "they begged like dogs." While he satirizes the rugged, frontier male as a mere blowhard, Twain also reveals that real violence does inhere in some of these rivermen, for, although it is often overlooked in criticism, Little Davy gives the two braggarts a genuine beating, not just to expose their prowess as bluster, but to prove he can—and for the sheer fun of it: "He snatched them, he jerked them this way and that, he booted

them around, he knocked them sprawling faster than they could get up"
(*HF* 109, 111–12). The violence here is matched at the other end of the
class spectrum by Sherburn's gunning down of Boggs and by the killings
in the Grangerford-Shepherdson feud. Twain insists that men—southern
gentlemen and riverboat ruffians alike—are fond of bloodletting.

Pap is jailed for "a-blowing around and cussing and whooping and carrying on" until midnight "all over town," but when he is released, Huck
tells us, "he said *he* was satisfied; said he was boss of his son, and he'd
make it warm for *him*" (*HF* 26). Having been curtailed by the law, Pap
reestablishes his sense of self by threatening to do violence to the weaker,
vulnerable Huck. (And of course he makes good on his threat.) Twain
makes this impulse to elevate the self by assailing—with words, or fists,
or guns—a weaker person a common denominator of the men. Pap beats
Huck; the judge jails Pap; the Shepherdsons kill Buck and other Grangerfords; Sherburn guns down Boggs; and, while it is a somewhat different
matter, the King and the Duke sell Jim. Twain criticizes in the men a need
for dominance that is most often satisfied by the assertion of strength over
weakness. The mobs, composed entirely of men, that threaten to lynch
Sherburn and to lynch "the whole gang" in the Peter Wilks affair only
act out collectively the desire for domination the men possess individually
(*HF* 256).

Twain's text is charged with the threat of male violence. When Huck
paddles off in the canoe to see if he and Jim have passed Cairo, he meets
a man in a skiff, setting a trotline, and innocently asks him, "Mister, is
that town Cairo?" The man replies, "Cairo? no. You must be a blame'
fool," and after Huck asks what town it is then, the man says, "If you
want to know, go and find out. If you stay here botherin' around me for
about a half a minute longer, you'll get something you won't want" (*HF*
129). The man's threat of violence is especially horrifying because it is
gratuitous. It is, however, indicative of the danger that truly stalks Huck at
every turn. Twain suggests the male lust for cruelty when he has the crowd
trying to discover the true Wilks brothers sing out, "The whole *bilin'* of
'm's frauds! Le's duck 'em! le's drown 'em! le's ride 'em on a rail!" (*HF*
256). Another mob, of course, does finally tar and feather the Duke and
the King and ride them out of town on a rail. Huck says, "They was all
over tar and feathers, and didn't look like nothing in the world that was
human—just looked like a couple of monstrous big soldier-plumes" (*HF*

290). Asserting their false manhood in violent acts, the men of the mob destroy the human in themselves as well as their victims. Huck's image—"monstrous big soldier-plumes"—is, appropriately for Twain's satire, a grotesque parody of a stock emblem of conventional manhood.

While Twain satirizes traditional forms of manhood, most recurrently those that involve physical strength and violence, he also enacts a positive vision of a true man. Paradoxically, the real man in the novel is the adventuring boy Huck Finn. He tells us in the beginning of his book that we "don't know" about him unless we have "read a book by the name of 'Adventures of Tom Sawyer,' but that ain't no matter" (*HF* 1). If we have read that book, we know that in it Huck worries over Muff Potter (though it is left to Tom, the book's hero, to save him) and that he acts to protect the Widow Douglas. We know, that is, that Huck is stirred by compassion. Unlike Tom, who must learn from his adventures to feel for others, to take them into account and adjust his actions to fit their needs, Huck is attuned to others from the first. The check to egocentricity and lock onto empathy that Tom must acquire to approach manhood Huck already has. Unlike Tom's, Huck's adventures do not lead him to manhood so much as they create occasions for his manliness to express itself. If, to return to Huck's disarming opening remarks, we "don't know" about him, that "ain't no matter" because Twain dramatizes his character throughout the novel named for him. In particular, he reveals over and over Huck's emotional responsiveness, his acute capacity for fellow feeling.

In his seminal essay on *Huck Finn*, Lionel Trilling long ago called attention to this remark of Huck's: "We looked away down into the village and could see three or four lights twinkling, where there was sick folks, may be" (*HF* 8). For Trilling, Huck's supposition—"there was sick folks, may be"—captures not the reality of night in St. Petersburg but Huck's concern for others, his "quick and immediate" sympathy (117). Huck's empathy is evident everywhere in the novel. He worries over—feels with and therefore for—the Widow Douglas, Jim, the thieves on the *Walter Scott*, the Grangerfords (especially Buck but also Miss Sophia), the Wilks sisters, the Duke and the King, Aunt Sally and Uncle Silas, as well as Tom Sawyer. His compassion is so quick and extreme that were it not concealed by Huck's colloquial language and flat, matter-of-fact tone, it would surely qualify him to be the heroine of a sentimental novel. Jim, who knows Huck intimately, calls him, somewhat surprisingly, "de ole true Huck; de on'y white genlman dat ever kep' his promise to ole Jim" (*HF* 125). Huck is always a gentle man.

Henry Nash Smith once pointed out the presence in Twain's novel of "a residue of the eighteenth-century cult of sensibility" (117), and there is, I believe, an obvious connection between this cult of sensibility and Huck himself. The historical emphasis on sensibility carried well beyond the eighteenth century, of course, becoming a prominent feature of nineteenth-century Victorian life and art, especially the so-called "feminized" American version of it (Douglas). In attending to such emotionalism Twain was not only being true to his novel's setting in the 1830s or '40s, he was also commenting on current postures in his own culture. The sentimental was, in short, very much with Mark Twain, and, as I've argued in the first chapter, it was also *in* him. Twain's burlesque of the cult of sensibility in *Huckleberry Finn* is in part a check against his own susceptibility and in part a diversion calculated to deflect our attention away from Huck's own overabundance of emotion. A further disguise of "de ole true Huck" is provided by Huck's role *as critic* of the sentimental. Huck memorably dismisses emotional outpourings as "tears and flapdoodle," "soul-butter and hogwash," "rot and slush" (*HF* 213). But Huck himself is governed by intense emotions, and at times he gives voice to them in fairly sentimental ways. Unlike the various imposters in the novel who call themselves gentlemen, weeping soulful tears only to perpetrate violent acts, Huck is genuinely softhearted and never violent. His tenderness is extraordinary. For he is, I believe, Twain's version of the eighteenth-century Man of Feeling.

The ideas that generated the Man of Feeling may be summarized as follows: first, the identification of virtue with acts of benevolence and with feelings of universal goodwill; second, the assumption that good affections, benevolent feelings, are the natural outgrowth of the heart of man; third, the conviction that tenderness is manly; and fourth, the belief that benevolent emotions, even anguished ones, result in pleasant, self-approving feelings (Crane). The first three of these fit Huck's character perfectly, and the notion that tenderness is manly encapsulates, I believe, Twain's own conception of manhood. Twain's departure from the archetype of the Man of Feeling lies in his rejection of the fourth engendering idea: the notion that pleasure can be derived from even painful benevolent emotions. This is a crucial variation, one that saves Twain's character from absurd postures of self-approving joy and, more important, one that makes Huck a *comic* Man of Feeling. Huck never feels good about his goodness; his altruistic emotions—with the possible exception of his aid to Mary Jane—never give him egoistic satisfaction. For of course Huck always thinks that in following his fine feelings he is acting immorally. His confusion is the source of both our laughter and our moral approval.

Twain's conception of manhood in this novel, with its emphasis on tenderness as the defining characteristic, is thus something of a throwback to an earlier age, though in the prevailing nineteenth-century confusion over the masculine there were, as I've suggested, models of the softhearted male. Twain's most elaborated demonstration of the poignant fellow-feeling that constitutes Huck's manhood, of course, is his struggle over whether to turn Jim in. Twain stages the conflict between Huck's tender heart and his conventional conscience twice; and in each case, the heart wins out. Huck has everything backward, of course, for when he honors his tender feelings over his conscience he believes he is doing wrong. He also believes—and this has generally been overlooked in criticism—that he is unmanly. When he first tries to violate the prompting of his heart and turn Jim over to the slave hunters, only to fail, he says, "I warn't man enough—hadn't the spunk of a rabbit" (*HF* 125). But just as he does right, thinking he is doing wrong, so he acts like a man, believing he has lacked manliness. Unlike the typical hero of boy-adventure, Huck never gets to feel satisfied with his resolve, nor does he ever realize that he possesses true manhood. To be sure, his resolve seems called into question by his willingness to go along with Tom Sawyer's preposterous plans for freeing Jim, but his manliness, his sympathy for Jim, remains steadfast, even though he acts so obliquely on it out of deference to Tom.

What Twain does rather clearly in the end is to turn emphatically against the genre of boy adventure. Tom's Great Evasion, as he calls it, is finally neither exciting nor funny. Twain's parody of adventure fictions is farcical, but its critical design is unmistakable. The end of *Tom Sawyer* upholds adventure, as Tom's time in the cave not only validates his growing manly concern for others but also yields material rewards. In contrast, the end of *Huck Finn* (or the near end) not only mocks adventure as it renders its elements ludicrous but also problematizes its moral content in the treatment of Jim. In the aftermath of the Evasion, however, Twain stages one final demonstration of Huck's manly empathy. As he does so, he releases Huck from his comic (and often poignant) confusion, from his conflict between heart and conscience, and the release is tantamount to an affirmation. Stranded at Aunt Sally's (still in disguise as Tom), wondering what has happened when the doctor visited the wounded Tom and the hidden Jim, Huck longs to run off, but Aunt Sally—after seeing him to bed and mothering him "so good"—tells him, "The door ain't going to be locked, Tom; and there's the window and the rod; but you'll be good, *won't* you? And you won't go? For *my* sake?" Huck longs to go, but avers, "after that, I wouldn't a went, not for kingdoms" (*HF* 350). For once Huck does what is "good," which is also what his heart feels is right. Compassion is triumphant in this gentle moment. In the end, Huck gives up his current adventure out of love (though he later seconds Tom's scheme to "go for howling adventures amongst the Injuns" [*HF* 361]), and in so doing illustrates Twain's sense of what it is to be a true man. In the end, Huck has far more spunk than a rabbit and is man enough.

In February 1885, one month after he began writing *Kidnapped*, Stevenson wrote to his friend John Addington Symonds, "Have you read *Huckleberry Finn*? It contains many excellent things; above all, the whole story of a healthy boy's dealings with his conscience, incredibly well done" (*Letters of RLS* 5:80). It seems very likely that *Huck Finn* had a shaping influence on *Kidnapped*. Critics have pointed out multiple similarities: two boys are newly orphaned; their lives are threatened by greedy men; both are kidnapped by relatives; both fake their deaths; both have interludes on islands; both then journey with a man who is a fugitive from justice; both undergo extensive wanderings through the heart of a country; and both struggle with their conscience to accept their outcast companions, a slave in one case, a defeated rebel in the other (see Eiger 79–80). The similarities are intriguing, but David Balfour is no Huck Finn.

While Huck is from the first of his adventures deeply selfless, David is preoccupied with himself, measuring his strength, intellect, and spirit at every turn. Where Huck is uncertain, self-denigrating, and largely without purpose (beyond helping Jim), David is determined, often prideful, and intent upon recovering his inheritance. Huck could not possibly say, as David does, that he had "the upper hand" in outwitting an adversary, nor could he, as David does, assault an enemy, saying with pride, "I was a strong lad" (*K* 113, 111). Nor could Huck wound and kill others, as David does in the siege of the roundhouse aboard the ironically named brig *The Covenant*. David moralizes in a manner foreign to Huck, observing, for instance, that "men should never weary of, goodness and humility," and unlike Huck, he congratulates himself: "I was a good deal puffed up with my adventures and with having come off, as the saying is, with flying colours" (*K* 122). Yet like Huck, David is often moved by pity: he feels sorry for the half-witted cabin boy, Ransome; he feels sorry for the first mate who kills Ransome; he feels sorry for the captain who kidnaps him; he feels sorry for the rebellious Highlanders; he feels sorry for the Red Fox who oppresses them; and he even feels sorry in the end for the rapacious, cruel uncle who has usurped his birthright (*K* 42, 61, 80, 87, 129, 227). Much like Huck, David is a Man of Feeling.

At first glance, Stevenson would seem to be as intent on satirizing varieties of bogus manhood as Twain is. David's minister is as good, and as ineffectual, as Silas Phelps; his uncle Ebenezer, though a miser rather than a drunk, is as cruel, as lost to common humanity, as Pap; and the Red Fox is reported to be (we never see him act) as hard, arrogant, and murderous as Colonel Sherburn. James of the Glens and Cluny are hardened warriors (though James is also a concerned husband and father). Certainly the two men David meets on the road to Torosay are as deceitful, greedy, and threatening as the Duke and the King, as one cheats him and menaces him with a knife and the other tries to rob him using a pistol. The world David moves through is as fraught with the likelihood of male violence as Huck's. But David's world has recently been through civil war, the Jacobite uprising of 1745, and is still torn by political conflict ready to erupt yet again into armed warfare. Violent men are called forth by the times.

However, Stevenson further complicates his critical depiction of men in the commanding figure of Alan Brock Stuart. For Alan embodies many of the traits censored in the other men. He is a Highland warrior: bold, aggressive, confident, violent, but also cunning, full of guile, duplicity, and sweet-tongued talk. He is, rather clearly, a variant of Long John Silver. Stevenson's fondness for such an ambivalent admixture of the authentic and the fraudulent, of admirable talents and contemptible traits, tips in this novel from the mild disapproval registered in *Treasure Island* to near celebration. He does laugh gently at Alan for his overbearing self-conceit. David observes, for instance, that while Alan "had a great taste for courage in other men," he "admired it most" in himself (*K* 91). But Stevenson nonetheless makes him a glittering hero. Once he appears, Alan's presence dominates the narrative, easily overshadowing the upright but unremarkable David. Alan's bold and manly cries reverberate throughout the novel: "Am I no a bonny fighter?"; "It will be as it must"; "Forth, Fortune! and take a cast among the heather"; "As well one death as another" (*K* 75, 94, 134, 150). In terms that are both dire and dramatic, he lays out for David the hardships and dangers they will face as they flee across the Highland heather: "But mind you," says Alan, "it's no small thing. Ye maun lie bare and hard, and brook many an empty belly. Your bed shall be the moorcock's, and your life shall be like the haunted deer's, and ye shall sleep with your hand upon your weapons. Aye, man, ye shall taigle many a weary foot, or we get clear! I tell ye this at the start, for it's a life that I ken well. But if ye ask what other chance ye have, I answer: Nane." Alan's daring spirit is irresistible; indeed, he embodies the allure, the excitement, the exoticism of adventure itself. And he not only represents but also articulates a recurrent standard of manhood in the novel. "To be feared of a thing," he tells David, "and yet to do it, is what makes the prettiest kind of a man" (*K* 133, 147).

But for all his attraction to Alan Breck Stuart, and despite Alan's dominating presence in David's adventures, Stevenson's tale does not totally sanction either Alan or his kind of manhood. Paradoxically, he makes Alan, the manly hero, the epitome of the adventurer, the definer of manhood, something of a boy. He is vain, peevish, and moody. Oddly, like Tom Sawyer, he delights in his attire. Above all, however, he has what David calls a "childish propensity to take offense and to pick quarrels" (*K* 91).

Stevenson's ambivalent portrayal of Alan is a wonderfully complex commentary on both exciting adventure and one common ideal of manhood. Though David grows as fond of Alan as Huck does of Jim, there is no simple issue of emulation in Stevenson's novel. Priggish at times (whiggish always), David seems to possess from the beginning of his adventures the requisite qualities of manhood upheld in this novel: courage, endurance, loyalty, and—perhaps most importantly—empathy. Though steadfast, he is as unglamorous as Alan is bewitching. However much Stevenson admired Twain's depiction of a heart locked in combat with a conscience, he avoids such polarities in his account of David's experience.

David makes two critical decisions: he decides to aid Alan and determines to confront the Red Fox and his retinue. He explains his resolve to help Alan this way: "My mind was made up all in a moment. I have no credit by it; it was by no choice of mine, but as if by compulsion"; and he gives this account of his daring to halt the Red Fox: "I had no sooner seen these people coming than I made up my mind (for no reason that I can tell) to go through with my adventure; and when the first came alongside of me, I rose up from the bracken and asked him the way to Aucharn" (*K* 68, 125). At both of these critical junctures, David acts thoughtlessly, impulsively. While Stevenson thus seems to slip by the very conflicts that should tear and divide David (Twain's creation of Huck's struggle seems bold and honest in contrast), David is not always mindlessly impulsive. He not only thinks carefully about but finally acts on another, even more crucial issue: should he continue to aid Alan? (His reflection on this stands in stark contrast to his other spontaneous acts.) He realizes that while Alan thinks he is saving him, he is in fact putting him in jeopardy. David would be safer going it alone without the well-known rebel at his side. He says, "Alan's society was not only a peril to my life, but a burden on my purse." His eventual decision to stay with Alan, to see things through with him for better or worse, is the fullest expression of his nascent manhood, for here—as in Twain's novel—ultimate manhood resides in loyalty born of love. As moral counterpoint to David's commitment, in the much-praised Quarrel in the Heather, Alan is told by David, "Ye should think more of others, Alan Breck" (*K* 159, 180). This is just what David, the boy adventuring into manhood, has done in determining to stay with Alan. For all the swashbuckling bravery and martial antics in this novel, the final measure of a man for Stevenson—as for Twain—is dedication to another at whatever risk, or affliction of conscience, or public humiliation.

Boy adventure for both Stevenson and Twain thus transcends thrills, danger, excitement, though both provide plenty of those, to arrive at a representation of manhood that confounds some of the commonplace notions at large in their culture in its time of confused, contested versions of the manly. Both affirm the tender man.

While the gentle is ultimately upheld, however, both Stevenson and Twain also acknowledge the forceful. Jim Hawkins has his Long John Silver, Tom Sawyer his Injun Joe; Huck Finn listens to Colonel Sherburn, David Balfour to Alan Breck Stewart. Stevenson pursued such divisions most arrestingly in *Doctor Jekyll and Mr. Hyde* and *The Master of Ballantrae*.[11] Twain placed the oppositions that mark his two boy novels at the very center of Hank Morgan, for his Connecticut Yankee in King

Arthur's Court is both tearfully compassionate and determinedly, even destructively, assertive. But these later fictions are not boy adventures. The luminous world of the unknown, the realm Stevenson and Twain experienced in their travel and recuperated in their adventure fictions, faded for both writers. As they aged, both writers turned away from the world of exhilarating experience beckoning boys on the way to manhood.

# Mark Twain
# & Rudyard Kipling

*Saved from the jaws of the cowcatcher, me wandering*
*devious a stranger met.*

RUDYARD KIPLING, 1889

The story is a good one, the tale of the first meeting between Twain and
Kipling, and Kipling told it well. He wrote it up as a journalistic scoop
with verve and dash, with a jaunty confidence amounting to cockiness,
publishing it first in an Indian newspaper, the *Allahabad Pioneer*, then
reprinting it in the *New York Herald*, and eventually revising it for inclusion in *From Sea to Sea*. The actual encounter took place in August 1889,
as Kipling, returning to England from India, traveled across America from
San Francisco to New York. Kipling was writing up his experiences in a
series of travel letters for the *Pioneer*, but he went out of his way to meet
Mark Twain.

Kipling turns his attempt to find the famous author—whom he greatly
admired—into nothing less than a comic quest. He reports seeking him
first in Buffalo, where he is told that Twain is either in Hartford or sum-
mering in Europe. The thought that Twain is abroad and that he would
therefore miss him so upsets Kipling that he embarks on "the wrong train"
and is "incontinently turned out by the conductor three-quarters of a mile
from the station, amid the wilderness of railway tracks." "Have you ever,"

he asks his readers, "encumbered with great-coat and valise, tried to dodge diversely-minded locomotives when the sun was shining in your eyes?" Saved, he says, from "the jaws of the cowcatcher," "wandering devious," he meets a stranger who tells him Twain can be found in Elmira, New York, "not two hundred miles away." He immediately takes a train to Elmira, where he is warned that Twain may have gone "East somewhere" and instructed to find his brother-in-law. Kipling is so dismayed he spends a restless night. "The idea," he says, "of chasing half a dozen relatives in addition to Mark Twain up and down a city of thirty thousand inhabitants kept me awake" (*Portable K* 668–69).

After his sleepless night he finally finds a policeman who assures Kipling that he has seen Twain or "some one very like him." Kipling is delighted: "Fancy living in a town where you could see the author of 'Tom Sawyer' or 'some one very like him,' jolting over the pavements in a buggy." Sent three miles up the steep East Hill to Quarry Farm, Kipling is told there that Twain "has just walked downtown" to his "brother-in-law's." Hurrying downhill and then to the home, Kipling hesitates on the doorstep: "It was in the pause that followed between ringing the brother-in-law's bell and getting an answer that it occurred to me, for the first time, Mark Twain might possibly have other engagements than the entertainment of escaped lunatics from India, be they never so full of admiration" (*Portable K* 669–70).

He need not have worried, for he is ushered in, seated in the drawing room, and greeted by Twain with a joke: "Well, you think you owe me something, and you've come to tell me so. That's what I call squaring a debt handsomely" (*Portable K* 671).

The interview itself strikes one today as more perfunctory than original. Occasionally guided by Kipling but most often just following his own whim, Twain seems to talk about potentially substantive topics but to say little of significance about them—and often little that is new as he trots out pet ideas. (This was an almost necessary tactic for a famous man like Twain, increasingly subject to interviews. The very familiarity of some of the ideas at least authenticates Kipling's report of the interview.) Much in the manner of celebrity interviews, now as well as then, Kipling tries to create a sense of Mark Twain's presence. He notes his advanced years, his playful eyes, his "grizzled hair" and "brown moustache," his slow drawl, his slouching body posture, his incessant pipe-smoking, and his occasional pacing about the room "in his slippers." Twain holds forth about copyright (it should be treated like real estate), about *Tom Sawyer* (in a sequel Tom would end up either in Congress or on the gallows, an "angel" or a "rip"), about the force of conscience (a nuisance that should be treated like a child, spanked when "rebellious"), about truth in literature (everyone lies, especially in autobiography, though the reader can usually discern the fraudulent from the true), and about current fiction (he prefers reading factual books and only reads fiction for the "workmanship"). Although Kipling trumpets the wisdom as well as the greatness of Twain—"Attend," he commands his readers, "to the words of the oracle" (*Portable K* 671–79)—Twain's remarks are, for a man so likely to say something unexpected and so skilled at saying even the commonplace in arresting ways, curiously tepid and flat. The presence that sparkles in the interview is not Twain but Kipling.

While Twain sounds ponderous and dull, Kipling is sprightly and provocative. Playing the admiring, humble acolyte, he nonetheless surpasses the master in playfulness. From his opening self-mockery—he is one of the many "rampageous outsiders" who seek Twain—to his mockery of Elmira—its streets are "desolated by railway tracks," its suburbs devoted to the "manufacture of door-sashes and window-frames"—to his fawning description of himself and celebratory elevation of Twain—"when the old lion roars, the young whelps growl. I growled"—to his paradoxical evocation of future nostalgia—"I should have ample time to look back to that meeting across the graves of the days"—it is Kipling himself who stands out (*Portable K* 669–79). His report effects a curious displacement: the upstart journalist from India supersedes, at least in humor and lively phrasing, the elder humorist and consummate talker.

Kipling's article is, to be sure, full of lavish praise for Twain. Indeed the basic design of the piece casts Kipling as the devoted admirer of a great author and Twain as nothing less than a literary god, with the admirer being totally unworthy of attention (a conceit redolent of extravagant oriental courtesy) but delighted to the point of swagger at having received it. In this vein he begins with a journalistic "grabber" by calling British commissioners, lieutenant-governors, holders of the Victoria Cross, and even viceroys a "contemptible lot" since they have not, as he has, "seen Mark Twain." Early in the interview he serves up this vignette: "I was shaking his hand. I was smoking his cigar, and I was hearing his talk—this man

I had learned to love and admire fourteen thousand miles away." And in mid-interview he interrupts his account of Twain's talk, first to suggest comically that he covets Twain's pipe since it would give him "a hint of his keen insight into the souls of men" but never finds it "within stealing reach," and then to note a special favor that bestows grandeur: "Once, indeed, he put his hand on my shoulder. It was an investiture of the Star of India, blue silk, trumpets, and diamond-studded jewel, all complete" (*Portable K* 668–76).

But these celebrations of Twain are oddly counterpointed in suggestive ways. The very first thing that Kipling notes about Twain is that he is "an elderly man," though he modifies this by finding youth in his eyes. When he jokes about stealing Twain's pipe, he offers this curious analogy: "I understood why certain savage tribes ardently desired the liver of brave men slain in combat." He describes the moment of actual first meeting as a time "to be remembered" but adds, "the landing of a twelve-pound salmon was nothing to it." And he ends his sketch with this peculiar notion: "If so experienced a man could by any means be made drunk, it would be a glorious thing to fill him up with composite liquors, and, in the language of his own country, 'let him retrospect'" (*Portable K* 671–80).

Kipling's ironic counterpoint to his adulation of Twain creates a kind of equality with, or even superiority to, his idol. To compare his meeting to fishing is surely to reduce its significance, comically of course. To picture Twain drunk to the point of loquacious reminiscence is far from flattering (and for the genteel of the time it would have put both Kipling and Twain in a dim light). His suggestion that in wanting to steal Twain's pipe he comprehends the savage ritual of cutting out a brave warrior's liver is shocking and grotesque, however casually he presents it. These equalizing or demeaning turns in Kipling's sketch create a fanciful subtext, one rendered with the utmost good will: Twain is old, likely to falter, subject to manipulation by a younger author. It is hard not to see here some anxiety of influence, something of a not-too-hidden desire to supplant a revered precursor.

According to Kipling, Twain made a joke on first meeting him about Kipling's owing him something. Twain was just breaking the ice with a stranger, putting him at ease by giving him an entrée into explaining who he was and why he was there. But Kipling did, in fact, owe Twain something. Indeed, his debt was twofold: he was indebted to Twain for his having demonstrated the power—the energy, versatility, and newness—of the vernacular in literature, and he was indebted to him for showing the attractiveness of the figure of a good bad boy, like Tom Sawyer or Huck Finn, both as a compelling literary type and as a foil for satire. Kipling had an even greater debt. In the revised version of the interview, there is one glaring omission: Kipling never asks Twain anything about *Adventures of Huckleberry Finn.* If absence is presence, and omission is acknowledgment, Twain's novel must have loomed powerfully in Kipling's mind. In time, however, Kipling paid all his debts to Twain in full. He exploited the vernacular with great skill not only in his ballads but also in his stories, and *Stalky & Co.* is a boarding-school version of *Tom Sawyer,* while Kipling's finest work, *Kim,* is nothing less than a tale of Huckleberry Finn in India.

When Kipling visited Twain, Twain did not know who he was—in fact had never heard of him or his writings (*MTE* 309–12). But a year or so later, when his friend George Warner introduced him to *Plain Tales from the Hills,* he quickly remedied this. He not only bought—and read—Kipling but also came to admire his works, perhaps as much as Kipling admired him. Eventually he owned some twenty-five individual volumes of Kipling, along with a twenty-seven-volume collected edition, *The Works of Rudyard Kipling* (Gribben, *MT's Library* 375–82). He loved to read Kipling aloud, both his poems and his stories (Kipling replaced Robert Browning in Twain's repertoire of authors to read publicly), and he never ceased to praise his artistry. At one time he considered using Kipling's jungle creatures in one of his own (eventually unwritten) stories; he did incorporate references to Kipling into several of his late fictions. He remembered lines from Kipling's poetry, weaving them naturally into his conversation and autobiographical reminiscences. Feeling the poignancy of Kipling's phrase, "The Light that Failed" (the title of Kipling's 1890 novel, one that failed), he thought repeatedly of his beloved Susy's early death in precisely these terms (*Love Letters of Mark Twain* 325). He found "On the Road to Mandalay" the "most fascinating" of all Kipling's poems and saw in it, heard in it as he and others read it aloud, "mingled pathos and humor" (Gribben, *MT's Library* 379)—the combination that he seems to have sought often in his own writing (see the first chapter). Kipling became, in short, a small but significant touchstone for Twain in his later writing, public performances, and private life.

Though a generation apart in time, the careers of Twain and Kipling (1865–1936) have some notable parallels. Setting aside juvenilia—early poems in Kipling's case, comic sketches in Twain's—both really began as journalists. Both then turned to travel writing, Twain spectacularly so with *The Innocents Abroad*, Kipling rather quietly with a series of travel letters first published in Indian newspapers and eventually collected in *From Sea to Sea*. Both were slow to tackle novels, spending most of their early work on short stories, sketches, and essays—and in the case of Kipling, poems. In their most successful and significant work, both plumbed their childhood, Twain most notably in *Tom Sawyer* and *Huck Finn*, Kipling in "Baa, Baa, Black Sheep," *Stalky & Co.*, and *Kim*. And many of their late works, like Kipling's *Puck of Pook's Hill* and Twain's the Mysterious Stranger tales, exploit fantasy (Twain imagined that he saw something, though he did not say what, of his own Mysterious Stranger in Kipling's Puck [Gribben, *MT's Library* 381]).

Both arguably began as provincial writers, only to end as cosmopolitan ones, and both had at one time or another in their careers problems with recognition and acceptance. Beginning as a western humorist and then vagabond travel writer, Twain was estranged from but aspired to become a part of the eastern literary establishment in America. Similarly, Kipling started out as an alien to the literary center, as a member of the Anglo-Indian culture, but longed, at least initially, to be acknowledged by the clubby world of literary London. Both writers became immensely popular, but each had difficulty securing critical acclaim; indeed, Twain was often dismissed as a low vulgarian, and Kipling was sometimes denounced as the voice of the hooligan. Perhaps in retaliation for their slow and mixed reception by sophisticated critics, both Twain and Kipling would in time decide that they wrote principally, as Twain once put it, for the "Belly and the Members" not for the "Head"—for the general public, that is, not the elite (*CH* 334–36). In time they succeeded so well with the elite as well as the masses that both received honorary degrees from Oxford in 1907. At the encaenia they talked together before the ceremony, then walked side by side in the procession to the cheers of the people who lined the streets and often shouted, at least according to Kipling, "good old Mark" (RK, *Letters* 3:249). (Kipling would receive the even greater honor of the Nobel Prize later in the same year.) Both writers left their mark not only on their time but on subsequent ones; both, to use one of Twain's favorite metaphors, blazed like comets across the sky of literature.

The acknowledgment of their work in the Oxford degrees must have gone a long way toward erasing any memories of adverse criticism suffered in the past. Whatever they might have lacked in critical recognition in the uneven course of their careers, however, Twain and Kipling more than made up for in mutual admiration.[1] Each praised the other unstintingly. In his late autobiographical reminiscences, Twain confessed, "Kipling's name and Kipling's words always stir me now, stir me more than do any other living man's" (*AMT* 286). And with extravagant playfulness, he insisted: "I am not acquainted with my own books but I know Kipling's—at any rate I know them better than I know anybody else's books." He avowed that some of Kipling's ballads had "a peculiar and satisfying charm" for him; he found the *Jungle Book*s "incomparable"; and he said that his long and difficult journey to India was worth the exhaustion just "to qualify" him "to read *Kim* understandingly and to realize how great a book it is." He claimed that he re-read *Kim* "every year" and found that Kipling's works "never grow pale," that they "keep their color," and that they are "always fresh." He marveled at Kipling's fame: "He has held this unique distinction: that of being the only living person, not head of a nation, whose voice is heard around the world the moment it drops a remark, the only such voice in existence that does not go by slow ship and rail but always travels first-class by cable" (*MTE* 311–12).

Kipling was no more restrained than Twain in his praise of the elder writer. He told his American publisher Frank Doubleday in 1903, "I love to think of the great and God-like Clemens. He is the biggest man you have on your side of the water by a damn sight, and don't you forget it" (qtd. in *MTL* 747). Twenty-five years after Twain's death, a year before his own, Kipling became chairman of the Mark Twain Centennial Committee in England. He wrote at the time to the committee chairman in America, Nicholas Murray Butler, the president of Columbia University: "To my mind he was the largest man of his time, both in the direct outcome of his work, and, more important still, as an indirect force in an age of iron Philistinism" (qtd. in Baetzhold, *MT and John Bull* 195).

In keeping with the Victorian notion—still alive then, though about to lose its hold in the Edwardian era—that literature served a large social purpose, that it had the power to direct society itself for good or ill, both Twain and Kipling in their praise see each other as a force in the world at large—a far cry from what would become the modernist sense of the alienated artist writing for a comprehending coterie of other estranged writers.

However, Kipling's final praise is odd at least, for he celebrates Twain as a "force" in "an iron age of Philistinism." Implicitly he thus makes Twain a force *against* Philistinism, an interpretation of Twain and his work that interestingly recalls Matthew Arnold's analysis of society as a composite of Barbarians, Philistines, and the Populace. But unlike Arnold, Kipling places Twain not among the Philistines, as Arnold had, but as a counter-force to them. It is a view that suggests, albeit vaguely, something of a conservative Twain—a Twain more like Kipling himself. Modern critics of Twain would not support such a reading of him, for he is most often seen today as a radical, even subversive writer. Yet no one would con-test the idea, clearly articulated by both Twain and Kipling, that they tried to address their age not only through their writings but also more di-rectly as moral spokesmen, as sages, to return to the Arnoldian connection, as personages of eminence and wisdom who had the power to illuminate by critique—sometimes casual, sometimes extended—the shortcomings of their culture. It is their fictions, however, that finally engage their culture most searchingly, for their pronouncements, however sharp, or forceful, or even humorous, lack the sustained exploration and revelation of their novels.

In the original version of his interview with Twain, finally published in no fewer than three newspapers, two in India, one in New York, Kipling ended the sketch with a single short paragraph expressing in an affected way his dismay—"Oh shame! Oh shock! Oh fie!"—over *A Connecticut Yankee in King Arthur's Court* because of its "yankee animal." He re-treated awkwardly from his alarm, declaring first that he did not believe that Twain "ever wrote it" and then adding that if he did, and if one examined it carefully, it would surely reveal "some crystal clean tale as desirable as Huck Finn" ("RK on Mark Twain" 321). Here, obliquely ex-pressed, to be sure, is praise for Twain's greatest novel, the one Kipling so pointedly failed to ask about. Kipling worried that he might have offended Twain with his remarks about the *Yankee*, but Twain seems not to have minded, perhaps because Kipling's censure was so vague, perhaps because it was offset by the praise of *Huckleberry Finn*, or perhaps because by then Twain had read far more adverse responses to his novel. Still, when he revised the interview for inclusion in *From Sea to Sea: Letters of Travel*, Kipling omitted the final, potentially offensive paragraph on *A Connecticut Yankee.*

In all versions of the interview, Kipling alters the facts of his actual visit in a very suggestive way. The facts Kipling changed are harmless enough but finally revealing, both of Kipling's strategy in the interview and of the formal structure that Kipling and Twain shared in a profound way. In the two versions of his encounter with Twain, the revised as well as the original, Kipling presents his final effort to find Twain as a mad dash, immediately undertaken upon learning where Twain was, from the uphill Quarry Farm to the downtown residence of the Langdon family: "With speed I fled, and the driver, skidding the wheel and swearing audibly, arrived at the bottom of that hill without accidents" (*Portable K* 670). In fact, in the actual event, Kipling did not rush away from Quarry Farm in hot pursuit of his idol. As Twain recalled in his autobiography, Kipling "sat on the veranda" with Twain's sister-in-law, Susan Crane, and his daughter Susy, "rested," chatted, and generally "refreshed himself" (*MTE* 309–10). The group was charmed (as so many were throughout his life) by Kipling's talk. Kipling omits this interlude not only to heighten the drama of his search for Twain but also to continue its essential form: that of a wandering journey.

The journey motif that Kipling uses so effectively in his interview points to the basic formal link that binds together *Adventures of Huckleberry Finn* and *Kim:* both are picaresque novels, novels in which an outsider, a sub-social picaro, journeys haphazardly across a landscape and awkwardly through the complex strata of society. Although the picaresque did not have the currency of the five other modes taken up so far in this study, it was still very much in evidence in the second half of the nineteenth century. It is a remarkably capacious form. It can—and in Twain and Kipling pretty much does—incorporate all the other modes considered here: it is sentimental, humorous, Gothic, sagely, and adventurous. Assimilating these forms, the picaresque raises the key issues central to each. It reflects the need for ethical grounding at the heart of the sentimental mode practiced by Harte and Twain; it examines the kind of class tension evident in the genteel/vulgar modes of humor indulged by Howells and Twain; it contains some of the metaphysical longing and physical brutality of the Gothic mode used by Stowe and Twain; it often exploits the assumption of authority at the center of the sage's role performed by Arnold and Twain; and it allows for the probing of masculinity that occurs in the adventure fiction of Stevenson and Twain. (The exception, at least in terms of *Huck Finn* and

*Kim*, might seem to be the mode of sage, but it too is certainly discernible in Kipling's third-person omniscient narrative, and it arguably emerges in *Huck Finn* when Twain extends Huck's restricted point of view to the breaking point by recording at length, in detail, and with precise rhetoric Colonel Sherburn's denunciation of the mob.)

Like the other modes, the picaresque arose—and reappeared—in response to cultural turbulence. Its inception, as critics have formulated it, suggests its pertinence (some three hundred years later) to both Twain and Kipling, for its emergence is conventionally attributed to "social disruption" (Monteser 1) or, more precisely, to "individual alienation from and loneliness within a coercive and chaotic social order" (Blackburn 9). That Twain's world and its temporal overlap with that of the younger Kipling witnessed social disruption does not need repeating here. Every relation—that is, kind of narrating—utilized by Twain, along with a fellow member of the guild of writers he felt he belonged to, examined in this study found importance, even in many cases popularity, because of the ongoing cultural crisis of the time. Both Twain and Kipling were deeply attuned to the temper of their age. However, the picaresque no doubt had a special appeal to each writer, as it invited a fictive recreation of the personal dislocation and subsequent wandering they had both actually experienced. Be that as it may, they used the form brilliantly. To take in the full significance of their common exploitation of the picaresque, a form predicated on odyssey, it is useful to consider first their two novels of fixity: *Tom Sawyer* and *Stalky & Co.*

Twain's original conception for *Tom Sawyer*, at least insofar as it can be deduced from his working notes, was quite different from the book he eventually wrote. His first plan was ambitious in scope, sweeping in setting, and finally cynical in outcome. He planned to track nothing less than the whole of Tom's life (had he succeeded, Kipling would never have needed to ask him what became of Tom when he grew up). Here are the phases he noted down: "1, Boyhood & youth; 2 y & early Manh; 3 the Battle of Life in many lands; 4 (age 37 to 40,) return to meet grown babies & toothless old drivelers who were grandees of his boyhood" (qtd. in *TS* 8–9). The most intriguing thing about his planned novel is that it was to follow Tom through "the Battle of Life" in "many lands." As he first thought of it, *The Adventures of Tom Sawyer* was likely to be a picaresque novel.

The one he ended up writing was such a far cry from the dark notes of his first imagining that Twain would call it a "hymn," that is, a song of praise (*MTL* 477). It was also a long way from, indeed nearly the opposite of, a picaresque novel, for the final *Tom Sawyer* is not only rooted in but also confined to a specific locale. Unlike a picaro, Tom never wanders far from home.

The novel opens with Tom on the run. Caught by Aunt Polly with jam on his hands, about to be switched, Tom tricks her into releasing him—"My! Look behind you, aunt!"—and manages to escape: "The old lady whirled around, and snatched her skirts out of danger. The lad fled, on the instant, scrambled up the high board fence, and disappeared over it" (*TS* 40). Twain's opening is a virtual paradigm of the novel's central concern: Tom in conflict with authority, and the fence he climbs is an emblem of what he seeks: the boundary between the staid and the untrammeled. Tom's long summer (the time seems to stretch into mythic time), from late school-time to vacation time, is all the same time insofar as it always gives Tom occasions to break free from the conventional in pursuit of the unfettered. From skylarking at home, to cutting up at school, to misbehaving in church and Sunday school, to lurking about in graveyards, to running off to Jackson's Island, to attending his own funeral, to disrupting the Examination Evening, to playing at war and love, to shocking a courtroom, to losing himself—and Becky—in the cave, Tom crosses traditional boundaries. But his transgressions do not really carry him far, either literally from home or morally from the standards of his community. The very geography of the novel suggests Tom's restricted rebellion. The places of freedom—Cardiff Hill, Jackson's Island, McDougal's cave—all lie within the purview of St. Petersburg, visually, legally, and morally. Tom lives and plays in a world that is fixed, confined, and stable, both spatially and normatively—the very antithesis of a picaresque one.

A number of critics have called attention to the fact that Twain leaves the town of St. Petersburg itself notably vague—or even not there at all. The main edifices—church, school, courthouse, jail, taverns, and private homes—are not described in specific detail. Twain also leaves out altogether the other buildings that would actually constitute a river town like St. Petersburg: the dockside sheds, the livery stable, the hotel, general store, bank, and blacksmiths. The town's principal inhabitants—doctor, lawyer, minister—are little more than names. Judge Thatcher, as both eminent citizen and father of Tom's sweetheart, is given some real presence, and the hated schoolmaster Dobbins is shown in some detail. But St. Petersburg is on the whole "a phantom town inhabited largely by ghostly presences" (Wolff 148–49), by types and shadow figures, many of whom are identified by the evanescent signifier of voice (Mitchell xxiii). One knows from "Old Times on the Mississippi," a text Twain wrote in the very middle of the composition of *Tom Sawyer*, how graphically Twain could, when he chose to, recreate a river town brought to life by the arrival of a steamboat. So this vagueness seems calculated to create the sense that somehow, despite their idiosyncrasy and extremity, Tom's adventures are those of every boy. Twain's deliberate vagueness also generates the sense that Tom's adventures are somehow as mythic as they are real.

If the place of Tom's adventures is paradoxically definite yet vague, his adventures themselves capture profound, if not universal, desires: they pit vagrancy against routine, spontaneity against discipline, play against work, freedom against self-sacrifice, power against submission, public attention—not to say acclaim—against private anonymity. They are the stuff of fantasy. Yet they are all bounded by, and transpire within, the sphere of the conventional. When play turns to injury as the time on Jackson's Island threatens to break Aunt Polly's heart, when personal safety and boyish resolve risk injustice and death as Muff Potter comes to trial, when vagrant freedom bodes instability as Huck evades the Widow Douglas, Tom knuckles under to his conscience. For he is from first to last, as Judith Fetterley puts it, only a "sanctioned rebel"—that is, a good bad boy who, for all his disruptive acts, "does not hold any values which are at root different from those of the community" (301). Shadowy about place, Twain's text is crystal clear about the need for conventional probity; indeed, it may well be read as a moral fable in which a phantom place and ghostly characters function to highlight moral imperatives. Though some critics are dismayed by it, there is nothing surprising about Tom's final curtailment of Huck in the name of conventional respectability. When Huck protests, "The widder eats by a bell; she goes to bed by a bell; she gits up by a bell—everything's so awful regular a body can't stand it," Tom's reply, "Well, everybody does that way, Huck," bespeaks his fundamental commitment to social normality, his acceptance of traditional ethics (*TS* 234).

The narrative of *Tom Sawyer* reflects what one critic has called a "battle of discursive modes" (Mitchell xxvi). In tension, if not conflict, within the narrative are oppositions between standard English and vernacular speech, sentimental rhetoric and anti-sentimental expression, inflated language and flat, factual idioms. Henry B. Wonham has even argued that in the difference between Twain's own narrative and Tom Sawyer's tale-telling the text reveals a "subtle competition for narrative authority" (230). What the multiple discursive modes disclose is the possibility of alternate systems of value—a vernacular one in place of the genteel, for instance, or even a romantic one instead of a realistic. Yet fractured as it is, Twain's third-person omniscient narrative not only creates this explicitly linguistic—and potentially normative—chaos but also controls it. It controls it simply by manifesting it. (If there is a competition among discursive modes, Twain's, not Tom's, wins.) For at work in Twain's narrative mode is nothing less than a principle of authority—one might say male authority, since the omniscient narrator mocks various forms of female utterance—that is the equivalent of the conventional conscience Tom finally exhibits. Which is to say that Twain's narrative mode, for all its curious and sometimes colliding discourses, is nonetheless a conservative one. It judges Tom by, and ultimately aligns him with, the traditional in language, lifestyle, and morality. Or to reverse the equation, the inescapable authority of Tom's conscience is at one with the conventional authority of Twain's narrative mode. However much one might wish otherwise, *Tom Sawyer* is a conservative text that sponsors as it exerts the authority of the status quo.

Kipling's inquiry in his interview with Twain as to the future of Tom Sawyer (would he marry Becky, would we learn of him as a man?) is in one sense misguided. For, while leaving the details of Tom's future completely unexplained, Twain's novel certainly makes clear what kind of man he will be: a thoroughly conventional one. Twain's reply—Tom would "turn out a rip or an angel"—is designed as a joke. But the two different futures would be possible, as Twain indicates, only if the close of the actual text were altered or extended. As Twain says, to create such differing outcomes would require giving "a little joggle to the circumstances that controlled" Tom (*Portable K* 674). As he is controlled in the text by the narrator and the events he creates, Tom could only be an angel. To make him a rip, the narrator—or some different one—would have to exert an alternate kind of authority and place him in a different world, subject him to other events, and so allow him to be shaped in some other way.

While Tom's submission to the authority of a traditional conscience defines him as conventional at the core, the attributes he not only possesses but also practices equip him for various unknown futures. As readers always notice, his play is often by the books, and this too marks his conventionality. But in his adventures he utilizes independence, risk-taking, guile, deviousness, cunning, manipulative skill, persuasive art, able deception, a ready comprehension of others, the power to command, and a knack for surprise. He deploys these considerable talents paradoxically in trampling orthodoxy while ultimately upholding conventional authority. In all this, he is the clear progenitor of Kipling's famous—or infamous—Stalky.

" 'Stalky' "—the word—Kipling explains at the start of the fourteen stories that comprise *The Complete Stalky & Co.*, means in the "schoolboy vocabulary" "clever, well-considered and wily, as applied to plans of action" (*S&C* 13).[2] Stalkiness is English boarding school for Tom Sawyerness.

Like Tom Sawyer, Stalky (whose true fictive name is Corkran) is bounded geographically. His world is confined in the first place by the boarding school (unnamed in the text but clearly a version of Kipling's own United Services College at Westward Ho! in north Devon), and within the school there are further places of restriction—classrooms, form rooms, the studies of house masters, and even the Head's office. As home, church, and tribunal as well as school, Stalky's boarding school is all in itself the equivalent of Tom's St. Petersburg. Where Tom escapes to hilltop, riverbank, and island to have his adventures, Stalky slips away to adjacent farmlands, woods, cliff-side, and channel shore. Tom can look up- (or down-) river, and Stalky can gaze cross-channel, but neither can really experience a world other than the one they are in. Neither has the freedom—burdened freedom, in most cases—of the picaro. And both finally accept not only the physical limits but also the moral constraints of their circumstance.

Kipling seems to have been most impressed by the plucky bad boy Tom Sawyer, the seeming rebel of endless imagination, resource, and will. This, at any rate, is the figure he creates—and admires—in Stalky. Stalky, along with his companions M'Turk and Beetle (the latter is Kipling's version of himself), defies school rules, plagues neighboring farmers, tricks and abuses fellow classmates (including at times his two comrades), bamboozles prefects, confuses school support staff, and generally hoodwinks, embarrasses, and defeats his housemasters. Although a master at crafting mayhem, he is not merely a lord of misrule. To be sure, at times he revels in creating general confusion and disorder; he does so exuberantly in the first of the Stalky stories when he secretly frees schoolmates locked in a barn by local farmhands for moving their cattle about, covertly locks up the farmhands in the same barn, clandestinely stampedes the cattle himself with his slingshot, boldly extorts from the incarcerated farmworkers a letter explaining how the trio's assistance in releasing them (he has blamed the other boys for locking them up) has delayed their return to college in time for call-over, gracefully flatters a fine tea from the farmer's wife, and then returns insouciantly to school where he first confounds the housemaster bent on punishment with his unimpeachable letter of gratitude and then torments the very boys he has rescued by refusing to divulge how he has managed the whole affair. In doing all this he exercises consummate Stalkiness—or what we might call Tom Sawyerness. Most often, however, Stalky does not create chaos for its own sake but for what he conceives of as justice. Operating Stalkily out of an eye-for-an-eye code, he inflicts retribution on all who slight or offend or even just impose on him and his company of two. When they are insulted, for instance, by the members of another house who say that they smell bad, Stalky and company retaliate by placing a dead cat beneath the floor boards of their adversaries' dormroom, creating in short order an unbearable stench. Stalky is clearly an avenging angel—or perhaps more precisely, an avenging little devil.

Early readers of *Stalky & Co.* found Kipling's tales of Stalky low, vulgar, coarse, and crude, offensive to good taste as well as sound morals. The year after the book appeared the case was put succinctly by Robert Buchanan, who insisted: "The vulgarity, the brutality, the savagery, reeks on every page" (31). Later readers, brought up on darker visions of human nature in general and boy nature in particular, have found the book more engaging than off-putting. Kipling himself seems to have found it outright hilarious. According to his cousin Florence Macdonald, when he was writing *Stalky & Co.*, he "kept going into fits of laughter." She describes his delight this way: " 'No one,' he said, 'gets more fun out of my stories than I do.' Then returning to his desk, having relighted his pipe, he added, 'And now what *shall* we make them do?' " (19).

Kipling imparts his own amusement at Stalky, M'Turk, and Beetle to the boys themselves. For again and again the boys find their subversive acts uproariously funny. "Gloats! oh gloats," Stalky says at one point, "Fids! oh, fids! Hefty fids and gloats to us!" (*S&C* 20), thereby expressing his delight in the humor of their most recent comic triumph. All three boys, but especially Beetle (the fictive version of Kipling), are repeatedly convulsed with laughter over their antics. They do not laugh aloud in public, however, for on the one hand they play the role of injured innocence, and on the other they adhere to a code of reticence in public. Beetle is often forced to seek a private space—the boot-cupboard under the staircase, for instance—in which "to loose the mirth that was destroying him" (*S&C* 67). While their laughter is self-serving, and perhaps therefore suspect, it nonetheless invites from the reader a comic view of the havoc they perpetuate. Most importantly, Kipling himself—or rather his narrator—endorses the three scamps. Kipling's narrator subjects them to little irony, lots of neutral description, and no small amount of outright approval.

The contrast with Twain is instructive. Although indulgent, indeed affectionate, Twain's narrative often mocks Tom and his acts in ways that range from extravagant burlesque to pointed irony to sharp sarcasm. Furthermore, where Twain's novel contains a clash of discourses, both within its narrative mode and between the narrative and Tom's way of storytelling, a clash which to a degree opens the fiction to multiple norms, Kipling's narrative is more purely univocal. He does endow characters with the idioms that define them, of course, as the headmasters are usually pompous and stilted in their speech, the farmers typically earthy and unlettered in their dialects, but his own narrative is not, as Twain's is, divided by conflicting idiolects. Whereas Tom speaks and narrates his adventures to others in a colloquial language that stands in contrast to the generally standard English of Twain's narrator, implying at least the possibility of an alternate system of values and creating the contest for authority that Wonham sees as central to the novel, Stalky and his comrades rely not on a separate vernacular but on slang. Their slang is, however, a willful departure from standard discourse, a kind of linguistic slumming. They clearly know the King's English, proper standard English, but choose to use instead an argot largely of their own creation. Or to put it another way, implicit in their deliberate defiance of proper speech is their command of it, and such command finally aligns them with the narrator's (here one longs to say, Kipling's) own orthodox language, his own perfectly correct style.

The standard critical interpretation of *Stalky & Co.* is that it records Kipling's sense of how boys are turned into men fit to manage the British empire (e.g., see Buchanan, Nayor, and Marcus). In his autobiography, Kipling explained the origin of his book: "There came to me the idea of beginning some tracts or parables on the education of the young. These, for reasons honestly beyond my control, turned themselves into a series of tales called *Stalky & Co.*" (*Something of Myself* 79). Kipling's acknowledgment of a didactic impulse, albeit one bent into fiction, seems to support the notion that his book is about how to create empire builders. Stalky's inventiveness, daring, dominance, and cunning—traits cultivated outside of the classroom and in defiance of school discipline—arguably qualify him to maintain empire as an officer in the military. Certainly the final story, a retrospective account by old boys of the school—which tells how Stalky, operating along the frontiers of England's far eastern empire, turns two tribes assaulting a beleaguered segment of the colonial army against each other by employing the same tactic he once used as a schoolboy to turn one school functionary unwittingly against a housemaster— drives home the value of Stalkiness for empire. Coming as it does at the end, this story—which leads the aging school chums to proclaim Stalky "the great man of his Century" (*S&C* 281)—seems contrived to provide not just closure but a way of interpreting—or reinterpreting—all the preceding tales. But I believe that the book is ultimately about something even more basic than the qualities of character requisite for the leaders of empire.

Kipling's *Stalky & Co.*, like Twain's *Tom Sawyer*, is finally about authority. Like Tom, Stalky defies the authority codified in rules and embodied in preceptors, and like Tom, he leads his two comrades (the boys of both books band together in threes, suggesting perhaps the influence of Dumas's three musketeers) into various actions against established order. They not only contest but also subvert the status quo. Like Twain, though, Kipling finally brings his wayward boys into line with authority. For all their insubordination, Stalky and his company submit themselves, not just of necessity, but willingly, to the rule—the word—of the Head. He inflicts punishment (canings) and requires amends both in accord with the facts (often ones obscured to most by Stalkiness) and in agreement with what he takes to be their just deserts, regardless of the exact facts. The boys readily accept the rightness of his rule. *Stalky & Co.*

thus upholds an authority quite different from Twain's in *Tom Sawyer*. Where Tom is caught by his conscience and by the conventionality of Twain's narrator, both expressions of the value system of the dominant culture, Stalky and his confederates are finally trapped by the dictates of one man, sponsored by Kipling's narrative, a man largely but not entirely in harmony with his society. At times the Head's acts toward the boys—his acts upon them—are mysterious, seemingly out of sync with their "crimes" and with the prevailing morals of the culture. (See, in particular, "The Satisfaction of a Gentleman.") But the boys always submit, and what's more, they always subscribe to the belief that whatever the Head does to them or requires of them is right. Twain's *Tom Sawyer* confirms a traditional authority based on society's moral compact, but Kipling's *Stalky & Co.* upholds authority even when it appears to be—and sometimes actually is—arbitrary. Both texts are profoundly conservative, but Twain's novel bases its conservatism on collective norms, whereas Kipling's founds its on authority per se, without the further sanction of social agreement.

There is one final difference between *Stalky & Co.* and *Tom Sawyer* worth mentioning, one that is perhaps as obvious as it is important. The difference, simply put, is between silence and performance. It is no doubt a difference rooted in each author's temperament, but it also signals cultural shapings at odds with each other. For all their similarities, Stalky and Tom are finally quite different boys. No matter what his achievements, Stalky never brags publicly about them; on the contrary, he deliberately and consistently refrains from both open explanation and celebration (although he does, of course, revel privately among his company). His code of reticence embodies two things: a personal stance of stoic self-possession and a public posture of self-effacement. Both are foreign to Tom Sawyer. Tom not only loves to announce his larks but also glories in having them exclaimed over by the town. Where Twain's tale moves again and again toward moments of personal self-aggrandizement and public acclaim, Kipling's steadfastly avoids such display. What Twain flaunts, Kipling curtails. Perhaps Twain is comfortable allowing his hero to preen in public because the authority he finally honors is communally sanctioned, while Kipling keeps his equally successful protagonist silent because at its furthest reach the authority he submits to is itself private—the arbitrary, not to say mysterious, rightness of a single figure of power.

After the publication of *Stalky & Co.* in 1899, Kipling soon returned to work on the novel of India that would eventually become *Kim*. (He had begun it as early as 1892 and taken it up again briefly in 1898.) In retrospect, he was dismissive of the critical row caused by *Stalky*. With a kind of brutality of his own, he attacked those who found his stories "irreverent, not true to life, and rather 'brutal,' " by asking "at which end of their carcasses grown men keep their school memories." As for his new work, he understood that it was "nakedly picaresque and plotless" (*Something of Myself* 79–80, 132).

Buoyed by Howells's favorable one, Twain bore the somewhat mixed reviews of *Tom Sawyer* with equanimity, awaiting what was always for him the all-important judgment: sales figures. But even before the novel was published, he was thinking of a follow-up. "By and by," he told Howells, "I shall take a boy of twelve & run him on through life . . . but not Tom Sawyer—he would not be a good character for it." He knew that he should write his future novel "in the first person"; indeed, he assured Howells that it would be "fatal to do it in any shape but autobiographically—like Gil Blas" (*MTHL* 92, 91). Conjured up here, along with the necessity of a first-person narrative, is the form that his projected novel should take, for *Gil Blas* is a picaresque novel, and that is what *Huckleberry Finn* would eventually become. Having completed, to their satisfaction if no one else's, their novels of literal stasis and moral fixity, Twain and Kipling both contemplated ensuing novels of mobility, novels that would in the end deal far more searchingly with the foundations of action for a boy or a man.

Beginning *Adventures of Huckleberry Finn* as an extension of *Tom Sawyer* but with the intention of writing not only a first-person narrative but also a picaresque tale, Twain faced a major problem. It was easy enough to let Huck begin to tell his own story (though the acquisition of literacy had to be accounted for), and Twain does this with humor as well as grace by letting Huck himself refer to Mark Twain's earlier book, thereby creating a curious sense of Huck's actuality: "You don't know about me, without you have read a book . . . made by Mr. Mark Twain" (*HF* 1). But the more difficult task was to get Huck on the road or rather, in this case, the river to begin his adventures as a picaro. Twain needed to disentangle Huck from the constraining, static world of St. Petersburg—from the home, church, school regimen of the Widow Douglas and from the equally confining robber and pirate play of Tom Sawyer. To effect Huck's escape, at least according to one critic, Twain first invented Miss Watson to make life at the Widow's truly unbearable (as opposed to just irritating), then returned Pap to St. Petersburg as a further way of prying Huck loose, and finally concocted a court hearing presided over by a new judge who "didn't know the old man" (*HF* 26) and thus rules in favor of restoring custody of Huck to his father (Lynn, "Welcome Back"). Pap's brutality toward Huck and his incarceration of him in the cabin, sometimes for as long as three days at a time, set the final stage for Huck's becoming a runaway. Twain creates these characters and events with such verve, ease, detail, and humor that one forgets that they are all strategies for getting his picaresque novel underway.

The main elements of the picaresque form to which Twain turned are familiar: a first-person narrator who is in one way or another a scamp; a series of loosely joined peripatetic adventures; a struggle on the part of the hero, who is really an antihero, for survival in a threatening world; a more or less detailed depiction of that hostile environment; a criticism or satire of the structure and values of the social world through which the antihero moves; and an open-ended—that is, not concluded—ending.[3] True to form, *Huck Finn* incorporates all of these. It is not, however, to the point here to create a taxonomy of the picaresque novel (and certainly not to apply any such listing mechanically to Twain's novel). But it is useful to see Huck, the quintessential picaro, on the run though the American South in relation to Kim, Kipling's vagabond, at large in India.

It is now more or less commonplace to see at least parts of *Huckleberry Finn* as engaging not the pre–Civil War South but the postwar problems of both Reconstruction and post-Reconstruction.[4] Illuminating commentaries have explored in particular the now obvious postwar problem of "freeing the free Negro" enacted—or travestied—in Twain's novel (Nilon 62). Most, if not all, of these analyses focus on the novel's end, trying in part to lay to rest the ghost of the controversy—instigated most forcefully by Hemingway—over the book's failed comic ending. These interpretations are compelling, but they promote once again in a curious roundabout turn the sense that the novel is flawed insofar as it is severely split between an initial segment on slavery in the prewar South and a final Reconstruction and post-Reconstruction section on the postwar South. However, like the two postbellum southern writers Twain singles out in *Life on the Mis-*

*sissippi*, Joel Chandler Harris and George Washington Cable, Twain uses the antebellum setting, from first to last, to explore postbellum issues. And this reveals, I think, a new link with Kipling, for both *Kim* and *Huckleberry Finn* can be seen as revolving about imperial rule, in the one case when it is present, in the other when it is absent. Whereas Kipling's *Kim* suggests the appropriateness of British rule in India, Twain's *Huck Finn* suggests the ills of the postwar South released from imperial control by the North.

The "Notice" prohibiting any search for motive, moral, or plot that begins *Huck Finn* probably echoes, as Neil Schmitz has observed, the "Civil War/Reconstruction orders" posted on the courthouses of southern cities and towns (79). The notice, most often unnoticed in criticism, thus signals the true postwar concerns of Twain's novel. The signature, "Per G. G., Chief of Ordnance," may playfully suggest General Grant, commander in chief of the victorious Union forces and president during radical Reconstruction. The notice bodes explosive events to come, and nothing was more explosive to the body politic than Reconstruction and its aftermath. The novel actually grapples with the postwar traumas of Reconstruction and failed—or abrogated—Reconstruction. It faces, as Louis J. Budd has pointed out, "the southern question" ("Southward Currents" 237).[5]

Postwar issues settle strongly into the novel's opening sequence. Directly or obliquely addressed are these: the horror of chattel slavery, or more precisely the continuation of it, for the war did not end slavery everywhere in the South; the ineffectuality of religious sentiment, the very emotion that had sustained the abolitionist cause; the unreliability of the legal system, which entered so definitively—and sometimes so disastrously—into postwar civic arrangements; and the voting and civil rights of the freedmen, rights first established and then curtailed in the postwar South. For Twain's postwar, post-Reconstruction audience, these show up refracted in Jim's circumstance, Huck's religious instruction, Pap's court claim to Huck, Pap's diatribe against the freedman from Ohio whom he encounters on election day, and Pap's equally virulent—and confused—claims to his own rights (see Wieck, chapter 3). If one accepts that Tom Sawyer emerges in the end as the post-Reconstruction southern aristocrat who assumes and exercises "the privileges of the powerful" (Nilon 70), Twain's opening treatment of him as a facile romantic trapped in his illusions to the point of inhumanity (his notions of incarcerating and torturing prisoners, along with his desire to tie Jim up just for fun, illustrate this) completes the picture of a benighted postwar South.

The chief victim of course is the freedman, or in this case, the not-freed Jim. Twain's first working note for *Huckleberry Finn* was, somewhat cryptically, simply "De Mule!" (underlined three times and then crossed out) (*HF* 714). At least one critic has surmised that this reveals Twain's interest in the postwar promise to the freedmen, one betrayed in practice, of "forty acres and a mule" (Wieck 100–101). This not only underscores Twain's true postwar focus throughout his novel but also centers it on the condition of the former slave. Twain enthusiastically signed on to support the Republican candidate for president in 1876, Rutherford B. Hayes, eventually the president who ended Reconstruction, because he believed that Hayes was for the rights of blacks as well as whites in the South.[6] Hayes's letter accepting the Republican nomination was, Twain assured Howells, "amply sufficient to corral my vote" (*MTHL* 143). Hayes had written to "assure my countrymen of the Southern States that if I shall be charged with the duty of organizing an administration, it will be one which will regard and cherish their truest interests—the interests of the white and of the colored people both, and equally; and which will put forth its best efforts in behalf of a civil policy which will wipe out forever the distinction between North and South" (qtd. in Wieck 61). Twain himself, in *Life on the Mississippi*, had advocated converting the backward South into a counterpart of the progressive North, thereby eliminating their differences. And he was committed to interests of black freedmen as well as white southerners, but he had witnessed the failure of anything even approaching the securing of those—often divergent—interests "equally." *Huck Finn* faces that failure and exposes its multiple causes.

The clearest sign of Twain's postwar interests in his prewar novel is his use of Pap. Pap's introduction facilitates the launching of Huck as a picaro, but Pap more obviously becomes the vehicle for Twain's representation of problems that begin in Reconstruction and continue through post-Reconstruction. These problems center on the voting rights and civil liberties of African Americans. Pap's drunken denunciation of the "free nigger" for his dress, the "whitest shirt on you ever see," and the "shiniest hat," and "a gold watch and chain," the garb of the well-to-do and respectable; for his learning, he "could talk all kinds of languages, and knowed everything"; and above all, for his right to vote—"they said he could *vote*"—reflects white anxiety and resentment over some freedmen's improved economic conditions, educational achievement, and enfranchisement. Pap's infuriation—expressed in heavy-handed irony directed at "a wonderful govment, wonderful," a "govment" that allows, even abets, such circumstances—echoes the anger of the South over the federal intervention that tried to secure such conditions for the freedmen during Reconstruction (*HF* 33–34). That Pap is, as the phrase of the time had it, poor white trash (a phrase echoed by Jim when he denounces Huck for the trick he plays on him in the fog [chapter 15]) indicts one troubled, vociferous, and finally vicious segment of the southern population. But one must realize that what Pap, a member of the lowest class of his society, says so blatantly—and crudely—was also believed by the likes of the respectable, the Judge Thatchers, Miss Watsons, and Widow Douglases of the South. Twain lets the bottom of the culture speak for the top (as well as for itself), for Pap's prejudice is more easily manifest than that of the refined who cover it with the veneer of respectability. While Miss Watson is transparently hypocritical as well as racist, the Widow Douglas is a more masked example of southern problems, but her ethic of Christian charity—one "must help other people, and do everything" one can "for other people" and "never think about" oneself (*HF* 13)—does not encompass the black population. Pap's ultimate response to the free African American—whose bearing, intelligence, and occupation not only threaten but also measure him—is violence, like that of other desperate whites in the postwar South: "I . . . shoved him out o' the way" (*HF* 34).

Once Pap has had his say, openly for himself, indirectly for the majority of the white southern community, and once Twain's irony has pilloried him for his dissipation, ignorance, racism, and violence, Huck's picaresque adventures begin. And almost at once Twain links Huck to Jim, thus creating the primary problem facing the postwar South: the relation of whites to blacks. Huck is initially his father's son: he treats Jim as an inferior and attempts to assert his superiority over him. But in their exchanges over royalty, King Solomon, and Frenchmen, Huck loses each debate and is forced to rely on sheer prejudice to maintain—like the South itself—his sense of white supremacy: "You can't learn a nigger to argue" (*HF* 98).

The violence Pap resorts to is shown in the Grangerford-Shepherdson feud to be a propensity of southern aristocrats as well as poor white trash. Indeed the threat of violence envelops Huck and Jim as they descend the river ever deeper into the South; it is embodied in raftsmen, town loafers, country farmers, and aristocrats, and it is no wonder that Huck's most recurrent emotion is fear. To make his condemnation of southern violence even more emphatic in the novel than it is, and to acknowledge who in the postwar decades was steadily becoming its chief target, Twain contemplated including a lynching in his novel. In his working notes he first recorded "**A lynching scene**," and then more pointedly— and revealingly—he jotted down, "They lynch a free *nigger*" (*HF* 731, 752).[7] In the end, he did not include the scene, but his thinking discloses not only his horror at southern violence but also his correct perception that the freedman was the object of it. Borrowing many of the ideas first articulated in *Life on the Mississippi* and then later excised from the final text, Twain clinches his case against southern violence not only in the actions but also the speech of Colonel Sherburn.[8] Sherburn's utterly unnecessary gunning down of Boggs exposes bogus southern pride in a most horrible way, and his subsequent denunciation of the mob that has come to lynch him, for all its probable truth about mob psychology, strips bare the cold inhumanity that grips the heart of the resurgent Bourbons. Having witnessed the killing and heard Sherburn's harangue, Huck is relieved to divert himself first at the circus and then at the Duke and the King's Shakespearean revival. He looks away at other things, at innocent entertainment and fraudulent performance, much as the North turned away its eyes from the South after the Compromise of 1877.

Although some readers have disliked their controlling presence in the middle section of Twain's novel, his introduction of the Duke and the King (two chapters before the Boggs-Sherburn episode) enables Twain to thrust his picaro into layers of southern society he would otherwise shun in his escape with Jim. But their intrusion into Huck's world also gives Twain a chance to enlarge his excoriation of the postwar scene. Often overlooked in criticism is the fact that both the Duke and the King pointedly board the raft toting "big fat ratty-looking carpet-bags" (*HF* 160). For himself at some level and for his alert contemporary reader, Twain thus suggests that the two scoundrels are examples of—or at least not altogether unlike— the plague of carpetbaggers that descended on the South after the war. To be sure, Twain's two deadbeats hold no political office, have no part in influential business, and play no role in civic affairs, but exaggerated as they are, they may be seen as representing the nefarious ethics and egregious self-interest of the exploitive carpetbagger. (Of course, many so-called carpetbaggers were perfectly upright.) Twain is writing not as a political analyst but as a humorist and a moralist, so he eschews the realities of the typical carpetbagger's position, makes his swindlers comic fools, and exposes chiefly their flawed character. In acts often too outrageous to credit but always hilarious to take in, the two rogues pervert religious sentiment, issue bogus legal documents (ones that would re-enslave Jim), control Huck, dehumanize Jim, provide salacious entertainments, and generally hoodwink the common folk. They are rapacious and ultimately cruel; first to last, they are money-grabbing materialists.

Huck's affiliation with the Duke and the King complicates his own moral character. For up until the Wilks episode he not only refrains from judging them but also acquiesces in their fraudulent activities. This places him in the morally ambiguous situation of the typical picaro, who skirts conventional norms, connives at wrongdoing, and even commits outright criminal acts. Huck's early discussions with Jim over "borrowing," like the minor thefts they rationalize, mark by contrast his essential moral innocence (see chapter 12). The picaresque novel thrives on the depiction of the moral underside of a society, in this case that of the postwar South, and its antihero's amorality makes all the more explosive the form's irony. For the more the picaro (Huck in this case) abstains from judging manifold corruption, the more that corruption evokes the reader's condemnation, as acceptance of wrongdoing provokes delight only up to a point. In Huck's case, that point comes first—and rather melodramatically—when the love-struck Huck cannot abide the Duke and the King's cheating of Mary Jane and her sisters. Then the point of moral opposition emerges more strongly—and credibly—in Huck's distress over the selling of Jim and his concomitant resolve to steal him into freedom.

In the novel's overarching context of postwar problems, Huck can be seen as a scalawag: a native southerner who "betrays" his homeland by conspiring with the North in its view of the African American. His moral struggle over Jim, regarded in virtually all the criticism as the moral center of the novel, turns on a conflict between the views of the retrograde white supremacists and those of the progressive white radicals, whether northern or southern: between, that is, the definition of the African American as an inferior, even subhuman creature and the vision of the freedman as, if not equal to the white, at least human enough to have freedom and rights. To the dismay of many recent readers, Twain's novel captures the complexity of its historical moment, for few northern radicals supportive of the freedman and few southern scalawags in sympathy with the radicals actually considered the freedmen the equals of whites. Thus, despite his discovery of Jim's similarities to whites—"I do believe he cared just as much for his people as white folks does for theirn"—and his decision to work to secure his freedom, Huck, like the typical scalawag, continues to think in racist ways: "I knowed he was white inside" (*HF* 201, 341). Huck represents not some paragon of racial enlightenment but the uncertain, internally divided, still racist southern scalawag.

From several perspectives Huck's ineffectuality in freeing Jim in the final Great Evasion sequence of Twain's novel makes perfect sense. As picaro, Huck is likely to be a passive, perhaps even feckless actor in events, for it is in the nature of the picaro to be more a dodger of than engager in significant action. And as a scalawag, Huck cannot really set Jim free and still reflect the historical reality of Reconstruction and especially post-Reconstruction. Looked at in this way, the famous problem of the ending of *Huck Finn* is no problem at all but rather a more or less inevitable and logical conclusion.

That ending sequence surely reflects, as Victor Doyno has suggested in his fine study, "the era when the post-bellum Reconstruction was obviously failing" (*Writing HF* 228). Huck flounders as well-intentioned scalawag, Tom emerges as abusive white Bourbon, and Jim suffers as a reincarcerated freedman. When Huck proposes a quick, sensible way to get Jim out of captivity in the Phelps's cabin, Tom says, "I bet we can find a way that's twice as long" (*HF* 293), echoing the deliberate postponement of true freedom for the former slaves in the South following the Civil War and the eventual collapse of Reconstruction. Tom's absurd antics, somehow amusing to Twain as a burlesque of the childish romantic imagination, create the confusions, delays, and, worse, the pains of freeing the freedman. Tom's attitude toward Jim here is no different from his callous, dehumanizing interest in playing tricks on him in the novel's opening. Freely construed as reflections of the behavior of many white southerners, Tom's shenanigans suggest the duplicitous, patronizing gradualism advocated by resurgent whites in the South; they smack of the bogus paternalism that marked both plantation slavery and postwar white southern politics. Rather brilliantly, Twain exposes not only how false all such pretenses are but also how they cover a rooted prejudice, indeed hatred, that could erupt at any time into lethal violence: after Jim is recaptured, Huck tells us, "some" of the white men want "to hang Jim, for an example to all the other niggers around there" (*HF* 352).

While Twain's ending thus climaxes his representation of postwar problems, while it fits neatly his general attention to the backward South that wanted to return to prewar racial arrangements, it is still disconcerting in its comic form. Twain's burlesque and farce in the end seem to trivialize the very issues they attack. One is tempted, then, to see the extravagance of the sequence as a kind of saturnalia, as a carnivalesque moment in which Tom becomes the Lord of Misrule, and the world of failed and failing Reconstruction is turned upside down. But what is upended in the carnivalesque is ultimately upheld, as Bakhtin has argued (see his introduction), so perhaps for all the outrageousness of Tom's protracted escapades, what Twain's *form* finally yields is both the grotesque horror of the South's treatment of the freedman and a nervous sense that it will be maintained.

Jim not only suffers but also seems debased, transformed from the figure who proclaims to Huck that he will either buy his family out of slavery or steal them out of it. In making Jim acquiescent in Tom's rituals of degradation Twain seems to have diminished the very humanity of the freedman he was at pains to reveal and insist upon—and whose abuse and repression he has critically disclosed. However, as Charles Nilon has observed, the reduction of Jim should be seen as *the consequence* of his mistreatment, a mistreatment that "prevents him from being a man," that "stimulates fear in him," and that thus injures him "emotionally and spiritually" as black people were injured "during the post-Reconstruction period" (69). This is a telling reading of the import of Twain's late depiction of Jim.

In having Jim give up his newfound freedom to aid the doctor who aids the wounded Tom, the analogical oppressor of the freedman, Twain confirms not just the compassion—and hence the humanity—of Jim, his representative of the black man still constrained in the South, but also his manhood. In 1885, speaking of former slaves, Twain observed, "We have ground the manhood out of them. The shame is ours, not theirs and we should pay for it" (qtd. in Fishkin, "Racial Attitudes" 613). In Jim's action he recuperates the manhood eradicated by southern slavery and suppressed in the ensuing struggles for true emancipation. Jim's act is "noble" beyond Tom's childish notions, and it is virtually a paradigm of Twain's own conception of what constitutes true manhood. In a telling moment in *A Connecticut Yankee in King Arthur's Court*, he depicts the true manhood of King Arthur by having him risk his life, sacrifice himself, to aid a young girl dying of smallpox: "Here was heroism at its last and loftiest possibility, its utmost summit" (*CY* 331). Jim's act is equally heroic and manly. As we saw in comparing the fictions of Twain and Stevenson, manhood for both, but especially for Twain, resided in compassion, fellow feeling, empathy. Jim has compassion for Tom even though he has suffered at his hands, and even though he thinks of Tom in estranging terms, in terms that acknowledge Tom's assumed and insisted-on superiority, as "mars Tom." Significantly, in contrast, he calls Huck "Huck" or, even more affectionately, "honey" and "chile" (*HF* 341, 154). Twain thus closes his novel by exposing white supremacy in Tom, by reaffirming abiding but ineffectual scalawag sympathy in Huck, and by disclosing the true manhood of the long-debased African American.

Huck's adventures end, as do those of all picaros, with the suggestion of further excursions to come. (The uncertainty of this future accords with his moral role as scalawag.) But the world he has already traversed reveals, I believe, Twain's deepest sense of life itself, life past, present, and future— life personal, social, political, and perhaps even metaphysical. As George C. Carrington Jr. has pointed out, the world of nature in *Huckleberry Finn* is indifferent to humankind, random in its occurrences, disorderly to the verge of chaos, and so in flux as to point to endless change and essential meaninglessness as the conditions of life itself (chapter 1).

Moments of natural erosion, of physical dissolution, mark Huck's picaro experience. The most pointed and striking occurs in Bricksville when Huck, off of the river, not entranced by the days and nights that swim along—"slid along," he says, "so quiet and smooth and lovely"—registers with mild alarm the true force of a powerful, erratic, and destructive river: "sometimes a strip of land as wide as a house caves in at a time," "sometimes a belt of land a quarter of a mile deep will start in and cave along and cave along till it all caves into the river in one summer" (*HF* 156, 183). While Huck tells wonderingly of star-fall over the river and of sunrise above it, he also records in his matter-of-fact way the river's corrosive force, an innocent acknowledgment of something entropic at work in his world: "the river's always gnawing"; "it was dangersome" (*HF* 183). Twain creates a subcurrent in his text that suggests an abyss filling with emptiness. In his illuminating analysis, Carrington argues that, given the natural world's disastrous turbulence, the human world of culture created through performance—"culture is drama"—becomes crucial as a way of creating meaning in the face of meaninglessness (60, chapter 2). But such performance, the creation of meaning in the face of nullity through culture, does not finally seem to me to capture the deepest import of *Huck Finn*. Indeed, nature gnaws at Huck's river world, at the human erections on it, but for all the significance human culture achieves in contrast to—in defiance of—the entropic force of nature, those human, cultural assertions and establishments are themselves without foundation. For Twain suggests over and over again that Huck's human world is as insubstantial as the physical one erected on the Mississippi's riverbanks. There is nothing, natural or human, to rely on.

As picaresque rapscallion, Huck resists virtually all the social institutions—along with their moral imperatives—that he encounters in his vagrant odyssey. But more to the point, Twain undercuts them through his multifaceted but steadily subversive humor. His comedy, variously asserted through Huck as a mask of innocence, destabilizes the entire human circumstance. It gently mocks or playfully contests or sharply confronts or savagely assaults all human constructs: religion, politics, economics, law, manners, mores, morals, and culture itself. In astounding contrast to *Tom Sawyer*, in which conventionality reigns, there is in Huck's world no sure, reliable, guiding—and therefore sustaining—authority. Almost nothing is left standing in Twain's novel, if one really takes in the full bore of its humor, except perhaps the fleeting, fragile relationship between Huck and Jim, and this affection is harshly compromised by Huck's racism and Jim's enforced subservience. As faltering scalawag and groping picaro, Huck encounters without fully realizing it a world of uncertainty, unreliability, a world of human as well as natural chaos. Whereas Tom Sawyer aligns himself with the authority sanctioned by Twain's conventional narrator, Huck contests every authority that confronts him. And Twain's humor suggests that he should, since they are all bogus. Whereas Tom Sawyer was rewarded for his covert acceptance of the status quo, Huck is, like the typical picaro, left at the end in uncertainty, in the dark about right and wrong, and very much on his own, for as he says so famously, he cannot stand to return to the civilization of Aunt Sally, which is the civilization of the Widow Douglas and all the rest. It gnaws at him as the river does the towns encroaching on its banks, both river and civilization seeming to lead, in Twain's dark comedy, only to a void.

Although *Kim*, like *Huckleberry Finn*, was a long time aborning, Kipling felt that it emerged rather spontaneously, that it surged up and then flowed almost without his control. He attributed this joyous process of creation to his "Daemon," borrowing the term from Socrates, to an inner feeling imposed by an external creative force that drove his writing at its best, in the grip of which he took care "to walk delicately, lest he should withdraw" (*Something of Myself* 122). That some outpouring of joyful recall and imagining shaped *Kim* seems indisputable. But Kipling's Daemon had a lot to work with. To create *Kim* Kipling drew upon an early, never published, soon abandoned, and eventually destroyed apprentice novel, "Mother Maturin"; upon a first working draft of *Kim*, entitled "Kim O' the Rishti" (preserved in the British Library as "Additional Manuscript 44840"); and, finally, upon his conversations and joint recollections with his father, John Lockwood Kipling (see Feeley). The latter were, at least as Kipling himself recalled, the most fecund. "In a gloomy, windy autumn," he said, "*Kim* came back to me with insistence, and I took it to be smoked over with my Father." Although he once consulted the India Office, he and his father recaptured endless "opulence of detail," "every step, sight, and smell" on Kim's "casual road" as well as "all the persons he met" (*Something of Myself* 82). Also informing Kipling's creative shaping, however, perhaps imposed on his vivid remembrances, were Twain's two books of boy-adventure, *Tom Sawyer* and *Huckleberry Finn*. For Twain was, as I've suggested, Kipling's most formative precursor, and as Harold Bloom has insisted, "*Huckleberry Finn* and *Tom Sawyer* are reflected inescapably in *Kim*" (3–4). While personal experience and shared recollections inspired the locale, the chance characters, and the picaresque drift of *Kim*, its deeper configuration seems to lie not in lived and recalled life but in literature—Twain's.

Like *Huck Finn*, *Kim* takes its imaginative shape against the backdrop of a war. For Twain that war was, of course, the Civil War, the horrendous conflict that sundered and devastated the country and finally divided Twain (then Clemens) himself. After being a staunch secessionist (and for a brief time a Confederate soldier), he gradually became, as Howells so memorably phrased it, "the most desouthernized Southerner" he knew

(*My MT* 30). He conducted his reconstruction principally in *Huck Finn* as he used the prewar setting to explore postwar issues. The war that loomed in the background of Kipling's consciousness, that finally hovered over his masterwork, was the 1857–58 Mutiny in India. Kipling recognizes that horrendous—and pivotal—event in *Kim* itself, but slips by it, skirting its causes as well as its horrors, and leaving unexplored the changes it wrought in British outlook and policy—and consequently in his own attitude. He evokes the mutiny as Kim and his lama, wandering haphazardly toward Benares, find themselves guided by "an old, withered man, who had served the Government in the days of the Mutiny" as a "native officer in a newly raised cavalry regiment" (*Kim* 94). Kipling makes this servant of British imperialism something of a hero, both in military valor, as a soldier who stood his ground in conflict, one of only three out of 680 to do so, and in moral character, for the lama, while disapproving of the man's occupation as well as his absorption in the world, finally accords him generous approval: "Thou hast clung to thy Way, rendering fidelity when it was hard to give, in that Black Year" (*Kim* 103).

The mutiny, which Kipling thus recalls from a colonial point of view and reduces to morality rather than politics, transformed Britain's entire approach to India. The uprising, largely centered in the Ganges plain and supported chiefly in the Kingdom of Oudh, has been viewed by some historians as a first stirring of Indian nationalism and by others as only a revolt of local landowners and provincial religious leaders who felt power and privilege slipping from them (Coates 18–20; Hibbert). Although the scale of the mutiny and its impact are disputed, the effect it had on British colonial policy and public opinion is clearer. The mutiny led Britain to increase its firm hold on India, to tighten its control, enlarging the white military presence and expanding the colonial administration; at the same time, it led the public in general to conceive of the native Indian as ineradicably barbarous. The mutiny seemed to the English to confirm the brutality of Indian nature, marking Indians as savages in need of containment by the civilized British. It opened an all but unbridgeable gulf between Indian and Briton, creating, in the words of one critic, "a distrust and dislike of 'native,' and a withdrawal from all but official and the most superficial contact with them that was to last, sometimes with increased intensity, as long as the Raj itself" (Paffard 6). In short, the mutiny deepened forever the separation between colonizer and colonized that marked Britain's rule in India and defined the world Kipling grew up in, both abroad in India and at home in England; it confirmed the apparently irreconcilable differences that Kipling would memorialize in verse in 1890: *"Oh, East is East, and West is West, and never the twain shall meet, / Till Earth and Sky stand presently at God's great Judgment Seat"* ("The Ballad of East and West," *RK's Verse* 233). Seeming to defy the certitude of his own ballad some eleven years after he wrote it, Kipling created in *Kim* a memorable and touching meeting of East and West.

North meets South in *Huckleberry Finn* insofar as Huck gradually acquires a northern conscience, or scalawag feeling, about Jim. In *Kim*, however, divergent races and cultures collide from the very first, when Kim—unknowingly a Sahib who will finally gather in if not fully embrace his birthright—meets the red lama from Tibet. Thereafter East not only meets West but enthralls it. For the lama, somewhat inexplicably, compels Kim's love from first sighting, and in turn the holy man from the East loves his disciple.

The ground of this affection, literally the land upon which it transpires, is as brilliantly realized in Kipling's novel as Twain's river is in *Huck Finn*. Both Kipling and Twain place the figures that captivate their moral imaginations and reflect the significant historical conflicts of their time in regions that are both real and magical, regions alive with beauty. Huck records sunrise over the "monstrous big river" in appreciative—one wants to say, loving—detail as he and Jim, freshened by a swim in the river, "cool off" and watch "the daylight come" until "everything" is "smiling in the sun" and the "songbirds" are "just going it!" (*HF* 156–57). Kim awakens to similar beauty on the Grand Trunk Road: "The diamond-bright dawn woke men and crows and bullocks together. Kim sat up and yawned, shook himself, and thrilled with delight" (*Kim* 121). Place thus evokes wonder and seems to make possible attachments—Kim with his lama, Huck with Jim—shunned, even prohibited, in less lustrous, enchanting, and magically transforming physical settings. Both Kipling and Twain unleash deep, transgressive feelings, emotions that defy the very cultures both adhere to, by casting them in the atmosphere of sudden beauty: the river at dawn, the road at sunrise. And both imagine such transfiguring—and transformative—moments as taking place unexpectedly for a displaced picaro in flight, on the lam, to he knows not where or what.

Harold Bloom, who has explored briefly the influence of Twain on Kipling, argues this: "Insofar as he is free but lonely, Kim is Huck; insofar as he serves the worldly powers, he is Tom" (4). And David Bromwich has suggested that the lama is Jim (191). These comparisons are intriguing, indeed provocative, but they finally seem to me more misleading than illuminating.[9] Without wanting to quibble, one needs to recall that Huck is rarely lonely and that Kim is almost never so; further, neither Huck nor Kim is truly free, for both are tethered by their innate morality. Tom Sawyer is, as we've seen, conventional at the core, but unlike Kim, he rarely acts in service to "the worldly powers"; most often he irritates such forces by disrupting their agendas. And while both Jim and the lama are figures of profound goodness, Jim has nothing of the lama's spiritual vision, nothing of his quest for transcendence, nothing of his indifference to the people and things of life in this world. Is Kim Huck?

Yes and no. In realization of their creators' design, both are picaros, roguish scamps, sent off onto river or road to live by their wits as they encounter a kaleidoscope of people and events. Both possess an untaught righteousness; both have an unerring sense of the authentic; both feel the prick of empathy; both embody a rare capacity for deep love; and, lest this comparison sound sentimental, both are adroit liars, artful dodgers of difficulty, clever swindlers, masters of feigned innocence, quick-change artists of identity. Both find contentment, even delight, in doing absolutely nothing—in just "lazying," as Huck puts it (*HF* 157). Both are keen observers of the minutiae of the world, the quotidian of existence, the sheer stuff of life itself. Both evoke—and return, though in notably different ways—an affection tantamount to love: Jim to Huck, "Jim won't ever forget you, Huck; you's de bes' fren' Jim's ever had" (*HF* 125); the lama to the world, "Was there ever such a *chela*?" (*Kim* 243). In their relationships, Huck with Jim, Kim with his lama, friendships that defy conventional norms and cross the boundaries of race, Huck and Kim seem not only most alike but also most thematically important.

Yet one is also struck by the many differences between Huck and Kim. Perhaps most obvious is the simple fact that Kim is reflective and self-conscious in a way that Huck isn't; Huck thinks less than Kim does. For all his talent as a picaro to cope with events and to fend for himself, Huck remains remarkably impervious to the world at large. Kim, in contrast, absorbs the world at every turn. He is knowing from the first, and his knowingness deepens as his travels unfold. Huck is naïve from the first, and his naïveté persists despite his adventures downriver. Which is to say, Huck retains his innocence, while Kim sheds his time and again along the road. And perhaps because of this, Kim is always at ease in the world, while Huck is always on edge. Finally, Huck is humble, in keeping with his limited awareness and moral confusion (and with Twain's use of him as a comic mask), where Kim is cocky, in keeping with his growing knowledge and moral certitude (and with Kipling's use of him as a figure of just imperial control).

Liberal critics, from Lionel Trilling to Irving Howe to Harold Bloom to Edward Said, have been hard-pressed to explain the wonders of *Kim* without explaining away its unmistakable—politically unacceptable—imperialism.[10] Some apologists point to Kipling's affectionate depiction of the land itself, to his masterful realization of the varied splendors of the subcontinent. From the plain along the Grand Trunk Road, with its bustle of life:

> The morning mist swept off in a whorl of silver, the parrots shot away to some distant river in shrieking green hosts: all the well-wheels within ear-shot went to work. (*Kim* 121)

> It was beautiful to behold the many-yoked grain and cotton wagons crawling over the country roads: one could hear their axles, complaining a mile away, coming nearer, till with shouts and yells and bad words they climbed up the steep incline and plunged on to the hard main road, carter reviling carter. It was equally beautiful to watch the people, little clumps of red and blue and pink and white and saffron, turning aside to go to their own villages, dispersing and growing small by twos and threes across the level plain. (*Kim* 111)

to the hills and mountains of the northeastern frontier:

> Through the speckled shadow of the great deodar-forests; through oak feathered and plumed with ferns; birch, ilex, rhododendron, and pine, out on to the bare hillsides' slippery sunburnt grass, and back into the woodlands' coolth again, till oak gave way to bamboo and palm of the valley, the lama swung untiring. (*Kim* 279–80)

> Above them, still enormously above them, earth towered away towards the snow-line, where from east to west across hundreds of miles, ruled as with a ruler, the last of the bold birches stopped. Above that, in scarps and blocks upheaved, the rocks strove to fight their heads above the white smother. Above

these again, changeless since the world's beginning, but changing to every mood of sun and cloud, lay out the eternal snow. (*Kim* 284)

Kipling does convey the loveliness of the land. But acknowledging India's magnificence does not gainsay his commitment to imperial control—indeed, the sheer beauty of the land may intensify the imperial desire to possess it.

Other apologists for the novel call attention to Kipling's sympathetic representation of the Indian people. To be sure, Kipling—like his Kim—delights in them. Early in his journeying Kim announces, "This country is full of good folk" (*Kim* 111). At every turning the "good folk" assist Kim and his lama, offering food and shelter and companionship, and, in a retrospective moment, Kim says definitively that they are "kindly and gentle" (*Kim* 281). (The contrast with Huck's world, where deceit, rapacity, and violence dominate, could hardly be starker.) Ascetic that he is, the lama often sighs as if in lament, "It is a great and terrible world" (*Kim* 83), but almost without exception (one priest does try to steal from the lama), the natives are not only gentle and kind but also generous, hospitable, and respectful. But at the same time Kipling thus celebrates the colonized Indians, he also denigrates them in stereotypes, in brief asides that betray his Western orientalism. Referring to them as Asiatic or Oriental, he suggests that the people are lazy, improvident, disorderly, laggardly, dishonest, indifferent to noise, likely to be dirty, and given to opium.[11]

Kipling places Kim squarely in two antithetical but intertwined worlds: the sphere of British colonial rule, represented by the Great Game, the spy network of the British Indian Government; and the realm of Eastern religion, embodied in the lama's search for the River of the Arrow, the holy waters in which one may be washed clean of impurity and begin to escape from the Wheel of Things. Kim embraces both worlds, serving with zest as an apprentice player in the Great Game, and becoming with passion a *chela*, or disciple, to the lama in his search. In the epithets bestowed on him, he is "Friend of all the World" and "Friend of the Stars" (*Kim* 96). Critics have stumbled over Kim's two friendships, his dual allegiance to the secular and the spiritual, to British rulers and to Indian mystics, none more so (and more influentially) than Edmund Wilson:

Kipling has established for the reader—and established with considerable dramatic effect—the contrast between the East, with its mysticism and sensuality, its extremes of saintliness and roguery, and the English, with their superior organization, their confidence in modern method, their instinct to brush away like cobwebs the native myths and beliefs. We have been shown two entirely different worlds existing side by side, with neither really understanding the other, and we have watched the oscillations of Kim, as he passes to and fro between them. But the parallel lines never meet; the alternating attractions felt by Kim never give rise to a genuine struggle. . . . The fiction of Kipling, then, does not dramatize any fundamental conflict because Kipling would never face one. (Wilson, *The Wound and the Bow* 123–24, 126)

Edward Said has corrected this misapprehension by pointing out that "the conflict between Kim's colonial service and loyalty to his Indian companions is unresolved not because Kipling could not face it, but because for Kipling *there was no conflict*" (146). There is no conflict because Kipling believed that the welfare of India depended on British colonial control (this is, of course, his imperial bias). Something of Kipling's own feeling, of his rationale for imperial rule, is suggested when the native soldier loyal to British dominion is asked by the lama, "What profit to kill men?" and the soldier replies, "Very little—as I know; but if evil men were not now and then slain it would not be a good world for weaponless dreamers" (*Kim* 100). Here Kipling posits a sanction not only for Britain's imperial control but also for its exercise of force to maintain it.

To create and preserve the wonder of the world in which Kim serves two masters, Colonel Creighton and the lama, Kipling erases almost all traces of any native oppositional views toward British rule. The Punjabi farmer whose child Kim treats for malaria and malnutrition exclaims in passing, "The Government has brought on us many taxes," and then even before his complaint can register, he adds, "but it gives us one good thing—the *te-rain*" (*Kim* 245–46). In the mountains near Shamlegh the men, Kipling says, "judged India and its Government solely from their experience of wandering Sahibs who had employed them or their friends," remembering in detail and with derision their incompetence as hunters, which for these men constitutes absolute insufficiency (*Kim* 306), but their view is both passed over and compromised by their provinciality. More telling, however, in terms of the wrongs of England's imperial presence is the story of the woman of Shamlegh, who has been lied to and betrayed by a sahib. Having accepted Christianity and British culture, she falls in love with a sahib, cares for him when he is ill, and believes him when he pretends to return her love and promises to marry her, only to leave forever. She concludes that "the Gods of the Kerlistians lied" (*Kim* 313). (Kipling retells here in capsule form his own early story "Lispeth.") This is perhaps the closest thing to a critique of the English in all of *Kim*, though the lama observes trenchantly, "The Sahibs have not *all* this world's wisdom" (*Kim* 240). But clearly what Kipling concedes is only the misconduct of an individual Englishman, a far cry from acknowledging that there is anything fundamentally wrong with British colonial rule itself.

Though it too is disconcerting, Kipling negotiates a resolution to the contrast (Said is correct in saying that there is for Kipling no actual conflict) between East and West that confronts Kim throughout his adventures. For the common denominator in Kim's experience is the need to submit to authority, Eastern as well as Western, spiritual as well as secular, native as well as colonial. The striking thing about Kim is that, as Kipling creates him, he is ready, even anxious, to yield to both the rules of the Great Game and the holiness of the lama; his posture in both cases is one of willing surrender. The idea that such concession is appropriate seems to lie at the very center of Kipling's multifarious novel, and this marks the novel's most profound difference from its engendering precursor, *Huckleberry Finn.* For of course Huck resists, with varying confidence and intensity, every authority he encounters. Twain's novel enacts a disease with, even a distrust of, authority that recurs and builds until the text seems to render any and all authority null and void. In contrast, Kipling's novel enacts a comfort with, a trust in, authority that recurs and builds until the text seems to insist that any and all authority is legitimate and valid. Here, I think, Twain and Kipling, who in their earlier fictions were both captivated by bad boys like Tom Sawyer and Stalky, part company for good.

Where Huck has not one reliable guide, Kim has no fewer than five, and where Huck has, at least by the end, no real or surrogate father, Kim has, in the end, two. In the course of his experience, Kim submits himself to the command and tutelage of the lama, his guide in holiness; Mahbub Ali, his general instructor in the Great Game; Colonel Creighton, the overseer of the Great Game; Lurgan Sahib, his tutor in the special arts of the Great Game; and Huree Babu, his comic but still effective fellow practitioner in the Great Game. It is revealing that the seemingly free picaro

Kim is so often constrained and that the apparently freedom-loving Kim is so submissive to authority. Kim is called by both the lama and Mahbub Ali an imp, but his mischievous impulses do not defy in any significant way the dictates of his various tutors. He does break some minor rules at school, and he does run away to the road for summer holidays (a breach of regimen finally sanctioned by Creighton), but these departures from strict rule do not demonstrate a nature resistant to discipline. To be sure, Kipling tantalizes—perhaps mystifies—by making Kim *seem* to be ungovernable. He gives us a Kim who roams, lies, dupes, teases, curses (vituperation is one of his art forms), capers, hoodwinks, runs, hides, and lurks, and in all these antics he appears to be a free spirit. Pointedly, Kipling has Kim ask of himself in three moments of troubled seriousness: "Who is Kim?" (*Kim* 166). And though it is not so easy to see (at least many readers and critics overlook it), the answer Kipling embeds in the text is that Kim is a person ready to resign himself to authority. When Mahbub Ali asks him if he meekly takes instruction from his schoolteachers, Kim answers with more honesty than guile: "It is an order," and then adds, "Who am I to dispute an order?" (*Kim* 181).

Kim, the Little Friend of all the World, seems loved by everyone he encounters. But he is finally most beloved by Mahbub Ali and the lama. Kipling ultimately casts both men as Kim's surrogate—admiring and affectionate—fathers. This functions in two ways: as a deepening of their uncontestable authority and as a kind of reward to Kim for submitting to it. Again, one feels the contrast with Huck, who has no such sponsorship, though to be sure Jim is fond of him and Aunt Sally stands ready in the end to mother as well as civilize him. Jim's affection is, however, disarmed by his status, whether free or enslaved, as a man of color in a racist society, and Huck resists, of course, Aunt Sally's adoptive concern. Interestingly, Kim submits to all authority except that of women. Like Huck, he keeps his distance from those women who would love and nurture him. Mahbub Ali, imparting something like the wisdom of a father, warns Kim against women in grim terms: "It is by means of women that all plans come to ruin and we lie out in the dawning with our throats cut" (*Kim* 225; of course, the "we" are the players of the Great Game). Ironically, however, Kim is aided most decisively, if not in fact saved, by women. The woman of Shamlegh provides food, money, and a litter to carry the sick lama (and Kim), as well as guides to enable Kim to rush his injured "father" down from the mountains to the plains. And the woman from Kulu sends her litter to complete the journey of rescue, houses both Kim and the lama, and nurses them back to health and sanity. Kipling makes both the woman of Shamlegh and the woman from Kulu sexual women, but he also dispels any threat or temptation their sexuality might pose—and thereby any power they might exert over Kim—by making both women very old. Needless to say, Twain keeps the women who try to assist Huck completely sexless.

For Kipling the point of submission is to create and maintain an ordered society. That society in *Kim* is the one shaped by British colonial rule. If his fiction in general "negotiates an uneasy series of truces between the resistance of the self to the authority of empire, and between the antithetical longings for empire" (Sullivan 1), in *Kim* the resistance is subdued and the longing fulfilled. In the loving bond between Kim and his lama, Kipling creates an idealized version of union between colonizer and colonized, between necessary power and unconditional love. He achieves this in part by making the lama something of a child, or perhaps more precisely, a precociously wise child. He is, as one critic has observed, "an ironically 'childish' counterpart to Kim's preternatural sophistication" (Bivona 45). Furthermore, insofar as the lama's search for transcendence, for release from the Wheel of Life, is a longing for permanence, it valorizes a kind of stability arguably akin to the need for social order implicit in the Great Game.

Kim loses himself—loses his very being—in illness at the end, only to be reborn into this world. Earlier he speaks of the possibility of losing himself in, of deliberately escaping into, the "great, grey, formless India" (*Kim* 143), but the India he faces (the one Kipling so marvelously creates) is neither chaotic nor entropic. Which is to say, that while Twain brings Huck into a world that realizes the full logic of the picaresque form, a logic that says finally that existence, like the universe itself, is random, a matter of meaningless motion, Kipling does not place Kim in any such place, physically or metaphysically. Kipling keeps Kim's India as real, as solid, as the political and social structure of empire the Great Game successfully preserves. The lama smiles at the end, Kipling says, "as a man may who has won salvation for himself and his beloved" (*Kim* 338), but it is not salvation Kim himself rejoices in but rather rebirth into human life. From feeling that his spirit is, in Kipling's famous metaphor, "a cog-wheel unconnected with any machinery," he awakens to—reconnects with—the machinery of life itself, a life far more solid and certain than the world in flux and disintegration with which Twain surrounds Huck. Here is Kim's recovery: "He did not want to cry—had never felt less like crying in his life—but of a sudden easy, stupid tears trickled down his nose, and with an almost audible click he felt the wheels of his being lock up anew on the world without. Things that rode meaningless on the eyeball an instant before slid into proper proportion. Roads were meant to be walked upon, houses to be lived in, cattle to be driven, fields to be tilled, and men and women to be talked to. They were all real and true—solidly planted upon the feet—perfectly comprehensible—clay of his clay, neither more nor less" (*Kim* 331). While Twain's picaro remains in motion—or at least vows to be—in a world, physical as well as social, that is itself fluid and uncertain, Kipling's picaro ends at rest in a world, physical as well as social, that is—or at least is said to be—real and true. Thus the very nature of things, the very constitution of life for Twain, problematizes authority, while the very nature of things, the very constitution of life for Kipling, sustains it.

Certainly Twain and Kipling had no inkling of the crucial differences between their interlinked novels. Each writer's masterwork bodied forth something basic in its author and important to his culture. But Twain, a lifelong reader of Kipling after he discovered him, seems to have intuited the essential character of the man that expressed itself subtly, indeed seductively, in *Kim*. In 1907 Twain confided to his private secretary, Isabel Lyon, a slightly murky but discernibly critical view of Kipling that he never revealed in public. Even though he voiced his notions in the atmosphere of confidentiality, he formulated them more as forgiving understanding than condemning indictment. He averred that Kipling's early life, his formative upbringing, "makes him cling to his early beliefs; then he loves power and authority and Kingship—and that has to show itself in his religion" (qtd. in Gribben, *MT's Library* 382). That democratic Twain would object to a monarchist Kipling is no surprise, nor is it unexpected that the skeptical Twain would look askance at any sign of a religious Kipling. What is eye-opening, however, is Twain's crystal-clear sense that Kipling is enthralled by power and in love with authority. It is a shrewd reading of the man, which also glosses *Kim* perceptively.

Although Twain kept private his sense of Kipling's weaknesses, preserving their friendship out of honest admiration for Kipling's talent and achievements, the ideological divergence between the two is plain. Kipling became the foremost spokesman for empire, the great—and famous—advocate of colonial rule. Writing, speaking, and poeticizing on behalf of imperialism, he reminded the Western world, for his audience remained vast even as his critical acclaim declined, of the moral necessity, god-ordained, to preserve the rule of the Western powers:

> God of our fathers, known of old,
>> Lord of our far-flung battle-line,
> Beneath whose awful Hand we hold
>> Dominion over palm and pine—
> Lord God of Hosts, be with us yet,
> Lest we forget—lest we forget! ("Recessional," *RK's Verse* 327)

He feared that civilization itself would decline, perhaps even fall, if the superior, enlightened races of the West did not maintain hegemony. For him, as W. H. Auden once observed, "Civilization . . . is a little citadel of light surrounded by a great darkness full of malignant forces and only maintained through the centuries by everlasting vigilance, will-power and self-sacrifice" (199). Skeptical in *Huckleberry Finn* of the civilization Huck shuns, Twain became increasingly critical of the very civilization Kipling believed in. The more he saw the tears and blotches in the fabric of Western civilization, the less he could countenance its imposition on other lands and peoples. And further, he imagined his way into the skins of those other peoples and realized the terrible destruction of individual freedom and autonomous selfhood that imperial ventures wrought.

The pivotal experience leading to Twain's late, anti-imperial outlook was his 1895–96 lecture tour, which took him to the colonized countries of Australia, New Zealand, Ceylon, India, Mauritius, and South Africa. He began as one predisposed to accept colonialism, but looking at it first-hand, he had second thoughts. As Budd has put it, he adjusted his "mental baggage to fit the realities he met" (*Social Philosopher* 169). He was inclined to approve of British rule in India (the colonial circumstance dearest to Kipling's heart), while criticizing it in other countries.[12] He seems to have arrived at dissatisfaction leaning toward critique by thinking of—

thinking into—the colonized themselves. Sometimes playfully, more often moralistically, he figures for himself as well as his readers the complexity of cultural superimposition:

> The Whites always mean well when they take human fish out of the ocean and try to make them dry and warm and happy and comfortable in a chicken coop; but the kindest-hearted white man can always be depended on to prove himself inadequate when he deals with savages. He cannot turn the situation around and imagine how he would like it to have a well-meaning savage transfer him from his house and his church and his clothes and his books and his choice of food to a hideous wilderness of sand and rocks and snow, and ice and sleet and storm and blistering sun, with no shelter, no bed, no covering for his and his family's naked bodies, and nothing to eat but snakes and grubs and offal. This would be a hell to him; and if he had any wisdom he would know that his own civilization is a hell to the savage—but he hasn't any, and has never had any; and for lack of it he shut up those poor natives in the unimaginable perdition of his civilization, committing his crime with the very best intentions, and saw those poor creatures waste away under his tortures; and gazed at it, vaguely troubled and sorrowful, and wondered what could be the matter with them. (*FE* 267)

After having supported the Spanish-American War, believing at first that it was a struggle to free Cuba, Twain read the Treaty of Paris and decided that the war was a fraud. From 1900 to the time of his death in 1910, he opposed global imperialism. He became vice president of the Anti-Imperialist League and vice president of the American Congo Reform Association, writing powerful essays for both causes. He was especially passionate about the immorality and the horror of the United States' war to subjugate the Philippines, a country colonized by Spain and ceded to the United States after the Spanish-American war in Cuba (for Twain's writings and speeches on the Philippines, see Zwick). Ironically, it was the colonization, or rather the re-colonization, of the Philippines that moved Kipling to write his most famous pro-imperialist poem, "The White Man's Burden." Starkly, he enjoined America to take possession of the savage, uncivilized Philippines for their own benefit (and for the good of universal civilization as well as the fulfillment of God's plan):

Take up the White Man's burden—
   Send forth the best ye breed—
Go bind your sons to exile
   To serve your captives' need;
To wait in heavy harness
   On fluttered folk and wild—
Your new-caught, sullen peoples,
   Half devil and half child. ("The White Man's Burden," *RK's Verse* 321)

Twain's criticism of imperialism often centered on just the question of how it functioned—or failed to function—"to serve [its] captives' need."

Coincidentally, seven months before *Kim* appeared in print (but well after it was written), Twain published his most scathing attack on global imperialism, the compelling and passionate "To the Person Sitting in Darkness." Viewing Twain's essay in relation to Kipling's novel, one is perhaps most struck by their differing use of the metaphor of the "game." By the time both Kipling and Twain wrote, imperialism itself, probably reflecting old aristocratic attitudes of insouciance (see Green, *Dreams of Adventure*), had been frequently described, with varying degrees of indifference or engagement, as a game "to be played for the sake of play" (Bivona 35). But where Kipling mystifies—and glorifies—the Great Game Kim learns to play for the sport of it (significantly, there is not one moment in the novel in which Kim reflects on the general import, the ideological assumptions, or the political impact of the game), Twain turns the metaphor into a derogatory term for the force and conniving and deception used to subjugate a people.

Conceptually, Twain's critique of international imperialism in "To the Person Sitting in Darkness" centers on three things: first, the hypocrisy with which the imperial powers pretend to colonize for the benefit of the colonized; second, the rapacious desire for economic gain that drives imperial ventures; and third, the wanton subjugation of indigenous peoples that deprives them of their freedom as well as their land. (For a discussion of Twain's rhetorical strategies in this essay, especially his exploitation of sentimental melodrama, see the first chapter; for a consideration of his use of the discourse of civilization in it, see the chapter on Twain and Arnold.) All three are telling objections, and he makes them with brilliant rhetoric, vivid images and metaphors, and bayonet-sharp irony. Though there is no evidence that he read Twain's essay, Kipling would no doubt have contested all three of Twain's criticisms.

Twain bolsters his attack on imperialism by suggesting that, at least in the case of America, it defies the very principles upon which the imperial country itself was founded: principles of freedom, democracy, and the right to self-governance. By invoking such foundational principles, along with the icons and symbols of America itself, Twain employed a tactic frequently used by the American anti-imperialists (Zwick xxx–xxxiv), who as a group were a strange mix of conservatives and liberals (see Beisner). Looked at in the largest sweep of U.S. imperialism, in the light of twentieth- and twenty-first-century American globalism, Twain seems to have deployed in opposition to imperialism the very ideology that America would most successfully use to sanction it. For as various historians and critics have pointed out, the United States exported the idea of freedom—with "the 'American Revolution' of 1776" as its "model"—to gain political influence over other countries and, in some cases, Cuba and the Philippines paramount among them, to establish actual imperial control (Jones 207).[13] Cuba and the Philippines had to be freed from Spain under the aegis of an anticolonial posture in order to become subject to the United States.

Twain spins the table one more time, however, turning the rhetoric invoked in seizing Cuba and the Philippines into an argument for their liberation. He pricks the conscience of his American audience, especially those who are oblivious to the paradox of a democratic country assuming totalitarian control over another country. He is especially effective when he casts the appeal to patriotism in lurid images: for America's conquered foreign lands he suggests, "we can have just our usual flag, with the white stripes painted black and the stars replaced by the skull and cross-bones" (*MTC2* 472–73). At his best he manages to provoke, to return to an Arnoldian formulation, "the free play of mind," prompting his audience to consider anew just what constitutes true patriotism. (Twain himself was never an uncritical, knee-jerk patriot.)

Running through his major anti-imperial essays, "To the Person Sitting in Darkness," "To My Missionary Critics," "A Defense of General Funston," and "King Leopold's Soliloquy," is a common thread. In every case he directs his attack at one or more powerful public figures, the monarchs or missionaries or politicians or generals who carry forward the imperial enterprise. This tendency is no doubt due in part to the fact that focusing on a public figure enables him to unleash the kind of ad hominem sarcasm at which he excels. It may also reflect a habit of mind—his tendency to see people rather than forces as the shapers of events (Budd, *Social Philosopher* 180). In any case, his attention to powerful figures takes us to a final contrast between Twain and Kipling. Both men, it must be said, enjoyed knowing prominent and powerful leaders in political and economic life. But when it came to such leaders of empire, Twain and Kipling once again diverged. The most obvious—and representative—example is Cecil Rhodes.

Kipling met Rhodes in casual social gatherings first in Cape Town in 1891 and then again in London in 1897, but it was not until Kipling spent three months in the Cape Town Colony from January to April 1898 that he and Rhodes really conversed and became friends. By then Rhodes had made a fortune in industry and in the diamond fields of South Africa, been elected to the Cape Parliament, and served as prime minister for the colony. He had also sponsored the famous Jameson raid into the independent Boer republic in the Transvaal, hoping, as he had for years, to extend British rule farther north. Rhodes believed firmly in the rightness of empire, in the justice of British dominion, and in this his outlook coincided perfectly with Kipling's. While something of a visionary in his plans to develop as well as extend the British African colonies—perhaps for Kipling the embodiment of "The Dreamer whose dreams come true!" ("The Fairies' Siege," *RK's Verse* 520)—Rhodes was above all a man of will, of power, of imperious control. He would bring his dreams into reality, even, if necessary, by force of arms. Besides sharing his vision, Kipling admired the man's practicality and sheer might; he memorialized him this way:

> As tho' again—yea, even once again,
> We should rewelcome to our stewardship
> The rider with the loose-flung bridle-rein
> And chance-plucked twig for whip,
>
> The down-turned hat-brim, and the eyes beneath
> Alert, devouring—and the imperious hand
> Ordaining matters swiftly to bequeath
> Perfect the work he planned. ("Rhodes Memorial," *RK's Verse* 210)

Clearly, for Kipling, Rhodes was the figure of consummate authority—the equivalent of Stalky's Head or Kim's Colonel Creighton—and so much did he share Rhodes's vision and admire his power that he lent his voice and his pen to Rhodes's causes. In his autobiography, Kipling recalled that the "inarticulate" Rhodes would fumble out his ideas and then ask him, "What am I trying to express? Say it, *say* it." And Kipling would say it for him (*Something of Myself* 101). When the Boer War, to which Rhodes's Jameson raid was the awkward, ineffectual prelude, was getting under way, Kipling celebrated its soldier-heroes with "The Absent-Minded Beggar":

> When you've shouted "Rule Britannia," when you've sung
>> "God save the Queen,"
> When you've finished killing Kruger with your mouth,
> Will you kindly drop a shilling in my little tambourine
>> For a gentleman in khaki ordered South?
> He's an absent-minded beggar, and his weaknesses are great—
>> But we and Paul must take him as we find him—
> He is out on active service, wiping something off a slate—
>> And he's left a lot of little things behind him!
> Duke's son—cook's son—son of a hundred kings—
>> (Fifty thousand horse and foot going to Table Bay!)
> Each of 'em doing his country's work
>> (and who's to look after their things?)
> Pass the hat for your credit's sake,
>>> and pay—pay—pay! (*RK's Verse* 457)

And when the war was in full swing he affirmed yet again the justice of the White Man's Burden:

> Now, this is the cup the White Men drink
>> When they go to right a wrong,
> And that is the cup of the old world's hate—
>> Cruel and strained and strong.
> We have drunk that cup—and a bitter, bitter cup—
>> And tossed the dregs away.
> But well for the world when the White Men drink
>> To the dawn of the White Man's day!

Now, this is the road the White Men tread
   When they go to clean a land—
Iron underfoot and levin overhead
   And the deep on either hand.
We have trod that road—and a wet and windy road—
   Our chosen star for guide.
Oh, well for the World when the White Men tread
   Their highway side by side! ("A Song of the White Men," *RK's Verse* 280)

For Kipling, Rhodes was one who undertook "to clean a land," and it was "well for the World" that he did so.

Twain's view of Rhodes could hardly be more different. Twain was in South Africa on his around-the-world lecture tour in May 1896, just four months after Jameson's incursion into the Transvaal. (He visited British prisoners in jail in Pretoria.) Back in England in August, he followed closely the testimony of Rhodes and Jameson (and others) before the Parliamentary Committee of Inquiry, and he read at least three books on the issue of the raid. In doing all this, he was in no way a disinterested observer, for as he explained to his friend and financial advisor Henry Huttleston Rogers, he had to enlarge the travel account of his tour, *Following the Equator*, to fill out the second volume and so "added 30,000 words," most of them about the South African situation (*MT's Correspondence with Henry Huttleston Rogers* 276). As he said in the book, the whole political situation was riddled with "conflicting" information, all but hopelessly "tangled," and consequently deeply confusing (*FE* 654–52).

Whether or not Twain sorted out the circumstances accurately, he became clear about one thing: Rhodes was a scoundrel. Twain enjoyed "chaffing Rhodes and making fun of his Jameson Raid" (*MT's Correspondence with Henry Huttleston Rogers* 276). He also amused himself—and his readers—by recounting the ineptitude of the Jameson forces and the martial skill of the Boers, but his chief target was Rhodes. Although he acknowledged opposing views of Rhodes, he labels Rhodes's work a "pirating expedition" and describes him and his chartered company as "highwaymen" (*FE* 686, 690). Where Kipling sees a visionary pursuing the good of the colonial lands and through that nothing less than the good of the world at large, Twain locates base self-interest and self-aggrandizement. For Twain, Rhodes is not a man interested in the common good but in his own power: "He wants the earth and wants it for his own." To this end, Twain believes, he deceives and tricks and exploits. Further, Twain sees him as horribly oppressing the indigenous people: "He raids and robs and slays and enslaves" (*FE* 709). The Twain who authored a Huck Finn resistant to control mocks the powerful Rhodes admired by Kipling, and so we are returned again to the fundamental difference between the two writers: Kipling cherishes authority, Twain challenges it. In terms of colonial affairs Kipling sanctions imperial dominion, finding it both necessary and just; Twain contests it, seeing it as both inappropriate and immoral. In a now-famous line, Twain concludes not only his account of Rhodes in particular but also, by implication, his overall view of the colonizer by saying, with lethal irony, of Rhodes: "I admire him, I frankly confess it; and when his time comes I shall buy a piece of the rope for a keepsake" (*FE* 710).

In 1899, when Kipling, seriously ill with pneumonia, seemed on the brink of death and the whole world watched and worried, Twain coined a bon mot that ingeniously linked not only the two writers but also their respective countries: "Since England and America have been joined in Kipling, may they not be severed in Twain" (qtd. in *MTB* 2:1087). But the two were, as we've seen, severed in their finest works, *Huckleberry Finn* and *Kim*, and were further divided in their views of imperialism. Privately Twain deepened their sundering by satirizing Kipling. In response to "The Absent-Minded Beggar" he wrote his own version:

> Duke's son, earl's son, son of the noovo rich,
> Bilk's son, snob's son, bastard son of a bitch,
>   None of 'm whine, they *all* jine,
>   Jine the cavalree,
> And hell they raise for God his praise
> In the Boer his counteree.
>   Pay, pay, goddam you, pay. (*On the Poetry of Mark Twain* 34)

Publicly, however, Twain concealed the breach between the two; he continued to exclaim over Kipling's art and to read his poetry aloud with appreciation. At the time of his *Following the Equator* lecture tour Twain playfully pretended that he would visit India (where it was rumored Kipling was about to go) solely to see Kipling:

Dear Kipling,—It is reported that you are about to visit India. This has moved me to journey to that far country in order that I may unload from my conscience a debt long due to you. Years ago you came from India to Elmira to visit me, as you said at the time. It has always been my purpose to return that visit and that great compliment some day. I shall arrive next January and you must be ready. I shall come riding my ayah with his tusks adorned with silver bells and ribbons and escorted by a troop of native howdahs richly clad and mounted upon a herd of wild bungalows; and you must be on hand with a few bottles of ghee, for I shall be thirsty. (*MTL* 629)

They did not meet in India, of course. By the time they did come together at Oxford to receive their honorary degrees in 1907, the differences between them on imperialism were glaring. True to his earlier quip, though, Twain did not let those radically divergent views, or anything else, sever the two friends. As Kipling remembered the occasion, they slipped off, like wayward schoolboys—like Tom Sawyer and Stalky—to sneak a smoke and share a laugh (RK, *Letters* 3:248–49). Kipling too preserved the friendship, though he must have known of Twain's outspoken attacks on the very imperial venture he enjoined America to undertake in the Philippines. Perhaps we should simply say that in their personal relations both Twain and Kipling were "wandering devious" to the end.

CONCLUSION

# Viewing Mark Twain

In an arresting moment in *Life on the Mississippi*, Twain visits the Washington Artillery building in New Orleans where he views "a fine oil-painting representing Stonewall Jackson's last interview with General Lee." Repeating the posture of art-ignoramus he made famous in *The Innocents Abroad*, he suggests that he cannot understand the painting: "it means nothing without its label" (*LOM* 315–16). He then playfully offers eight labels that might explain the painting:

> First Interview between Lee and Jackson.
>
> Last Interview between Lee and Jackson.
>
> Jackson Introducing Himself to Lee.
>
> Jackson Accepting Lee's Invitation to Dinner.
>
> Jackson Declining Lee's Invitation to Dinner—with Thanks.
>
> Jackson Apologizing for a Heavy Defeat.
>
> Jackson Reporting a Great Victory.
>
> Jackson Asking Lee for a Match. (*LOM* 316)

The problem so delightfully presented here is still a vexed issue: the uncertainty of reading a text, pictorial or written. Twain recognizes the problematics of what recent literary theory has so masterfully insisted upon. He posits the indeterminacy, the subjectivity, and the cultural relativity of reading a picture—or literary text, or historical figure. The slipperiness of interpretation grasped so firmly here for a moment still unsettles the criticism of the historical figure, the literary persona, Mark Twain.

In many ways Twain's last bid to be viewed as a writer was his auto-biography. From about 1870 on he began to write sketches that recalled segments of his life. Ironically, that life initially seemed most vivid to him when he was living abroad. Living in Vienna from 1897 to 1898, far from his homeland, he penned some ebullient recollections of his youthful years, and then in 1904, when he was living in Florence for the benefit of Livy's health, he began to dictate his life story. Interrupted by his wife's death—and the trials of emotional adjustment and literal relocation—he finally returned in 1906 to recalling his life. He used again the mode of dictation that was both physically easier than writing (he lay in bed smoking a cigar instead of sitting up at a table holding a pen) and psychologically satisfy-ing, as at times his recorder, his personal secretary, his financial advisor, and his designated literary executor were all in attendance, creating an audience of apparently approving, even enraptured, listeners. Whatever else the autobiography he thus created is, it is a final testament to his lifelong labor as a member of the literary guild.

The autobiography itself is a wonder—the sign either of eccentricity run amuck or of genius manifesting itself one last time. Twain was clear about the peculiarity he was creating. He deliberately casts his life story as a series of reminiscences without chronological, developmental, ideologi-cal, professional, or historical logic. He thus defies the very conventions of autobiography, which up to his time had insisted that one's life reflect a pattern of significance, yield a moral of one sort or another, by revealing a definitive conversion, or a personal evolution, or an economic progres-sion (rags to riches), or an unintended but apparent expression of history itself. Defying all these paradigms, Twain—perversely or playfully—opts for randomness. The haphazard is both the form of his autobiography and the content, as he tells it, of his life. He very purposefully creates not a co-herent narrative but a series of disjointed fragments, and muddying the line between the private and the public, the border along which individual life transpires, he dictated as a part of his autobiography the inclusion of documents, bits and pieces of news recorded in the daily newspapers. The principle governing it all was, he said, "a deliberate system, and the law of the system is that I shall talk about the matter which for the moment interests me, and cast it aside and talk about something else the moment its interest for me is exhausted. It is a system that follows no charted course and is not going to follow any such course. It is a system which is a complete and purposed jumble" (*MTOA* 4). Yet despite this avowal of—indeed delighted celebration of—"jumble," there is a centering to Twain's recollections. Again and again, inevitably one feels, he focuses on and returns to his life as a writer.

Twain's recurrent discussion of his life as the life of a writer ironically subverts his avowed intent to deny coherent meaning to his life. What it discloses, however, is something close to a fatality: he was to be, could not help but be, was abidingly, a writer. In the only version of his life he published during his lifetime, "Chapters from My Autobiography," printed in the *North American Review* in 1906 and 1907, he turns almost at once to his "experiences as an author." (He does in fact begin with an account of his ancestors that follows chronology until he includes fictitious "pirates" and "Satan," thereby subverting the autobiographical convention he seems to be honoring.) In passing, he acknowledges over and over his various literary endeavors, their origins, failures, successes, and incompletions. He defines his home life seriously as one alive with, even dominated by, "literary people," and playfully he says that he has spent his life "drowning the world in literary wisdom" (*MTOA* 12, 4–5, 110). As he centers his centerless life in his writing Twain also registers, haphazardly but with cumulative force, the fact that he has conducted his writing life in relation to others.

The number of writers named, remembered in brief, or recalled in some detail, is staggering—easily over a hundred. Clearly, his world was a world of novelists, poets, playwrights, historians, essayists, humorists, journalists, editors, and publishers. His acknowledgment of so many colleagues underscores what he emphasized in "The Turning Point of My Life," the essay that provided the point of departure for this study: he was—and thought of himself as—a member of a confederacy of craftsmen.

*Mark Twain & Company* has looked at his relations with only six of his fellow writers. These relations were both personal and literary. The personal ties ranged from a single meeting, as was the case with Stevenson, to a lifelong, close friendship, as with Howells. The nature of Twain's relations also varied from an abiding dislike, his feeling about Harte, to an invincible fondness, his feeling for Kipling, and in between these extremes we have seen these shadings: amused irony, tinged with real respect for Stowe; sharp annoyance, held somewhat in check by admiration, for Arnold; and esteem, strengthened by sympathy, for Stevenson. Twain's feelings for Howells transcend all these, for he venerated Howells, valued the man as much as his works, and felt for him a friendship beyond all others. In some ways, Twain's attachment to Kipling is the most revealing, however. Whatever it may suggest about the place of politics in his later life, Twain's refusal to let the profound disagreements between him and Kipling get in the way of their cordial friendship is testimony to his capacity for personal loyalty. This capacity is just the obverse of his unshakable contempt for Harte. For Twain, nothing could diminish Kipling, and nothing could redeem Harte. All six writers reciprocated Twain's response to them in their different ways. Their feelings for Twain and his work varied—from Arnold's supercilious dismissal of him (one tempered after he felt the full force of Twain's personality) to Stevenson's affectionate celebration. Perhaps the most important thing to say is just that, as their work interested Twain, so his engaged them. In the large, many-peopled guild of writers, Mark Twain clearly mattered.

Twain and the six other writers examined in this study all responded to the sudden and ongoing changes in their common trans-Atlantic culture. To shift from their personal connections to their *literary* relations, their modes of narrating all arise from the tensions and conflicts—the crises—in that culture. Their ways of storytelling are strikingly different, however. They assumed these forms: the sentimental, the humorous, the Gothic, the sagely, the adventurous, and the picaresque. One measure of Twain's versatility is the fact that he wrote in all six of these modes. A measure of his talent is that he succeeded in all six.

This study has proceeded in the way the fabled Noah's ark was loaded: two by two. I hope it has revealed how Twain's work corresponded with—or departed from—that of the six other members of the literary guild. Pairing Twain with one fellow writer after another has—perhaps unsurprisingly—signaled the multiple dimensions of his creative genius. Is it possible to put them all together? What kind of a Mark Twain can we see when we look at him in company?

If one were asked to name a nineteenth-century American writer who was sentimental, who expressed genteel New England concerns, who was absorbed in domesticity, a writer who used the Gothic for social protest, one who spoke as a sage with absolute assurance about social and cultural matters, who sponsored soft, compassionate masculinity, and who challenged the authority upon which civilization was grounded, I doubt that one would think first of Mark Twain. Yet, set alongside the six other writers examined here, Twain begins to emerge as this odd, disjunctive composite. The picture, to be sure, is still only a partial portrait, for Twain is nothing if not a multifaceted writer. But the picture, the portrait of Mark Twain in company, needs to find a place (it could be in a dimly lit corner) next to the other, more familiar paintings of Twain hanging in the critical gallery: Twain the southwestern humorist, Twain the adherent to vernacular values, Twain the subverter of conventions, Twain the literary comedian, Twain the social critic, Twain the explorer of human identity, and Twain the opponent of all orthodoxy, cutting out wildly on the loose.[1] These are luminous pictures. Looked at in even a small company of his fellow guild members, however, Twain appears even stranger. He is a writer who continues to elude exact critical focus.

# Notes

## Introduction

1. The poem in question, "Three Aces," was published in the *Buffalo Express* and signed "Carl Byng." Whether or not Twain wrote it is uncertain. In 1971, in what is still the fullest discussion, McCullough cautiously argued that the available evidence "suggests that Twain was indeed probably the author of the Byng sketches" ("MT and the Hy Slocum-Byng Controversy" 43). More recently, the editors of volume four of *Mark Twain's Letters* say, "a statistical comparison of the Byng texts with known texts by Mark Twain has suggested that Clemens did not write the Byng pieces" (*L4* 306, n. 3). In their fine collection of Twain's contributions to the *Buffalo Express*, McCullough and McIntire-Strasburg conclude: "Arguments for attribution of the Byng material [to Twain] remain too speculative to justify inclusion in this edition" (xxiii).

2. Blair *(MT & HF)* and Emerson *(The Authentic MT)* provide a number of illuminating comparisons between Twain's works and those of other writers, sometimes suggesting direct influence on Twain, but their discussions are always brief and therefore limited. Baetzhold's *Mark Twain and John Bull* is an exhaustive and often suggestive study of Twain and England as well as its writers. Various essays by Gribben also illuminate Twain's literary relations. Fulton makes a powerful case against the idea that Twain was unlettered and for his use of other texts in his process of composition (*MT in the Margins* 1–28).

3. In his lucid and moving study of four generations of American literary friendship, *A Common Life*, David Laskin takes a different approach, arguing that "the essential fact of nationality"—of the Americanness of his subjects, Melville and Hawthorne, James and Wharton, Porter and Welty, Bishop and Lowell—created a "common thread" (16). Indeed, the four friendships he studies, as he says, "bored deep into the core of what it

means to be American" (23). As much biography as critical study, his passionate book succeeds admirably in illuminating the country shared by the four sets of friends as well as their friendships.

4. While agreeing that there was a common Anglo-American culture, Sterner cautions us that there were nonetheless important differences between England and America; he points out four in particular: (1) the fact that America lacked a fully formed hereditary class structure; (2) the fact that political democracy was in place in America and only emerging in England; (3) the fact that there was no established church in America, as there was in England; and (4) the fact that there was greater and more widely shared abundance in America than in England (16–20).

## Wringing the Human Heart: Mark Twain & Bret Harte

1. Duckett's *Mark Twain and Bret Harte* is the most thorough account of the relationship, but she often defends Harte by attacking Twain, and she is inclined to mitigate Harte's shortcomings. A brief but insightful version of the relationship, one that sometimes corrects Duckett, is Thomas Schirer's *Mark Twain and the Theatre* (52–59). Scharnhorst's scattered comments on the two writers are always measured and sensible.

2. Again, Duckett, modified by Schirer, presents the essential facts of the final breakup, but Stewart provocatively observes, in what is still the best biography of Harte, that "there may never have been an out-and-out quarrel" (237).

3. Krause's chapter "Bret Harte: The Grumbling Realist's Friend and Foe" makes the case that Twain objected to Harte's lack of realism, largely by examining Twain's marginal notations in the books of Harte he owned (190–227). Booth has made these generally available, without much analysis.

4. Emerson provides a good review of Twain's compositional process, including his excisions (*Authentic MT* 100–106).

5. Twain was absolutely wrong in charging Harte with a failure to support his wife and family. Despite living apart from them, Harte sent his wife and family substantial sums of money, usually monthly, throughout his life (see Scharnhorst 67).

6. In "The Outcast of Literary Flat: Bret Harte as Humorist," Kolb explores the "astonishing gap" between the voice of Harte's narrator and his subjects, a gap that often provides irony.

7. For Twain's remarks about Walker, see *AMT* 113–14; and for a brief discussion of his significance for Twain, see Krauth 25–26.

8. Morrow provides a spirited defense of Harte's use of formula fiction (*BH as Literary Critic*, chapter 1).

9. Although he is not concerned with this question, in *Sentimental MT* Camfield shows convincingly that Twain was attuned to the "plastic and vital cosmology" of the sentimentalists (19). His trenchant study is virtually alone in placing Twain among the sentimentalists. While I agree with his analysis, my approach to sentimentality differs from his emphasis on the philosophical in stressing instead the rhetorical strategies and emotional impact of sentimentality.

10. Planned and financed by Twain, *Mark Twain's Library of Humor* was a collaboration by Howells and Twain, with the assistance of Charles H. Clark, a journalist known to both of them. Twain's work on the anthology was desultory until after both Howells and Clark had compiled their selections, at which point Twain made his decisions about their selections and rearranged the order of the whole book. For Howells's comments, see *MyMT* 17–18; for a succinct account of the joint venture, see Clarence Ghodes's foreword to a reprint of the original volume (vii–x).

## Creating Humor: Mark Twain & William Dean Howells

1. Although they may have treated each other as equals, Twain and Howells were not initially on a par. Howells, largely through his editorial position with the *Atlantic Monthly* but also through the popularity of his novels, established himself as an important presence in American literary culture well before Twain was given significant critical attention. Now the relative status of the two has been reversed, of course: the preeminence Howells achieved in his time, Twain commands in ours.

2. For commentaries on these ties between Twain and Howells, see Carter; Cady, *The Light of Common Day* as well as his biography; and Kolb, *The Illusion of Life*. For challenges to—often displacements of—the very idea of realism, see Bell, Amy Kaplan, and Michaels.

3. Studies of travel literature are now voluminous. I have found the following especially informative: Batten and Buzzard on forms, conventions, and cultural meanings; Pemble and Porter on the erotic aspect of travel; Pratt, Spurr, and Sara Mills on the politics of travel; William Stowe and Nathalia Wright on American travel books.

4. Howells's travels books, which grew out of sketches first published serially in magazines, were by no means the sole causes of his editorial appointments. In fact the *Atlantic* rejected the sketches later shaped into *Venetian Life*, but their publication in the Boston *Advertiser* not only made Howells

visible in the New England literary culture but also increased Lowell's admiration of his work, and Lowell was instrumental in securing Howells's advancement. Howells himself noted, with characteristic self-deprecation, that his skill as a printer was a major consideration when the *Atlantic* hired him away from the *Nation* (*Life in Letters* 1:104).

5. The types of humor—and their clashes—are surveyed in such standard studies as Blair *(Native American Humor)*, Blair and Hill *(America's Humor)*, and Rourke *(American Humor)*. Reynolds provides a more recent provocative account in *Beneath the American Renaissance* (see especially part 4, "The Grotesque Posture: Popular Humor and the American Subversive Style").

6. Howells felt guilty for not serving in the Civil War, as his brother Sam did, but his all-consuming desire was a literary career. Again in long retrospect, he would say of himself, "If there was any one in the world who had his being more wholly in literature than I had in 1860, I am sure I should not have known where to find him" (*Literary Friends* 7). When he received a letter of encouragement from Lowell in 1864, he described it in military terms that make it clear that his war was a fight for literary acceptance. The letter was, he wrote, "a trumpet call to battle, which echoed and reechoed in my soul and seemed to fill the universe with its reverberation" ("The Turning Point of My Life" 355–56). Lynn points out that government service like Howells's was "the most honorable alternative to military service" (*An American Life* 108).

7. For an account of the critical reception given Howells's first two travel books, see Woodress (56–61, 71–73).

8. One gropes to account for such assurance in a twenty-four-year-old self-educated young man, a would-be poet, a now-and-then journalist, with no previous European travel. To be sure, Howells taught himself Italian and did research for his writings on Italy, but these alone seem insufficient to generate the authority registered everywhere in his first two travel books. Authority in travel writing is usually based on—established by the announcement of—gender, race, class, and national identity. Howells quietly assumes his gender, making no parade of his masculinity; he never mentions his race; and he at most only implies his class (he never insists upon it) through his interests, his activities, and his narrative voice. His national identity is quietly announced as he acknowledges his position as U.S. Consul, but there is no return to it as a source of empowerment, as a basis for judgment. Howells did revel in being an American, privately assuring his sister at the time of his residence in Venice: "There is no life

in the whole world so cheerful, so social, so beautiful as the American," and later, when he had returned to Italy in 1883, he would insist "*we* have the country of the present and future" (*Life in Letters* 1:59, 338). But in *Venetian Life* and *Italian Journeys* he does not proclaim his identity as an American (as Twain would, sometimes shrilly, in *The Innocents Abroad*). Perhaps the best explanation of Howells's immense authority (apart from a deep conviction of personal ability) is just that it was born of overwhelming, inspiriting desire—Howells's desire to become a man of letters.

9. William Dean Howells, *Italian Journeys* (1867; rpt., Boston: Houghton Mifflin, 1881), 50–51. Subsequent references are to this edition, abbreviated *IJ*, and will be given parenthetically in the text.

10. William Dean Howells, *Venetian Life*, 2 vols. (1866; rpt., Boston: Houghton Mifflin, 1885), 1:46, 12. Subsequent references are to this edition, abbreviated *VL*, and will be given parenthetically in the text.

11. The basis for the dark strain in Howells, the dye that shows up in even his earliest travel books, is made clear in the biographies by Cady and Lynn, and it has received considerable attention by critics of his fiction. Crowley's *The Mask of Fiction* (1–13) provides a useful overview of Howells criticism, and his own varied studies of that work also explore the dark aspect of Howells's writings.

12. When he revised *Italian Journeys* in 1901, "taming its wild youthfulness," Howells expressed some dissatisfaction with the rowdy turns of his first version, noting that it was marred by "posing," "straining," unwarranted "omniscience," and "unseemly spites and resentments." With a comic grace that stands in contrast to the very faults he finds in his text, he summarizes its problem this way: "I had a sense of having put on more airs than I could handsomely carry" ("A Confidence," *Italian Journeys* [1901]).

13. For a representative sampling of critical responses to *The Innocents Abroad*, see Anderson, *CH* 21–45, and Budd, *MT: The Contemporary Reviews* 33–89. The most comprehensive treatment of Twain as a travel writer is Melton's recent *Mark Twain, Travel Books, and Tourism*.

14. Their private rapping at each other spilled into the public realm when the editorial "we" of the introduction to the anthology of humor they compiled slyly observes that if Twain "could have had his way throughout, this Library would have consisted solely of extracts from his own books" (*Mark Twain's Library of Humor* xii).

15. In an illuminating recent essay, Kiskis argues that we should consider Twain in the tradition of literary domesticity described by Gillian Brown, and that by doing so, we will discover new—or undervalued—dimensions

of the man and his work ("Twain and the Tradition of Literary Domesticity"). In a carefully nuanced essay, Doyno modifies some of the more
severe accounts of Twain as a husband and father (for these, see Hill, *MT:
God's Fool*; and Warren) by looking at new documents from Twain's home
life. His conclusion is that "judged within a realistic context of his own
era," Twain was "an extraordinarily good husband and father" ("Samuel
Clemens as Family Man and Father"). My consideration of domestic play
in the Twain-Howells letters supports both of these arguments, as does my
1974 essay, "Mark Twain: At Home in the Gilded Age."

16. It is interesting that both Howells and Twain tended to be grimmer about
aging and death in their correspondence to others than they were with each
other. This suggests, perhaps, how given to good humor they were inclined
to be with each other. In 1902 Howells wrote to Charles Eliot Norton, "My
mainstay for talk, this summer, has been Mark Twain, only forty trolley
minutes away. But how sad old men are! We meet, and strike fire and
flicker up, and I come away a heap of cold ashes" (*Selected Letters* 5:37).

17. William Dean Howells, *A Traveler from Altruria*, in *A Selected Edition of
W. D. Howells*, vol. 20, *The Altrurian Romances*, ed. Clara and Rudolf
Kirk (Bloomington: Indiana UP, 1968), 9. Subsequent references are to
this edition, abbreviated *TFA*, and will be given parenthetically in the text.

## Exposing the Body in Protest: Mark Twain
## & Harriet Beecher Stowe

1. For life at Nook Farm, see Andrews and Moers *(HBS and American Literature)* in particular, as well as the biographies of Paine, Kaplan, and
Hoffman on Twain, and Forrest Wilson and Hedrick on Stowe.

2. The idea of the Gothic body informs much of the current criticism on the
Gothic. In 1999 the International Gothic Association's biennial conference
was on "Gothic Spirits—Gothic Flesh." Two seminal studies of the Gothic
body are Bruhm, *Gothic Bodies: The Politics of Pain in Romantic Fiction*;
and Hurley, *The Gothic Body*. Bruhm defines the Gothic body as one that
is "put on excessive display" with "violent, vulnerable immediacy" (xvii).
Scarry's *The Body in Pain: The Making and Unmaking of the World* is a
profound meditation on the body in Western culture.

3. In *Trumpets of Jubilee* Rourke provides a fascinating account of Lyman,
Henry Ward, and Harriet. The best exploration of both the Beecher reli-
gion and its eventual varieties is Caskey's *Chariot of Fire: Religion and the
Beecher Family*.

4. Besides the standard biographies, Emerson's "Mark Twain's Quarrel with
God" illuminates the consequences of Twain's early religious training.

5. For discussions of the occult, spiritualism, and the scientific study of psychic phenomena in American culture, see Ebon, *They Knew the Unknown;* Kerr, *Mediums, and Spirit-Rappers, and Roaring Radicals;* Kerr and Crow, *The Occult in America;* and Kerr, Crowley, and Crow, *The Haunted Dusk.*

6. Besides Brooks and Varma, this dimension of the Gothic is illuminated by the various essays in Thompson, *The Gothic Imagination: Essays in Dark Romanticism.* The other major approach to the Gothic sees it not as a search for the disappearing sacred but as a psychological expression of the dark self. For versions of this idea in the American context, see Martin and Savoy, *American Gothic: New Interventions in a National Narrative,* especially part 1, "Framing the Gothic: Theories and Histories." The seminal and still provocative study of the American Gothic is Fiedler's *Love and Death in the American Novel.* Two useful general studies are Ringe, *American Gothic;* and Gross, *Redefining the American Gothic.* For women and the Gothic, see Moers, *Literary Women: The Great Writers;* Carpenter and Kolmar, *Haunting the House of Fiction;* and Masse, *In the Name of Love.*

7. For suggestive accounts of the American preoccupation with death in the nineteenth century, see Douglas, *The Feminization of American Culture,* chapter 6, "The Domestication of Death"; and Halttunen, *Confidence Men and Painted Ladies,* chapter 5, "Mourning the Dead."

8. Wecter, *Sam Clemens of Hannibal,* recounts the dark side of Twain's early years. The best accounts of his adult interest in various manifestations of the supernatural are Kerr, *Mediums,* chapter 7; and Gribben, " 'When Other Amusements Fail.' "

9. Harriet Beecher Stowe, *Uncle Tom's Cabin or Life Among the Lowly* (New York: Penguin, 1981), 488. Future references to this edition, abbreviated *UTC,* will be given parenthetically in the text.

10. Recent critics have disagreed over the functions of domesticity in the novel. Tompkins has seen it as Stowe's substitute for political and economic power (*Sensational Designs,* chapter 5), and Philip Fisher similarly defines domesticity as the critical foil used to illuminate and attack slavery (*Hard Facts,* chapter 2). However, in "Getting in the Kitchen with Dinah," Gillian Brown argues that Stowe "seeks to reform American society not by employing domestic values but by reforming them" (507). While one may thus dispute the social import of domesticity for Stowe—whether it is adequate as it is or in need of change—its desirability as a personal attribute is, I think, beyond contention.

11. Wilson *(Crusader in Crinoline)* chronicles Stowe's various bodily illnesses. The most extensive exploration of Stowe's illnesses in relation to her novel

that I know is Romero's "Bio-Political Resistance in Domestic Ideology and *Uncle Tom's Cabin.*" For an illuminating discussion of the use of the body in general in sentimental fictions concerned with disability, see Klages.

12. For the traits attributed to women in the much-discussed cult of true womanhood, see Welter and Berg. For Stowe's complex involvement in the women's movement, see Hedrick.

13. For a discussion of Stowe's difficulties, see Lentricchia; for an account of Twain's involvement, see Baender.

14. *Lady Byron Vindicated* (1870; rpt., New York: Haskell House, 1970), 428. Stowe's text incorporates her original *Atlantic* article, "The True Story of Lady Byron's Life." Subsequent references given parenthetically are to this edition.

15. While Twain and Stowe both use—and believe in—the gender types common to the cultural discourse of their era, the 1874 trial of Henry Ward Beecher for adultery complicated their responses if not their conventional thinking. Stowe could not imagine her brother as a Byronic lecher. He is, she wrote to George Eliot, using terms usually applied to the true woman, "purity, honor, delicacy," "sweet and perfect," and acknowledging her complete identification with him, she added, "he is myself" (*Life and Letters of HBS* 366). Twain, while apparently believing that Beecher was guilty—"let the worn stub of the Plymouth white-wash brush be brought out once more," he wrote to Howells (*MTHL* 227)—could not bring himself to condemn Beecher as he had Byron. Indeed, he continued his friendship with Henry Ward, and planned to publish not only his life of Christ but also his autobiography. (Beecher died before either was finished, but Twain's company did publish a family-written biography of Beecher himself.) Twain's loyalty and tolerance did not keep him from spoofing Beecher in his private notebook, much as he had laughed at Harriet Beecher Stowe herself in the same private space. He jotted down this hilarious note to a Lyceum Committee: "A minister with 16 sexual indiscretions proved against him . . . wishes to lecture. Stereopticon views. Terms $600 per night" (*N&J3* 214). A useful analysis of the entire affair in its cultural context is Waller's *Reverend Beecher and Mrs. Tilton: Sex and Class in Victorian America.*

16. Daniel Hoffman uses the term "black and white magic" in his seminal study of superstition in *Huckleberry Finn, Form and Fable in American Fiction* (317–42). While I consider chiefly Twain's comic treatment of such magic, Hoffman explores its serious thematic implications.

17. Kerr links the events Twain depicts in the Phelps sequence to several con-

temporary spiritualist phenomena, notably the Stratford rappings of 1850; he sees Tom and Huck as "unwitting poltergeists in a burlesque of spiritual manifestations" (*Mediums* 171–81).

18. Harriet Beecher Stowe, *Dred: A Tale of the Great Swamp* (Edinburgh: Edinburgh UP, 1999), 261. Further references to this edition, abbreviated *Dred*, will be given parenthetically in the text.

19. When the Civil War came, Stowe welcomed it and urged ever more violent military assaults on the South. Gossett concludes that she saw it as a "holy crusade" (312), and he cites multiple examples of her own righteous rhetoric, which echo *Dred*'s. Very much in the spirit of Dred, she viewed the destruction of the South as just retribution for sin and crime. For a provocative account of the violence of Stowe's imagination, see Cox's "Harriet Beecher Stowe: From Sectionalism to Regionalism."

20. Baetzhold outlines Twain's use of Ball (*MT and John Bull* 131–32, 151–52, 349 n. 33, 352 n. 39), as does Williams ("The Use of History").

21. In his late, usually unpublished essays, Twain sometimes rails against the body. In "Man's Place in the Animal World," for instance, he itemizes with pleased bitterness some seventy infirmities, ranging from measles to cancer ("but why continue the list," he asks), to which the body is subject. He concludes that man is "but a basket of festering offal provided for the support and entertainment of swarming armies of bacilli,—armies commissioned to rot him and destroy him" (*What Is Man?* 88).

## Holding Up the Looking Glass: Mark Twain & Matthew Arnold

1. Trilling suggests that Arnold used his humor to keep his friends "at a distance" (*Matthew Arnold* 24). Howells observed a similar aloofness, a masked quality, in Twain: "You were all there for him, but he was not all there for you" (*MyMT* 26). In terms that describe the dilemma Twain would face when he wanted to be taken seriously, Arnold explained the unfortunate result of his humor: "I laugh too much and they [his friends] make one's laughter mean too much. However, the result is that when one wishes to be serious one cannot but fear a half suspicion on one's friends' parts that one is laughing, and, so, the difficulty gets worse and worse" (qtd. in Honan 72.)

2. References to Arnold's poems will be given by title only, since there are many reliable editions (and no definitive one). I have used *Poetry and Criticism of Matthew Arnold*, ed. A. Dwight Culler. For the prose, references will be identified by title and then by volume and page number to

the standard edition, *The Complete Prose Works of Matthew Arnold*, ed. R. H. Super.

3. The reasons for Arnold's abandonment of poetry have been much discussed. He himself seems to have felt that his poems failed to match his own conception of what poetry should be (see his preface to the 1853 edition of *Poems*). Kermode analyzes Arnold's difficulties, stressing an alienation typical of romantic poets (24–32). Honan takes note of various conflicts and pressures in Arnold (209–10, 272–75, 282–86, 300–301).

4. The pattern I trace here is in some ways analogous to the one fully and elegantly (if somewhat rigidly) laid out by Culler, who interprets the whole of Arnold's poetry in terms of these symbolic realms: "the Forest Glade, the Burning or Darkling Plain, and the Wide-Glimmering Sea" (4). Roper's "The Moral Landscape of Arnold's Poetry" has also guided my reading of the poems.

5. Familiar but still illuminating accounts of Victorian change, on both sides of the Atlantic, are Houghton's *The Victorian Frame of Mind*, Buckley's *The Victorian Temper*, Jones's *The Age of Energy: Varieties of American Experience, 1865–1915*, and Lear's *No Place of Grace*. In *Priests of Culture* Sterner emphasizes the loss of "authority" in Victorian culture and sees it arising from "the crisis of faith and a maelstrom of social change" (16).

6. For other views of Arnold's belief or lack of belief, see apRoberts, Cockshut, Eliot, and LeRoy. In a striking study, Daniel Riede uses the religious to explore the linguistic. He examines the basis of Arnold's language, arguing that "the great debate between the religious faithful and the 'men of fact' polarized the issue of language" and that Arnold "wanted to believe in both" (25). Twain, as Sewall has made clear, rejects the idea, dear to the transcendentalists, of language as a fixed universal medium rooted in nature sustained by God. Instead, he treats it as a diverse social construct, unstable, varied, subject to multiple contradictions (see Sewall 1–14).

7. Sterner notes that Arnold's concept of culture is "vague" but unmistakably full of "hopefulness" and therefore valuable (25). Carroll argues that Arnold establishes "a coherent cultural theory" that is "intelligible both in its own right and as a conscious contribution to the main currents of eighteenth- and nineteenth-century criticism" (xviii, xix). Raymond Williams's now standard study, *Culture and Society, 1780–1950*, provides the historical context for Arnold's idea of culture and gives an illuminating analysis of it (110–29). Weisbuch slyly observes that Arnold's culture is as "meta-theological as it is meta-everything" (89).

8. To his mother (and his audience may well account for his avowals) he

repeatedly insisted that he disliked conflict. "I had rather live," he assured her, "in a purer air than that of controversy" (*Letters of MA* 2:122), yet equally evident in his letters to her is his delight in the notoriety his contentious writings brought him. He is, to cite just one instance, flattered at a farewell dinner for Charles Dickens when he is first invited to the high table, then asked by Dickens himself to speak, and finally taken in to dine by Lord Lytton. "It shows what comes, in the end," he wrote his mother, "of quietly holding your own way and bantering the world on the irrationality of its ways without losing temper with it" (*Letters of MA* 3:186–87). Realizing perhaps that his mother saw through his disavowals of enjoying controversy, he sometimes couched his protestations running counter to her view, as in this 1868 letter: "You will laugh, but fiery hatred and malice are what I detest, and would always allay or avoid, if I could" (*Selected Prose* 439).

9. A now famous exchange between Arnold and his sister "K" is revealing in this regard. When she accused him, in his words, of "becoming as dogmatic as Ruskin," he answered by saying that the difference between them was that Ruskin was "dogmatic & *wrong*" (*Letters of MA* 2:234).

10. In what is still a useful analysis of Arnold's style, Lewis E. Gates, writing in 1898, identified four styles in Arnold, which may be summarized as: (1) a severe and exact style; (2) the familiar essay style; (3) a harsh argumentative style; and (4) an emotional, highly wrought style (lix–lxxvi). Though E. K. Brown seconds the idea of a highly wrought style, I find such a style more an anomaly in Arnold's writing than a fundamental characteristic of it. For a different approach to Arnold's style, one that emphasizes its "experiential and revelatory" quality, see Buckler (29–65).

11. Krause provides a full and perceptive discussion of Twain's attitudes toward Macaulay (227–45), daring to hazard that if there were one writer other than himself Twain would have liked to be "it would have been Macaulay" (229), while Fulton explores Macaulay's direct influence on *A Connecticut Yankee* (*MT in the Margins* 47–62 and appendix 2).

12. Hamlin Hill's suggestion in "Mark Twain and His Enemies" that as a flamboyant personality Twain resented Arnold's praise of Grant's self-effacing modesty (524–25), while true to Twain's propensity to personalize things and true to his tendency to let annoyance escalate into anger, discounts Twain's seriousness about ideas, the very core of his performances as sage. I think that Twain responded to Arnold's ideas so vigorously because he had—and felt passionately about—contrary ones, as I hope my exposition of their conflict will indicate. In addition to the texts just cited, in which

Twain "replied" to Arnold, he seems to have let his fury infiltrate *A Connecticut Yankee* in various ways (see Baetzhold 110–19; Hoben; and Krauth 193–94).

13. Twain believed in government by the "best men" and became a mugwump—that is, one who abandoned his political party (in Twain's case, the Republican party) in the interest of general moral reform—in 1884, advocating a broad range of moral principles as crucial to proper government. For his alignment with the "best men," see Budd, *MT: Social Philosopher* 107–10, and Krauth, *Proper MT* 192–93.

14. The passage quoted here by Twain does not appear in exactly this form in either the original essay or in the Boston reprint. John Y. Simon believes that Twain was "borrowing freely" from a reply to Grant published in the *North American Review* (April 1887) by James B. Fry, provost marshal general during the Civil War (7–9). While both Fry and Twain raise similar issues, for the most part obvious ones, there is little specific likeness between the two essays. Fry does not quote the passage Twain uses—and changes—here. Twain omits two sentences that occur in Arnold's original between the second and the third sentences he does quote, and he italicizes eight third-person pronouns unemphasized by Arnold. The omitted intervening sentences contain only two such pronouns. Twain's omission creates a sudden rush of pronouns, a veritable clutter, and his added emphasis intensifies them for comic confusion. Twain's alterations make the passage more intoxicating than it really is.

15. *Microfilm Edition of Mark Twain's Previously Unpublished Letters*, vol. 3, *Letters Written from 1886 through 1890* (Berkeley: U of California P, 2001).

16. Gibson posits that throughout his career Twain wrote many pieces "in the spirit of the social critic, satirist, reformer, judge, political partisan, moralist, and Old Testament prophet" and suggests that "the humorist found the prophetic role congenial from the first" (132–33). This is, I think, to find the mature bird in the fledgling, but Gibson provides an arrestingly lengthy list of the different topics Twain spoke out on during his career (134–35). Budd also points out the great variation in the causes he took up (*MT: Social Philosopher*, chapter 9).

17. *Microfilm Edition of Mark Twain's Previously Unpublished Letters*, vol. 3, *Letters Written from 1886 through 1890* (Berkeley: U of California P, 2001).

## Assaying Manliness: Mark Twain & Robert Louis Stevenson

1. *Microfilm Edition of Mark Twain's Previously Unpublished Letters*, vol. 3, *Letters Written from 1886 through 1890* (Berkeley: U of California P, 2001).

2. Robert Louis Stevenson, *Travels with a Donkey in the Cevennes* (New York: P. F. Collier & Son, 1912), 1:194. Subsequent references to this edition, abbreviated *TWD*, will be given parenthetically in the text.

3. For a discussion of Stevenson's actual trip and of the changes made to his texts, see Hart's introduction to Stevenson's *From Scotland to Silverado*.

4. In the descriptions that follow I draw on such standard studies of the Victorian world as Houghton *(The Victorian Frame of Mind, 1830–1870)*, Buckley *(The Victorian Temper)*, Young *(Victorian England)*, and the various essays in Howe *(Victorian America)*. For changes in the family structure, I follow Aries and Walker *(The Age of Enterprise)*. For gender roles in general and the doctrine of the two spheres in particular, I rely on Welter, Cott, Ryan, and Gillian Brown.

5. Despite their occasional denigration of romantic adventure, both Stevenson and Twain enjoyed the works of Frederick Marryat, one of the age's most popular writers of adventure fiction. Stevenson cited Marryat's *The Phantom Ship* as a direct influence on *The Master of Ballantrae* (Eigner 189), and it seems clear that Stevenson's *The New Arabian Nights* owes something to Marryat's *The Pacha of Many Tales* as well as the original *Arabian Nights*. Twain gave Marryat's *The Children of the New Forest* to his daughters (*My Father, Mark Twain* 25), and he used Marryat's *A Diary in America* in composing *Life on the Mississippi* (see Ganzel). When he was in Venice in October 1878 Twain recorded that he took a gondola trip in the rain, closed the boat windows, put his slippers on, lit a cigar, felt "wonderfully snug & cozy," and settled down to read "Marryatt's Pacha of Many Tales" (*N&J3* 209).

6. Other useful commentaries on adventure can be found in Cawelti, Day, and Nerlich. In *Sexual Anarchy*, Showalter discusses "the male quest romance" in late-nineteenth-century British fiction (chapter 5).

7. *Treasure Island* (New York: Penguin, 1981), 17. Subsequent references to this edition, abbreviated *TI*, are given parenthetically in the text. As various Stevenson critics point out, the collected editions of Stevenson (and there are many) are not authoritative; indeed, in some cases, they alter Stevenson's own original texts. For the fiction, then, I have used two readily available paperbacks, which reprint the first editions. The edition cited later for *Kidnapped* is the Penguin edition of 1987; it is abbreviated for parenthetical reference as *K*.

8. For an account of the popularity of boy books, see Jacobson (chapter 1); for a provocative description of the form, see Cady (*The Road to Realism* 12); for a consideration of Twain's use of the genre, see Gribben ("I Did Wish

Tom Sawyer Was There"). Cowley provocatively explores childhood sexuality in the boy book ("Polymorphously Perverse"). Jacobson's approach is to see the boy book as encoding a conflict with the father (24). None of these studies takes up directly the issue of manhood I find central. In "Boy Culture: Middle-Class Boyhood in Nineteenth-Century America," Rotundo explores the actual experience of boys in America, noting in particular how boy-life conflicts with domesticity and how boys' pastimes prepare them for the adult male world.

9. In 1881, writing in the *Athenaeum* (25 June), Henley reviewed Arnold's selection of Byron's poetry, and while he calls Arnold a great critic, he finds that he is out of sympathy with Byron, failing to do justice to the rebellious poet of powerful emotions. His criticisms are in keeping with his private remarks to Stevenson about Arnold. However, four years later when he reviewed Arnold's own poetry, again in the *Athenaeum* (22 Aug. 1885), he not only praised it but even celebrated it as "modern" poetry.

10. For an account of Stoddard's life, career, and sexual orientation, see Austen's *Genteel Pagan: The Double Life of Charles Warren Stoddard.*

11. As biographers have often pointed out, Twain was fascinated by Stevenson's *Dr. Jekyll and Mr. Hyde*, perhaps because his own personality was divided, perhaps because he believed that every personality was. In any case, he ruminated on the puzzle of multiple selves, using *Dr. Jekyll and Mr. Hyde* as a point of departure for his own speculations (see *Mark Twain's Notebook* 348–52). Intriguing as this connection between Twain and Stevenson is, it lies beyond their representation of boys adventuring into manhood.

## Wandering Devious: Mark Twain & Rudyard Kipling

1. For passing comments on their friendship, see the biographies of Twain by Paine, Kaplan, and Hoffman, and those of Kipling by Carrington, Wilson, and Ricketts. Baetzhold (*MT and John Bull* 187–95) and Graver provide more extensive discussions.

2. The Sussex Edition of Kipling's works (1937–39), reprinted in the American Burwash Edition of Kipling's works (1941), includes Kipling's own revisions, but it is not a scholarly definitive edition, and it is not readily available. For *Stalky & Co.* I cite here a modern edition based on the 1929 one issued by Kipling himself in which he added five stories not included in the first edition. In referring to *Kim* I cite a modern edition based on the Sussex one.

3. In describing the characteristics of the picaresque novel, I draw on the

standard studies by Lewis, Alter, Miller, Whitbourn, and Blackburn. In *Picaresque Narrative, Picaresque Fictions*, Wicks provides a review of research, a guide to familiar picaresque novels, and a useful bibliography of critical studies of the picaresque. Cady sheds light on Twain's use of the form in *The Light of Common Day* (chapter 5).

4. For studies attuned to *Huck Finn*'s postwar dimensions, see in particular Budd ("Southward Currents"), Spencer Brown, Schmitz, Gollin and Gollin, Nilon, Beaver, Fishkin *(Was Huck Black?)*, and Doyno *(Writing HF)*.

5. Twain's feelings about the South in general have been traced by Turner ("MT and the South"), Rubin, and Pettit. Pettit locates no fewer than three views of the South held by Twain: he sees Twain as imagining an innocent, beguiling, pastoral South, defined by a landscape of beauty; a debased, corrupt South, created by racial prejudice; and a progressive, changing one, driven by economic forces.

6. I am indebted here to Wieck (59–61), whom I follow closely.

7. Twain's outrage over southern lynchings is evident in his 1869 note in the *Buffalo Express*, "Only a Nigger" *(MTBE* 22–23), and in his 1901 essay, "The United States of Lyncherdom" *(MTC2* 479–86). Most of the working notes seem to be reminders to include authenticating details of the river world—"Dog-fight—describe in detail," "Country quilting," "Candypulling," "Country funeral," for instance—but some, like "De Mule," the lynching notes, and this astounding entry, "Teaches Jim to read & write," suggest Twain's deeper concerns *(HF* 727–28, 753). No one knows why he decided not to include the twice-contemplated lynching, but a reasonable surmise would be that he did not want to lose either young readers with too much violence or southern ones with too stark a condemnation of the South.

8. Although he stages a double attack through Sherburn's speech, excoriating mobs but also revealing Sherburn's own arrogance, Twain himself believed in much of what he had Sherburn say. He had first penned some of Sherburn's ideas as his own views in *Life on the Mississippi*, though he eventually omitted them from the final text. For the omitted passages, see Cox's edition of *Life*, which reproduces them (332–36).

9. In *The Art of Rudyard Kipling*, Tompkins offers a brief but evocative comparison of *Kim* and *Huck Finn* that stresses the differences between the two fictions (29–32).

10. See Trilling, *The Liberal Imagination* (126–35); Howe, "The Pleasure of *Kim*"; Bloom's introduction to the *Modern Critical Interpretations* vol-

ume; and Said, *Culture and Imperialism* (132–62). The literature on imperialism is voluminous, as is that on Kipling and imperialism. For imperialism in general, I have found, in addition to Said's, the studies by Brantlinger, Bivona, Faber, and Bhabha especially enlightening. Commentary on Kipling and imperialism ranges from the biographer Carrington's apologetics to George Orwell's philippic. These recent studies illuminate various dimensions of Kipling's imperial fictions: Kemp, Paffard, Randall, Sandison, and Sullivan. Coates reviews such studies provocatively (13–36).

11. For Kipling's derogatory stereotypes, see *Kim* 112, 154, 185, 188, 190, 254, and 255. For his orientalism, see in particular Patrick Williams and Said. For his views of India and Indians, see Rao. For English views of India and Indians in general, see Paffard (chapter 1).

12. Baetzhold observes that "*Following the Equator* shows its author very close to his British friend's paternalistic concern for the 'lesser breeds without the Law'" (*MT and John Bull* 192).

13. The most searching, up-to-date account of U.S. imperialism that I know is Rowe's *Literary Culture and U.S. Imperialism*, the first of a planned two-volume study. Although he is principally concerned with imperialism in relation to literary culture, his first chapter provides a fine overview of approaches to and major studies of American imperialism in general. Rowe devotes a chapter to Twain (chapter 6), which, unlike my commentary, focuses on *A Connecticut Yankee in King Arthur's Court*.

## Conclusion: Viewing Mark Twain

1. I allude here to only seven of the many illuminating critical studies of Twain, seven that suggest the wide range of interpretation: the studies of Lynn, Smith, Cox, Sloane, Budd, Gillman, and Michelson. There are other vivid pictures of Twain drawn by scholars, and, needless to say, I value many of the other studies greatly.

# Works Cited
# and Consulted

Aaron, Daniel. *The Unwritten War: American Writers and the Civil War.* New York: Alfred A. Knopf, 1973.

Adams, Henry. *The Education of Henry Adams.* 1907. Rpt., Boston: Houghton Mifflin, 1961.

Alter, Robert. *Rogue's Progress: Studies in the Picaresque Novel.* Cambridge, Mass.: Harvard UP, 1964.

Ammons, Elizabeth. "Heroines in *Uncle Tom's Cabin.*" In *Critical Essays on Harriet Beecher Stowe.* Ed. Elizabeth Ammons. Boston: G. K. Hall, 1980. 152–65.

———. "Stowe's Dream of the Mother-Savior: *Uncle Tom's Cabin* and American Women Writers Before the 1920s." In *New Essays on "Uncle Tom's Cabin."* Ed. Eric J. Sundquist. Cambridge: Cambridge UP, 1986. 155–95.

Anderson, Frederick, ed. *Mark Twain: The Critical Heritage.* London: Routledge & Kegan Paul, 1971.

Andrews, Kenneth R. *Nook Farm: Mark Twain's Hartford Circle.* Cambridge, Mass.: Harvard UP, 1950.

apRoberts, Ruth. *Arnold and God.* Berkeley: U of California P, 1983.

Arac, Jonathan. *Huckleberry Finn as Idol and Target.* Madison: U of Wisconsin P, 1997.

Ariès, Philippe, and Georges Duby, eds. *A History of Private Life.* 5 vols. Cambridge, Mass.: Belknap Press of Harvard UP, 1987.

Arnold, Matthew. *The Complete Prose Works of Matthew Arnold.* Ed. R. H. Super. 11 vols. Ann Arbor: U of Michigan P, 1960–1997.

———. *The Letters of Matthew Arnold.* Ed. Cecil Y. Lang. 4 vols. Charlottesville: UP of Virginia, 1996.

———. *The Letters of Matthew Arnold to Arthur Hugh Clough.* Ed. Howard Foster Lawry. London: Oxford UP, 1932.

———. *Matthew Arnold: Selected Prose.* Ed. P. J. Keating. New York: Penguin, 1970.

———. *Poetry and Criticism of Matthew Arnold.* Ed. A. Dwight Culler. Boston: Houghton Mifflin, 1961.

Auden, W. H. "The Poet of the Encirclement." In *Prose.* Vol. 2 of *The Complete Works of W. H. Auden.* Princeton: Princeton UP, 2002. 198–203.

Austen, Roger. *Genteel Pagan: The Double Life of Charles Warren Stoddard.* Ed. John W. Crowley. Amherst: U of Massachusetts P, 1991.

Baender, Paul. "Mark Twain and the Byron Scandal." *American Literature* 30 (Jan. 1959): 467–85.

Baetzhold, Howard G. "Arnold, Matthew." In *The Mark Twain Encyclopedia.* Ed. J. R. LeMaster and James D. Wilson. New York: Garland, 1993. 36–38.

———. *Mark Twain and John Bull.* Bloomington: Indiana UP, 1970.

Bakhtin, Mikhail. *Rabelais and His World.* Trans. Helene Iswolsky. Bloomington: Indiana UP, 1984.

Bataille, Georges. *Eroticism: Death and Sensuality.* Trans. Mary Dalwood. 1962. San Francisco: City Lights, 1986.

Batten, Charles L., Jr. *Pleasurable Instruction: Form and Convention in Eighteenth-Century Travel Literature.* Berkeley: U of California P, 1978.

Baym, Nina. *Women's Fiction: A Guide to Novels By and About Women in America, 1820–1870.* Ithaca: Cornell UP, 1978.

Beaver, Harold. *Huckleberry Finn.* London: Allen and Unwin, 1987.

Bederman, Gail. *Manliness and Civilization: A Cultural History of Gender and Race in the United States, 1880–1917.* Chicago: U of Chicago P, 1995.

Beisner, Robert L. *Twelve Against Empire: The Anti-Imperialists, 1898–1900.* New York: McGraw-Hill, 1968.

Bell, Michael Davitt. *The Problem of American Realism: Studies in the Cultural History of a Literary Idea.* Chicago: U of Chicago P, 1993.

Berg, Barbara J. *The Remembered Gate: Origins of American Feminism, the Woman and the City, 1800–1860.* New York: Oxford UP, 1978.

Bhabha, Homi K. *The Location of Culture.* London: Routledge, 1994.

Bivona, Daniel. *Desire and Contradiction: Imperial Visions and Domestic Debates in Victorian Literature.* Manchester, Eng.: Manchester UP, 1990.

Blackburn, Alexander. *The Myth of the Picaro: Continuity and Transformation of the Picaresque Novel, 1554–1954.* Chapel Hill: U of North Carolina P, 1979.

Blair, Walter. *Mark Twain and Huck Finn.* Berkeley: U of California P, 1960.

———. *Native American Humor.* New York: American Book Co., 1937.

Blair, Walter, and Hamlin Hill. *America's Humor: From Poor Richard to Doonesbury.* New York: Oxford UP, 1978.

Bloom, Harold. Introduction to *Modern Critical Interpretations: Rudyard Kipling's "Kim."* New York: Chelsea House, 1987. 1–8.

Booth, Bradford A. "Mark Twain's Comments on Bret Harte's Stories." *American Literature* 25 (Jan. 1954): 492–95.

Brantlinger, Patrick. *Rule of Darkness: British Literature and Imperialism, 1830–1940.* Ithaca: Cornell UP, 1988.

Brashear, Minnie M. *Mark Twain: Son of Missouri.* Chapel Hill: U of North Carolina P, 1934.

Bridgman, Richard. *Traveling in Mark Twain.* Berkeley: U of California P, 1987.

Brodhead, Richard H. *Cultures of Letters: Scenes of Reading and Writing in Nineteenth-Century America.* Chicago: U of Chicago P, 1993.

Bromwich, David. *A Choice of Inheritance: Self and Community from Edmund Burke to Robert Frost.* Cambridge: Harvard UP, 1989.

Brooks, Peter. *The Melodramatic Imagination: Balzac, Henry James, Melodrama, and the Mode of Excess.* New Haven: Yale UP, 1976.

Brown, E. K. *Matthew Arnold: A Study in Conflict.* 1948. Rpt., Chicago: U of Chicago P, 1966.

Brown, Gillian. *Domestic Individualism: Imagining Self in Nineteenth-Century America.* Berkeley: U of California P, 1990.

———. "Getting in the Kitchen with Dinah: Domestic Politics in *Uncle Tom's Cabin.*" *American Quarterly* 36, no. 4 (fall 1984): 503–23.

Brown, Spencer. "*Huckleberry Finn* for Our Time: A Re-Reading of the Concluding Chapters." *Michigan Quarterly Review* 6 (winter 1967): 41–46.

Bruhm, Steven. *Gothic Bodies: The Politics of Pain in Romantic Fiction.* Philadelphia: U of Pennsylvania P, 1994.

Buchanan, Robert. "The Voice of the Hooligan." In *Kipling and the Critics.* Ed. Elliot L. Gilbert. New York: New York UP, 1965. 20–32.

Buckler, William E. *Matthew Arnold's Prose: Three Essays in Literary Enlargement.* New York: AMS Press, 1983.

Buckley, Jerome H. *The Victorian Temper: A Study in Literary Culture.* Cambridge, Mass.: Harvard UP, 1951.

———. *William Ernest Henley: A Study in the "Counter-Decadence" of the Nineties.* New York: Octagon Books, 1971.

Budd, Louis J. *Mark Twain, Social Philosopher.* Bloomington: Indiana UP, 1962.

———. *Our Mark Twain: The Making of His Public Personality.* Philadelphia: U of Pennsylvania P, 1983.

———. "The Southward Currents under Huck Finn's Raft." *Mississippi Valley Historical Review* 46 (September 1959): 222–37.

————, ed. *Mark Twain: The Contemporary Reviews.* Cambridge: Cambridge UP, 1999.

Buell, Lawrence. *New England Literary Culture: From Revolution through Renaissance.* Cambridge: Cambridge UP, 1986.

Burns, Rex. *Success in America: The Yeoman Dream and the Industrial Revolution.* Amherst, Mass.: U of Massachusetts P, 1976.

Buzzard, James. *The Beaten Track: European Tourism, Literature, and the Ways to "Culture," 1800–1918.* New York: Oxford UP, 1993.

Cady, Edwin Harrison. *The Light of Common Day: Realism in American Fiction.* Bloomington: Indiana UP, 1971.

————. *The Realist at War: The Mature Years, 1885–1920, of William Dean Howells.* Syracuse, N.Y.: Syracuse UP, 1958.

————. *The Road to Realism: The Early Years, 1837–1885, of William Dean Howells.* Syracuse, N.Y.: Syracuse UP, 1956.

Camfield, Gregg. *Necessary Madness: The Humor of Domesticity in Nineteenth-Century American Literature.* New York: Oxford UP, 1997.

————. *Sentimental Twain: Samuel Clemens in the Maze of Moral Philosophy.* Philadelphia: U of Pennsylvania P, 1994.

Campbell, Joseph. *The Hero with a Thousand Faces.* 1949. Rpt., New York: World Publishing, 1956.

Cardwell, Guy A. *The Man Who Was Mark Twain: Images and Ideologies.* New Haven: Yale UP, 1991.

————. *Twins of Genius.* East Lansing: Michigan State College P, 1953.

Carpenter, Lynette, and Wendy K. Kolmar, eds. *Haunting the House of Fiction: Feminist Perspectives on Ghost Stories by American Women.* Knoxville: U of Tennessee P, 1991.

Carrington, Charles. *Rudyard Kipling: His Life and Work.* Rev ed. London: Macmillan, 1978.

Carrington, George C., Jr. *The Dramatic Unity of "Huckleberry Finn."* Columbus: Ohio State UP, 1976.

Carroll, Joseph. *The Cultural Theory of Matthew Arnold.* Berkeley: U of California P, 1982.

Carter, Everett. *Howells and the Age of Realism.* Philadelphia: Lippincott, 1954.

Caskey, Marie. *Chariot of Fire: Religion and the Beecher Family.* New Haven: Yale UP, 1978.

Cawelti, John G. *Adventure, Mystery, and Romance: Formula Stories and Popular Culture.* Chicago: U of Chicago P, 1976.

————. *Apostles of the Self-Made Man.* Chicago: U of Chicago P, 1965.

Clemens, Clara. *My Father, Mark Twain.* New York: Harper & Brothers, 1931.

Coates, John. *The Day's Work: Kipling and the Idea of Sacrifice.* Madison, N.J.: Fairleigh Dickinson UP, 1997.

Cockshut, A.O.J. *The Unbelievers: English Agnostic Thought, 1840–1890.* London: Collins, 1964.

Comfort, Mary S. "Nook Farm." In *The Mark Twain Encyclopedia.* Ed. J. R. LeMaster and James D. Wilson. New York: Garland, 1993. 544–46.

Cook, Don L. "Realism and the Dangers of Parody in William Dean Howells' Fiction." *The Old Northwest* 8 (spring 1982): 69–80.

Cott, Nancy F. *The Bonds of Womanhood: "Woman's Sphere" in New England, 1780–1835.* New Haven: Yale UP, 1977.

Cox, James M. "Harriet Beecher Stowe: From Sectionalism to Regionalism." *Nineteenth-Century Fiction* 38 (1984): 444–66.

———. "Humor and America: The Southwestern Bear Hunt, Mrs. Stowe, and Mark Twain." *Sewanee Review* 83 (1975): 573–601.

———. *Mark Twain: The Fate of Humor.* Princeton: Princeton UP, 1966.

Crane, R. S. "Suggestions Toward a Genealogy of the 'Man of Feeling.'" *ELH* 1 (1934): 205–30.

Crowley, John W. *The Mask of Fiction: Essays on W. D. Howells.* Amherst, Mass.: U of Massachusetts P, 1989.

———. "Polymorphously Perverse? Childhood Sexuality in the American Boy Book." *American Literary Realism* 19, no. 2 (winter 1987): 2–15.

Crozier, Alice C. *The Novels of Harriet Beecher Stowe.* New York: Oxford UP, 1969.

Culler, A. Dwight. *Imaginative Reason: The Poetry of Matthew Arnold.* New Haven: Yale UP, 1966.

Curtis, Susan. "The Son of Man and God the Father: The Social Gospel and Victorian Masculinity." In *Meanings for Manhood: Constructions of Masculinity in Victorian America.* Ed. Mark C. Carnes and Clyde Griffen. Chicago: U of Chicago P, 1990. 67–78.

Daiches, David. *Robert Louis Stevenson and His World.* London: Thames and Hudson, 1973.

Dawson, Carl, ed. *Matthew Arnold: The Poetry, The Critical Heritage.* London: Routledge & Kegan Paul, 1973.

Dawson, Carl, and John Pfordresher, eds. *Matthew Arnold: Prose Writings, The Critical Heritage.* London: Routledge & Kegan Paul, 1979.

Day, William Patrick. *In Circles of Fear and Desire.* Chicago: U of Chicago P, 1985.

DeLaura, David J. *Hebrew and Hellene in Victorian England: Newman, Arnold, and Pater.* Austin: U of Texas P, 1969.

Detienne, Marcel. *Dionysus Slain.* Baltimore: Johns Hopkins UP, 1979.

DeVoto, Bernard. *Mark Twain's America.* Boston: Little Brown, 1932.

Dickinson, Emily. *The Complete Poems of Emily Dickinson.* Ed. Thomas H. Johnson. Boston: Little Brown, 1960.

Douglas, Ann. *The Feminization of American Culture.* New York: Knopf, 1977.

Doyno, Victor A. "Samuel Clemens as Family Man and Father." In *Constructing Mark Twain: New Directions in Scholarship.* Ed. Laura E. Skandera Trombley and Michael J. Kiskis. Columbia: U of Missouri P, 2001. 28–49.

———. *Writing "Huck Finn": Mark Twain's Creative Process.* Philadelphia: U of Pennsylvania P, 1991.

Duckett, Margaret. *Mark Twain and Bret Harte.* Norman: U of Oklahoma P, 1964.

Eble, Kenneth E. *Old Clemens and W.D.H.: The Story of a Remarkable Friendship.* Baton Rouge: Louisiana State UP, 1985.

Ebon, Martin. *They Knew the Unknown.* New York: World Publishing, 1971.

Eigner, Edwin M. *Robert Louis Stevenson and Romantic Tradition.* Princeton: Princeton UP, 1966.

Eliot, T. S. "Arnold and Pater." In *Selected Essays.* London: Faber and Faber, 1951. 431–43.

———. "Matthew Arnold." In *The Use of Poetry and the Use of Criticism.* London: Faber and Faber, 1955. 103–19.

Emerson, Everett. *The Authentic Mark Twain: A Literary Biography of Samuel L. Clemens.* Philadelphia: U of Pennsylvania P, 1984.

———. "Mark Twain's Quarrel with God." In *Order in Variety: Essays and Poems in Honor of Donald E. Stanford.* Ed. R. W. Crump. Newark: U of Delaware P, 1991. 32–48.

Emerson, Ralph Waldo. "The Comic." In *The Works of Ralph Waldo Emerson.* 14 vols. Standard Library Edition. Boston: Houghton, Mifflin, 1883–93. 8:149–66.

Faber, R. *The Vision and the Need: Late Victorian Imperialist Aims.* London: Faber and Faber, 1966.

Feeley, Margaret Peller. "The *Kim* Nobody Reads." In *Modern Critical Interpretations: Rudyard Kipling's "Kim."* Ed. Harold Bloom. New York: Chelsea House, 1987. 57–74.

Fetterley, Judith. "The Sanctioned Rebel." *Studies in the Novel* 3 (1971): 293–304.

Fiedler, Leslie. *Love and Death in the American Novel.* 1960. Rpt., Cleveland, Ohio: World Publishing, 1962.

Fisher, Philip. *Hard Facts: Setting and Form in the American Novel.* New York: Oxford UP, 1987.

Fishkin, Shelley Fisher. "Racial Attitudes." In *The Mark Twain Encyclopedia.* Ed. J. R. LeMaster and James D. Wilson. New York: Garland, 1993. 609–15.

————. *Was Huck Black? Mark Twain and African-American Voices*. New York: Oxford UP, 1993.

Foner, Philip S. *Mark Twain, Social Critic*. New York: International Pub., 1958.

Fulton, Joe B. *Mark Twain in the Margins: The Quarry Farm Marginalia and "A Connecticut Yankee in King Arthur's Court."* Tuscaloosa: U of Alabama P, 2000.

————. *Mark Twain's Ethical Realism: The Aesthetics of Race, Class, and Gender*. Columbia: U of Missouri P, 1997.

Fulweiler, Howard W. *"Here a Captive Heart Busted": Studies in the Sentimental Journey of Modern Literature*. New York: Fordham UP, 1993.

Furnas, J. C. *Voyage to Windward*. New York: William Sloane, 1951.

Ganzel, Dewey. "Twain, Travel Books, and *Life on the Mississippi*." *American Literature* 34 (1962): 40–55.

Gardner, Joseph H. *Dickens in America: Twain, Howells, James, and Norris*. New York: Garland, 1988.

————. "Mark Twain and Dickens." *PMLA* 84 (Jan. 1969): 90–101.

Gates, Lewis E. Introduction to *Selections from the Prose Writings of Matthew Arnold*. New York: Henry Holt, 1898. ix–lxxxvii.

Geismar, Maxwell. *Mark Twain: An American Prophet*. Boston: Houghton Mifflin, 1970.

Ghodes, Clarence. Foreword to *Mark Twain's Library of Humor*. New York: Bonanza Books, 1969. vii–x.

Gibson, William M. *The Art of Mark Twain*. New York: Oxford UP, 1976.

————. Introduction to *Mark Twain's Mysterious Stranger Manuscript*. Berkeley: U of California P, 1969.

————. "Mark Twain and Howells: Anti-Imperialists." *New England Quarterly* 20 (1947): 435–70.

Gilbert, Sandra M., and Susan Gubar. *The Madwoman in the Attic*. New Haven: Yale UP, 1979.

Gillman, Susan. *Dark Twins: Imposture and Identity in Mark Twain's America*. Chicago: U of Chicago P, 1989.

Gollin, Richard, and Rita Gollin. "*Huckleberry Finn* and the Time of Evasion." *Modern Language Studies* 9 (spring 1979): 5–15.

Gossett, Thomas F. *"Uncle Tom's Cabin" and American Culture*. Dallas: Southern Methodist UP, 1985.

Green, Martin. *The Adventurous Male: Chapters in the History of the White Male Mind*. University Park: Pennsylvania State UP, 1993.

————. *Dreams of Adventure, Deeds of Empire*. New York: Basic Books, 1979.

————. *The Problem of Boston: Some Readings in Cultural History*. New York: Norton, 1966.

Gribben, Alan. "'I Did Wish Tom Sawyer Was There': Boy Book Elements in *Tom Sawyer* and *Huckleberry Finn.*" In *One Hundred Years of "Huckleberry Finn."* Ed. Robert Sattelmeyer and J. Donald Crowley. Columbia: U of Missouri P, 1985. 149–70.

———. *Mark Twain's Library: A Reconstruction.* 2 vols. Boston: G. K. Hall, 1980.

———. "'When Other Amusements Fail': Mark Twain and the Occult." In *The Haunted Dusk: American Supernatural Fiction, 1820–1920.* Ed. Howard Kerr, John W. Crowley, and Charles L. Crow. Athens: U of Georgia P, 1983. 171–89.

Griffen, Clyde. "Reconstructing Masculinity from the Evangelical Revival to the Waning of Progressivism: A Speculative Synthesis." In *Meanings for Manhood: Constructions of Masculinity in Victorian America.* Ed. Mark C. Carnes and Clyde Griffen. Chicago: U of Chicago P, 1990. 183–204.

Griswold, Robert. "Divorce and the Legal Redefinition of Victorian Manhood." In *Meanings for Manhood: Constructions of Masculinity in Victorian America.* Ed. Mark C. Carnes and Clyde Griffen. Chicago: U of Chicago P, 1990. 96–110.

Gross, Louis S. *Redefining the American Gothic.* Ann Arbor: UMI Research P, 1989.

Grossberg, Michael. "Institutionalizing Masculinity: The Law as a Masculine Profession." In *Meanings for Manhood: Constructions of Masculinity in Victorian America.* Ed. Mark C. Carnes and Clyde Griffen. Chicago: U of Chicago P, 1990. 133–51.

Habegger, Alfred. *Gender, Fantasy, and Realism in American Literature.* New York: Columbia UP, 1982.

Hall, David D. "The Victorian Connection." In *Victorian America.* Ed. Daniel Walker Howe. Philadelphia: U of Pennsylvania P, 1976. 81–94.

Halttunen, Karen. *Confidence Men and Painted Women: A Study of Middle-Class Culture in America, 1830–1870.* New Haven: Yale UP, 1982.

———. "Gothic Imagination and Social Reform: The Haunted Houses of Lyman Beecher, Henry Ward Beecher, and Harriet Beecher Stowe." In *New Essays on "Uncle Tom's Cabin."* Ed. Eric J. Sundquist. Cambridge: Cambridge UP, 1986. 107–34.

Harris, Susan K. *Mark Twain's Escape from Time: A Study of Patterns and Images.* Columbia: U of Missouri P, 1982.

Harte, Bret. *The Letters of Bret Harte.* Ed. Geoffrey Bret Harte. Boston: Houghton Mifflin, 1926.

———. *Poems.* Boston: Houghton Mifflin, 1912.

———. *Selected Letters of Bret Harte.* Ed. Gary Scharnhorst. Norman: U of Oklahoma P, 1997.

————. *Selected Stories and Sketches*. Ed. David Wyatt. New York: Oxford UP, 1995.

————. *The Writings of Bret Harte*. Standard Library Edition. 20 vols. Boston: Houghton, Mifflin, 1896–1914.

Harte, Bret, and Mark Twain. *California Sketches: Mark Twain and Bret Harte*. New York: Dover, 1991.

Heilman, Robert. *Tragedy and Melodrama: Versions of Experience*. Seattle: U of Washington P, 1968.

Hendrick, Joan D. *Harriet Beecher Stowe: A Life*. New York: Oxford UP.

Henley, W. E. Review of *Poems* (1885), by Matthew Arnold. *Athenaeum*. August 22, 1885. 229–30. Rpt. in *Matthew Arnold: The Poetry, The Critical Heritage*. Ed. Carl Dawson. London: Routledge & Kegan Paul, 1973. 287–90.

————. Review of *Poetry of Byron* (1881), by Matthew Arnold. *Athenaeum*. June 25, 1881. 839–40. Rpt. in *Matthew Arnold: Prose Writings, The Critical Heritage*. Ed. Carl Dawson and John Pfordresher. London: Routledge & Kegan Paul, 1979. 349–54.

Hibbert, Christopher. *The Great Mutiny: India, 1857*. New York: Viking, 1978.

Hill, Hamlin. *Mark Twain: God's Fool*. New York: Harper & Row, 1973.

————. "Mark Twain and His Enemies." *Southern Review* 4, no. 2 (spring 1968): 520–29.

Hoben, John B. "Mark Twain's *A Connecticut Yankee:* A Genetic Study." *American Literature* 18 (Nov. 1946): 197–218.

Hoffman, Andrew J. *Inventing Mark Twain: The Lives of Samuel Langhorne Clemens*. New York: William Morrow, 1997.

————. "Mark Twain and Homosexuality." *American Literature* 67, no. 1 (1995): 23–49.

Hoffman, Daniel G. *Form and Fable in American Fiction*. New York: Oxford UP, 1961.

Holloway, John. *The Victorian Sage: Studies in Argument*. London: Macmillan, 1953.

Honan, Park. *Matthew Arnold: A Life*. New York: McGraw-Hill, 1981.

Hooker, John. *Some Reminiscences of a Long Life: With a Few Articles on Moral and Social Subjects of Present Interest*. Hartford, Conn.: Belknap and Warfield, 1899.

Houghton, Walter E. *The Victorian Frame of Mind, 1830–1870*. New Haven: Yale UP, 1957.

Howe, Daniel Walker. "Victorian Culture in America." In *Victorian America*. Ed. Daniel Walker Howe. Philadelphia: U of Pennsylvania P, 1976. 3–28.

Howe, Irving. "The Pleasures of *Kim.*" In *Modern Critical Interpretations: Rudyard Kipling.* Ed. Harold Bloom. New York: Chelsea House, 1987. 31–41.

Howells, William Dean. "A Confidence." In *Italian Journeys.* Rev. ed. Boston: Houghton, Mifflin, 1901. 1–2.

———. "The Country Printer." In *Criticism and Fiction and Other Essays.* Ed. Clara Marburg Kirk and Rudolf Kirk. New York: New York UP, 1959. 290–98.

———. *Criticism and Fiction and Other Essays.* Ed. Clara Marburg Kirk and Rudolf Kirk. New York: New York UP, 1959.

———. *Italian Journeys.* Enlarged ed. Boston: James R. Osgood, 1872.

———. *Italian Journeys.* Boston: Houghton, Mifflin, 1881.

———. *Life in Letters of William Dean Howells.* Ed. Mildred Howells. 2 vols. Garden City, N.Y.: Doubleday, Doran, 1928.

———. *Literary Friends and Acquaintances: A Personal Retrospect of American Authorship.* Ed. David F. Hiatt and Edwin H. Cady. Bloomington: Indiana UP, 1968.

———. "The Man of Letters as a Man of Business." In *Criticism and Fiction and Other Essays.* Ed. Clara Marburg Kirk and Rudolf Kirk. New York: New York UP, 1959. 298–309.

———. "Mark Twain: An Inquiry." In *My Mark Twain: Reminiscences and Criticism.* 1910. Rpt., Baton Rouge: Louisiana State UP, 1967. 143–62.

———. *My Literary Passions.* New York: Harper & Brothers, 1895.

———. *Selected Letters of W. D. Howells.* Ed. George Arms et al. 6 vols. Boston: Twayne, 1979–83.

———. *Selected Literary Criticism.* Vols. 1–3. Ed. Ulrich Halfmann. Bloomington: Indiana UP, 1993.

———. *A Traveler from Altruria.* In *The Altrurian Romances.* Ed. Clara and Rudolf Kirk. Bloomington: Indiana UP, 1968.

———. "The Turning Point of My Life." In *Criticism and Fiction and Other Essays.* Ed. Clara Marburg Kirk and Rudolf Kirk. New York: New York UP, 1959. 353–62.

———. *Venetian Life.* 2 vols. 1866. Rpt., Boston: Houghton, Mifflin, 1885.

Hurley, Kelly. *The Gothic Body.* Cambridge: Cambridge UP, 1996.

Jacobson, Marcia. *Autobiography and the American Boy Book.* Tuscaloosa: U of Alabama P, 1996.

James, Henry. "The Art of Fiction." In *Selected Literary Criticism.* Ed. Morris Shapiro. Cambridge, England: Cambridge UP, 1981.

———. *The Art of the Novel.* Ed. Richard P. Blackmur. 1934. Rpt., New York: Charles Scribner's Sons, 1962.

———. *Hawthorne*. 1879. Rpt., Ithaca, N.Y.: Cornell UP, 1956.

———. "Howells's Italian Journeys." In *Literary Reviews and Essays on American, English, and French Literature*. Ed. Albert Mordell. New York: Grove P, 1957. 198–202.

———. "Matthew Arnold." In *Matthew Arnold, the Poetry: The Critical Heritage*. Ed. Carl Dawson. London: Routledge and Kegan Paul, 1973. 276–86.

———. *A Small Boy and Others*. New York: Charles Scribner's Sons, 1913.

———. *William Wetmore Story and His Friends*. 2 vols. Boston: Houghton Mifflin, 1903.

Johnson, James L. *Mark Twain and the Limits of Power: Emerson's God in Ruins*. Knoxville: U of Tennessee P, 1982.

Jones, Gareth Stedman. "The History of U.S. Imperialism." In *Ideology in Social Science: Readings in Critical Social Theory*. Ed. Robin Blackburn. New York: Pantheon, 1972. 207–37.

Jones, Howard Mumford. *The Age of Energy: Varieties of American Experience, 1865–1915*. New York: Viking, 1971.

Kaplan, Amy. *The Social Construction of American Realism*. Chicago: U of Chicago P, 1988.

Kaplan, Justin. *Mr. Clemens and Mark Twain*. New York: Simon & Schuster, 1966.

Kemp, Sandra. *Kipling's Hidden Narrative*. New York: Basil Blackwell, 1988.

Kermode, Frank. *Romantic Image*. 1957. Rpt., London: Fontana, 1971.

Kerr, Howard. *Mediums, and Spirit-Rappers, and Roaring Radicals: Spiritualism in American Literature, 1850–1900*. Urbana: U of Illinois P, 1972.

Kerr, Howard, and Charles L. Crow, eds. *The Occult in America: New Historical Perspectives*. Urbana: U of Illinois P, 1983.

Kerr, Howard, John W. Crowley, and Charles L. Crow, eds. *The Haunted Dusk: American Supernatural Fiction, 1820–1920*. Athens: U of Georgia P, 1983.

Kiely, Robert. *Robert Louis Stevenson and the Fiction of Adventure*. Cambridge, Mass.: Harvard UP, 1964.

Kipling, Rudyard. *The Complete Stalky & Co.* Ed. Isabel Quigly. New York: Oxford UP, 1987.

———. *Kipling: Interviews and Recollections*. 2 vols. Ed. Harold Orel. Totowa, N.J.: Barnes & Noble, 1983.

———. *Kim*. Ed. Edward W. Said. New York: Penguin, 1987.

———. *The Letters of Rudyard Kipling*. 3 vols. Ed. Thomas Pinney. Iowa City: U of Iowa P, 1990–96.

———. *The Portable Kipling*. Ed. Irving Howe. New York: Penguin, 1982.

———. "Rudyard Kipling on Mark Twain." In *Mark Twain: Life as I Find It*. Ed. Charles Neider. Garden City, N.Y.: Hanover House, 1961. 310–21.

————. *Rudyard Kipling's Verse: Definitive Edition.* New York: Doubleday, Doran, 1940.

————. *"Something of Myself" and Other Autobiographical Writings.* Ed. Thomas Pinney. New York: Cambridge UP, 1990.

Kiskis, Michael J. "Mark Twain and the Tradition of Literary Domesticity." In *Constructing Mark Twain: New Directions in Scholarship.* Ed. Laura E. Skandera Trombley and Michael J. Kiskis. Columbia: U of Missouri P, 2001. 13–27.

Klages, Mary. *Woeful Afflictions: Disability and Sentimentality in Victorian America.* Philadelphia: U of Pennsylvania P, 1999.

Knoepflmacher, U. C. "Dover Revisited: The Wordsworthian Matrix in the Poetry of Matthew Arnold." *Victorian Poetry* 1 (January 1963): 17–26.

Kolb, Harold H., Jr. *The Illusion of Life: American Realism as a Literary Form.* Charlottesville: UP of Virginia, 1969.

————. "The Outcast of Literary Flat: Bret Harte as Humorist." *American Literary Realism* 23 (winter 1991): 52–63.

Kolko, Gabriel. "Brahmins and Business, 1870–1914: A Hypothesis on the Social Basis of Success in American History." In *The Critical Spirit: Essays in Honor of Herbert Marcuse.* Ed. Kurt H. Wolff and Barrington Moore Jr. Boston: Beacon, 1968. 343–63.

Krause, Sydney J. *Mark Twain as Critic.* Baltimore: Johns Hopkins UP, 1967.

Krauth, Leland. "Mark Twain: At Home in the Gilded Age." *Georgia Review* 28 (1974): 105–13.

————. *Proper Mark Twain.* Athens: U of Georgia P, 1999.

Kristeva, Julia. *Desire in Language: A Semiotic Approach to Literature and Art.* Ed. Leon S. Roudiez. Trans. Thomas Gora, Alice Jardine, and Leon S. Roudiez. New York: Columbia UP, 1980.

Landow, George P. *Elegant Jeremiahs: The Sage from Carlyle to Mailer.* Ithaca, N.Y.: Cornell UP, 1986.

Laskin, David. *A Common Life: Four Generations of American Literary Friendship and Influence.* Hanover, N.H.: UP of New England, 1994.

Lawrence, D. H. *Studies in Classic American Literature.* 1923. Rpt., Garden City, N.Y.: Doubleday, 1951.

Lears, T. J. Jackson. *No Place of Grace: Antimodernism and the Transformation of American Culture, 1880–1920.* New York: Pantheon, 1983.

Lentricchia, Frank, Jr. "Harriet Beecher Stowe and the Byron Whirlwind." *Bulletin of the New York Public Library* 70 (April 1966): 218–28.

Leonard, James S., Thomas A. Tenney, and Thadious M. Davis, eds. *Satire or Evasion? Black Perspectives on "Huckleberry Finn."* Durham, N.C.: Duke UP, 1992.

LeRoy, Gaylord C. *Perplexed Prophets: Six Nineteenth-Century British Authors.* Philadelphia: U of Pennsylvania P, 1953.

Lewis, R. W. B. *The Picaresque Saint: Representative Figures in Contemporary Fiction.* Philadelphia: J. B. Lippincott, 1959.

Lewis, Sinclair. "The American Fear of Literature." In *The Man from Main Street: Selected Essays and Other Writings, 1904–1950.* Ed. Harry E. Maule and Melville H. Cane. 1953. Rpt., New York: Pocket Books, 1962. 3–17.

Lynn, Kenneth S. *Mark Twain and Southwestern Humor.* Boston: Little, Brown, 1959.

————. *William Dean Howells: An American Life.* New York: Harcourt, 1971.

————. "Welcome Back from the Raft, Huck Honey!" *American Scholar* 46 (1977): 338–47.

Macdonald, Florence. "Some Memories of My Cousin." In *Kipling: Interviews and Recollections.* Ed. Harold Orel. 2 vols. Totowa, N.J.: Barnes and Noble, 1983. 1:16–21.

Macnaughton, William R. *Mark Twain's Last Years as a Writer.* Columbia: U of Missouri P, 1979.

Maixner, Paul, ed. *Robert Louis Stevenson: The Critical Heritage.* London: Routledge & Kegan Paul, 1981.

Marash, Margaret. "Suburban Men and Masculine Domesticity, 1870–1915." In *Meanings for Manhood: Constructions of Masculinity in Victorian America.* Ed. Mark C. Carnes and Clyde Griffen. Chicago: U of Chicago P, 1990. 111–27.

Marcus, Steven. *"Stalky & Co."* In *Kipling and the Critics.* Ed. Elliot L. Gilbert. New York: New York UP, 1965. 150–62.

Martin, Robert K., and Eric Savoy, eds. *American Gothic: New Interventions in a National Narrative.* Iowa City: U of Iowa P, 1998.

Massé, Michelle. *In the Name of Love: Women, Masochism, and the Gothic.* Ithaca: Cornell UP, 1992.

McCarthy, Justin. "Mrs. Stowe's Last Romance." 1869. Rpt. in *Critical Essays on Harriet Beecher Stowe.* Ed. Elizabeth Ammons. Boston: G. K. Hall, 1980. 169–72.

McCullough, Joseph B. "Mark Twain and the Hy Slocum-Byng Controversy." *American Literature* 43 (March 1971): 42–59.

McCullough, Joseph B., and Janice McIntire-Strasburg. Introduction to *Mark Twain at the "Buffalo Express": Articles and Sketches by America's Favorite Humorist.* Dekalb: Northern Illinois UP, 1999.

Melton, Jeffrey Alan. *Mark Twain, Travel Books, and Tourism: The Tide of a Great Popular Movement.* Tuscaloosa: U of Alabama P, 2002.

Messent, Peter. *Mark Twain.* New York: St. Martin's, 1997.

Meyer, D. H. "American Intellectuals and the Victorian Crisis of Faith." In *Victorian America*. Ed. Daniel Walker Howe. Philadelphia: U of Pennsylvania P, 1976. 59–77.

Michaels, Walter Benn. *The Gold Standard and the Logic of Naturalism: American Literature at the Turn of the Century*. Berkeley: U of California P, 1987.

Michelson, Bruce. *Mark Twain on the Loose*. Amherst, Mass.: U of Massachusetts P, 1995.

———. "Mark Twain the Tourist: The Form of *The Innocents Abroad*." *American Literature* 49, no. 3 (1977): 385–98.

Mill, John Stuart. "Civilization." In *Collected Works of John Stuart Mill*. 33 vols. General ed. John M. Robson. Toronto: U of Toronto P, 1963–91. 18:117–47.

Miller, David C. *Dark Eden: The Swamp in Nineteenth-Century American Culture*. New York: Cambridge UP, 1989.

Miller, J. Hillis. *The Disappearance of God: Five Nineteenth-Century Writers*. Cambridge, Mass.: Belknap Press of Harvard UP, 1963.

Miller, Stuart. *The Picaresque Novel*. Cleveland: Case Western Reserve UP, 1967.

Mills, Sara. *Discourse and Difference: An Analysis of Women's Travel Writing and Colonialism*. New York: Routledge, 1991.

Mitchell, Lee Clark. Introduction to *The Adventures of Tom Sawyer*. New York: Oxford UP, 1993.

Moers, Ellen. *Harriet Beecher Stowe and American Literature*. Hartford, Conn.: Stowe-Day Foundation, 1978.

———. *Literary Women: The Great Writers*. New York: Doubleday, 1976.

Monteser, Frederick. *The Picaresque Elements in Western Literature*. Tuscaloosa: U of Alabama P, 1975.

Morrison, Toni. Introduction to *Adventures of Huckleberry Finn*. New York: Oxford UP, 1996.

Morrow, Patrick D. *Bret Harte: Literary Critic*. Bowling Green, Ohio: Bowling Green U Popular P, 1979.

Mott, Frank Luther. *Golden Multitudes: The Story of Best Sellers in the United States*. New York: Macmillan, 1947.

Naylor, Carol. "Shaping Boys into Men: 'Imperial Manliness' in Kipling's *Stalky & Co.*" *Kipling Journal* 74, no. 295 (Sept. 2000): 62–71.

Nerlich, Michael. *The Ideology of Adventure*. Minneapolis: U of Minnesota P, 1987.

Newman, Judie. Introduction to *Dred: A Tale of the Great Dismal Swamp*, by Harriet Beecher Stowe. Edinburgh, Scotland: Edinburgh UP, 1999.

Nilon, Charles. "The Ending of *Huckleberry Finn*: 'Freeing the Free Negro.'" *Satire or Evasion? Black Perspectives on "Huckleberry Finn."* Ed. James S. Leonard, Thomas Tenney, and Thadious M. Davis. Durham: Duke UP, 1992. 62–76.

Ohmann, Richard. "A Linguistic Appraisal of Style." In *The Art of Victorian Prose*. Ed. George Levine and William Madden. New York: Oxford UP, 1968. 289–313.

Orwell, George. "Rudyard Kipling." 1942. Rpt. in *Collected Essays*. Ed. Sonia Orwell and Ian Angus. 4 vols. New York: Harcourt Brace Jovanovich, 1968. 2:184–97.

Paffard, Mark. *Kipling's Indian Fiction*. New York: St. Martin's, 1989.

Pemble, John. *The Mediterranean Passion: Victorians and Edwardians in the South*. New York: Oxford UP, 1987.

Persons, Stow. *The Decline of American Gentility*. New York: Columbia UP, 1973.

Pettit, Arthur G. *Mark Twain and the South*. Lexington: UP of Kentucky, 1974.

Porte, Joel. "In the Hands of an Angry God: Religious Terror in Gothic Fiction." In *The Gothic Imagination: Essays in Dark Romanticism*. Ed. G. R. Thompson. Pullman: Washington State UP, 1974. 42–64.

Porter, Dennis. *Haunted Journeys: Desire and Transgression in European Travel Writing*. Princeton: Princeton UP, 1991.

Pratt, Mary Louise. *Imperial Eyes: Travel Writing and Transculturation*. New York: Routledge, 1992.

Raleigh, John Henry. *Matthew Arnold and American Culture*. Berkeley: U of California P, 1961.

Randall, Don. *Kipling's Imperial Boy: Adolescence and Cultural Hybridity*. New York: Palgrave, 2000.

Rao, K. Bhaskara. *Rudyard Kipling's India*. Norman: U of Oklahoma P, 1967.

Reynolds, David S. *Beneath the American Renaissance: The Subversive Imagination in the Age of Emerson and Melville*. Cambridge, Mass.: Harvard UP, 1988.

Ricketts, Harry. *Rudyard Kipling: A Life*. New York: Carroll and Graf, 2001.

Riede, David G. *Matthew Arnold and the Betrayal of Language*. Charlottesville: UP of Virginia, 1988.

Ringe, Donald L. *American Gothic: Imagination and Reason in Nineteenth-Century Fiction*. Lexington: UP of Kentucky, 1982.

Robbins, William. *The Arnoldian Principle of Flexibility*. Victoria, B.C.: U of Victoria P, 1979.

———. *The Ethical Idealism of Matthew Arnold: A Study of the Nature and Sources of His Moral and Religious Ideas*. Toronto: U of Toronto P, 1959.

Romero, Lora. "Bio-Political Resistance in Domestic Ideology and *Uncle Tom's Cabin*." In *The "American Literary History" Reader*. Ed. Gordon Hunter. New York: Oxford UP, 1995. 111–30.

Roper, Alan H. "The Moral Landscape of Arnold's Poetry." *PMLA* 77 (1962): 289–96.

Rotundo, E. Anthony. "Boy Culture: Middle-Class Boyhood in Nineteenth-Century America." In *Meanings for Manhood: Constructions of Masculinity in Victorian America.* Ed. Mark C. Carnes and Clyde Griffen. Chicago: U of Chicago P, 1990. 15–36.

Rourke, Constance. *American Humor: A Study of National Character.* New York: Harcourt, Brace, 1931.

———. *Trumpets of Jubilee.* New York: Harcourt, Brace, 1927.

Rowe, John Carlos. *Literary Culture and U.S. Imperialism: From the Revolution to World War II.* New York: Oxford UP, 2000.

Rubin, Louis D., Jr. *The Writer in the South.* Athens: U of Georgia P, 1972. 34–81.

Ryan, Mary. *Cradle of the Middle Class: The Family in Oneida County, New York, 1790–1865.* New York: Cambridge UP, 1981.

Said, Edward W. *Culture and Imperialism.* New York: Alfred A. Knopf, 1993.

Salomon, Roger. "Gothic." In *The Mark Twain Encyclopedia.* Ed. J. R. LeMaster and James D. Wilson. New York: Garland, 1993. 332–33.

———. "Mark Twain and Victorian Nostalgia." In *Patterns of Commitment in American Literature.* Ed. Marston LaFrance. Toronto: U of Toronto P, 1967. 73–91.

Samuels, Shirley, ed. *The Culture of Sentiment: Race, Gender, and Sentimentality in Nineteenth-Century America.* New York: Oxford UP, 1992.

Sanchez-Eppler, Karen. *Touching Liberty: Abolition, Feminism, and the Politics of the Body.* Berkeley: U of California P, 1993.

Sandison, Alan. *The Wheel of Empire.* New York: St. Martin's, 1967.

Scarry, Elaine. *The Body in Pain: The Making and Unmaking of the World.* New York: Oxford UP, 1985.

Scharnhorst, Gary. *Bret Harte.* New York: Twayne Publishers, 1992.

Schirer, Thomas. *Mark Twain and the Theatre.* Nuremberg: Verlag Haus Carl, 1984.

Schmitz, Neil. "Mark Twain's Civil War: Humor's Reconstructive Writing." In *The Cambridge Companion to Mark Twain.* Ed. Forrest G. Robinson. New York: Cambridge UP, 1995. 74–92.

Scott, Arthur L. *Mark Twain at Large.* Chicago: Henry Regery, 1969.

Sewell, David R. *Mark Twain's Languages: Discourse, Dialogue, and Linguistic Variety.* Berkeley: U of California P, 1987.

Simmel, Georg. *On Individuality and Social Forms.* Chicago: U of Chicago P, 1971.

Simon, John Y. Introduction to *General Grant by Matthew Arnold, with a Rejoinder by Mark Twain.* Carbondale: Southern Illinois UP, 1966.

Skandera Trombley, Laura E. *Mark Twain in the Company of Women.* Philadelphia: U of Pennsylvania P, 1994.

Skandera Trombley, Laura E., and Michael J. Kiskis. Introduction to *Constructing Mark Twain: New Directions in Scholarship*. Columbia: U of Missouri P, 2001. 1–12.

Sloane, David E. E. *Mark Twain as a Literary Comedian*. Baton Rouge: Louisiana State UP, 1979.

Smith, David L. "Huck, Jim, and American Racial Discourse." In *Satire or Evasion? Black Perspectives on "Huckleberry Finn."* Ed. James S. Leonard, Thomas A. Tenney, and Thadious M. Davis. Durham, N.C.: Duke UP, 1992. 103–20.

Smith, Henry Nash. *Mark Twain: The Development of a Writer*. Cambridge, Mass.: Belknap Press of Harvard UP, 1962.

Spender, Stephen. *Love-Hate Relations: English and American Sensibilities*. New York: Random House, 1974; Rpt., New York: Vintage, 1975.

Spengemann, William C. *The Adventurous Muse: The Poetics of American Fiction, 1799–1900*. New Haven: Yale UP, 1977.

———. *A Mirror for Americanists: Reflections on the Idea of American Literature*. Hanover, N.H.: UP of New England, 1989.

Spurr, David. *The Rhetoric of Empire: Colonial Discourse in Journalism, Travel Writing, and Imperial Administration*. Durham, N.C.: Duke UP, 1993.

Stahl, J. D. *Mark Twain, Culture and Gender: Envisioning America Through Europe*. Athens: U of Georgia P, 1994.

Stein, Gertrude. "Composition as Explanation." In *Selected Writings of Gertrude Stein*. Ed. Carl van Vechten. New York: Vintage, 1990. 513–23.

Sterner, Douglas W. *Priests of Culture: A Study of Matthew Arnold and Henry James*. New York: Peter Lang, 1999.

Stevenson, Robert L. *An Inland Voyage*. In *The Works of Robert Louis Stevenson*. Vol. 1. Vailima Edition. New York: P. F. Collier & Son, 1912.

———. "Diogenes." In *The Works of Robert Louis Stevenson*. Tusitala Edition. London: William Heinemann, 1924. 5:189–97.

———. "A Fable." In *The Works of Robert Louis Stevenson*. Tusitala Edition. London: William Heineman, 1924. 1:223–26.

———. *From Scotland to Silverado*. Ed. James D. Hart. Cambridge, Mass.: Belknap Press of Harvard UP, 1966.

———. "A Gossip on Romance." In *The Lantern-Bearers and Other Essays*. Ed. Jeremy Treglown. New York: Cooper Square Press, 1999. 172–82.

———. "A Humble Remonstrance." In *The Lantern-Bearers and Other Essays*. Ed. Jeremy Treglown. New York: Cooper Square Press, 1999. 192–201.

———. *Kidnapped*. New York: Penguin, 1987.

―――. *The Letters of Robert Louis Stevenson.* Ed. Bradford A. Booth and Ernest Mehew. 8 vols. New Haven: Yale UP, 1994–95.

―――. "My First Book—*Treasure Island.*" In *The Lantern-Bearers and Other Essays.* Ed. Jeremy Treglown. New York: Cooper Square Press, 1999. 277–84.

―――. *Selected Letters of Robert Louis Stevenson.* Ed. Ernest Mehew. New Haven: Yale UP, 1997.

―――. *Travels with a Donkey in the Cevennes.* In *The Works of Robert Louis Stevenson.* Vol. 1. Vailima Edition. New York: P. F. Collier & Son, 1912.

―――. *Treasure Island.* New York: Penguin, 1981.

Stewart, George R., Jr. *Bret Harte: Argonaut and Exile.* Boston: Houghton Mifflin, 1931.

Stewart, J.I.M. *Rudyard Kipling.* New York: Dodd, Mead, 1966.

Stoddard, Charles Warren. "Early Recollections of Bret Harte." *Atlantic Monthly* 78, no. 469 (Nov. 1896): 673–78.

Stone, Albert E. *The Innocent Eye: Childhood in Mark Twain's Imagination.* New Haven: Yale UP, 1961.

Stone, Donald D. *Communications with the Future: Matthew Arnold in Dialogue.* Ann Arbor: U of Michigan P, 1997.

Stoneley, Peter. *Mark Twain and the Feminine Aesthetic.* New York: Cambridge UP, 1992.

Stowe, Harriet Beecher. *Dred: A Tale of the Great Dismal Swamp.* Ed. Judie Newman. Edinburgh, Scotland: Edinburgh UP, 1999.

―――. *A Key to "Uncle Tom's Cabin."* 1853. Rpt., Bedford, Mass.: Applewood Books, n.d.

―――. *Lady Byron Vindicated: A History of the Byron Controversy, From Its Beginning in 1816 to the Present Time.* 1870. Rpt., New York: Haskell House, 1970.

―――. *Life and Letters of Harriet Beecher Stowe.* Ed. Annie Fields. Boston: Houghton, Mifflin, 1897.

―――. *Uncle Tom's Cabin or, Life Among the Lowly.* New York: Penguin, 1981.

Stowe, William W. *Going Abroad: European Travel in Nineteenth-Century American Culture.* Princeton, N.J.: Princeton UP, 1994.

Sullivan, Zohreh T. *Narratives of Empire: The Fictions of Rudyard Kipling.* New York: Cambridge UP, 1993.

Svaglic, Martin J. "Classical Rhetoric and Victorian Prose." In *The Art of Victorian Prose.* Ed. George Levine and William Madden. New York: Oxford UP, 1968. 268–88.

Thomas, Brook. *American Literary Realism and the Failed Promise of Contract.* Berkeley: U of California P, 1997.

Thomas, Jeffrey F. "Bret Harte and the Power of Sex." *Western American Literature* 8 (fall 1973): 91–109.

Thompson, G. R., ed. *The Gothic Imagination: Essays in Dark Romanticism.* Pullman: Washington State UP, 1974.

Tillotson, Geoffrey. "Matthew Arnold's Prose: Theory and Practice." In *The Art of Victorian Prose.* Ed. George Levine and William Madden. New York: Oxford UP, 1968. 73–100.

Tompkins, Jane. *Sensational Designs: The Cultural Work of American Fiction, 1790–1860.* New York: Oxford UP, 1985.

Tompkins, J.M.S. *The Art of Rudyard Kipling.* London: Methuen, 1959.

Towers, Tom H. "Love and Power in *Huckleberry Finn.*" *Tulane Studies in English* 23 (1978): 17–37.

Trilling, Lionel. *The Liberal Imagination: Essays on Literature and Society.* 1951. Rpt., London: Penguin, 1970.

———. *Matthew Arnold.* Rev. ed. New York: Meridian, 1955.

Turner, Arlin. "Comedy and Reality in Local Color Fiction." In *The Comic Imagination in America.* Ed. Louis D. Rubin Jr. New Brunswick: Rutgers UP, 1983. 157–64.

———. *Mark Twain and George W. Cable: The Record of a Literary Friendship.* East Lansing: Michigan State UP, 1960.

———. "Mark Twain and the South: An Affair of Love and Anger." *Southern Review* 4 (1968): 493–519.

Twain, Mark. *Adventures of Huckleberry Finn.* Comprehensive ed. Ed. Victor Doyno. New York: Ballantine, 1996.

———. *The American Claimant.* Vol. 21 of *The Writings of Mark Twain.* Author's National Edition. New York: Harper & Brothers, 1899–1920.

———. *Huck Finn and Tom Sawyer Among the Indians and Other Unfinished Stories.* Ed. Dahlia Armon and Walter Blair. Berkeley: U of California P, 1989.

———. *Letters from the Earth.* Ed. Bernard DeVoto. New York: Harper & Row, 1962.

———. *Life on the Mississippi.* Ed. James M. Cox. New York: Penguin, 1984.

———. *Love Letters of Mark Twain.* Ed. Dixon Wecter. New York: Harper & Brothers, 1949.

———. *Mark Twain's Correspondence with Henry Huttleston Rogers.* Ed. Lewis Leary. Berkeley: U of California P, 1969.

———. *Mark Twain's Letters to Will Bowen: "My First & Oldest & Dearest Friend."* Ed. Theodore Hornberger. Austin: U of Texas P, 1941.

———. *Mark Twain's Notebook.* Ed. Albert Bigelow Paine. New York: Harper & Brothers, 1935.

———. *Mark Twain's Travels with Mr. Brown*. Ed. Franklin Walker and G. Ezra Dane. New York: Alfred A. Knopf, 1940.

———. "Mark Twain Talks Mostly about Humor and Humorists." Ed. Louis J. Budd. *Studies in American Humor* 1 (1974): 4–22.

———. *Mark Twain to Mrs. Fairbanks*. Ed. Dixon Wecter. San Marino, Calif.: Huntington Library, 1949.

———. "My Literary Shipyard." In *Mark Twain: Tales, Speeches, Essays, and Sketches*. Ed. Tom Quirk. New York: Penguin, 1994. 407–10.

———. *On the Poetry of Mark Twain with Selections from His Verse*. Ed. Arthur L. Scott. Urbana: U of Illinois P, 1966.

———. *The Prince and the Pauper*. Ed. Victor Fischer and Lin Salamo. Berkeley: U of California P, 1979.

———. *Pudd'nhead Wilson and Those Extraordinary Twins*. Ed. Sidney E. Berger. New York: Norton, 1980.

———. *The Washoe Giant in San Francisco*. Ed. Franklin Walker. San Francisco: George Fields, 1938.

———. *What Is Man? and Other Philosophical Writings*. Ed. Paul Baender. Berkeley: U of California P, 1973.

———. "William Dean Howells." In *Mark Twain: Collected Tales, Sketches, Speeches, and Essays, 1890–1910*. Ed. Louis J. Budd. New York: Library of America, 1992. 722–30.

Twain, Mark, and William Dean Howells. Introduction to *Mark Twain's Library of Humor*. 1888. Rpt., New York: Bonanza Books, 1969. xii–xiv.

Varma, Devendra P. *The Gothic Flame*. London: Barker, 1957.

Walker, Robert H. *The Age of Enterprise, 1865–1900*. 1967. Rpt., New York: Paragon Books, 1979.

Waller, Altina. *Reverend Beecher and Mrs. Tilton: Sex and Class in Victorian America*. Amherst: U of Massachusetts P, 1982.

Wecter, Dixon. *Sam Clemens of Hannibal*. 1952. Rpt., Boston: Houghton Mifflin, 1961.

Weisbuch, Robert. *Atlantic Double-Cross: American Literature and British Influence in the Age of Emerson*. Chicago: U of Chicago P, 1986.

Welter, Barbara. "The Cult of True Womanhood, 1820–1860." *American Quarterly* 18, no. 2 (summer 1966): 151–74.

———. *Dimity Convictions: The American Woman in the Nineteenth Century*. Athens: Ohio UP, 1976.

Westbrook, Perry D. *A Literary History of New England*. Bethlehem, Pa.: Lehigh UP, 1988.

Whitbourn, Christine J., ed. *Knaves and Swindlers: Essays on the Picaresque Novel in Europe*. Oxford UP, 1974.

Wicks, Ulrich. *Picaresque Narrative, Picaresque Fictions: A Theory and Research Guide.* Westport, Conn.: Greenwood P, 1989.

Wieck, Carl F. *Refiguring "Huckleberry Finn."* Athens: U of Georgia P, 2000.

Willey, Basil. *Nineteenth Century Studies: Coleridge to Matthew Arnold.* 1949. Rpt., New York: Harper & Row, 1966.

Williams, James D. "The Use of History in Mark Twain's *A Connecticut Yankee.*" *PMLA* 80 (1965): 102–10.

Williams, Patrick. "*Kim* and Orientalism." In *Kipling Considered.* Ed. Phillip Mallet. New York: St. Martin's, 1989. 33–55.

Williams, Raymond. *Culture and Society, 1780–1950.* 1958. Rpt., New York: Harper & Row, 1966.

————. *Marxism and Literature.* London: Oxford UP, 1977.

Wilson, Angus. *The Strange Ride of Rudyard Kipling.* New York: Viking, 1978.

Wilson, Edmund. *Patriotic Gore: Studies in the Literature of the American Civil War.* New York: Farrar, Straus and Giroux, 1962.

————. *The Wound and the Bow.* New York: Oxford UP, 1947.

Wilson, Forrest. *Crusader in Crinoline: The Life of Harriet Beecher Stowe.* Philadelphia: J. B. Lippincott, 1941.

Wolff, Cynthia Griffin. "*The Adventures of Tom Sawyer:* A Nightmare Vision of American Boyhood." In *Critical Essays on "The Adventures of Tom Sawyer."* Ed. Gary Scharnhorst. New York: G. K. Hall, 1993. 148–59.

Wonham, Henry B. "Undoing Romance: The Contest for Narrative Authority in *The Adventures of Tom Sawyer.*" In *Critical Essays on "The Adventures of Tom Sawyer."* Ed. Gary Scharnhorst. New York: G. K. Hall, 1993. 228–41.

Woodress, James L., Jr. *Howells and Italy.* Durham, N.C.: Duke UP, 1952.

Worley, Sam McGuire. *Emerson, Thoreau, and the Role of the Cultural Critic.* Albany: State U of New York P, 2001.

Wright, Nathalia. *American Novelists in Italy: The Discoverers, Allston and James.* Philadelphia: U of Pennsylvania P, 1974.

Wyllie, Irvin G. *The Self-Made Man in America: The Myth of Rags to Riches.* New York: Free P, 1954.

Zweig, Paul. *The Adventurer: The Fate of Adventure in the Western World.* New York: Akadine P, 1999.

Zwick, Jim. Introduction to *Mark Twain: Weapons of Satire.* Syracuse, N.Y.: Syracuse UP, 1992. xvii–xlii.

# Index

Howells, William Dean (*continued*)
work, 50–51, 52, 77–78; dark strain in, 58–59, 75–76, 78, 267 (n. 11); early travel abroad of, 55–56; friendship with Twain, 49–51, 69, 260–61; on Harte, 30; humor of, 51–52; humor of, in *A Traveler from Altruria*, 79–82, 85; humor of, in letters to Twain, 69–76; humor of, regional source of, 77–78; humor of, in travel books, 57–62, 64; and New England culture, 53–54, 62–63; persona of, in letters to Twain, 72–73; persona of, in travel books, 57, 62–63; on Twain, 2, 11, 12–13, 50–51, 52, 77–78; Twain letters to, 4, 50, 69–76, 82–83, 137; on *Uncle Tom's Cabin*, 89. *See also entries for specific works*
"A Humble Remonstrance" (Stevenson), 173
Humor, 12; American, 160; Arnold's, as sage, 138, 152–53, 154–55; conflicting modes of, 55; frontier, 107–8; in Howells, 51–52, 57–62, 64, 77–78; in *Huckleberry Finn*, 237; New England, 54–55; and pathos, 24, 39, 45; regional sources of, in Twain, 77–78; in Twain-Howells letters, 69–77; Twain's, as sage, 137–38, 152, 153–54, 154–55. *See also* Arnold: humor; Howells: humor; Twain: humor

Imperialism: and Harte, 30–31, 47; and Kipling, 249–51; and Twain, 43, 47, 249–53. See also *Adventures of Huckleberry Finn*; *Kim* (Kipling)
*An Inland Voyage* (Stevenson), 169
*The Innocents Abroad*, 3, 7, 17, 20, 36, 53, 54, 60, 143, 170, 171, 214, 258; as exposé of travel, 65–66; the Gothic in, 108–9; Howells's review of, 52; New England aspects of, 66–69; reviews of, 63–64
Intertextuality, 5
*Italian Journeys* (Howells), 52, 54, 56, 57–63

James, Henry, 11, 12, 21, 46, 146, 168; on Arnold, 128–29; "The Art of Fiction," 173; on Howells, 56–57; on *Uncle Tom's Cabin*, 89–90
*The Jungle Books* (Kipling), 215

Keller, Helen, Twain letter to, 4–5
*A Key to Uncle Tom's Cabin* (Stowe), 101
*Kidnapped* (Stevenson), 168; adventure in, 197–98; compared to *Huckleberry Finn*, 204–5, 207; manhood in, 205–7
*Kim* (Kipling), 213, 218, 227, 239, 251, 256; authority in, 245–48; compared to *Huckleberry Finn*, 240–42, 245–47; imperialism in, 242, 243–45; as a picaresque novel, 217, 227, 248; sources for, 238; Twain on, 215
Kipling, Rudyard, 7, 9, 11, 12, 30, 260, 261; and authority, 225–26, 243–48; career compared to Twain's, 214; on Cecil Rhodes, 253–55; and imperialism, 249–51, 253–56; on Twain, 209–13, 215–16; Twain letter to, 257; Twain on, 213, 215, 248, 256. *See also entries for specific works*
Kristeva, Julia, 5